THE STORY OF
MODERN
ARCHITECTURE
OF THE 20th CENTURY

With contributions from Wolfgang Hoffmann and Philipp Meuser

Drawings: Meuser Architects, Berlin

© h.f.ullmann publishing GmbH

Managing Editor: Peter Delius
Project management: Ulrike Reihn-Hamburger
Editing and layout: Ulrike Sommer
Coverdesign: Simone Sticker
Cover: All images: © Archiv für Kunst und Geschichte, Berlin, except for:
Front cover top left and top middle right
Back cover bottom: © British Architectural Library Photographs Collection

Original title: *Geschichte der Architektur*
ISBN 978-3-8480-0564-2

© for the English edition: h.f.ullmann publishing GmbH

Translation from German: Susan Bennett in association with Goodfellow & Egan, Cambridge
Editor of the English-language edition: Philippa Youngman in association with Goodfellow & Egan, Cambridge
Typesetting: Goodfellow & Egan, Cambridge
Project Management: Jackie Dobbyne for Goodfellow & Egan, Cambridge
Overall responsibility for production: h.f.ullmann publishing GmbH, Potsdam, Germany

Printed in China, 2013

ISBN 978-3-8480-0562-8

10 9 8 7 6 5 4 3 2 1
X IX VIII VII VI V IV III II I

www.ullmann-publishing.com
newsletter@ullmann-publishing.com

Jürgen Tietz

THE STORY OF MODERN ARCHITECTURE OF THE 20th CENTURY

h.f.ullmann

Contents

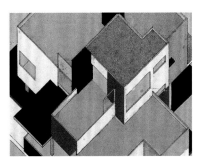

1890

1910

1920

1920

1930

1945

1960

1970

1980

1990

2001

Stocktaking
and impulses

Architecture at the turn of the century

1890–1910

THE ROOTS IN THE 18TH AND 19TH CENTURIES

The world around us

Our everyday life is conditioned to a significant degree by the architecture that surrounds us each day – at home, in the workplace, out shopping. Even during our leisure time, at the pool or in the football stadium or at the museum, architecture creates the necessary architectural environment for our activity. Without architecture, human society would be impossible.

Our cities present a colorful, multilayered world. Buildings from many centuries mingle with contemporary architecture to form a living organism. Towering next to Gothic cathedrals are high-rise buildings made of steel and glass, or with reflecting granite façades. Exciting museum buildings, almost like sculptures large enough to walk in, coexist with soberly functional factories or dreary administration buildings.

Architecture at the end of the 20th century is as multifaceted as life itself. We experience cities as bewildering assemblages of a variety of functions, to which architecture, in all its widely differing manifestations, lends the necessary framework.

New worlds …

The swift development of architectural technique and form in this century has roots that go as far back as the 18th century. The Enlightenment, which enhanced the significance and the social status of every citizen, was accompanied by a fundamental change in political culture. Centuries-old monarchies gave way to democratic constitutions whose stock of ideas spread outwards in ever-increasing circles. It was these thoughts that were enshrined in a comprehensive and enduring form in the American Declaration of Independence (1776), and found direct political expression in the French Revolution (1789).

Following the start given by the 18th century, it was almost inevitable that the 19th should be an era of revolutionary changes affecting every area of life. The industrial revolution, which spread from England to the whole of Europe and North America, created a new type of worker: the wage-laborer or proletarian, who earned a hard living in the ever more numerous factories. A symbol of the increasing mechanization of the world was the steam engine, invented by Watt in 1785, whose proliferation into newly built machine shops and iron foundries engendered an appropriate type of building.

A second, no less meaningful symbol of the new age was the railway. In 1830, Crown Street Station was built in Liverpool, the first station intended for passengers, who could now travel comfortably by rail between

1833: First law against child labor in England.

1837: Victoria crowned queen of England.

1842: China cedes Hong Kong to England, and opens its ports to west European forces.

1848: Karl Marx publishes his *Communist Manifesto*

1861: Abraham Lincoln becomes US president and abolishes slavery.

1869: The Suez Canal is opened, shortening the sea route to India.

1871: Founding of the German Empire after the end of the Franco-Prussian war.

1876: Alexander Graham Bell patents his "membrane speaking telephone." International Centennial Exhibition held in Philadelphia.

1886: The Statue of Liberty erected in New York, a present from the French Republic commemorating the anniversary of the Declaration of Independence.

1889: Paris hosts an international exhibition, the Exposition Universelle. Completion of the Eiffel Tower.

1895: Wilhelm Conrad Röntgen discovers X-rays. Sigmund Freud lays the foundations of psychoanalysis. First film shows given by Max Skladanowsky in Berlin and the Lumière brothers in Paris.

1899: First peace conference held in The Hague to discuss the peaceful settlement of international conflicts; passing of the Convention relating to the Laws and Customs of Warfare on Land. The United Fruit Company sets up the first monopoly trade in bananas in Central America.

1900: Exposition Universelle and Olympic Games held in Paris.

1900-01: Boxer rising in China, put down by an expeditionary force of the European powers.

1901: Theodore Roosevelt becomes US president. Thomas Mann's novel *Buddenbrooks* published. Picasso's "Blue Period" begins, with scenes from Parisian life, and the lives of circus people. Pavlov begins his experiments in animal psychology.

1903: Margarete Steiff presents the first toy teddy bear at the Leipzig Fair.

1904: First performance of Puccini's *Madame Butterfly*. Death of Anton Chekhov.

Max Skladanowsky with his bioscope (projecting equipment) in 1895

1905: Erich Heckel, Ernst Ludwig, and Karl Schmidt-Rottluff found the Expressionist art movement "Die Brücke."

1906: San Francisco destroyed by earthquake and fire.

1907: Maria Montessori opens her first "Children's House." Sun Yat-sen announces his program for a Chinese democratic republic with social legislation.

1908: Matisse coins the word "Cubism" for a painting by Georges Braque.

1909: First permanent wave in London. Ford specializes in the mass production of the Model T: around 19,000 are sold in this year alone.

1910: Japan annexes Korea. The 13th Dalai Lama, fleeing from the Chinese, takes temporary refuge in India. Robert Delaunay completes his painting *The Eiffel Tower*. Feininger begins to make his mark with his characteristic Cubist/Expressionist style.

Liverpool and Manchester. A whole network of railway lines spread over Europe, and made it possible for both people and goods to be transported over immense distances very much faster than by coach. This in turn had consequences for architecture, for, in order to cross valleys and mountains, tunnels and massive bridges made of either stone or *iron* were required – real masterpieces of *civil engineering*. Within a short time railway stations were springing up, palatial buildings of ever greater size and splendor, which, because of the amount of space they took up, were generally placed on the edge of town.

... new buildings ...

It was not only technical progress that found expression in the architecture of the 19th century, but also new democratic forms of government. Thus, prestigious parliament buildings sprang up, such as the Houses of Parliament in London, designed by Charles Barry (1839–52), the German Reichstag in Berlin by Paul Wallot (1884–94), Imre Steindl's Budapest parliament (1885–1902), and town halls that served as centers of state government and administration, while at the same time gave emphatic expression to

the newly developed self-confidence of the bourgeoisie. This self-confidence was also reflected in numerous other architectural models that arose at almost exactly the same time, such as the museum – for example Klenze's Sculpture Gallery in Munich, Germany (1816–34) or Smirke's British Museum in London (1823–47). These "temples of the muses," open to all, took the place of the aristocratic private collections: a concrete proof of the will of the middle classes to educate themselves.

While this was going on, metropolises such as Paris, London, and Brussels saw the birth of the first great department stores and arcades – roofed-in shopping streets – which became synonymous with the burgeoning commercial world of the 19th century.

... familiar forms

The requirements that architecture was being called upon to fulfill were changing fundamentally in the 19th century, and totally new tasks for the builder were constantly arising. Yet a great deal of architecture at this time was marked above all by the need to create an imposing effect – a need which the rising bourgeoisie inherited from the aristocracy as

Joseph Paxton, *Crystal Palace*, London 1851, moved to Sydenham 1855, destroyed by fire 1936

A pure space carved out of the atmosphere – that was the impression created by the Crystal Palace, erected by the gardener and architect Joseph Paxton for the Great Exhibition of 1851, the first international exhibition to be held in London. Its basic module was the largest sheet of glass that it was then possible to produce. All the component parts of the exhibition building were standardized and prefabricated industrially. It was thus possible to erect the great hall – 750,000 square feet (70,000 square meters) – in less than five months, and then remount it in Sydenham.
Bare of all the ornamentation then in fashion, the *iron*, glass, and wood construction of the Crystal Palace is stripped of all sense of solidity. As the first high point of the new field of *architectural engineering*, it inspired a great deal of emulation. At the beginning of the 20th century it was celebrated as a breakthrough into modernity.

Gustave Eiffel, *Eiffel Tower,* Paris 1889

The Eiffel Tower, erected by Gustave Eiffel and Maurice Koechlin in 1889 for the Exposition Universelle, came to symbolize the highest point of both *architectural engineering,* and the Parisian skyline. Eiffel, engineer and entrepreneur, concentrated all the experience that he had gained in the construction of innumerable bridges and railway stations into it. For 40 years the tower, besides being almost free of any practical utility, was also the tallest construction in the world. Its then unimaginable height of 1000 feet (300 meters) was achieved by means of a framework of prefabricated iron girders riveted together, offering maximum stability with minimal weight. The dispersal of forces is visible from its shape. Only the four arches linking the legs were added later for decorative effect. They did not stop the Parisians finding it hard to live with, describing it as "naked architecture" and seriously debating whether to pull it down. But by 1900 the Eiffel Tower had already become the symbol of Paris, and was discussed as a work of art.

they replaced them in the function of running the state. As early as 1828 the German architect Heinrich Hübsch asked "In what style should we build?," putting into words the general uncertainty of the 19th century as to what architectonic *style* was appropriate to the requirements of the day.

The search for an appropriate and universally valid style of building is one of the most characteristic features of architecture in the 19th and early 20th centuries. One of its foundations was intensive scientific research into architectural history – an enterprise that had already begun in the 18th century. For example, the results of lengthy research trips to Athens, Rome or Sicily to visit what was left of the monuments of antiquity were published as large-format collections of engravings, which made them available for the first time to numerous architects throughout Europe.

Besides the archaeological study of antiquity, the new disciplines of history and fine art also focused on the *Romanesque,* the *Gothic,* the *Renaissance,* and the *Baroque.* An important impetus for this engagement with the most varied facets of history was the search for the national roots of states, as well as of building styles. The century of nationalism had begun. For instance, the *neo-Gothic* style flourished with especial vigor in Prussia in the first half of the 19th century, because it was assumed that the Gothic had German roots – until research uncovered the fact that the Gothic style had arisen in medieval France.

Not only did the people of the 1800s begin a scientific study of the architectural relics of previous eras, they handled the buildings themselves with new respect. Efforts were made to preserve them (conservation) or, if they were already severely damaged, to rebuild them (restoration). The era of the conservation of historic monuments had begun.

As research penetrated ever deeper into the contexts and developments of architectural history, contemporary architects suddenly had at their disposal a whole spectrum of building styles that they could use in their own work. Heinrich Hübsch answered his own question about what style he should build in by opting for a *round-arched* style borrowed from the Romanesque. But the 19th century offered many additional answers to Hübsch's question. Whereas the 1800s brought forth a

Europe-wide flowering of *classicism,* with buildings that looked back to ancient Greece, Gottfried Semper also established the neo-Renaissance as a suitable style for large buildings with his Dresden Opera, which was built between 1838 and 1841. (It was recon-structed between 1871 and 1878. The present opera house was built in 1985.) A different trend, destined to sweep all before it, the *neo-Baroque,* was initiated by Charles Garnier with his new Paris Opera (1861–75). This growing tendency to look to history as a source of inspiration, which reached its apogee in the second half of the 19th century, is generically termed *historicism,* whatever epoch or style individual architects took as their reference.

For a long period in the 20th century it was usual to look down somewhat on the architecture produced by historicism, for supposedly not having any creative force of its own. So it came about that in the wake of the *Neues Bauen* (new building) movement of the 1920s, people simply threw away the façades of houses dating from those formative years. Cities that had already been markedly depleted by the wars of the 20th century thus suffered further losses that were not possible to repair.

The aspect of the town

With the change in architecture, the aspect of towns changed. The small town that could be taken in at a glance, which was still the general rule in 1800, had been replaced at the end of the 19th century by the Moloch big city. The medieval walls had long crumbled, and the city boundary was extending ever further into the countryside. But, most significantly, the factories and industrial installations were surrounded by the dwellings of millions of workers and their families, who, in the hope of work and better living conditions, had turned their backs on their homes in the country.

Speculation in land favored erection of the notorious and ever increasing tenements, with their numerous stone back yards, into which neither light nor healthy air could penetrate. Crushed together into the smallest possible spaces, whole sections of the population became increasingly enfeebled and ill, whereas the more affluent members of the bourgeoisie cultivated the lifestyle of the nobility, that which they had previously disparaged.

Toward the end of the 19th century these living conditions gradually began to change. Light and air were permitted to enter the homes of the less privileged members of the population. Raymond Unwin and Barry Parker built Letchworth (in Hertfordshire, England), the first garden city, between 1898 and 1914, and in 1893 Alfred Messel built the blocks of flats for rent in the Sickingenstrasse in Berlin, thus laying the foundation for the housing reform movement that reached its height in the ambitious housing developments of the first half of the 20th century.

Glass, iron, concrete – new building materials create new possibilities

Alongside the familiar building materials that had been in use for millennia – wood, stone, and brick – in the 19th century new materials such as iron, zinc, steel, and glass increasingly found their way into architecture. As they were not always used in a visible way, it could quite easily happen that a building that looked historicist on the outside had modern encroachments on the inside: a daring roof-construction in iron perhaps, or a glass skylight.

As early as the mid-19th century a single-material building was created: the Crystal Palace in London. This glass palace, erected for the first of the international exhibitions, the Great Exhibition of 1851, was free of all traditional styles. Paxton created a monumental structure that consisted purely of a supporting iron frame with walls made not of stone but of sheets of glass. Today, in an age marked by glassy high-rise buildings, it is difficult to imagine how revolutionary the people of that time felt this novel construction to be, when all that was around it was stone.

The erection of this iron and glass exhibition building was the first step in a development that was to lead to a systematic reduction of architecture to its functional components. Most of the buildings inspired by historicism were still marked by a taste for luxuriant and ostentatious decoration, which was applied regardless of their function – whether as factories, or administrative buildings, or simply dwellings. In opposition to this the demand arose that every architectural undertaking should be carried out in the most functional way, avoiding all superfluous decoration. This thinking is summed up in one pregnant phrase, attributed to the American architect Louis Sullivan: "Form follows function." It was to become one of the guiding principles of modern architecture in the 20th century.

Paxton's glass palace also demonstrated that innovation in 19th-century architecture could be found, not least, in the masterpieces of the civil engineer. Another modern icon, the Eiffel Tower, was also built by engineers: Gustave Eiffel and Maurice Koechlin. The construction of the tower at the edge of central Paris on the old Champ de Mars, as part of the Exposition Universelle of 1889, met with considerable opposition at the time. Eiffel judged that only a framework of iron girders would do for building a tower 1000 feet (300 meters) high; a more solid construction would offer too large a surface area to the wind, and would be bound to collapse.

Glass, iron, and steel changed the face of architecture, but it took a mixture of sand, gravel, and cement to revolutionize it. Only when concrete came along was it possible to produce the architecture that has set its stamp on our cities, both positively and negatively, right up to the present day. Concrete, being relatively light and not requiring plaster, opened up an extraordinarily rich spectrum of forms that was unattainable with traditional materials like stone, which was heavier, or wood, which was more fragile.

Although the new material had been developed in the 1890s, the French building entrepreneur Auguste Perret was the first to use it to very striking effect in 1902, for a residential building: the apartment block at 25 rue Franklin in Paris. The startlingly simple core of the building is a grid of *reinforced concrete*, reinforced, that is, with an iron skeleton to give it stability. The *façades* between the concrete load-bearing elements could thus be filled with patterned *ceramic tiles* in Art Nouveau style. The banks considered Perret's plan of constructing a residential building out of concrete such a risky undertaking that they refused to give him credit.

The Arts and Crafts movement

Although the breakthrough into modern architecture had already begun in the middle of the 19th century, the swiftly growing metropolises were largely dominated right till the end of the century by stone colossi, all displaying the same unfeelingly reproduced "Gothic" or

Auguste Perret, *House in the rue Franklin,* Paris, 1902–03

A completely open ground floor, and above it projections and recesses and differing ground-plans: 25 rue Franklin, by Auguste Perret, was the first demonstration in a multi-story building of the potential of a new material, reinforced concrete. With this technique, only the skeleton of piers and beams is set firm; the wall areas can be filled in as desired. Accordingly, the façades had large areas of glass and were richly decorated with floral tiles.

Victor Horta, *Hôtel Tassel*, Brussels, 1893

The year 1893, in which Victor Horta built a house for Paul-Emile Tassel, can be considered as the beginning of Art Nouveau. Its greatest novelty lay in the fact that the architect had no longer drawn his forms from the established canons of architectural history, but from a precise study of nature. Horta's floral shapes were more than a decoration added on to a building, they were stylistic elements that turned the house into a consistently designed organic whole. The basic design was no longer the sum of clearly separated rooms and corridors, but a single interconnecting space. All of the ornamented interior, from the sweeping ironwork to the beautifully crafted mosaics, supports the dynamic of this architect's first pure Art Nouveau building.

"classic" ornamentation. The real picture of the city and its inhabitants was one of grim clusters of tenements with five or more courtyards behind, erected at breakneck speed. At the end of the century, therefore, people were as disappointed with the inability of this architecture to cope with social problems as they were with its didactic academicism.

General disaffection with the traditional architectural forms of the 19th century was the starting point for the search for a new means of expression, a new *style*. In a period of growing industrialization, boundless faith in progress, and ever-increasing urbanization, the Arts and Crafts movement arose in England. As early as the mid-19th century, its adherents began campaigning for a return to the craft tradition of the Middle Ages.

It was the object of the Arts and Crafts movement, under the leadership of the artist-craftsman William Morris, the architect Philip Webb, and the influential writer, art, and

architecture critic John Ruskin, to fill people's everyday lives with quality products made in the art and craft tradition, so that mass-produced industrial goods did not gain the upper hand and destroy the aesthetics of objects. William Morris, who was much influenced by the symbolist painting of the Pre-Raphaelite artist Dante Gabriel Rossetti, opened up his own business in 1861, making products ranging from furniture and glassware to fabrics and wallpapers, which he decorated with repeating patterns of stylized flowers. Although Morris, the most prominent figure in the Arts and Crafts movement, was not himself an architect, his work had an astonishing influence over architecture right into the 20th century.

ART NOUVEAU

Vegetal forms spread across Europe

Since history plainly did not offer any style that could adequately express the new era, people turned to the models provided by nature in their search for a new way. From the middle of the 19th century, painters, especially in France, had been going out into the countryside and putting up their easels in the midst of nature, instead of working shut up in a studio as they had done before. This intense involvement with nature led to new themes in painting and to new types of representation. People began to translate the crooked lines of a tree or the involuted petals of a bud into a new formal language of *ornamentation*, generally rather two-dimensional in appearance, which broke entirely with the repertoire of forms in use before this. In architecture too, these *vegetal* forms drawn from the natural world joined with the new building materials of glass and iron to create a new formal language, and as the new materials were placed unadorned next to traditional ones like brick, *freestone*, and marble, the way was opened not only to a new style but also to a previously unknown material aestheticism.

In Germany, the movement was called Jugendstil – a programmatic-sounding name, somewhat out of keeping with its floral inspiration and its idealistic evocation of renewal, awakening, and youthful freshness, which it derived from the art magazine *Die Jugend* (Youth). This had been published since 1896 in Munich, which had become a center of the new art movement through the activities of Richard Riemerschmid, Bruno Paul, and August Endell, three architects.

Like *classicism* in the 1800s, Art Nouveau captured the whole of Europe at the beginning of the century. But, in contrast to classicism, which permitted only a slight deviation from the canons of traditional architectural form, it developed as many different names as regional variants: the French "Art Nouveau" was "Jugendstil" in Germany, "Modern Style" in England, "Stile Liberty" in Italy, "Modernismo" in Spain. Luxurious and playful in the work of Victor Horta in Brussels, fantastic in Antoni Gaudí's Barcelona, emotional in Raimondo D'Aronco's Constantinople and Turin, cubic and severe in the work of Josef Hoffmann in Vienna and Charles Rennie Mackintosh in Glasgow, there were as many national variants as there were names. What united all of Art Nouveau's facets, however, was their unconditionally innovative character compared with the *historicism* of the outgoing century.

Brussels and Paris

The year 1893, in which the Belgian architect Victor Horta designed a house for Emile Tassel, a professor of geometry, at 6 rue Paul-Emile Janson in Brussels, was also the year in which Art Nouveau architecture was born. From the curving door handle to the vegetal sweep of the banisters, the slender iron pillars and the coiling patterns of the mosaic floor, Horta created a delicate and total work of Art Nouveau with a unified underlying design.

Between 1896 and 1899 Horta realized a completely different building project: the Maison du Peuple for the Belgian Socialist Party, which was to become the model for numerous 20th-century buildings with a similar purpose. In this "house for the people," Horta united technical innovation and new-style decoration in exemplary form. The spacious assembly hall on the top floor was roofed by a bold ironwork construction, which was not only without supports, but was also elegantly curved. The whole building was dominated by glass and iron. Despite its importance for architectural history, it was ruthlessly pulled down in 1969.

A Frenchman, Hector Guimard, was as extravagantly decorative as Horta in his design for the entrances to the underground stations

in Paris. Visitors to the Exposition Universelle were able to admire these in 1900, whereas the Métro itself only came into operation the following year. The entrances were constructed of *moulded iron* in a wide spectrum of playful floral shapes. Guimard differentiated between the various types of Métro entrances, according to whether they were either roofed-in or open.

But the limitations of Art Nouveau itself were already visible at the 1900 Exposition. Next to Guimard's playful but nonetheless crisp ornamentation, tendencies to rococo-like excess appeared. By way of example, one might quote the striking formal language of the Italian Raimondo d'Aronco, whose pavilion at the Turin arts and crafts fair of 1902 was almost theatrical in its *mise en scène* of architectural forms and sculptures.

A review of Art Nouveau in France would be incomplete without a look at the most important craft of this period: the works of art

Hector Guimard, *Entrance to a Métro station,* Paris 1900

Hector Guimard's entrances to the Parisian Métro are some of the most impressive examples of French Art Nouveau. With a lavish profusion of forms, they conduct the dynamic of the city traffic under the earth into a new world. The plant-like cast-iron shapes of the leek-green street lamps, railings and glass roofs growing out of the pavement reconcile the world of technology, as it increasingly took over areas of everyday life, with that of nature – admittedly in appearance only. For in truth these floral pavilions had nothing to do with the Métro, either symbolically or functionally. They involuntarily laid bare not only the novelty of the transport system but also a basic problem of Art Nouveau. More than any preceding style, it quickly degenerated into overblown decoration – and it was soon to swamp all Europe.

Antoni Gaudí i Cornet, *Casa Batlló*,
Barcelona 1904–06

Balconies like masks, a roof in the form of a dinosaur's back, a layout without right-angles – the block of luxury flats Casa Batlló demonstrates to the full the imagination and the technical mastery of a totally unique artist, the Catalonian architect Antoni Gaudí. The above view, taken from the street, shows one of the typical cylindrical side towers of the house, the façade of which has a changing pattern of *natural stone* and colorful *small ceramic tiles.* Unlike the products of other representatives of Modernismo or Art Nouveau, Gaudí's organic, close-to-nature forms are not *ornamentation* that has been added on; they pervade the whole building, determine its construction: architecture becomes sculpture.

in glass created by the school of Nancy and its chief representative Emile Gallé. He created costly objects, glasses like jewels, covered with stylized floral patterns or shaped in vegetal forms. Their effect is enhanced by their delicate coloring, sometimes gleaming with a matt sheen, sometimes brilliantly sparkling. This has made them into highly prized collectors' pieces. The only work that approaches the art of Gallé is that of the American Louis Comfort Tiffany.

Gaudí and Modernismo in Spain

The work of the Catalan Antoni Gaudí is unique in architectural history. Gaudí, almost all of whose buildings are in Barcelona, was the most important representative of Modernismo, the Spanish variant of Art Nouveau. Ignoring functionality, Gaudí developed an opulent formal language that included *Gothic* and *Moorish* elements as well as creations of his own. Fragments of glass and bits of pottery were assembled by Gaudí into lively *mosaics* that animate the façades of his houses and the undulating benches in the Güell Park, named after his most important patron, Eusebi Güell.

The height of Gaudí's success in his lifetime were the two residential buildings, the Casa Batlló and the Casa Milà. Instead of a conventional façade, Gaudí gave the Casa Batlló one that went in and out, and was sometimes gently bowed, with an iridescent surface additionally enlivened by small round *ceramic* plates. The ground floor takes its character from pillars like elephants' feet; the weird window-openings on the first floor look like the gaping mouths of prehistoric beasts. Bizarrely formed mask-like balconies enliven the already richly alive façades. Rounded forms predominate in the interior as they do in the exterior, with windows and doors of a species all their own, created by Gaudí's fertile imagination. The house is crowned by a roof reminiscent of a dinosaur's spine, and the chimneys arising out of the loft behind a *fascia,* shaped like the crest of a wave look like a congregation of unearthly giants.

Gaudí's abstract architectural fantasies awaken a crowd of associations in the mind that can never, however, really be pinned down, so that in spite of all the imagination that has been displayed, the beholder is still left somewhat perplexed.

The Sagrada Familia cathedral in Barcelona, started a hundred years ago, is still awaiting completion. It is hardly surprising that Gaudí occupies the position of a much-admired bird of paradise in the history of architecture, but is without a successor. Not only would the wild extravagance to which Gaudí's houses bear witness represent a budgetary factor that any architect would underestimate at his peril, but his sheer unquenchable creativity would by no means be easy to emulate.

The Jugendstil in Germany

The work of the Belgian Henry van de Velde demonstrates, perhaps more clearly than any other, that the Jugendstil, like the Arts and Crafts movement, is much more than an architectonic fashion. His vision of an art that was youthful amounted to a liberation from all traditional constraints and conventions, not only in architecture, but in all areas of life. Each everyday object was recognized as a craft product that could be shaped with artistry, and must be subjected to a specific design process. So van de Velde's œuvre encompasses not only costly bookbindings, new styles of lettering, and stylish furniture with curving lines, but designs for women's dresses representing, as he put it in the title of a book, "women's apparel raised to the level of art."

After his first artistic sojourns in Brussels – in the neighborhood of which, in Uccle, he created a house for himself, the Bloemenwerf house – and in Paris, van de Velde went on to create his most important work in Germany. Between 1901 and 1902 he created the interior decor for the Folkwang Museum, which was erected by the industrialist Karl Ernst Osthaus in Essen. Van de Velde's friend and mentor Harry Graf Kessler, whose diaries are still considered to be some of the most impressive sources of turn-of-the-century cultural history, brought him to Weimar to the court of the Grand Duke, Wilhelm Ernst. There, from 1907 to 1914, he designed, and then directed, the school of applied art, out of which came Walter Gropius's Bauhaus after the First World War.

Another Weimar nobleman, Ernst Ludwig von Hessen, commissioned Jugendstil additions to his residence. In 1899 he invited a number of artists to Darmstadt, including Joseph Maria Olbrich from Vienna. The artists' colony that grew up at the Mathildenhöhe in the following years, under the patronage of Ernst Ludwig, achieved great importance as a center of the German Jugendstil, especially through the realization of architectural projects, which went on right until Olbrich's untimely death in 1908.

Olbrich's best-known building in Darmstadt, apart from the Ernst-Ludwig-Haus, which served as a workshop for the artists in the colony, was the Wedding Tower. The red brick tower is crowned by five arched elements like fingers, covered in blue ceramic tiles.

The Mathildenhöhe is dominated by the late work of Olbrich, but it was here that another artist, Peter Behrens (see page 23) took his first steps as an architect, after previously distinguishing himself as a painter and craftsman. He was later to become one of the most influential personalities of European architectural history.

Cube instead of curve: Glasgow and Vienna

Just as Horta's work in Brussels and Gaudí's buildings in Barcelona stamped their image on those cities, so the work of Charles Rennie Mackintosh became the trademark of the Scottish metropolis of Glasgow. His key work, the school of art, provoking violent controversy among his contemporaries, was not plant-like, but heavily *stereometric* in its basic design. Smooth, almost menacing façades of natural stone are opened up by large windows.

In 1900 Mackintosh was invited to present his work in Vienna. His furniture designs, with their largely cubic forms, gave the impetus to the founding by Josef Hoffmann of the Vienna workshops in 1903, and they were to remain a center of applied art production until they were closed down in 1933. Mackintosh's work was displayed in Vienna in the Secession exhibition building, which Joseph Maria Obrich had built just before he moved to Darmstadt.

In 1897 a highly varied collection of artists, from the painter Gustav Klimt and the sculptor Max Klinger to the architect Josef Hoffmann, had withdrawn from the traditional Vienna art world and its exhibitions of academic art, and

Joseph Maria Olbrich, *Wedding Tower,* Darmstadt-Mathildenhöhe, 1908

Grand Duke Ernst Ludwig von Hessen was one of the few German aristocrats who promoted political reform together with reform in visual art. He called seven artists to Darmstadt and put Mathildenhöhe at their disposition, to create a "document of German art of enduring worth." When their studios were opened to the public in 1901, it was the first art exhibition of that kind. Joseph-Maria Olbrich, a pupil of Otto Wagner, designed a "five-fingered" wedding tower for the second anniversary of the grand duke's marriage, completing one of the most important ensembles of Modernist work.

Henry van der Velde, *Karl Ernst Osthaus Museum,* Brunnenhalle, Hagen, 1901–02

The interior of the Folkwang-Museum, whose basic structure was built by C. Gerard, belongs to the most important early works in Germany of the Belgian van de Velde. He was contracted by the banker's son Karl Ernst Osthaus, a major patron of the arts. Van de Velde had established himself as a leading exponent of the Jugendstil with the *vegetal* formal language that is to be seen in this impressive museum, but it is particularly noticeable for its economic use of materials. Stone, wood, glass, and metal work together to define their own new aesthetic: an aesthetic that has its counterpart in the great works of engineering of that time. The impact of the materials on the senses is underlined by the flowing, yet flattened shapes created by van de Velde, as can be seen in the top-lighted pillars in the fountain court (*Fountain with Boys* by Georges Minne 1901).

Charles Rennie Mackintosh, *Glasgow School of Art,* 1896–1909

Viewed in passing, the Glasgow School of Art, created by the Scottish architect Charles Rennie Mackintosh, appears a radically sober, rational building. Outside it is angular, cubic; its block-like enclosed quality is further emphasized by the use of *natural stone*, and a row of large north-light windows indicating the studios that lie behind. Inside, it has a flexible layout that predates Mies Van der Rohe by many years with its use of moveable partition walls. But the rough-hewn clarity of the whole is overlaid by delicate, fluid details, which are not applied to the building as decor, but which humanize and animate it: the arches over the entrance, the filigree alcoves, the sweeping stair-rail, and the interior details in wood and metal, all bear witness to Mackintosh's penetrating graphic imagination.

In the harmony between these two principles of form lies the strength of Mackintosh's architecture, and it was this that made him a model for the Vienna *Secession* and the moderns.

founded the Vienna Secession, which dominated the art scene at the turn of the century in the Austro-Hungarian capital. The newly founded association of artists was to become the model for other secessions, such as those in Munich and Berlin.

But it was not only the unusual Secession building, with its crowning cupola of iron laurel leaves, that was different from the general architectonic picture of the city: the Secession exhibitions themselves presented an extremely different image to the familiar traditions of exhibiting. Instead of walls so full that it was impossible to see anything

adequately, with pictures hanging several rows deep, the exhibitions favored selection and presentation, which gave each work of art an appropriate space within which to develop its effect.

The architecture of the Vienna Jugendstil, with its severe tectonic language, was clearly different from either the work of Horta with its leaning toward *vegetal* models, or the overflowing fantasy of Gaudí. This gave it a particularly important role as a link to the predominantly functionalist development of modern architecture. Although Otto Wagner did cover the façades of his so-called "Majolika House" at 40 Linke Wienzeile Strasse with luxuriantly floral decoration, the formal language of his buildings in general is cubic, and much more restful.

An example of this is the large cashiers' hall of the Vienna post office savings bank, laid out on a severe rectilinear grid, and overarched by a gently curving glass skin through which light floods into the room. An additional stroke of artistry on Wagner's part was to light the rooms under the hall through ceiling areas made of glass blocks.

A very similar paring-down of form can be seen in the work of another Viennese architect, Josef Hoffman, whose key work is the Palais Stoclet in Brussels. This house, built for the banker Adolphe Stoclet, is characterized by its interpenetrating cubic blocks, and its economical use of decoration on the *façade*: elements that look forward to modern architecture after the First World War, when the

Otto Wagner, Austrian Post Office Savings Bank, Vienna 1904–06

The interior of this trapezoid building, especially the large cashiers' hall, is of an elegant economy. Free of any decoration, it derives its charm from the reduction of its elements to the simplest form: the extremely narrow steel supports in the arched glass roof, and the columns that, for structural efficiency, grow narrower toward the base. The construction of the roof, which Wagner derived from the principle of the suspension bridge, is given particular emphasis by the fact that the pillars plainly do not support the roof, but run right through it. The post office savings bank underpins Otto Wagner's *Theses on modern architecture*, which he had propounded in 1896 in the book of the same name. In it he argued for a modern style appropriate to the time bringing together architecture and engineering in a new, practical, total artwork. "Anything impractical cannot be beautiful."

ADOLF LOOS

Adolf Loos belongs to the architect-writers among the moderns, who were able to translate their theories into designs. Whereas Adolf Loos, who was hard of hearing, couched his thoughts in flowery parables and imaginative essays, when formulating ideas about design he favored unadorned architecture and archaic forms. His texts constantly reflect a search for a "pure architecture" freed from the influence of other disciplines. Architecture, according to Loos, was not art in three dimensions, but the organisation of space. As a *functionalist* he campaigned for a rejection of decorative elements, for instance *stucco* in interiors, demanding that his fellow architects concentrate on the technical aspects of a building's use. A combination of dandy, artist, architect, and art critic, lifelong friend of the writer Karl Kraus, Adolf Loos was one of the most brilliant and multitalented personalities of 20th-century architecture.

He was born in Brünn, in Moravia, and started out, oddly enough, as a member of the Vienna Secession – a group who, in the tradition of the English Arts and Crafts movement, believed in the merging of crafts and architecture. He was a member of the so-called "Coffee house trio," the other two members being Joseph Maria Olbrich and Josef Hoffman, who were enthusiastic proponents of the Jugendstil. But in 1898, Loos broke away from the circle on

Adolf Loos, circa 1930

matters of principle, and later became one of its most vehement critics.

From then on he promoted the thesis that lack of ornament was a sign of spiritual strength, and that "the evolution of culture implies the removal of ornament from objects of use." By this dissociation from art, Loos sought to strengthen the authenticity both of art and architecture. He saw this separation as the precondition for cultural modernity, even going so far in his work as journalist and writer to leave his texts in lower case, in order to break away from the ornamental capitals used in printing at the time.

While he was studying in Dresden, Loos spent three years (1895–98) in the United States, where he visited the World's Fair and became acquainted with the *Chicago School* (see page 42). There he studied the theories of Louis Sullivan, who had suggested as early as 1885 in his essay "Ornament in Architecture" that decorative elements in architecture should be abandoned, for a few years at least, since they unnecessarily disrupted the organic relationship between function, form, material, and expression.

Loos developed this proposal further by decrying ornament as socially and economically wasteful. All that the builder was actually paid for was the house itself. Ornamentation was regarded as on a level with "wasted labor and spoiled materials."

What the architectural consequences of this attitude were, Loos himself revealed in his design for the building on the Michaelerplatz (built in 1909–11 and reconstructed 1981), which finally brought about his breakthrough into architecture. Commissioned by the tailoring firm Goldman and Salatsch, he erected a spare, plastered building, whose only decorative feature – dictated by the materials – was the *natural stone* of the ground floor. The building was both a dwelling and a shop, and is remarkable for the sensitivity with which Loos incorporated elements from the neighboring buildings (such as the portal of the Michaelerkirche), and for the fact that the owner gave town planning considerations precedence over economic by placing the building in a commanding position with one wall facing the square, rather than opting for maximal use of the site in the traditional way by building it on the corner. Loos is famous both for his open fight against decorative building but also for his idea of "spatial planning," though in fact this was not formulated by him, but was a response to his works. The essence of spatial planning is to work out the dimensions for individual rooms in a building by their functional and display roles. Loos took his idea of having rooms of different heights from England, where the gallery-construction of the medieval hall had found its way into country houses. Always a provocateur, he maintained that an architect should not do sketches, design façades or do cross-sections. Much more important was to "design space." The result of this was that Loos designed buildings that were sets of boxes within boxes, joined by staircases, as in the Moller

The building incorporating residential floors and a shop for the tailoring firm Goldman & Salatsch on the Michaelerplatz in Vienna, 1909–11

building (Vienna, 1928) or the Müller house (Prague, 1930). The latter is the most worked-out translation into practice of spatial planning by Loos himself. The living room, dining room, library, and ladies' drawing-room were all on different levels, together composing a coherent open organisation of space. Every room is in expensive materials – marble, mahogany, lemon-wood – which underline Loos's starting point: that the artifice of ornament should be replaced by the effect of noble materials.

Among the best-known works of Loos, which relates to his experience in the USA, is the Kärnter Bar in Vienna (1908) which incorporates the American idea of the bar where you stand to drink. Four highly polished marble columns support a sharply projecting canopy roof portraying a stylized banner of the Stars and Stripes. The lettering is so artistically executed in brightly colored broken glass, that it almost makes a nonsense of Loos's edict about the forcible separation of architecture and art. Loos had laid down that only a small part of architecture belonged to the realm of art – tombs and monuments, neither of which had any architectural sense or function, except perhaps of a symbolic nature.

However, the most convincing interpretation of Loos's theories came not from their originator but from the philosopher and architect Ludwig Wittgenstein who, in 1926–29, together with Loos's pupil Paul Engelmann, erected a building made up of unadorned cubes fitted within one another, which looked just as if it had been carried out by the "master" himself.

Unadorned: the flat symmetrical garden side of the houses (completed 1910) for Lilly and Hugo Steiner in Vienna, which exemplify Loos's battle against decorative architecture

FRANK LLOYD WRIGHT

To be the "greatest architect in America," that was the wish of Frank Lloyd Wright's mother for him when he was born in 1869. When he died, 90 years later, he had indeed given a direction to the architecture of his country.

Frank Lloyd Wright, 1957

Wright left behind well over 400 buildings and projects, many of the rank of icons, which can barely be subsumed under any academic category since so many styles and stylistic variants are expressed within them. He was forerunner, protagonist, contemporary, and executor of the greatest overarching line of development of 20th-century architecture: Modernism.

At first sight it appears that it is only Wright's own will to design everything that unites his work. The foundations for the perfectionist urge, which caused him to work personally through every stage of a project from the long-distance view to the details of the furniture, and to give his personal stamp to even such rebarbative projects as the Romeo and Juliet windmills (1896), were laid when he worked in Louis Sullivan's studio (1887–93). While everyone was drowning their buildings with *historicist* decoration, and long before the Modernists had made a criterion of the thesis (attributed to Sullivan) "form follows function," Sullivan himself was carrying it out in practice, developing the design of a building to work in unison with its construction, and the construction to work in unison with the material.

Wright did not, however, enjoy the benefit of having been to a specialist college, which would have given him a theoretical grounding in architecture. Because of a lack of money he was only able to take a draftsmanship course at the third-class state university of Wisconsin, which he dropped in order to work for Sullivan. In 1894 he set up his own studio in Chicago. In 1906 he traveled to Japan, where the art made a deep impression upon him. In Europe, which he visited in 1910, he exhibited in Berlin, and the

description of his work published by the publisher Wasmuth ensured his importance in Europe as a stimulator of innovation. But he did not personally engage much with the concepts of his sternly rationalistic colleagues Gropius, Le Corbusier, and Mies van der Rohe. Although he did take note of almost all of the themes of Modernism, it was not in an abstract, theoretical way, but practically, in his designs. An example of this is the "machine." Whereas his European colleagues translated the way it worked into making buildings, for Wright it was an instrument for creating art. So it was that he created the Charles Ennis house out of industrially produced prefabricated concrete blocks in 1924, thoroughly in the spirit of Modernism. But Wright used the technology in an Arts and Crafts way and decorated the façades in Mayan style, whereas Modernism rejected such things, in the spirit of Adolf Loos's dictum "Ornament is criminal."

The real theme that the self-taught Wright developed himself, and spent his life propagating with missionary zeal, was that of organic architecture: "A building is only organic when the exterior and the interior exist in unison, and when both are in harmony with the character and nature of its purpose, its reason for existence, its location, and the time of its creation."

His first step in this direction was the "Prairie House," the layout of which was of a revolutionary freedom for that time, with the whole living area assembled around a hearth. Under wide projecting roofs, set on a massive base, the house opens on to the landscape through an expanse of windows that occupy all sides. With their dominating horizontals the buildings "make it credible," as Vincent Scully has said, "that the Americans had been living on their continent for ever." From 1910 dozens of buildings of this type were produced.

Later on the buildings became more individual, adapted to the particular requirements of the project and terrain. The Kaufmann house of 1936 is simply named "Falling Water," due to its perfect symbiosis with the waterfall over which it is constructed. Other buildings, such as the Marin County Civic Center of 1957, are enthroned like fantastic apparitions on a hill. But the basic motifs developed in the prairie houses remain the same.

Wright took up his own position in the landscape. Born in a little town in Wisconsin, the son of a preacher, he spent his whole life far from the centers of civilization. In 1911 he moved back to Spring Green, Wisconsin. In the valley of his forefathers he built Taliesin (first completed 1914, renovated following a fire 1925). In Taliesin

Perfect symbiosis with the waterfall: the Kaufmann house, named "Falling Water"

architecture became a model for life. The property was dwelling, studio, and farming enterprise all together. In 1938, the very deliberately named Taliesin West was created in Scottsville Arizona. In the depths of the prairies, under the steep wooden frame of the drawing hall, Taliesin College students and their egocentric father-figure came together in almost spiritual communion.

Anyone who lives that way must have a hostile attitude to the town. Wright wrote of Chicago: "It was so cold, so black, and so damp! The dreadful bluish-white sheen of the arc lamps dominated everything. I shivered." Consequently Wright built mainly in the open landscape. His few constructions in a city context all turn away from the city and create their own rich inner worlds. The Larkin building in Buffalo, New York (1905), is a brick fortress on the outside, but its large interior, lit solely from above, is a revolutionary design for a commercial headquarters. This same effect is achieved by the factory buildings for the Johnson Wax Company in Racine, Wisconsin (1936–39). An internal road places the entrance within the complex. Under a forest of mushroom-like pillars there is one of the most impressive single-room interiors ever seen. In the Guggenheim Museum in New York (see illustration on page 63), a lift sucks the visitor up from Fifth Avenue into the heights. A spiral ramp

Under a forest of mushroom-shaped supports, the large central office space of the Johnson Wax Company in Racine, Wisconsin (USA)

leads him down through an interior space so breathtaking that he forgets both city and art.

Wright designed an anti-urban countermodel to set against metropolises such as New York. In "Usonia" everyone would live as he did in Taliesin. Unlike the European garden city, Usonia does not start with the community, but with the freedom of the individual, upon which American societies are based. So Wright demanded for each family a minimum of one hectare of land and stressed the right of each person to have his own car. Finally in 1935 he developed a plan intended to bring about the harmony of individuals with each other and the landscape: Broadacre City (see pages 40–41).

This vision came to life simply as a faceless suburb. The architect did not become, as he had dreamed, the savior of modern American culture. In his "Testament" Wright acknowledged with resignation: "The United States is the only civilization to go from barbarism to degeneracy with no culture in between."

Hendrik Petrus Berlage, *Stock Exchange,* Amsterdam, 1896–1903

A plastered wall was "an untruthful thing" according to Hendrik Petrus Berlage. In reaction to the *eclecticism* of the 19th century, he strove for "an honest baring of the problems of architecture," for simplicity and craftsmanlike construction that was true to the nature of the materials. His stock exchange (1903) reveals the magic of brickwork, and was responsible for the founding of the Amsterdam School (see page 24). Its main hall consists of a brick shell, incorporating a simple supporting frame designed on engineering principles. Whereas the arched walls in brick achieved a self-contained quality unknown since the *Romanesque* period, the iron skeleton is put on show, in anticipation of modern principles. "What is the issue? To have a style again! Not just a kingdom, but Heaven itself for a style! That is the despairing cry: that is the great lost happiness. The issue is to fight fake art, i.e. the lie, to have back the real thing, not the appearance." So wrote Berlage in his *Reflections on style in architecture.*

influence of movements such as De Stijl in the Netherlands (see page 31) or the Bauhaus in Germany (see page 33) was dominant.

Despite its innovative aspects, the Palais Stoclet is clearly the last extravagant flowering of the Jugendstil. Extravagant in its use of materials too, the whole façade of the house is clothed in sheets of marble, set in borders of bronze. In the interior Gustav Klimt's mosaics melt into the decor, which Hoffmann carried out in cooperation with the Vienna workshop, to form a single, unique work of art.

Elemental architecture

The idea of reducing forms to their appropriate and necessary shape was the guiding principle of the Dutch architect Hendrik Petrus Berlage, who both as an architect and as a theoretician was one of the most important forerunners of the modern architecture of the first half of the 20th century. His work not only exerted a direct influence on subsequent Dutch architecture of the De Stijl movement, but also on German architects such as Peter Behrens or Ludwig Mies van der Rohe.

When designing the Amsterdam stock exchange, Behrens moved away from the formal repertoire of historicism in favor of an architecture based upon fundamental *tectonic* needs, which used materials in the most appropriate way.

When Adolph Loos turned away from the Jugendstil, pronounced ornamentation to be a criminal offense, then produced the extremely pared-down Steiner house and the Michaelerplatz building, the first phase of 20th-century architecture was drawing to its close.

American architecture at the end of the 19th century had virtually nothing to do with the developments taking place in Europe. It was only with the work of Frank Lloyd Wright, with his free designs ranging widely into the surrounding countryside which revolutionized the architecture of the single-family house, that American architecture gained a direct influence over European practitioners.

Josef Hoffmann, *Palais Stoclet,* Brussels, 1904–11

Whereas the general external appearance of Josef Hoffmann's Palais Stoclet is one of *rationalist* aesthetic severity, the detail is rich and recherché almost to the point of decadence. This duality makes the work a prime example of the transition in architecture from the 19th to the 20th century.

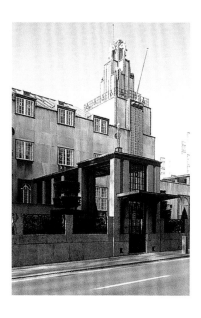

Reform and Expressionism
The First Moderns

1910–1920

MODERNIZATION AND INDUSTRIALIZATION

The age of imperialism ends in the First World War

Retrospectively, the European march toward the First World War has an ineluctable logic to it. At the beginning of the century the great powers – England, France, Austro-Hungary, and Germany – were making ever more threatening imperialist gestures at each other. At the same time the balance of power, which had been so laboriously established at the end of the 19th century, was beginning to shift again. The nationalist strains were sounding ever louder, and the arms race drove an ever deeper wedge of mistrust and ill-will between the European nations. In both politics and economics, it was national self-interest, driven by an unhealthy spirit of competition, which dictated the actions of the power-holders.

The murder in Sarajevo on 28 June 1914 of the Archduke Franz Ferdinand, the heir to the throne of Austro-Hungary, accelerated this process in spite of intensive secret diplomacy, and resulted a few weeks later in the outbreak of the First World War.

But the euphoric war fever of the first few weeks and months was destined to be short-lived. Years of disputing the same positions in the trenches at Verdun or on the Somme quickly brought home to English, French, and Germans alike that this war was a daily succession of horrors. The First World War brought the end of the "long 19th century." The era that had begun with the French Revolution of 1789 finally submerged in the bloody fever of a world war.

The German Werkbund

At the beginning of the 19th century the gap in economic development between Great Britain and Germany had been still wider. Intensive efforts were made on the Continent to challenge the British Empire's long and undisputed supremacy, and to compete with it in terms of *industrialization*. But Germany had a great way to go before it could make its industries and their products competitive on the world market.

While William Morris and his Arts and Crafts movement (see page 10) strove to renew art through a romantic harking back to the lost craft traditions of the Middle Ages, the forces for reform in prewar Germany went a different route toward reaching their goals. By using industrialization and mechanization, their aim was to turn out well-designed, high-quality products, as well as to achieve a new style in architecture. The combined economic and artistic strivings of industrialists, artists, and craftspeople came together in 1907 in the "Deutsche Werkbund" (German artwork union). The enlightened goal of the Werkbund was to achieve a better quality of design in objects for everyday use, and in ordinary life in general.

1911: Revolution in China under the leadership of Sun Yat-sen; the governors of several provinces join the revolution, and the Manchu Dynasty (established 1644) relinquishes power. IBM (International Business Machines Corp.) founded.

1912: The Italian film *Quo Vadis?* and the Russian film *War and Peace* shown in cinemas. 90% of all films shown in the world are of French origin. Sinking of the *Titanic*.

1913: The Indian poet and philosopher Rabindranath Tagore receives the Nobel Prize for Literature.

1914: The assassination of Archduke Franz Ferdinand of Austria in Sarajevo leads to the outbreak of the First World War (ends 1918). Henry Ford begins the assembly-line manufacture of the Model T. Mahatma Gandhi, who has been in South Africa since 1893, returns to India. Opening of the Panama Canal.

1915: Einstein begins developing his theory of relativity.

1916: Battle of Verdun. Ferdinand Sauerbruch constructs moveable false limbs. The German Expressionist painter of animals, Franz Marc, is killed in action. The Dada art movement comes into being in Zurich and Geneva (this ends around 1922).

1917: Nobel Peace Prize awarded to the International Committee of the Red Cross in Geneva. The October Revolution in Russia ends czarist rule. Lenin, Trotsky, and Stalin found the Soviet Union. George Grosz completes his collection of socially critical lithographs: *The face of the ruling class*.

1918: Otto Hahn and Lise Meitner

discover the radioactive element protactinium. The Russian Kasimir Malevich paints his monochromatic *White square on a white ground*, the high point of Suprematism.

1919: Peace conference begins in Paris. Founding of the League of Nations. Signing of the Treaty of Versailles. The leading left-wing socialists Rosa Luxemburg and Karl Liebknecht murdered by far-right officers. The Weimar Republic declared. Commencement of Prohibition in the USA.

1920: Gandhi begins his non-violent campaign for Indian independence. Mary Wigman opens her dancing school in Dresden, launching "expressive dance." The English writer Hugh Lofting brings out the children's *Dr. Dolittle* books. The Expressionist film, *The Cabinet of Dr. Caligari*, is premiered.

Production of the Model T Ford in Detroit. Photo dated 1913

Sociopolitical and economic interests merged in the Werkbund to reform German craft. Among the founder members of the union were such important architects as Hermann Muthesius, whose writings in particular had great influence on residential building in Germany, and Peter Behrens (see page 23), who rose to become the house architect and designer of Emil Rathenau's Allgemeiner Elektricitäts-Gesellschaft, AEG.

The Werkbund had a great influence on modern architecture in Germany right up till 1933, and it was an architect from Munich, Theodor Fischer, who became its first president. Fischer, the creator of the Garnisonskirche in Ulm, was likewise an extremely influential teacher for many architects of the next generation. The Werkbund's program-setting exhibition, held in 1914 in Cologne only a few weeks before the outbreak of the First World War, offered an overview of the various architectural currents of the time. Henry van de Velde called for a more strongly individualized and more craft-oriented direction. He was a champion of the Jugendstil, and had built the Werkbundtheater for the exhibition. This somewhat retrospective position was successfully opposed by Hermann Muthesius, who demanded a thoroughgoing move to industrial production, even of products that were traditionally handcrafted, and in this he included architecture.

Glass brings us the new age – industrial culture

The outstanding architectural event of the Werkbund exhibition in Cologne was the Glass Pavilion by Bruno Taut.

Set upon a curving *base*, the building was spanned by a *cupola* made of lozenge-shaped panes of glass. With its delicate many-colored brightness, the building was an example, inside as well as out, of the early Expressionism of German architecture with its *Gothic* derivation. Taut's glass architecture was inspired by the utopian verses of the poet Paul Scheerbart, whose aphoristic text also adorned the *façade* of his friend Taut's pavilion. "Glass brings us the new age, the culture of brick gives us only pain."

A year earlier, in 1913, Taut had produced another agenda-setting work, the monument to iron in the steel industry for the building exhibition in Leipzig, which served as a

model by means of its use of new forms and materials. Instead of *historicist ornamentation* or the floral decoration of the Jugendstil, the monument showed an exemplary respect for its materials. Even from the outside it was a clear demonstration of the principles of *building in iron*.

It was these same principles that gave its exceptional quality to a factory for making shoe-lasts, the Fagus Factory in Alfeld an der Leine, designed by Adolf Meyer and Walter Gropius (1911 – 13). It is rightly regarded as one of the founding buildings of 20th-century Modernist architecture. Scarcely anyone in Europe had until then designed so clear and functional an industrial building where every constructional element was on display without ornament: not even Peter Behrens, in whose office Gropius and Meyer had worked till 1910.

The model for these new factory buildings, with their functional, technical language of forms, were American silos and industrial buildings, whose persuasive functionality was now increasingly recognized to have an aesthetic dimension. The publication by Gropius of a collection of American "industrial architecture" in the Werkbund's yearbook for 1913 brought about a widespread appreciation of these exemplary buildings.

Also influential in Europe were the factory buildings with concrete skeletons that Albert Kahn and the engineer Ernest Ransome erected for the industrialist Henry Ford's thrusting new automobile works in Detroit.

Bruno Taut, *Glass Pavilion,* Werkbund exhibition in Cologne, 1914

19th-century engineers had used glass exclusively as a rational facing material. Now Bruno Taut showed off its many-sided potential in his pavilion for the German glass industry at the Cologne Werkbund exhibition. He was also making a point: in a time overshadowed by war, he made a construction in which everything had either mirrors or colored glass in it, from the roof to the steps, including a glass cascade with water bubbling down it, in a vision of a new, paradisiacal world. The building style, as well as the aphoristic texts by Paul Scheerbarts that decorated the exterior, elevated material to the status of a component in a new morality. Taut later developed this design into a whole series of fantastic sketches of crystalline "city crowns," none of which, however, were built.

Walter Gropius and Adolf Meyer,
Fagus Factory, general view (right) and
detail of the stairwell (below), Alfeld,
1911 – 13

The Fagus factory was Gropius's first
important building. The long workshop
block of this shoe-last factory is of
convincing, unadorned simplicity. In it, he
discriminates between the load-bearing
structure and the non-load-bearing
façade, which is constructed as a curtain
wall. The impression of lightness stems
chiefly from the all-glass corners, whose
vertical sheets of glass seem to hang from
the jutting cornice above because the
columns are recessed. There are no
columns within, so that the stairways float
freely in their glass towers. These
elements, and also the fact that all the
parts of the building (with the exception of
the chimney) are given equal significance,
made the Fagus factory into *the* stylistic
model of modern architecture.

The name of Ford is still linked above almost
any other with the sweeping success of the
car in the 20th century. His revolutionary
economic and social initiatives had to be
matched by production buildings that were
just as revolutionary. Ford's motor company
had began producing cars in 1903. His recipe
for success was signal in its modernity: only a
few mass-produced parts were needed to
assemble each car. The stringent rationality
with which each task followed the next, the
increased division of labor, and the resultant
low production costs all contributed to making
Henry Ford one of the most successful car
manufacturers of his day. Comparatively high
pay and low working hours increased his
employees' motivation.

Kahn's buildings reflect this sternly economic
point of view with its total renunciation of
display, in that they are soberly cubic in form
without any superfluous decoration. Being
constructed of concrete, the buildings were
relatively cheap to produce. The production
sheds with their conveyor belts were rationally
designed, laid out all on one level, and were
notable for their bright interiors, full of natural
light coming in through large windows set
into the supporting concrete skeleton. The
great art of Kahn's utilitarian buildings lies in
their renunciation of everything traditionally
considered artistic.

In Europe, on the other hand, architecture
was not yet as clearly modern as Kahn's
buildings or the early work of Gropius and
Meyer. Modern and *historicist* elements were

still often mixed together. This situation is
hardly to be wondered at when considering
the centuries-old – in some cases thousand-
year-old – regional building traditions in
Europe. The synthesis of building traditions
is exemplified in the early works of the Berliner
Hans Poelzig, whose own idiosyncratically
expressive architectural language increasingly
takes center stage, as in the case of the
chemical factory that he built between 1911
and 1912 in Lubau, near Posen. The brick
building could be seen to be composed of
geometrically stacked cubes, thus putting its
industrial nature clearly on display. In Breslau
in 1911 Poelzig designed an office building
entirely of reinforced concrete, notable for its
horizontal lines of windows and its rounded
corners, both motifs that were to recur
frequently in the 1920s in the work of other
Modernist architects such as Erich Mendelsohn
and Hans Scharoun.

The triumph of concrete

New materials were proving themselves to an
ever greater degree. Materials that at first
were used only for industrial and utilitarian
buildings gradually conquered the field of
traditional building projects. It was above all
the previously unheard-of possibilities of
concrete that revolutionized architecture.

Suddenly it became possible, using the new
materials, to roof an immense hall without
needing to put in any additional support in the
form of pillars, which would decrease the view
within the space. The first example of this was

Max Berg, *Centennial Hall,* general view (left), elevation and plan (below), Breslau (now Wrocław in Poland), 1910–13

Over 200 feet (65 meters) of unsupported space: the *reinforced concrete* stepped *dome* spanned three times the space of the dome of St. Peter's in Rome and weighed only half as much. Max Berg was the city architect of Breslau and erected the building for the celebrations commemorating the uprising against Napoleon. It had to serve as an assembly room and also have the technical and lighting provisions necessary for exhibitions. In it he demonstrated the huge spaces that could be spanned using the new material. He took advantage of the structural necessities of the work to produce a powerful impression of monumentality. The 32 curved radial ribs of the dome, between which light enters the building, are openly on view. The exposed concrete, roughened by the formwork, anticipates the bare-concrete aesthetic of Le Corbusier.

the Jahrhunderhalle (Centennial Hall) built by the city architect of Breslau, Max Berg. Although the *dome* of the Hall was three times bigger than the stone-built dome of St. Peter's in Rome, Berg's inspired creation with its reinforced concrete ribs weighed only half as much!

The more concrete, with its vast potential as a building material, entered architects' fields of vision, the more their approach to it changed. Gradually it was recognized as having an aesthetic value of its own in its unadorned form.

Whereas August Perret had covered the construction of the concrete supports in his apartment house in the rue Franklin in Paris with ceramic tiles, by 1905, when he built the garage at 51 rue de Ponthieu, he showed the reinforced concrete grid quite openly; it was simply painted to protect it from the weather. The wall spaces between the supports were completely filled with glass.

Cars were swiftly becoming popular in Paris at the beginning of the century, and making a building to park them in was an entirely new task for the architect. Perret's response was appropriately new, inside as well as out. Using the potential of concrete for *spanning* a large space, Perret was able to produce a relatively unobstructed covered area, which could be set up to service all the requirements of short- and long-term parking.

The movement in which Perret was instrumental, which aimed to reduce architecture to a functional supporting armor of concrete, reached its spiritual peak in his church,

Notre-Dame-du-Raincy, built near Paris in 1924. The vaulted roof of the nave, made out of unadorned concrete, rests on slim pillars, and the walls are so pierced with openings that daylight can stream into the church almost unhindered.

The Swiss architect Charles-Édouard Jeanneret – who under the name Le Corbusier was to become one of the most important Modernist architects, and who for a time had been employed in Auguste Perret's office – was keen to use *architecture in reinforced concrete*, which had been developed by Perret, for residential building. As early as 1915 he had developed the "Dom-ino-System" for re-building Flanders, which had been devastated by the battles of the First World War. This was a plan for mass-produced housing, whereby it should be possible to construct a concrete skeleton within a few weeks. The precondition for this was a far-reaching uniformity in the construction units, particularly the formwork for the concrete. The Dom-ino houses represent Le Corbusier's first attempt at thoroughgoing rationalization and total functionality. Although his plans remained an unrealized project, they were characteristic of the later development of his views on architecture and town planning.

NEOCLASSICISM

In search of a national style

Although a few modern buildings were being planned and realized in 1910, the rationalist

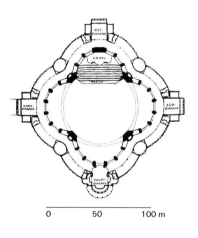

| 0 | 50 | 100 m |

Auguste Perret, *The Church of Notre-Dame-du-Raincy,* near Paris, 1924

The pioneer of *reinforced concrete* used it for a religious building drawing on the traditions of *antiquity* and the *Gothic* era. The concrete is visible everywhere, still rough from the formwork. Ornamentation is spare and dictated by the structure. The walls consist of ready-made concrete elements set with colored glass. They create a room out of light, in a way that is comparable to Gothic cathedrals. The church, with its three naves and barrel vaulting, belongs to the basic typology of a Romanesque basilica.

and functionalist trends in architecture were far from being the only ones in the prewar period. Far from it: a heterogeneous mix of the most varied *styles* prevailed in towns. Many buildings were indeed an *eclectic* jumble of historicist, Modernist, and Jugendstil forms.

At the beginning of the century the question of the *right* style suddenly dominated discussion again, a question that stemmed entirely from the 19th century, especially from *classicism* and the *neo-Renaissance.* The few really modern buildings that had so far been realized were in sharp contrast to the continuing tradition of grandiose *historicist* buildings, which employed an architectonic repertoire that had been handed down over the centuries. Yet the conservative shell of a *neo-Baroque* palace might have a steel skeleton or a concrete construction concealed under its luxuriant stucco decoration.

In the search for a national style that would also correspond to the nation's external self-image, *neo-Classicism* became, around 1910, the dominant doctrine, adding a further facet to the already rich spectrum of contemporary architecture.

Peter Behrens in particular, in his important buildings for AEG, including the Turbine Room in Berlin, tried to make a clear use of models from the history of architecture. The *rough-cast,* slightly curved corner *quoins* of his turbine room were very clearly reminiscent of ancient Egypt. Through this borrowing from history, the factory – a project quite without spirituality – managed to achieve a unique nobility that lifted it directly on to a plane with the temples of ancient Egypt

despite all the modernity in its functioning. In the St. Petersburg embassy of 1911, Behrens increased his classical borrowings. The result was an at that time unrivalled *Doric* monumentalism that made clear the conscious grandeur and power of those who had commissioned it.

But it was not only in Germany that neo-Classicism took root, and carried on right into the 1920s and 1930s. Edwin Lutyens used the style, which was generally understood to be the language of power at the time, to demonstrate the imperialist pretensions of Great Britain in the new buildings of New Delhi in India (1915–24).

Henry Bacon used the same monumental formal language in his Lincoln Memorial, which was designed in 1917 in Washington DC, feeling that he was under an obligation to reflect the classicist style of the old government buildings. The acceptance of this old architectural language for new buildings and national monuments deliberately placed them within the older tradition, with its connotations of upholding the state.

Classicism and Modernism

Heinrich Tessenow used an even more reduced language of form than Behrens or Lutyens. But even his Festspielhaus (festival hall) at Hellerau near Dresden was inspired by the classicist repertoire of forms. So the main façade had a monumental *pillared portico* as high as itself, supporting the tympanum of the steep pitched roof. The interior of the hall was constructed in such a way that it could be variously configured for different types of performance, and could be used for new artistic manifestations such as eurythmics, modern music, and free dance.

Likewise, Mies van der Rohe (see page 59), who had worked in Behrens' office, kept faith with a model of purified *classicism* in the early villas he built for well-heeled clients in Berlin and Potsdam.

Mies van der Rohe was very much involved, right through till his late work in the 1960s, with the architectural heritage of Karl Friedrich Schinkel, the most important Prussian architect of the 19th century. Mies realized better than anyone else how to transfer Schinkel's innovative use of materials – for example his early use of iron and zinc – and his strict articulation of space into his own work. Little

PETER BEHRENS

When Peter Behrens built a house for himself in 1901 in the Mathildenhöhe artists' colony in Darmstadt, it created a sensation. A native of Hamburg, he was already a respected figure in Germany, having made his name as an exponent of the Jugendstil both as a painter and a craftsman. But in architecture he was a newcomer.

Perhaps it was through this versatility and openness to the various art forms that Behrens was destined to become one of the most influential all-round artists in Germany in the first half of the 20th century. Today he is best known as an architect, but he was also a book designer, a designer of typefaces, and craftsman, so that he has to be seen as one of the earliest "designers."

A milestone in Behrens's career, as well as in the history of German art, was his connection with Emil Rathenau's AEG (General Electricity Company), which was the biggest industrial concern in Germany around 1910. In 1907, industrialist and designer began a partnership that was at that time unique. Through his work for AEG, designing their products according to artistic criteria, Behrens provided a model for that cooperation between art, craft, and industrial production that was one of the goals of the *Deutscher Werkbund*, founded in the same year. He thus became one of the grandfathers of "industrial design" and "corporate identity." But it was not only his industrial products for AEG that brought him public notice. There was also his turbine factory (1909), designed for the company in Berlin, which even today, and despite its

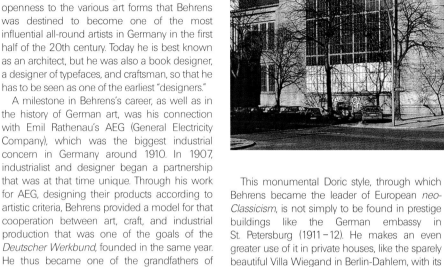

The dawn of a light-flooded era: the AEG Turbine Factory in Berlin, built in 1909

building so interpenetrate each other that the flat roofs of the lower parts of the block serve as terraces for the dwellings above.

The Nazis, who were attracted by the neo-Classicist side of Behrens, also tried to get him to build for them. Just before his death he was going to build the new AEG headquarters on the north-south axis planned by Albert Speer for Berlin. But the project went no further than the models (1937–39), and it foundered with the Third Reich.

This monumental Doric style, through which Behrens became the leader of European *neo-Classicism*, is not simply to be found in prestige buildings like the German embassy in St. Petersburg (1911–12). He makes an even greater use of it in private houses, like the sparely beautiful Villa Wiegand in Berlin-Dahlem, with its

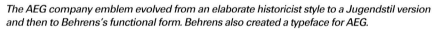

The AEG company emblem evolved from an elaborate historicist style to a Jugendstil version and then to Behrens's functional form. Behrens also created a typeface for AEG.

An Expressionist brick building: the entrance hall of the head office of the Hoechst dyeworks. (1920–24)

unique pillared hall. Apart from his enthusiasm for the industrial production of artistically valid objects, this pared-down neo-Classicism was the main theme he handed on to his younger colleagues in his Berlin architectural practice. Many were to number among the most important architects of the succeeding generation: Le Corbusier, Ludwig Mies van der Rohe, and Walter Gropius among others.

It was one of Peter Behrens's attributes as an architect that he was very much in tune with the spirit of the times and was able to render the demands and desires of those who commissioned him in architectural forms appropriate to the times. His openness to new styles and forms of artistic expression is shown in the brick building for the headquarters of the Hoechst dyeworks company, the high, cathedral-like entrance hall which displays all the colors of the rainbow. Behrens, a neo-Classicist before the war, here joins the *Expressionist* movement, with a building inspired by the *Amsterdam School.*

Behrens was a part of the next evolution of architecture too, from Expressionism to *Neues Bauen*. It was not a surprising move: the most important representatives of Modernism in architecture had been his pupils and colleagues. As a founder-member and leading representative of the Deutscher Werkbund, he had contributed to the Stuttgart building complex, the Weissenhofsiedlung (see page 39), a stepped apartment block. Behrens had a masterly grasp of how to put the contemporary forms of Neues Bauen to personal use. The cubic volumes of the

Behrens as industrial designer: the AEG-Sparbogenlampe was devised specifically for interiors with limited hanging space

monumental feel, remains one of the icons of modern architecture with its pared-down language of form. These were to become even more reduced in his AEG assembly shop (1912) in the Voltastrasse, the façade of which, with its clear lines and its total absence of decoration, gives it an almost revolutionary character, comparable with the early major works of Gropius and Kahn.

The outstanding feature of Behrens's buildings, apart from their functionality, is their imposing monumentality, for example in the turbine factory or in AEG's small motors factory of 1910. This quality is achieved through the buildings' sternly cubic volumes, but also through their *classical* formal language, mainly employing the *Doric* order.

by little, Mies van der Rohe succeeded in translating the classicist repertoire of forms employed by Schinkel, without any *historicist* motifs, into abstract modern architecture.

EXPRESSIONISM

The way to variety in color and form

A completely new direction in architecture began in around 1905. It occurred almost simultaneously with a completely new direction in painting: that taken by the Fauves, led by Henri Matisse and Maurice de Vlaminck in France, and the German Brücke group in Dresden including Erich Heckel, Karl Schmidt-Rottluff, Ludwig Kirchner, and Max Pechtsein.

Heinrich Tessenow, *Festival Hall,*
Hellerau near Dresden, 1910

The most ambitious housing project before the First World War was the garden city for the Hellerau workshops near Dresden. In the middle was the festival hall by Heinrich Tessenow, completed in 1910. The heart of this cultural center was a revolutionary flexible hall, with a single stage made up of mobile elements, dedicated to the promotion of social harmony through the art of movement. The exterior was equally high-minded, but more traditional in its formal language, for which Tessenow had abstracted elements of *classicist* architecture.

Glowing colors and strong brush strokes were among the revolutionary innovations of this emotional, boundlessly subjective painting, as was its radical reduction of forms to the verge of *abstraction*. The exponents of the new painting were open to influences of all kinds. For them, art could be creating sketch-like nudes with a few brush strokes in an open-air setting, or connecting to the so-called "primitive art" of Africa or Oceania: themes that had not till now been considered valid parts of artistic endeavor. Another creative involvement of these Expressionist painters was with the energetic forms of *Gothic* architecture, with its pointed arches and immense spirituality.

Just before the First World War architects also began to be interested in Expressionism. Thus, concurrently, with the functional formal language of for example Walter Gropius, there emerged another lively branch of Modernism, the mobile language of Expressionism.

Expressionism was expressed in architecture largely through the materials of *brick* and glass. Glass and Crystal Expressionism was a utopian architectural project that was initiated in 1914 by Bruno Taut's glass pavilion at the Werkbund exhibition. Expressionist architecture in brick held sway right into the 1920s, especially in the Nordic countries, which could look back on a continuous tradition that dated back to Gothic times. The red-brown through to bluish-violet coloring of the bricks, in addition to their differing surface textures, ensured that the façades were full of variety in both color and form. The individualized production of bricks made them particularly suitable for the frequently small-scale and extremely detailed Expressionist decoration.

The Amsterdam School – new directions in the Netherlands

Early on a group of architects who named themselves the "Amsterdam School" formed in the Netherlands, whose imaginative and expressive designs quickly became famous.

The prelude to Expressionist art in brick in the Netherlands was at the same time its climax. This was the Schiffahrtshaus (shipping building) erected between 1912 and 1916 by Johann Melchior van der Mey, together with Michel de Klerk and Pieter Kramer. This striking office building derived its name from the Amsterdam shipping companies who commissioned it as the base for their representatives. Following their demand for a "not too sober building in brick," van der Mey designed a façade decorated with a multitude of *ornaments*, sculptures and *friezes* made up of small parts. The imagery, drawn from the realms of shipping, sea, and trade with inexhaustible imaginative flair, exerts such a direct spell over the beholder that he almost forgets that the playful brick surface of the shipping building is simply the icing on top of the load-bearing concrete structure underneath. Van der May was reproached by rationalist critics with the fact that the façade was a surface, but it is perfectly in keeping with the picturesque charm of the building. Even this early example of Expressionist architecture shows how very much its exponents saw their buildings also as sculptures, and ornamented them accordingly, or else treated them as complete entities whose role was that of *architecture parlante*.

With his housing complex at the Spaarndammerplatsoen, which was built in several stages between 1913 and 1920, Michel de Klerk made his most important contribution to residential building in Amsterdam at that time. It was a step in the direction of housing reform, albeit of a bourgeois type, which was only practicable in small countries like Holland. The complex may not be as lavishly ornamented as the shipping building, but it is remarkable for its combination of the most varied expressive motifs and types of window, from the semicircular to the trapezoid, so that there is no monotony in the façades, and de Klerk's individual signature is clearly recognizable.

Together with his friend and colleague Pieter Kramer, de Klerk began putting up the workers' housing development De Dageraad in 1918, for the cooperatively organized workers' organization of the same name in the south of Amsterdam. Extensive town-planning initiatives devised by Hendrik Petrus Berlage took place in the same area. At De Dageraad – once again using *brick* – de Klerk developed an extraordinarily rich spectrum of the most varied types of building that even for his contemporaries evoked a wide range of associations. There are cubic shapes, wave motifs, cylinders, quotations from ship-building, roofs that extend far down the side of the buildings, and sculptures in brick. De Dageraad was a short-lived but innovative showcase of dynamic building ideas, which nonetheless fitted together as a whole.

De Dageraad was an artistic statement, but it was also a social and political one; it was a rejection of the barrack-like tenements built under *historicism*. The dominant theme in this housing development for working-class families was light and air in a richly varied environment. The cooperative nature of the body that commissioned it was a further element in the social commitment of De Dageraad.

Although residential building in the 1920s – as carried out by De Stijl (see page 31) in Holland and also in places in Germany where a great deal of it was going on (such as Frankfurt and Berlin, see page 37) – differed markedly from the expensive Expressionist architectural language of Klerk and Kramer, the estate which they built at De Dageraad was a decisive step forward in the reform of working-class housing.

The architectonic spectrum of the 1920s is very broad. However, if you mentally transport yourself to that era, it becomes clear that the first transposition of Frank Lloyd Wright's clear cubic shapes in reinforced concrete to Europe was the Villa in Huis ter Heide, designed by Robert van't Hoff when the members of the Amsterdam School were developing their multiform Expressionistic architectural language.

From the Einstein Tower to the Chile Building – Expressionism in Germany

Expressionism in architecture began in Germany with Bruno Taut's Glass House at the Werkbund Exhibition in Cologne in 1914. Its major creations did not arise until after the First World War.

Building activity almost ceased in Germany between 1914 and 1918. It seemed that architectonic endeavor had exhausted itself in laying out war cemeteries, or in producing

Johann Melchior van der Mey, Michel de Klerk, and Pieter Kramer, *Schiffahrtshaus*, Amsterdam, 1912–16

Three leading members of the Amsterdam School built the headquarters for a group of shipping companies. They faced the *reinforced concrete structure* with a variety of materials including tiles, concrete, and terracotta. The richly exotic, sculptural forms seek to establish a symbolic link with shipping and the distant worlds it opens up. The building is thus an early example of the sculptural inventiveness of Expressionism, and an *architecture parlante*.

Robert van't Hoff, *Villa,* Huis ter Heide, 1916

Van't Hoff's villa imports characteristic features from the work of the American architect Frank Lloyd Wright, who had become known in Europe though the publication of the famous Wasmuth edition of his works (1910–11) and an exhibition in Berlin. These included the strip windows, the skylights, and in particular the emphasis on the horizontal through the clear cubic form and gray-painted horizontal blocks of the reinforced concrete structure. The Dutch architect had studied in the USA, where he had got to know Wright personally and helped compile an inventory of his works. This enabled him to incorporate in the villa a union of French *Cubism* with Wright's theses, even before the Dutch De Stijl group was formed in 1917, around the three artists Piet Mondrian, Theo van Doesburg, and Gerrit Thomas Rietveld.

Erich Mendelsohn, *Einstein Tower,* Potsdam, 1920–24, sketch

As he was preparing his first important commission, Erich Mendelsohn created with a few strokes of the pen, a key work of architectural drawing. The completed building became *the* icon of Expressionism. Its purpose is not rationally expressed in its structure, but symbolically in its form. With its heavy *plinth* and its upwards-striving tower, the building, which housed a powerful telescope, an underground laboratory, a workroom at ground-level, and sleeping accommodation, mediated between heaven and earth. The sculpture in concave and convex planes was intended originally to be cast in *reinforced concrete,* which would have made the ultimate use of the plasticity of the medium. But because of technological difficulties, the walls above the plinth were constructed in the conventional way and plastered.

visionary and Expressionist drawings and watercolors. To promote the circulation and discussion of such ideas, Bruno Taut set up the forum "Gläserne Kette" (glass chain), which lasted from 1919 to 1921.

He expressed his utopian concepts of a new society and an ideal architecture for the cities within it, in his legendary essays *Alpine Architektur* (1918) and *Stadtkrone* (City crown) (1919). However, he did not carry out these visions during his tenure as city architect for Magdeburg (1921–23) nor when he went to practise as an architect in Berlin. Instead, he engaged in a pragmatic, socially committed program of *working-class housing,* becoming the leading architect in this area in the 1920s.

One of the few people who was able to put his vision into practice was Erich Mendelsohn. Mendelsohn translated the organic language of forms, which he too first envisioned in drawings, into a real building: the Einstein Tower in Potsdam. Built as an observatory and astrophysical institute for the study of Albert Einstein's theory of relativity, this striking tower brought Mendelsohn immediate fame.

The design he drew for the building in 1920 with only a few strokes of the pen, but which displayed all the concentrated dynamism characteristic of him, has become an icon of modern architectural drawing.

The thought-through plasticity of the Einstein Tower and the organic interweaving of its forms are strongly reminiscent of the buildings of the Amsterdam school of architects, who on the completion of the tower very logically invited him to Amsterdam to study what they themselves had built.

But, surprisingly enough, behind the formally innovative exterior of the Potsdam tower there are traditionally built walls. This came about chiefly because of the difficulty at that time of making appropriate formwork for the curved façade that Mendelsohn had designed to be made in concrete.

Very much more *stereometric* in design when compared with the Einstein Tower was the hat factory (its site now inevitably largely built over) that Mendelsohn designed for Steinberg Hermann and Co. in Luckenwalde (1921–23). It also represented a transition to the rationalist offices and department stores that Mendelsohn created after 1925. The Luckenwalde hat factory united functional design and technical innovation (like the arrangement for dispersing the poisonous fumes emanating from the dyeing installation) with what was, for the 1920s, an unusually expressive form for an industrial building

Shortly after the First World War another Berlin architect, Hans Poelzig, designed a huge theater, holding 5,000 spectators, in the center of Berlin for the renowned theater director Max Reinhardt in 1919. It was pulled down in 1986. From the interior of its crowning *dome* hung elongated shapes, making it look like a cave of stalactites. Not long afterwards (1920–22) Poelzig carried out a very similar design for a theater in Salzburg, cave-like and intricate as the icing on a cake.

German Expressionist architecture reached another peak in the brick buildings of the Hamburg architect Fritz Höger, who was for a time on the committee of the Deutscher Werkbund. One of his main works is the Chilehaus in Hamburg, which he built for a shipping company in the form of a giant ocean liner. One of the building's best-known features is its southeast corner which is sharply pointed like the bow of a ship.

The building was constructed in dark red *clinker*. Höger's inspiration for the building was not only marine architecture but the *Gothic* cathedrals constructed in brick that are widespread in the northern part of Germany. These borrowings are also evident in the arcades within the building, some of which also narrow toward the end, and the accent on the vertical in the whole edifice, chiefly achieved by the architect's use of *external piers* to articulate the façade. In order to ventilate the gigantic complex adequately, and to supply sufficient light for all the rooms, Höger built it around three big inner courtyards.

The Chilehaus and the Amsterdam Schiff-fahrtshaus built ten years earlier are, for all their many differences, linked as buildings in the Expressionist style, by their function and their use of brick, and also in their manifold small-scale ornamentation.

CUBISM

Architectonic independence in Prague

In Prague around 1911 there was a group of intellectuals whose work was influenced by

the clear *stereometric* architecture of Otto Wagner, who was a representative of the Vienna Jugendstil. The other important model and influence for them was the work of Robert Delaunay, Georges Braque, and Pablo Picasso, with its radically deconstructed and then reassembled forms.

While he was in Paris, Delaunay had been through a stylistic phase in which the object represented was broken down into basic geometric forms – the cube, ball, and circle. Delaunay's Cubist pictures, such as that of the Eiffel Tower or the giant composition City of Paris, were dramatic in effect, full of the dynamism of the big city, and the Prague Cubist architects took them as the inspiration for the façades

Fritz Höger, *Chilehaus,* Hamburg, 1921–24

This office building was designed by Fritz Höger for a shipping company. Inside and out it evokes a giant liner. There are lines of identical office cells like cabins. The set-back strips and horizontal railings emphasize the prow-like point of the triangular building. The dark red clinker on the façade and the arching ribs within are also reminiscent of the tradition of north German Gothic construction in brick.

Josef Gočár, *"The Black Madonna" Department Store,* Prague 1911–12

Josef Gočár was one of the leading representatives of Cubism in architecture, and kept up a lively intellectual exchange with the writers and artists of his time. He originally designed the department store in the modern classicist mode. But after fundamental revision, the *reinforced concrete skeleton* acquired its distinctive cubic elements, in particular the front entrance, the dormer windows and the *capitals* on the columns of the façade. This design lays particular emphasis on the effect created by shadow, which stresses the three-dimensional quality of the building. The architect's design continues in the interior, including a Cubist café on the top floor, which, however, was quickly disfigured by alterations. To this day the harmonious insertion of this building – a provocative one for its day – in its historic neighborhood is exemplary. The mansard roof can be seen as a concession to the heritage conservation lobby.

Josef Chochol, *Hodek Apartment Block,* Prague, 1913–14

The architecture of Josef Chochol includes some of the most thorough-going translations of Cubist theories of surface and space. One typical example is the shape he gives to the windows of the ground floor of the Hodek building, which itself stands out in a point on a steeply sloping site. The building, housing several families, is totally in the spirit of the day, down to the last detail. Even the corner rooms are polygonal.

of their houses, which they decorated with rows of cubic or prismatic shapes. As with the contemporary *Expressionist* movement, the whole building was treated in sculptural terms, so that it conveyed something of the impression of being a sculpture capable of being lived in.

The Prague architects could also cite the example of late *Gothic* architecture, with its almost abstract vaulting, of which Prague has, even today, a great deal. For a long time the Cubist architecture of Prague was wrongly interpreted as a purely regional manifestation, but now it has been re-evaluated as a related but independent alternative to northern European Expressionism.

Josef Gočár's department store, *The Black Madonna*, which is one of the most important works of Prague Cubism, clearly demonstrates the differences between Expressionist and Cubist architecture. Instead of the intricate, figurative ornamentation that characterizes the buildings of the *Amsterdam School*, Gočár designed a lucid, clearly structured building. The crystalline shapes that break up the façade create a fascinating play of light and shade, giving the building a particular, almost living, charm.

A similar architectural language is employed in the five-story Hodek apartment block that was designed by Josef Chochol.

In spite of being modeled in cubes and prisms, the façade is actually subdivided according to a strict grid of both vertical and horizontal elements. The ground floor in particular is given a specific emphasis with its unusually shaped six-cornered windows. The diamond shapes above the windows are echoed in the jagged relief of the jutting-out cornice that tops the façade, thus giving the building, in spite of its dynamic feel, a harmonious conclusion.

FUTURISM

Italy breaks out into modernity

The problem of human perception and appropriation of the world was one of the central themes of art at the beginning of the century. Whereas the approach of the *Expressionists* would be to conjure up an extremely subjective view of the world on their canvases, the *Cubists* favored the dissection of everyday objects, such as a chair or a guitar, into their basic geometric structures. They would then put them back together in a way that was both surprising and disorienting for the viewer. The object that had originally seemed familiar to the eye became something else. At the same time the viewer was challenged into a new, critical perception of the original object – the real chair or the real guitar. The result of this was in any case a sharpened perception of reality.

The Italian Futurists' experimentation took a different turn from that of the Cubists: dissecting the phases of the movement and reassembling them on a single plane.

The artistic concept of Futurism, which was first developed in painting, poetry, and sculpture before it moved on to architecture, was to make visible phases of movement and the power of speed derived from them, a dynamism that they recognized as a defining characteristic of the future. Although the Italian Futurists were denied the realization of their architectonic and town-planning designs, their drawings, expressive of both a denial of the past and a belief in progress, place their visions among the important trends of modern art in the 20th century.

A leading exponent of Futurism was Antonio Sant'Elia, who, in his manifesto of July 1914 on futurist architecture, took a clear stand against all "solemn, theatrical, and decorative building." Instead, he wanted to "invent and build the futurist city. It must be like a great resounding shipyard and be swift, mobile, and dynamic in every part:, the futurist house must be like a giant machine." Sant'Elia's sketches of a "Città Nuova," with its intersecting traffic planes for cars, railways, and aircraft, its electricity works and its glassy exterior lifts on residential buildings, reflect his conception of a really modern technological world. However, they remained only a vision. He published his revolutionary visions of architecture in Milan in 1914 ("Architecture means the ability to bring man and his environment freely and boldly into harmony with each other"). Tragically, two years later he was killed in the First World War, without having had the chance to realize them.

However, it was largely his futuristic architectural visions of stepped skyscrapers and monumental, emphatically vertical electricity works, which started the move away from 19th-century *historicism* and toward rationalist architecture in Italy. This made it possible after the war to link with contemporary movements and especially with the Russian avant-garde.

Antonio Sant'Elia, *Electricity Works,*
Architectural Vision 1914, Consuelo Accetti collection, Milan

The technology and the entirely new potential of electricity was a leitmotif of the Futurists and their innovatory thinker Sant'Elia. They transposed the concentrated energy and dynamism of the electric current into their sketches for architecture imbued with the spirit of technology and into urban visions that broke radically with traditional forms and conceptions of the city. This spirit is precisely conveyed by this drawing by Sant'Elia in which the pressure lines hurtle rather than fall, the chimneys rear up from a low-angle perspective, and the electric cables flow powerfully out of the picture: a new aesthetic for modern architecture takes shape from industrial forms.

Modernity establishes
itself

The International Style

1920–1930

ARCHITECTURE AFTER THE WAR

The war destroys the old world

Long before the First World War, movements for political and cultural reform had gathered strength in Europe and the United States. New directions in art such as *Art Nouveau* and, shortly afterwards, *Expressionism*, *Futurism*, and *Cubism* broke with traditional art and searched for new concepts and forms of artistic expression in a world that was progressing at lightening speed and was marked by continuous technical innovation. But it was only following the First World War that the foundations of the traditional world order finally crumbled. The centuries-old hegemony of Europe was destabilized. Not only did the Austro-Hungarian state with its multiple races disappear from the map of Europe, but the monarchies of Russia and Germany were swept away by revolutions, and while the United States stepped on to the world stage for the first time, the British Empire, which had previously spanned the world, slowly began to break up.

The First World War was the defining experience of a whole era. Modern weapons, such as tanks and aircraft, had been brought to a high degree of technical perfection and were employed for the first time. Soldiers no longer faced their opponents face to face, but as the anonymous "enemy", hidden behind gas masks and in the trenches. Already existing social and economic problems increased, and the economic uncertainty of the postwar era brought to the fore the demand for a solution to the misery of hunger, unemployment, and homelessness.

Programmes for dealing with social need

The generalized deprivation that had struck whole areas of the population was a challenge to artists and writers, as well as to politicians. At this time, artistic and political programs went hand in hand, from Moscow to Amsterdam, with aims of changing the face of the world and the ways of being that it offered, both in society as well as in art. The increasing political commitment of art expressed itself in themes such as social criticism – as seen in George Grosz's biting pictures – or in fiery outcries against the inhumanity of war as Henri Barbusse put forward in his novel *Le Feu*.

In architecture too, there was a thoroughgoing drive to develop functional new ways of building and to use new building materials: glass, concrete, and steel. The new, more rational and economical building methods were not just an expression of the spirit of the times, with its repudiation of *historicist* buildings covered in outdated ornamentation. They also had a definite social component, especially when applied to the *housing developments* that were carried out with a great deal of urgency to address the problem of homelessness.

The period 1900–20 was a determining one for the direction of modern art and architecture. But from 1920 to 1930, following the disaster of the First World War, an

1921: Washington agreement on the banning of the use of poison gas as an element of international law. Discovery of insulin as a treatment for diabetes. Arturo Toscanini becomes director of the Scala, Milan. Nobel Prize for Physics awarded to Albert Einstein for the discovery of the photon and his work in theoretical physics. Charlie Chaplin's film *The Kid* premiered in America. Women start wearing their hair bobbed.

1922: Following a fascist coup in Italy, Mussolini is named prime minister by the king. James Joyce completes his novel *Ulysses*.

1923: Kemal Atatürk becomes president of Turkey. Hitler putsch in Munich.

1924: Death of Lenin. Submission of the Dawes plan for the settlement of German reparations. Première of Gershwin's *Rhapsody in Blue*.

1925: Geneva Convention banning chemical and bacterial warfare. The "king of jazz," Louis Armstrong, sets up his Combo Hot Five.

1926: Founding of the British Commonwealth of Nations. First performances of Fritz Lang's *Metropolis* and Sergei Eisenstein's *Battleship Potemkin*. First successful television transmission in London. Walt Disney's *Mickey Mouse* cartoons first screened.

1927: After a murder trial in Massachusetts (USA) arousing international controversy, Sacco and Vanzetti are executed. Charles Lindbergh flies non-stop across the

Atlantic. Sven Hedin begins his expedition into the interior of Asia. Martin Heidegger's *Being and Time* is published, initiating a secular philosophy, existentialism. Proust publishes the seventh and last volume of his *Remembrance of Things Past.* Josephine Baker, the American-born French dancer and singer, takes Paris by storm.

1928: Briand-Kellogg pact outlaws war as a means of resolving international differences. Chiang Kai-shek unites China. Penicillin discovered by an English bacteriologist, Alexander Fleming.

1929: The Wall Street crash precipitates a world economic crisis.

George Grosz, *The Pillars of Society,* 1926

undreamed-of period of revolt and euphoria broke out. Now at last a new, more relevant, architecture, which was backed by social purpose, joined the cityscapes.

DE STIJL

Geometry and abstraction in the Netherlands

As early as the Expressionist architecture of the *Amsterdam School* (see pages 24–25), Dutch architects had been ahead of the field in architecture and, since the country had not become embroiled in the conflicts of the First World War, other avant-garde tendencies could develop there at a particularly early period compared with the rest of Europe.

Some architects thought that the intricate *ornamentation* and the use of *brick* in Expressionist architecture was too indivi- dualistic and saw them as a sign of conservatism. Influenced by the buildings of Frank Lloyd Wright, which had appeared in the Wasmuth editions of 1910 and 1911, and by the French *Cubists*, they had a vision of a different sort of architecture, one structured in plain cubes with interpenetrating planes such as was exemplified in Walter Gropius's Fagus factory.

The work of the Dutch painter Piet Mondrian was especially meaningful for the development of these architects. Mondrian's early work was composed of largely conventional neo-impressionist pictures, but as early as 1907 he began making the objects he was depicting ever more abstract, and gradually submitted them to a cubic structuring of forms. At the end of this development – around 1914 – he produced those famous, object-less pictures, in which the pictorial space was made into a harmonious structure by a framework of black lines. But this grid enclosed a number of squares and rectangles that were either left white, or were colored in. The colors he used were dominated by flatly painted primary colors – red, blue, or yellow – without any shaping or shadow. Mondrian's artistic concept consisted in the abnegation of any desire to depict the world of objects, but rather to explain their basic structures in a clear geometric system.

Gerrit Thomas Rietveld, *Schröder House,* Utrecht, 1924

The cabinet maker Gerrit Thomas Rietveld, creator of the red and blue chair, was given one of the few chances granted the De Stijl group to translate their ideas into buildings. Following the principle whereby in 1917 he deconstructed the armchair into boards and squared pieces of wood, then put it together again, he and Truus Schröder, a woman architect specializing in interiors, deconstructed the cubic form of a house. The planar walls are arranged as a composition of independent rectangles, which project beyond the points at which they join. The flat roof and the balustrade of the balcony seem to be floating on air. The impression is heightened by the large panes of glass at the corners of the building. But the real revolution was the replacement of solidly divided rooms by a freely transformable ground plan. The walls throughout the first floor could all be folded up or pushed round, so that the inhabitants could vary it like children's building blocks, including having an uninterrupted open space.

The ideas that Mondrian had developed in abstract painting were now taken up by the architects Theo van Doesburg and Gerrit Thomas Rietveld, who was also a cabinet-maker, in three-dimensional form. In 1917, with some other artists, including the architects Jacobus Johannes Pieter Oud and Jan Wils, they formed the De Stijl group, whose organ was the periodical of the same name, which appeared up till 1932.

The name means simply "The Style," which expresses how the group saw themselves: in contrast to the historical *styles* of *Classicism* or the *Baroque*, the artists of De Stijl saw their language of forms – abstract, unadorned, constructivist – as Style itself.

In a manifesto that appeared in 1918 in the second issue of *De Stijl*, the intellectual leader of the group, Theo van Doesburg, gave a broad outline of their complex theoretical goal. The dominance of the individual, which had reigned in the art of the 19th century, should be relinquished in favor of an equilibrium with the universal. The condition for the realization of De Stijl's new world, which they called "consciousness of the times," was the removal of all the fetters of tradition.

The vision that van Doesburg and De Stijl conjured up for artists was of a renunciation of all traditional ornamental decoration as it had been cultivated by *historicism* or even *Expressionism*. Instead, buildings should be as radically simplified as Mondrian's pictures.

Starting out from the principle of the right angle, interpenetrating cubic volumes would create a complex, quasi-sculptural experience of space. The color scheme of the buildings, which were indeed treated very like sculptures, was bright, but reduced to primary colors only. The result of this artistic concept, which was driven primarily by van Doesburg, was the neo-plastic art of De Stijl.

The influence of the De Stijl group, which was of a constantly changing composition throughout its existence, was by no means confined to Holland. In particular van Doesburg had a direct influence on the Bauhaus, founded by Walter Gropius after the First World War. Gropius invited him there as a guest in 1921.

The first famous embodiment of the ideas of De Stijl was the red and blue chair made by Gerrit Thomas Rietveld. Once again taking inspiration from Mondrian's pictures, in 1917 Rietveld designed a framework of black pieces of squared timber, which were joined to each other in strict right-angles.

Into the load-bearing frame of wood thus created, brightly colored sheets of wood were inserted to make the seat and the backrest, which were both given a slope by placing the squared timber at different heights.

As van Doesburg's architectonic sketches of this period remained unrealized, it once more fell to Rietveld to give the first practical expression to the aesthetic conceptions of De Stijl, this time in the field of architecture.

THE BAUHAUS

Even today the Bauhaus is synonymous with the radical modernization of art. There was no area of life that Bauhaus art was not out to reform or redesign. Far from being confined to fine art and architecture, its principles extended to dance, theater, photography, and design. Even toys (the *sailing boat*) were designed in its workshops. In having such a comprehensive brief, the Bauhaus resembled its predecessors, the English *Arts and Crafts movement* and the *Deutscher Werkbund*. Even today many of its products feature among the classics of design in their uncompromising modernity, such as Marcel Breuer's tubular steel chair or the Bauhaus table lamp.

In March 1919, when Walter Gropius took over the leadership of the Weimar Art School founded by Henry van de Velde, and united it with the former Art and Craft School to form the "staatlicher Bauhaus Weimar," his aim was to create a new unity between art and craft. The purpose itself points to the sociopolitical meaning acquired by the Bauhaus in postwar Germany. Gropius wanted to join all the creative forces into a unified "house of building", in which building not only implied architecture but a lot

A classic of Bauhaus design: Marianne Brandt's teapot with internal strainer (1924)

more besides. Gropius was entirely in tune with his time when following the catastrophe of the war and the collapse of the old order to erect a new society, he aimed to use his art to build a new mankind.

In order to achieve these elevated, socially utopian aims, all the masters at the Bauhaus followed a preordained sequence of courses with their students. A preliminary course introduced the students to working with the most various materials: wood, metal, textiles, glass, coloring materials, clay, and stone. The preliminary course was run by Johannes Itten in the early years in Weimar. It was largely due to Itten that the Bauhaus had at first a strongly Expressionist direction, and was formally modeled on the organization of the medieval guilds.

In mid-1921 Theo van Doesburg, the first and leading thinker of the Dutch De Stijl movement, came to Weimar. Under his influence the Bauhaus underwent a radical change to a technical, constructionist concept of art, which conditioned the second stage of its development. Marcel Breuer was stimulated by the red and blue chair created by the De Stijl artist Gerrit Thomas Rietveld to develop his tubular steel chairs.

But of all the masters at the Bauhaus, the new trend in art education is most clearly associated with the Hungarian László Moholy-Nagy, who

took over the introductory course from Itten. Dressed in a workman's boiler suit, he left no doubt that modern artistic production must be carried out from a technical point of view suited to the time. How broad the artistic spectrum of the Bauhaus remained, even under the influence of Moholy-Nagy, can be seen from the activity there of such diverse artistic personalities as the painters Oskar Schlemmer, Wassily Kandinsky, and Paul Klee.

While the Bauhaus was becoming the leading cultural force in the German – indeed the European – avant-garde, it was also coming under increasing political pressure. The progressive art school, which wore its political commitment on its sleeve, was a thorn in the flesh of the conservative forces that were once again gathering strength. In 1925 the Weimar Bauhaus had to close. A new beginning was undertaken in Dessau.

In Walter Gropius's Bauhaus building, the art school at last had an architectonic frame to match its inner concept. The architecture clearly expressed the various functions of individual parts of the building. So the workshop area was dominated by an uninterrupted wall of glass, providing the optimal amount of light. The façade of the students' living quarters on the other hand was characterized by an individual balcony for each room. It went without saying that Gropius's new building should have a flat roof, which in the 1920s was synonymous with modern architecture.

In 1928 Walter Gropius resigned as director of the Bauhaus. His successor was a Swiss, Hannes Meyer, who, like Gropius, was an architect. Under Meyer the social orientation of the Bauhaus became even more pronounced than under Gropius. Constructivism with an aesthetic bias was replaced by a style of artistic production that proclaimed itself to be strictly scientific. The components of this were an increasing standardization in the production of art-objects, and a growing collectivization of the production process that took the place of individual craftsmanship. The conscious politicization of the Bauhaus mobilized the right-wing press, which led in turn to the dismissal of Hannes Meyer by the mayor of Dessau.

It then became the task of Meyer's successor, the established architect Ludwig Mies van der Rohe, appointed in 1930, to steer the school into quieter waters. Political agitation had never been Mies's style, but even his move to concentrate on craft training could not prevent the Dessau Bauhaus from being closed down at the instigation of the Nazis. Mies's subsequent attempt to reestablish the Bauhaus in Berlin also failed.

Demonstrating the Expressionist roots of the Bauhaus: Lyonel Feininger's woodcut for the title page of the 1919 Bauhaus manifesto Cathedral

Architecture that corresponds to content: the Bauhaus building erected by Walter Gropius at its new site in Dessau in 1926

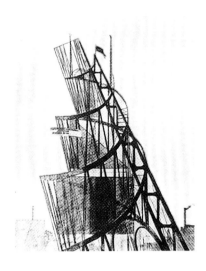

Vladimir Tatlin, *Sketch for the Monument to the Third International*, 1919

The victory of the Bolshevik revolution and belief in technical progress gave wings to the dreams of the Russian avant-garde. One of their boldest designs was by the constructivist Vladimir Tatlin. The office and conference building of the communist world organization the Third International depicted in his sketch was not only dynamic in its aesthetic effect, but actually moved. A steel spiral 980 feet (300 meters) high was to enclose three transparent volumes: a square assembly hall, a pyramidal administration area, and a cylindrical press office.

El Lissitzky, *Sketch for Cloud Props at the Nikitskiya Gate in Moscow*, 1923–26

The discussions about town planning that took place in the Soviet Union in the 1920s raised the need for designs for the new towns demanded by the stepped-up industrialization of the first Five-Year Plan. El Lissitzky's plan for a "horizontal skyscraper" for Moscow, which never got beyond the design stage, expressing both belief in progress and fascination with technology, is an attempt to transpose his Proun compositions into architecture.

A traditional 19th-century house had to satisfy certain conceptions of grandeur and monumentality in the minds of its inhabitants. But it was quite other aspects that Rietveld was interested in expressing in the Schröder house. How new and unusual it was, with its flat *roof* instead of the usual pitched or hipped roof, can be appreciated by comparing it with the rest of the conventional terrace of which it was to be the end house.

Among the radical innovations in the Schröder house, besides the startling façade with its flat white plaster and the walls that intersected and reached out into space, were the wide expanses of window-glass. The inside, too, was full of revolutionary design solutions. On the first floor it was possible to remove the walls that divided the rooms, producing a completely open space, very different from the immutable sequence of rooms imposed by solid walls.

The Schröder house was a fundamental challenge to conventional house-building. Its variable layout, its inconspicuous flat roof, and the almost industrial sobriety of its façades set an entirely new standard, which were from then on regarded as milestones of modern architecture.

CONSTRUCTIVISM

Revolution and avant-garde in the Soviet Union

While the Bauhaus in Germany and the De Stijl movement in the Netherlands were centers of progressive activity, it was above all the avant-garde of the young Soviet Union that gave artistic and architectural expression to the revolutionary political changes that occurred after 1917.

Russian art in the 19th century had been narrowly dependent on developments in western Europe. It was only able to free itself gradually from this dependence toward the end of the century by going back to themes and forms derived from folklore and traditional Russian models from the Middle Ages. But by the beginning of the First World War, art in Russia had not only connected with the developments in avant-garde art in western Europe, it was even taking a leading role in them.

Kasimir Malevich's 1918 painting *White square on a white ground* reduced painting

absolutely as far as possible, to point zero, creating thereby an icon of modern art. Malevich advocated a "pure abstraction" in which feeling must have the prime role. Accordingly he named his work Suprematism (from the Latin *supremus* – "the highest"). This style of painting, which reduces art even more than does Cubism to basic geometric structure, influenced the De Stijl group and the Bauhaus. In Russia it was El Lissitzky who developed his own brand of the abstraction prescribed in the works of Malevich. With Vladimir Tatlin, El Lissitzky became the leading representative of a current in art that, like De Stijl, advocated a synthesis of painting and architecture.

In 1920 Lissitzky developed his famous "Proun" (a shortening of Pro UNOWIS, from the Russian words meaning "project for the creation of new forms in art"), abstract compositions made up of various geometrical elements that could be realized in both two and three dimensions, clearly showing the influence of Malevich's suprematist painting. Lissitzky saw his Proun as a contribution to the continuous search for new forms in art. His definition was therefore deliberately vague, so that it could be adapted to the constantly changing conditions of artistic production.

The concept was by no means confined to two-dimensional paintings; he also applied it to interior design and to architectonic sketches. It was Lissitzky's view, derived from painting and at first expressed only in painting, that architecture should be pared down to only its most necessary functional elements, so that it was dominated by construction. This view he shared with his contemporary Malevich.

Like the Italian Futurists of the prewar period (see page 29), the members of this Russian art movement were characterized by a belief in progress and fascination with technology. This new, avant-garde concept of art expressed the view that the young Soviet Union had of itself after the communist revolution of 1917, an ideology that had broken with everything outdated and belonging to the past. Accordingly the Soviet state used Constructivism for its own propagandist purposes for a few years, up to the consolidation of Stalin's power.

The most important architectonic project of these years was "Cloud Props", which El

Lissitzky, who had joined the De Stijl group in Amsterdam in 1922, designed with Mart Stam, who was Dutch. This sketch for a giant office complex, which was never built, presents a technicist-looking building, resting horizontally on very few supports and apparently floating almost weightlessly in space.

That another famous constructivist project, Vladimir Tatlin's Monument to the Third International, also proceeded no further than the design stage, is very understandable in the light of the politically still confused and above all economically strained situation in the post-revolutionary Soviet Union. In a similar way to Lissitzky, Tatlin was concerned not only with architecture but with sculptural form, and consequently his design for the Moscow monument is a synthesis of both architecture and sculpture.

The building was to consist of a structure of metal girders standing at an angle of nearly 45 degrees. It was intended to bore upwards into the heavens in a tapering spiral 980 feet (300 meters) wide at the base and higher than the Eiffel Tower, thereby emulating the old human dream of the tower of Babel. Three transparent volumes were to be suspended within the structure: a cylinder, a pyramid, and a smaller cylinder (with an extra hemisphere attached). Tatlin intended these edifices to be used by various state organizations.

The cosmic dimension to this monument only becomes apparent when you take into account the fact that the individual edifices were all intended to rotate on their axes in different rhythms: individually, once a year, once a month, and once a day. The planned monument thus united constructive as well as dynamic aspects in an entirely original way. Through the work of the Soviet institutions in the various edifices within the structure, and because of its transparent sculptural form, the Monument to the Third International would have been much more than a revolutionary constructivist building, in essence it would have represented the revolution and consequently the new order established within the Soviet Union itself. But whereas the model Tatlin had put together for the monument had been constructed out of old cigar boxes and tin cans, the actual realization of the gigantic building would, like that of Lissitzky's Cloud Props skyscraper, have

swiftly turned out to be beyond both the technical and financial capacity of its time.

Just as revolutionary as Lissitzky's and Tatlin's work was the Wesnin brothers' plan for a building for the newspaper *Pravda* in Leningrad (St. Petersburg). It was their intention to build a skyscraper out of basic cubic blocks, on a site just 20 feet (6 meters) square. The plan included a sign saying *Pravda* (as it appeared on the newspaper), in huge letters. Glass lift-shafts added an additional futuristic note to the plan.

A notable aspect of the utopian and revolutionary works of Soviet Constructivism was that, although they were embodied in a wide and ambitious program and were extensively and vigorously disputed among Russian intellectuals, only a very few of them were ever realized.

One of those that was realized was the Rusakov workers' club in Moscow, built of concrete, which was designed by Konstantin Melnikov. The heart of the building is an assembly hall for 1,400 people. The cubic blocks housing the seating stick out sharply between the vertical strips of windows in the façade, giving the building a dramatic as well as a dynamic feel.

However, Constructivism, in a similar way to modern art in general, was allowed only a relatively short flowering. As early as 1931, when a competition was held for a "Palace of the Soviets" in Moscow, all the Modernist submissions, including those of Le Corbusier and Walter Gropius, were rejected in favor of a

Konstantin Stepanovitsch Melnikov, *Rosakow Workers' Club,* Moscow, 1928

Most of the dreams of the Russian avant-garde never got beyond the drawing-board. One of the few buildings to be completed was the Rusakow workers' club. Appropriately for a building that was to serve as a center of cultural education for the proletariat, Konstantin Melnikov gave it a semi-industrial appearance. Like Melnikov's Soviet Pavilion for the Exposition des Arts Décoratifs in Paris in 1925, the reinforced concrete building was dominated by intersecting irregularly shaped geometrical volumes and sharp diagonals. Hidden within the cubic shapes that project far out from the façade of the Moscow building is seating for an audience of 1,400.

Giuseppe Terragni, *Casa del Fascio,*
Como, 1932–36

In Italy, which was less developed than
Germany, it was easier for the fascists to
see themselves as the party of
modernization, and Rationalism was
sanctioned as the official architecture of
the state. The purest example is the Casa
del Fascio, erected in Como by Giuseppe
Terragni. In accordance with the classical
theory of proportion, Terragni designed
the headquarters of the local fascist party
as a square whose elevation, 54 feet (16.5
meters), was exactly half the length of
each side of the plan. The visibility of the
structural grid of *columns* and beams on
the entrance side was a modern
interpretation of the façade of the
Colosseum and gave the community
building a symbolic transparency. The
alternation of dazzling white marble and
hollow spaces unfolds a dramatic play of
light and shade. The Casa del Fascio
demonstrates that modern and classical
architecture in Italy, unlike many other
European countries, were not inimical
opposites.

neo-classical design corresponding to what
was to become the favored Stalinist form of
state architecture.

RATIONALISM VERSUS NEOCLASSICISM

Giuseppe Terragni and Italian Rationalism

As in many European states, the political
situation after the First World War in the
kingdom of Italy was far from stable. Society
was polarized at the extremes of the political
spectrum. There was a strong communist
party, and there was also a fascist party
which was rapidly gaining influence. Benito
Mussolini's march on Rome in 1922
established the first fascist regime in Europe.
Aside from the futurist projects of the prewar
period, which never got past the drawing-
board, Italy had no tradition of modern
architecture worth the name. Whereas in
Germany between 1918 and 1933 the
Neues Bauen movement was both reforming
and predominantly socialist in aim, new
building in Italy was by no means anxious
to outlaw traditional architecture. The cause
for this may have been that Modernism
was only able to become established in
Italy under the fascist system. This also
explains the circumstance that, unlike in
Germany where after the Nazi seizure of
power in 1933 the modern buildings of
the Weimar Republic and their architects
were widely despised, in fascist Italy modern
architecture was part of the innovatory

character of the system, and was even
attributed a certain role in the upholding of
the state.

In general terms, fascist Italy between 1920
and 1940 can be said to have had two
competing architectonic currents, both of
which based themselves in different ways
upon the heritage of classical Rome. Both
currents can be personified in their main
protagonists: on the one side there was
the *neoclassicist* Marcello Piacentini, and
on the other Giuseppe Terragni. The latter
joined up with six other architects from Milan,
who gave themselves the name "Gruppo 7"
and called for a radical modern architecture.
In so doing, Terragni saw no contradiction
between maintaining the traditional Italian
heritage of building that had been in
existence since antiquity, and developing a
new architecture. In their *Manifesto of Italian
Rationalism* which the group published in
1926–27, they demanded an architecture
based strictly upon the laws of logic and
proportion (otherwise named "ratio," which
caused the movement to be called
"Rationalism"). Influenced by the machine
aesthetic of the Futurists and the revolutionary buildings of Le Corbusier, Rationalism
established itself chiefly in the north of
Italy with its flourishing commercial and
industrial centers in Milan and Turin, where
the increasingly important car industry
was based.

The clearest expression of Rationalism's
formal and aesthetic priorities is to be found
in the Novocomum building, a block of rented
apartments in Como built in 1928, and in the
famous Casa del Fascio, the local office of the
fascist party in Como, which like the
Novocomum was built by Giuseppe Terragni.

The buildings incorporated an equal
balance between the aesthetic demands of
modernity and the classical theory that had
dominated the architecture of the Italian
peninsula since the days of the Roman
Empire. Terragni's grid of *columns* on the
entrance side of the Casa del Fascio is an
updating of the classical *portico*. His ground
plan, 110 square feet (33 meters), with an
elevation of 55 feet (16.5 meters), exactly half,
relates to the idea of *proportion*, already held
to be decisive by Vitruvius, whose influential
theories on building date back to Roman days.
At the same time the Casa del Fascio took up

the theme of transparency, an important aspect of the party's public image, by a symbolically open-looking façade.

Although Terragni's Italian Rationalism continued on into the 80s (see pages 94 ff.), it gradually lost influence after 1935. It was pushed aside by the classicist monumentalism of Piacentini. If Terragni's work presented a balanced synthesis of classical and modern, which came out in the fine detail and aesthetic sensitivity of his buildings, no such sensitivity is present in the stiff classicism of Piacentini, which became the preferred state architecture of Italy.

NEW BUILDING IN GERMANY

Housing developments in Berlin and Frankfurt

One of the most pressing problems facing the democratic Weimar Republic after 1918 was to find a solution to the housing shortage, which was one of the main causes of social distress. Even before the war there had been some initial moves to change the way in which new housing was constructed, especially in the largest German city, Berlin. The aim had been to replace the speculatively built working-class tenement blocks, with their warrens of dark, damp courtyards, with dwellings offering better conditions and an improved style of life. Instead of the large, dark apartments without adequate sanitary facilities, which were shared by several different groups of tenants, smaller units were to be constructed with increased light and ventilation.

But it was only from 1924 that the economic situation in Germany, which had been severely hit by the payment of reparations to the victorious Allies, began to pick up. This consolidation provided the conditions for a scheme conducted by the city architect for Berlin, Martin Wagner, which was unique in Europe: a *popular housing program*, providing tens of thousands of new homes in Berlin, and ending only with the world economic crisis of 1930.

Hans Scharoun, Walter Gropius, Ludwig Mies van der Rohe, and Bruno Taut were among the most important architects of these

Berlin housing schemes. They found ways to unite the social purpose inherent in the often cooperatively built apartment blocks, with a language of forms that was as functional as it was modern. A flat *roof* and white or brilliantly-colored façades characterize their buildings, as do quotations (such as round windows) from naval architecture, which Hans Scharoun in particular uses very frequently, following the lead given by Le Corbusier. In order to meet the challenge of producing serviceable buildings at low cost, thereby ensuring a low rent, the architects had to make them as standardized as possible and needed to use the most economical building materials.

These housing projects of the 1920s did not produce a multitude of single houses, like the Garden City movements at the turn of the century in England and Germany (see pages 40–41). They produced small, complete districts, laid out in an unstructured way with a great variety of apartment blocks. The social impetus that underlay these housing projects was notably expressed in the inclusion of communal facilities such as laundry rooms and roof-terraces. This, like the green environment in which the buildings were placed, was intended to promote healthy living and a sound social relationship among the inhabitants.

Apart from Berlin, the other big German city to face up to the general lack of housing by launching a systematic housing development scheme was Frankfurt, under the supervision

Hans Scharoun, residential block, *Siemensstadt Estate,* Berlin, 1931

The revolutionary upheavals following the First World War engendered strenuous efforts, in Germany as elsewhere, to solve the housing crisis. Hans Scharoun's residential blocks on the Siemensstadt estate, constructed as part of the state housing development scheme, are a prime example of the Modernist promise of a living space full of light and air for the working masses. Scharoun was one of the few architects of the modern movement to inhabit one of his superbly crafted apartments himself.

Margarete Schütte-Lihotzky, *The Frankfurt Kitchen,* 1928

Margarete Schütte-Lihotzky designed the prototype of all the fitted kitchens produced in the decades that followed. The elements are positioned to suit kitchen routines, and are fitted into the smallest possible space. A step that was intended to make light of housework also transformed the kitchen from a family living area into a purely functional space – all with the purpose, however, of giving the housewife more leisure or enabling her to go out to work.

of the city architect Ernst May. By building with industrially prefabricated parts, the cost of the scheme – and thus the level of rents – could be kept down. The apartments were relatively small, but they had the benefit of the space-saving "Frankfurt kitchen" designed by a female architect, Margarete Schütte-Lihotzky, which created a supremely rational work space making the cumbersome kitchen dresser a thing of the past. Schütte-Lihotzky's creation, which was the forerunner of all modern fitted kitchens, was the first to be mass-produced and ready-made, and until 1930 was fitted into 10,000 apartments in the Frankfurt housing schemes. Into a space of just 21 square feet (6.5 meters) the architect fitted everything necessary for a fully working kitchen, from the sink to the cooker.

Architects like Ernst May and Margarete Schütte-Lihotzky believed they had found the social model for the future in the revolutionary

USSR. So, when the world economic crisis practically put a stop to building in Germany, they tried briefly to put their architectonic ideas into practice in the USSR. However, these plans came to grief because of the totally inadequate infrastructure in the Soviet Union, which made a building program like that which had been achieved in Germany quite impossible.

The modern as program: the Weissenhof estate in Stuttgart

Like a magnifying glass placed over a page, the building exhibition of 1927 organized by the *Deutscher Werkbund* in the Weissenhof housing development in Stuttgart highlighted what was newest in the architecture of the day. For one more time, before National Socialism outlawed it, the Deutscher Werkbund was able to offer foreign practitioners of Modernism such as Le Corbusier and Jacobus Johannes Pieter Oud, and German architects such as Scharoun, Gropius, Behrens, and Mies van de Rohe, a forum in which to present the new building styles and their rationale systematically to the public. Flat roofs, white façades, glass, and metal were as much a part of the picture presented by the exhibition as the functionality and the stacked-cube construction of the buildings. Even today the Stuttgart estate, despite the extensive rebuilding that has occurred, gives an impression of the idea behind this new residential housing.

But in contrast to the *housing schemes* in Berlin and Frankfurt, it was not the working classes who were being offered a new lifestyle with the new architecture. In comparison, the Stuttgart Weissenhof estate, which started out under the direction of Ludwig Mies van der Rohe, was aimed at a well-off, university-educated public of bourgeois origin, as is apparent from the presence of the servant's room that is included in the ground-plans of the apartments.

This concentrated display of modern architecture at a time when it was still unusual evoked as much passionate enthusiasm as emphatic dislike. The white cubic shapes were compared to African buildings, and a humorous postcard shows them surrounded by dromedaries, palms, and people wearing turbans. Behind such criticism lay a deep and not unfounded mistrust of what was seen as modish architecture cut off from regional traditions. The *heritage protection movement*, which was very well represented in Germany via the architect Paul Schmitthenner and the Stuttgart school, accused the scheme of not having taken account either of the landscape or of the traditional buildings around it.

Astonishingly enough, in view of the large number of architects involved and the recognizably different styles that went into the details of their buildings, taken as a whole the buildings form a remarkably homogenous group. Although the architects came from different countries, bringing with them a highly diverse architectonic heritage, and were also all of different ages, the forms and materials they employed were broadly of a kind.

In the few years since the First World War a completely new architecture had developed, and in the Stuttgart Weissenhof estate it became clearly evident for the first time that this was not a specific style with a regional stamp, but a worldwide development.

CIAM and the International Style

In reaction to the stir caused by the Weissenhof scheme as an entity and as the product of an international team of architects, in 1928 Le Corbusier and Siegfried Giedion created the CIAM (Congrès Internationaux d'Architecture Moderne), to be a yearly forum for Modernist architects. It carried on until 1956, having met a total of ten times, each session being devoted to different social and architectonic themes. For example, under the leadership of Ernst May there was a debate on the theme "the minimal living unit," Gropius insisted on a debate about "rational building methods." But there were also debates on such themes as "the new city."

In face of the rapid worldwide triumph of the new building style exemplified by the Weissenhof estate, it is not surprising that it was christened the "International Style" by the architectural critic Henry-Russell Hitchcock on the occasion of an exhibition of recent Modernist architecture in the Museum of Modern Art in New York in 1932. This international style conquered almost the whole world in the years before the Second World War. With its cubic units in cement, steel, and glass it unified the visual aspect of cities, and dominated almost the whole of architectural development right into the 60s.

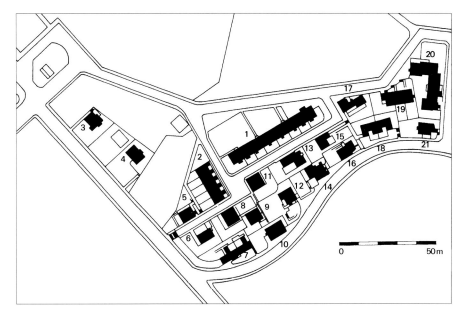

The Weissenhof estate, residential block by **Ludwig Mies van der Rohe**, Stuttgart, 1927, and **general plan**

Mies van der Rohe, who had the idea of laying out the scheme on an overall basis of cubic elements, also designed the apartment block that dominates the estate. The *steel skeleton construction* has all the advantages of the variable-plan interior. The Weissenhof exhibition is regarded as the final breakthrough for *Neues Bauen* in the Weimar Republic, when 21 different models of houses by various architects were on display.

Buildings, numbered by architect:
1 Ludwig Mies van der Rohe, **2** Jacobus Johannes Pieter Oud, **3** Victor Bourgeois, **4/5** Adolf Gustav Schneck, **6/7** Le Corbusier, **8/9** Walter Gropius, **10** Ludwig Hilberseimer, **11** Bruno Taut, **12** Hans Poelzig, **13/14** Richard Döcker, **15/16** Max Taut, **17** Adolf Rading, **18** Josef Frank, **19** Mart Stam, **20** Peter Behrens, **21** Hans Scharoun

TOWN PLANNING IN THE 20TH CENTURY

1850–1930

For centuries the town had functioned so well as an almost unchanging, easily comprehensible, coordinated fabric of relationships that its laws had become invisible. Then with the industrial revolution of the 19th century it turned almost overnight into a Moloch. The flight from the land brought an urban explosion. The problems arising from this could not be removed by technology or architecture alone. So a new discipline was born: town planning, which looked at the city as a whole for the first time. The planners found their first models in the place where the people who had caused all these urban problems had come from: the country. There they designed new towns as antitheses to the old ones.

The urban crisis at the end of the 19th century

During the 19th century the balance between town and country, which had until that time generally been fairly harmonious, suffered a dramatic change. The town became the theater of the industrial revolution. Its new economic structure produced an enormous growth in population. The country became depopulated; the cities exploded. In Great Britain, which spearheaded the change, there were fewer than 9 million inhabitants in 1800, 80 percent of them living in the country. Some 100 years later there were 36 million, 72 percent of them clustered in the big cities. In Germany over the same period the number of inhabitants shot up from 24.5 to 65 million. When the German state came into being in 1871, two-thirds lived outside the main centers of population, but scarcely half a century later this had dropped to 37 percent.

This unprecedented growth led – in cities whose structure dated back to anywhere between medieval times and the 17th century – to indescribable problems. The technological infrastructure could not keep pace with the change, the narrow streets could not contain the massively increasing pressure of traffic. New transport systems such as the railway could only be placed at the edges of towns because of the enormous amount of space they took up. Unregulated economic forces created a jungle of different usages, with factories wedged into living areas. These became so overcrowded due to the constant influx of people, that the most elementary necessities of life were no longer guaranteed. In the English city of Bristol, for instance, 46 percent of families had only one room between them. People who had to live in houses that backed onto lightless, airless yards were becoming ill. Infectious diseases spread through the tenements. Child mortality was high. There were no compensatory open spaces, parks, or squares. The housing question became a question of power. Economic freedom led to a widening gulf in city life between rich and poor, causing people to challenge the existing model of the city, and ultimately, the political order itself. The pressure of circumstances led in about 1900 to a new discipline – town planning.

Town planning

Town planning is a young discipline that looks back over a long tradition. The term was not used until the late 19th and early 20th century. But as long ago as the first urban groupings of distant antiquity, people began thinking about the most advantageous organization and structure for these residential and economic centers, taking into account strategic and climatic factors. While many towns were springing up "naturally," the first planned towns were coming into being, most according to a geometrical chessboard-like schema (Milet, Priene). Certain functions, as for instance that of the marketplace (the Greek agora), were allotted a specific position in the Greek city of antiquity. At the same time, standardized dwellings were erected according to a unified design.

The notion of the ideal city built according to a geometrical plan occurs over and over again in architectural theory over the centuries. It was in the era of the baroque that plans for an ideal city were transformed into buildings (Freudenstadt 1599, Mannheim 1607), in cities shaped by the ruling concept of society.

In Europe in the 19th century the flight from the land and the overall growth of the population led to

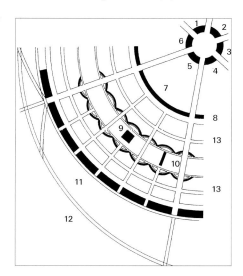

Ideal plan for an English Garden City, 1902

1 Hospital, **2** Library, **3** Theater, **4** Concert hall, **5** Town Hall, **6** Museum, **7** Central park, **8** Crystal Palace, **9** School, **10** Church, **11** Allotments, **12** Large farms **13** Residential area

ever greater urban concentrations, which made a serious reconsideration of the structure of the city essential on social and public health grounds. The initial steps in that direction look rather modest, in that they sought to enlarge and improve the organization of what already existed.

The first move was the "Commissioners' Plan" proposed for New York in 1811. It increased six-fold the area to be covered by the commercial settlements which had until then been concentrated at the southernmost point of Manhattan, and laid a regular grid over the whole island. From east to west ran 155 narrow Streets, all exactly 3 miles (5 kilometers) long, and from north to south ran 12 wider Avenues, all exactly 12 miles (20 kilometers) long. As befitted the ideal of an egalitarian society each of the 2,082 blocks measured 650 by 2,600 feet (200 by 800 meters) and each plot was 25 by 100 feet (7.5 by 30 meters). Only in 1853 was it decided to leave Central Park as a public space, only in 1916 was the

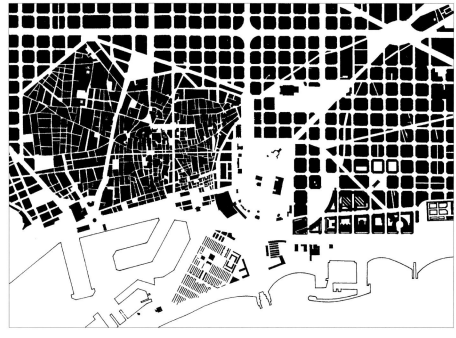

Inner-city Barcelona today: bottom, the sea; left, the confused network of streets in the old city; right and above, the grid of blocks created by Cerdà's extension of the city in 1859. It has grown outwards a great deal since then.

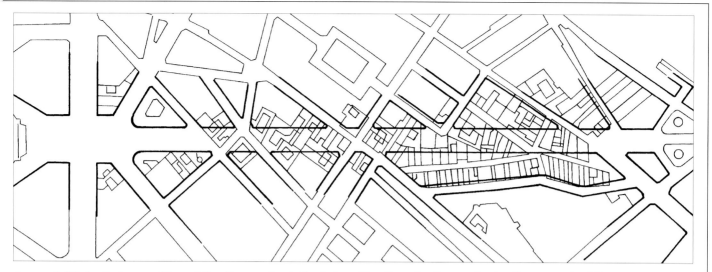

Avenue de l'Opéra, Paris, carved through the city according to the design of the city prefect Georges Eugène Haussmann in 1862

zoning law enacted to regulate the height of buildings, and only in 1961 was any law regarding land usage laid down. There is no traffic plan to this day. The "Commissioners' Plan" designated a terrain on which the forces of growth could develop freely and took no measures to prune them if they got out of hand.

The first attempt to address social needs was made by Ildefonso Cerdà, with the enlargement of Barcelona. In order to gain public space, his plan, which divided the city up into a grid of boulevards 165 feet (50 meters) wide, also sliced off the corners of the 440 by 440 feet (133 by 133 meter) blocks so that the intersections took on the character of public squares. But his idea that each block should only be built up on two sides failed because there were no mechanisms for enforcing it. Private owners continued to use their land as intensively as possible. Instead of buildings with courtyard spaces between them full of greenery, a crowded mass of blocks arose, which are still a dominant feature of the city.

It was with very much greater powers at his disposal that the Paris prefect, Georges Eugène Haussmann, undertook the transformation of that city. He proposed building a network of new boulevards which would give the city a "pleasing aspect," solve traffic-problems, and get rid of sources of infection in the poor quarters (and also increase the mobility of the army, enabling it to nip social disturbances in the bud). But the pressure for change was beyond the control of the existing city and state. Insurrection – the Paris Commune of 1870 – brought down the Empire. Though demolition and rebuilding under government control had at least been established as a method, nothing at this stage was able to resolve the city's problems. Radical concepts which also took issue with society were the order of the day. Even when socialist thinking did not result in a revolution, it changed the self-image of the state and its functionaries. The socially oriented state arose, taking responsibility for the lives of its citizens in all kinds of areas. The builder of cities changed into the technician of the city, and finally to the builder of a new society.

A new society

All the utopias that were developed at the beginning of the 20th century said goodbye to the old city and tried instead to remove the tensions between town and country. In 1898 an Englishman, Sir Ebenezer Howard, developed the idea of the garden city. He proposed the creation of new towns independent of the old cities, of limited dimensions and whose inhabitants would be self-supporting through arable farming and cattle-rearing. A settlement of a maximum of 32,000 people was to radiate out from a central park. The garden city was to be fully 400 hectares in total, of which half should be for productive use. The first garden city, Letchworth, was created some distance from London in 1903 by Barry Parker and Raymond Unwin. The age-old ideal of a rural commune did not, however, fit with the contemporary economic system. The garden cities failed as self-sufficient entities, but they succeeded outstandingly on the export market as a model for living. Many smart agglomerations of private houses were built in Germany under the name of garden cities, and in England the idea gave rise to the "new towns" of the 1960s, which were actually nothing but collections of houses.

Of greater success were the American Frank Lloyd Wright's anti-urban reflections (see page 16). He gave the name "Usonia" to the utopia in which the architect brought individual and countryside together to live in organic unity. His most extended elaboration of the idea was in his plans for Broadacre City (1935). Here city space becomes landscape. The primary building block of Broadacre City was the Usonian house, dovetailed into the landscape, in which people were to live and work. Every family was intended to cultivate their garden, so houses were built on large plots of land. Wright's demand for half a hectare per family was not at all unrealistic in view of the size of America. The whole population of America at that time could have been housed in the state of Texas. All the usual public buildings were to be placed in open countryside. Complexes comprising school, library, administration and meeting halls would form the social center of a neighborhood. Industry was to be accommodated in separate industrial parks. At the nodal points for traffic, skyscrapers housing offices would be built. Here Wright placed market centers where every citizen would offer his produce for sale.

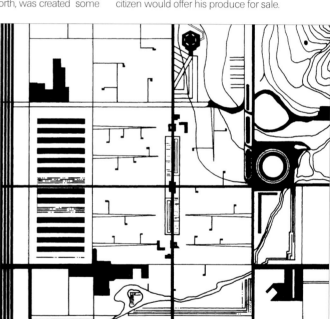

Instead of overcrowded working-class areas, single houses for free individuals. But the scheme that was intended as a replacement for the old metropolises developed not in opposition to them but with them: Broadacre City (above, part of the "Broadacre" project, Frank Lloyd Wright, 1935) became a model for suburbs everywhere.

This new style of building was the ancestor of the malls of today. The functional buildings, which were set at a distance from each other, are joined by a hierarchical street-system. Without the car, one of which Wright intended every citizen to own if at all possible, Broadacre City would not work. Today Wright's vision seems to have been realized in the worldwide phenomenon of the suburb, except that in practice Wright's individualistic ideal was to prove incompatible with his projections of a centralized plan (see pages 66–67).

The way to the skies

American Architecture

1920–1940

Cass Gilbert, *The Woolworth Building*,
New York, 1913

Frank Woolworth, the founder of the retail chain, gave Cass Gilbert the task of designing an imposing symbol of his power. The architect faced the challenge of seamlessly welding traditional aesthetics with the demands of a very tall new office building.
The result was for 17 years the tallest building in the world. Gilbert chose to make it in the *Gothic* style, with its arches, little towers, flying buttresses, which had already adorned the French cathedrals of the Middle Ages: historical vocabulary camouflaging technical innovation.

LAND SPECULATION AND ARCHITECTURAL ENGINEERING

The roots of the American passion for skyscrapers

To this day the fascination of the skyscrapers in American cities continues unabated. They dominate the skyline, majestic symbols of economic power and social prosperity.

It only took a few years at the end of the 19th century to establish the basic preconditions for building skyscrapers several hundred yards high, and to resolve the complex technical and static problems that the new type of building posed for architects and engineers. Fireproofing was a particular concern, as were the problems relating to the access to such tall buildings.

Yet, however great the aesthetic fascination of these masterpieces of *architectural engineering*, their creation was by no means an end in itself. Economic causes had led almost inevitably to ever taller buildings, since increasing land prices in the thrusting centers of American economic activity necessarily led to the exploitation of every single square foot of a plot of land. After the problems of constructing tall buildings had been solved, a price spiral set in: the more effectively a piece of land could be exploited through ever taller buildings, the more gigantic the sums which could be earned from it on the real-estate market.

The Chicago fire

If New York, the throbbing heart of economic life, was the first center of this new architectural movement, it was soon more than rivaled by Chicago. The all-engulfing fire which raged there between 8 and 10 October 1871 had razed large tracts of the city to the ground. Yet, terrible though the consequences of the fire were, it also acted as a trigger for the construction of a new city, of which the skyscrapers, mounting story upon story, were the most distinctive component. Chicago saw the creation of such extraordinary early skyscrapers as the *round-arched* Marshall Field Warehouse by Henry Hobson Richardson (1885–87) or the first building with a steel skeleton, the Home Insurance Building by William Le Baron Jenney (1883–85). One of the leaders of the American skyscraper culture at this time was

Louis Sullivan, the chief representative of the *Chicago School*, the general label given to the most important architects of the new Chicago.

Although Sullivan did add some ornamental decorations to his buildings, at the turn of the century he was already beginning to formulate one of the leitmotifs of modern architecture in his tall buildings: the strict grid-like articulation of their façades. In this way the façade of the Garanty Building in Buffalo (1894–95) looked as though it was striving heavenward, an effect that was heightened by the perpen-dicular strips of masonry between the rectangular windows. By contrast, the Carson, Pirie & Scott Store in Chicago (1899–1904), also by Sullivan, displays an energetic balance between horizontal and vertical elements. Whereas the two parts of the store facing on to the street tended to create the impression of a grid of horizontal layers, the rounded corners clearly expressed verticality.

Neo-Gothic cathedrals of consumerism

Although it was an unheard-of innovation to have as many people as would normally inhabit a small American town suddenly all working and shopping in the same building, surprisingly enough no specific new architectural language was at first evolved for the new genre.

Most of the leading American architects did not take much note of the debates on architectural reform in Europe, dismissing them as intellectual. So the development of architecture in the United States between 1900 and 1925 proceeded, with a few exceptions, along its own path. Instead of relating to modernist work in Europe, American architects rifled the store-cupboard of historical models and dressed their technically highly innovative tall buildings with *historicist* façades which often seem to us today quite inappropriate to their time. Although Louis Sullivan in Chicago had already started the breakthrough into a new skyscraper architecture, other American architects of the same era were unceremoniously mingling *Art Nouveau, Classicism, Romanesque,* and, especially, *Gothic.* The end result of this was that many American tall buildings did not differ much from their historical forebears, the Gothic cathedrals of Europe, the "skyscrapers of the Middle Ages," which had the same ornamental repertoire of tracery around their windows, the same crockets and merlons.

The high point of this *eclectic* skyscraper architecture remained for many years the Woolworth building, erected in 1913 by Cass Gilbert for the American retail chain. At 850 feet (260 meters) it was the tallest building in the world for 17 years. The tower of the Woolworth building not only dominated the skyline of the city, it also powerfully expressed the enormous wealth and the economic might of the concern which had commissioned and now possessed it. In the consumption-oriented society of the United States, skyscrapers were not only signs of technical and social progress. They served, years after their construction, as important status symbols and advertisements, sometimes to the point of being modeled, as with the Chrysler building, on parts of the product being advertised.

The *Chicago Tribune* competition

In 1922, the *Chicago Tribune* announced a competition for a new building for the newspaper in that city. The requirements were not exactly modest; the terms of the competition demanded that it should be the most beautiful building in the world – and naturally it would be another skyscraper.

Surprisingly enough, European architects also took part. Previously they had been hindered from constructing very tall buildings by the mature, often medieval structure of European cities, but after the First World War, the longing to build "towers" had awakened. Many representatives of the *new building* movement saw the American competition as an opportunity to use the formal language of European Modernism in a skyscraper. Eliel Saarinen from Finland, the group composed of Walter Gropius, Adolf Meyer, Adolf Loos, Bruno and Max Taut, and Hugo Häring were among the best-known European architects who submitted designs for the newspaper building. Yet despite the epoch-making quality of the contributions – discussed many times thereafter in architectural publications and used as models by many other architects – the Americans opted for an utterly conservative design, that of Raymond Hood and John Mead Howell's *Gothic-inspired* skyscraper, whose climbing tracery seemed to mock the development of European architecture.

Eliel Saarinen, *Chicago Tribune Competition,* design drawing 1922

Saarinen's entry for the competition to design a building for the *Chicago Tribune* newspaper was consigned to second place, but even the winner, Raymond Hood, thought it better than his own design. Saarinen's thrusting conception, monumental yet mobile, exerted a strong influence over the later development of skyscraper architecture.

Raymond Hood, *McGraw Hill Building,* New York, 1928–29

Hood concentrated all the impact of this skyscraper into the horizontal strip windows and glazed windowsills, which was immediately interpreted as an engagement with European Modernism. But the symmetry and ziggurat shape of the building are entirely in the tradition of American skyscrapers.

Nonetheless, it was a representative of European architecture, Eliel Saarinen, who was awarded the second prize. His sketch was quite without frills, achieving a distinctive vertical effect through the articulation of the façade, with its emphatic corners, by masonry bands, a device previously used by Sullivan. This effect is further emphasized by the skillful stratification of volumes in the skyscraper. Through the use of narrowing steps at increasing intervals, Saarinen creates a pyramidal effect. The building narrows as it goes up, culminating in a tower which appears to rise from out of the building and dominates the whole complex.

From the Gothic to the Modern: the skyscrapers of Raymond Hood

In the years that followed, Raymond Hood set about becoming the uncrowned king of the American skyscraper. In the forceful 21-story, black and gold Radiator Building (1924) he once more gave free rein to his Gothic fantasies. But the vaguely Gothic formal language of the building that seems to rear up in the way of something from a painter's imagination, crowned once more by a tower-like structure, had now clearly become more abstract than his design for the Chicago Tribune building had been.

The versatility of Hood's architectural language can be seen from the steel skeleton construction of the McGraw Hill Building (1928–29). Suddenly all the "Gothicism" was gone, and in its place came borrowings from the treasury of contemporary European architecture. The absence of rich ornamentation on the façade, the quieter formal language, the stratified rectilinear volumes all agreed with the conceptions of Modernist architects, as did the horizontal strip-windows, which had become the trademark of big-city avant-garde architecture in the 1920s. All of which may have been why Hood's McGraw Hill Building was the only American skyscraper awarded the distinction of being included in Henry-Russell Hitchcock and Philip Johnson's 1932 exhibition "The International Style."

Articulated into clearly defined grids, the stories of the greenish McGraw Hill Building were stacked in tiers. The only reminder of Hood's earlier passion for richly detailed decoration is the tower which crowns the building, giving it a monumental appearance.

In the Daily News building in New York which Hood designed only a little while later (1930) he changed his design principles yet again. Instead of the tiers of the McGraw Hill building, he now ordered the building in a strictly vertical direction. Only the stepping of the volumes, which Saarinen had already proposed in his design for a tall building for the Chicago Tribune, gave some life to the shiny façade of the skyscraper.

EUROPE MEETS USA

Residential buildings by Schindler and Neutra

It was only towards the end of the 1920s that Hood reacted to modern architectural developments in Europe and took leave of his neo-Gothic formal language. By then two young Austrian émigrés, Rudolph Schindler and Richard Neutra, had already given Modernism a toehold in America. Influenced by the country houses of Frank Lloyd Wright, in whose studio Schindler had worked for a time, they did not, interestingly enough, break into the American domain of the skyscraper but started with private houses, where they developed new architectural concepts that, in many respects, went further than the contemporary buildings of Le Corbusier or Mies van der Rohe.

Rudolph Schindler was strongly influenced by the abstract *Cubist* formal language of his teacher Otto Wagner and the buildings of the Vienna *Secession*. In 1921 he built his own house in California, which also had room for two friends – a married couple. As an experiment in communal living Schindler created private as well as communal areas for both couples. Like Rietveld in the Schröder house in Utrecht (see page 32), Schindler entirely abandoned the sequence of rooms that had been traditional for prestigious homes in the 19th century. Instead he aimed for an interpenetration of interior and exterior. Large sliding doors opened out onto the garden, thus creating a relationship between the inhabitants' studios and the natural world around. An interior courtyard with an open-air hearth took over the function of the traditional living room. The bungalow-like building was unusual even in its use of materials. The walls were constructed from thin prefabricated concrete slabs. Ceilings and window frames were of dark wood, which, in conjunction with the simple interior fittings also designed by Schindler, gave the building a feeling of being both natural and close to the earth. In its spare sobriety and reserved charm, with its sliding doors and horizontal window bars, and its mingling interior and exterior, the house bears witness to the influence of the traditional home culture of Japan.

Schindler was constantly experimenting in his buildings with new materials and forms, as can be seen in the famous Lovell Beach House, which he built for a doctor client, Phillip Lovell, as his holiday house by the ocean.

The unusual appearance of the house, almost reminiscent in its formal language of technical buildings, is simply a playful conceit of the architect's. Schindler erected the modern holiday house upon five concrete stilts, cast in the form of a figure of eight, which served many purposes. The upper story, which was almost fully glazed, had an uninterrupted view over the neighboring buildings to the sea, and since the upper story overhung the bottom story there was a protected roofed area at the front of the house which could be used for the children to play in. The decisive advantage of this construction, which was expensive to build, was its safety in the event of an earthquake. California is one of the most endangered areas of the world as regards earthquakes, and in fact the Lovell Beach House, standing as it did on stilts, withstood one such quake only a few years after it was built, during which nearby buildings were destroyed.

For the same client, Richard Neutra, who had worked for a while in Schindler's office, built the Lovell Health House. The entrance to the building, situated on a slope in Beverly Hills, is via the top floor. The living area, with its lavish use of glass, works like an enclosed space that has been placed in a frame composed of horizontal strips of concrete, painted a bright white, and the vertical steel skeleton. This latter was put up in only 40 hours. The close relationship of the house with the natural world around, which is spread out in an overwhelming panorama in front of the building, is also reflected in the outward reaching concrete walls which serve now as windowsills and now as roofs to terraces, but also compose an abstract spatial boundary, an extension of the building line.

Neutra's façades, in the same way as Schindler's, have the quality of an abstract multi-dimensional sculpture, a design which is continued in the interior through the interpenetration of individual living areas.

The two Austrians did not simply reproduce the work of their teacher, they developed it further in their own architectural language, at the same time opening up American architecture to contemporary European developments.

ART DECO

Advent of a new taste

In 1925, the "Exposition internationale des arts décoratifs et industriels modernes" was held in Paris, France. It was an international exhibition of work in progress, covering the various contemporary developments in the areas of decorative art and design and

Rudolph Schindler, *Lovell Beach House*, Newport Beach, California, 1926 (top)

Richard Neutra, *Lovell Health House*, Beverley Hills, Los Angeles, 1929 (above)

Rooms and landscape flow into each other. Taking a lesson from their teacher Frank Lloyd Wright, Rudolph Schindler and Richard Neutra made the dream reality. Instead of conventional walls, they used modern construction methods: In the case of the house built for Phillip Lovell, a doctor, five figure-of-eight shaped concrete supports sustain an upper story that is almost entirely of glass. From every point of the open, interconnected space there is a dreamlike view of the Pacific ocean.
The same effect was achieved by Richard Neutra in the hills of Los Angeles with an entirely different construction. In the Lovell Health House each story-level is suspended on a light steel skeleton by steel cables.

architecture. This concentrated presentation of new trends brought a change in the artistic landscape. The great influence which the Paris exhibition of "arts décoratifs" had on art in the 1920s and early 1930s can easily be gauged by the fact that it gave its name to a new style: Art Deco.

From clothing and jewelry to cutlery and cars, and even architecture and painting, the geometric shapes of Art Deco with their semi-circular forms and rounded corners were to be found everywhere. A touch of *Cubism*, a pinch of *Expressionism*, a little of the practicality of the *Neues Bauen*, and some of the technicity of the machine aesthetic – this was Art Deco's successful recipe for catching the tone of the times. The style is not always elegant; sometimes there is a certain amount of clumsiness about it, deriving in part for the preference for heavy materials such as steel, silver, and especially brass.

In America as well as Europe, Art Deco quickly became the symbol of the Roaring Twenties with their elegant charm but also their decadence. Advertising, which burgeoned with the American economic boom of the 1920s, was filled with the streamlined, glittering chrome of Deco. Advertising awakened in the prosperous classes of society, especially in towns, a continual longing for new products, which stimulated demand and increased production and sales.

But right next to this glittering world there was the America of the poor. Poverty was at its most visible in the slums which were a by-product of the continued rapid growth of the big cities, where hundreds of thousands of immigrants and black Americans lived in hope of a better life – all too often in vain.

In the United States it was the era of Prohibition, the infamous Al Capone and the Mafia, and the rise of the film industry in Hollywood, which challenged the European cinema and brought in new stars for the sound movies which were gradually replacing the old silent pictures. The public loved to see Harold Lloyd, at once comic and tragic, hanging terrified but still witty from the dizzy height of a skyscraper façade, the street like a narrow ribbon below with cars, oblivious of his plight, racing along it like toys.

The boom, which inspired the massive demand for cars and was synonymous in its early stages with the name of Henry Ford (whose architect was Albert Kahn), continued on its way with the automobile company of Walter P. Chrysler. The Chrysler Building was to be the visible expression of the seemingly unlimited might of the car magnate. Originally designed for another client, William van Alen's 77-story skyscraper, which bores 1000 feet (319 meters) up into the sky over New York, was not only for a short while the highest building in the world; it also became an icon of Art Deco and was reproduced thousands of times over.

To what irrational and technically complex lengths architects were prepared to go in their competition to erect the tallest building in the world in New York City is illustrated by the story of the top of the Chrysler tower. In order to prevent his competitors from garnering the coveted title of builder of the world's tallest skyscraper, van Alen had the seven-story tower which was intended to cap the building constructed inside the building. In a surprise coup which trumped the opposition, he then anchored the complete tower within a few hours on to the top of the skyscraper.

The top of the Chrysler Building, with its pinnacle, is, in fact, a splendidly theatrical crown to the building. Its semi-circular segments of decreasing size rise one on top of each other like a telescope to a sky-piercing point, so that it seems even today to be striving up and up into the clouds. The three-cornered window openings in the semi-circles add a dynamic, jagged quality to this dramatic structure, which could almost be part of a film set such as is seen in Fritz Lang's visionary classic *Metropolis*. On top of all this there is the delicate coloring of the tower-top, which is covered with reflecting, glittering steel, and offers an extraordinary spectacle when illuminated at night.

However, the Chrysler Building was not just the tallest construction in the world. It also functioned as a giant advertisement for the automobile company. Original wheel caps from Chrysler cars were used on the façade, and giant radiator mascots imitated *Gothic* gargoyles at the corners of the building. But it is the slightly decadent elegance which the Chrysler building continues to exude in defiance of the changing face of fashion which gives it its unique charm. It is this charm which secures its leading role among the numerous skyscrapers of New York, even though the Empire State Building took its place as the highest building in the world only a few years after it was constructed.

Although the Empire State Building, which for years dominated the staggering New York skyline, has long since lost the title of tallest building to the skyscrapers of southeast Asia, it retains its position as the star of New York's tourist attractions, a myth which Hollywood played a considerable role in cultivating and propagating. What would King Kong be, without his pose at the top of the (then) tallest building in the world? And the building still plays an unbilled lead in many films , like *An Affair to Remember* or *Sleepless in Seattle*, where decisive encounters take place on its observation platform, with New York lying at the actors' feet.

With its somewhat cool effect, and its use of noble materials, the Empire State Building was the parting shot of the American variety of Art Nouveau. It was an act of daring in the face of the growing economic problems in the United States at the end of the 1920s, to erect a building that makes such a bold statement. In fact it was impossible to find tenants for the offices for a long time, and it quickly became known to a mocking general public as the "Empty State Building."

The Chrysler Building and the Empire State Building were essentially visions in stone of the "American Dream" of the 20th century, whereas in the MacGraw Hill Building and the Daily News Building, Raymond Hood showed himself open to the formal language employed by the European avant-garde. In their skyscraper for the Philadelphia Savings Fund Society (PSFS) in New York (1926–31) George Howe and William Lescaze tried to effect a synthesis between the demands of European Modernism and the traditional American skyscraper. The strip windows girdling the building are given a rhythm by the supporting elements; this brings the whole into an interesting balance. The functionality, which was the chief aim of the PSFS building, was visibly expressed in the structure of the façades. Howe and Lescaze used dignified materials throughout, except for the mechanical services floor,

which made a clear break in the façades' composition.

Dance on the volcano

Just how fragile the hard-won postwar prosperity of the 1920s was – not just in the United States – was shatteringly revealed by the world economic crisis. Worldwide, the 1920s were both economically and socially a "dance on the volcano," a tightrope walk over the abyss without a rope or a safety net.

This dangerous situation is strikingly captured by Louis W. Hine in his photographs, which document the construction of the Empire State Building. Surrounded

William van Alen, *Chrysler Building*, New York, 1930

A gleaming needle pierces the New York sky. With its steel-covered, telescopically narrowing point, the Chrysler Building seems to grow out from itself. It was the tallest building in the world when it was erected, and even today it remains the most symbolic, an advertisement for skyscrapers as well as for the company that commissioned it. Wheel caps and radiator mascots from the products of the car manufacturing giant decorate the Art Deco façade of the 1000-foot (319-meter) building.

Shreve, Lamb & Harmon, *Empire State Building,* New York, 1931

The Empire State Building broke all conceivable records and its height was only one of them; at 1250 feet (381 meters) it was to remain for more than 40 years the tallest building in the world. Immediately after its construction the world economic crisis ended the struggle to beat the record for height. People shrank from putting up buildings whose use was symbolic rather than practical. That the Empire State Building, which is certainly not architecturally breathtaking, became synonymous with the idea of the skyscraper, was undoubtedly due to its media image. Millions of cinema-goers saw King Kong fall to his death from its roof – a symbol of the downfall of the mighty.

by steel girders and cables, iron, and cranes, the building workers seem almost to hover over the city, which stretches out hundreds of feet below them. Man and technology seem to have entered into a daring pact: one false move, one wrong step and the harmony of the moment would break, and they would hurtle into the abyss. This is exactly what happened on 24 October 1929, when the bottom fell out of the stock market on Wall Street, the financial center of New York, turning millionaires into beggars within the space of a few hours.

The effects of the Wall Street Crash were felt across the world, and in the wake of the ensuing economic crisis, unemployment and inflation, which it had taken immense efforts to combat, began once again to rise. The economic existence of workers and middle classes alike was threatened, leading to more political radicalization, against which in many countries no adequate countermeasures could be found. The brief postwar boom gave way to a deep depression, the "dance on the volcano" ended in a fall.

That such extensive building projects as the Empire State Building or especially the Rockefeller Center were nonetheless undertaken in this economically and politically

tense situation, was largely due to the fact that they had been planned and begun before "Black Friday," as the day of the Wall Street crash subsequently became known, and that basic changes in concept were accepted in order to complete them. In the case of the Rockefeller Center there was also the knowledge that despite all the economic problems there was nonetheless a financier – John D. Rockefeller – in the background, who had a large and solid fund of capital.

The plans for the Rockefeller Center had begun in the late 1920s. Numerous architects were originally employed on the project, once more among them was the highly successful Raymond Hood. Hood was responsible for the actual focal point of the enormous site, the thin slab that is the 70-story RCA Building. Stepped at the sides, it rose elegantly from among the numerous buildings of lesser height that surrounded it. These had various functions: the Rockefeller complex was a predecessor of modern media centers – a city within a city – including the Radio City Music Hall which could accommodate as many as 6,200 visitors, and a movie palace for an audience of 3,500.

Yet the length of time that it actually took to build the Rockefeller Center – it was finally completed in 1940 – also serves to make clear the serious problems that such an ambitious project had to face in those economically difficult times.

The New Deal

Under the leadership of President Franklin D. Roosevelt the United States began in 1933 to master against the economic crisis that had been brought on by the stock market crash with a whole catalog of national measures. These had decisive consequences for the economy, for communities, and for the social whole. The breakthrough was the New Deal introduced by Roosevelt. The heart of this economic program was a range of economic measures designed to combat unemployment in industry as well as in agriculture, while at the same time targeting homelessness and urban slums

A gigantic work-creation program provided for the construction of canal systems, streets, theatres, gardens and parks, schools, law courts, town halls, and hospitals. Since there were enough workers, materials, and supporting funds, and no time constraints, the simplest technology and the most basic of working methods were used.

Important technical projects such as the building of a total of 32 cofferdams, headed by the architects and engineers of the Tennessee Valley Authority did not just create work. Realized in a forward-looking and ambitious formal language, they expressed the dynamic new start taken by the American economy, and demonstrated the gradual return to national self-confidence after the shock of the economic crisis.

For prestige buildings on the other hand, the traditional forms of *Classicism* were preferred, giving a reassuringly familiar image in these uncertain times. For example, the classical monumentality of the United States Mint erected in 1937 by architect Gilbert Stanley Underwood in San Francisco leaves no doubt that the stability of the dollar is once again now guaranteed.

The measures for economic advancement undertaken by President Roosevelt in the New Deal also had the effect of laying the foundations for the successful rise of the United States to the position of top industrial nation after the Second World War.

Reinhard and Hofmeister; Corbett Harrison and MacMurray; Hood and Fouilhoux, *Rockefeller Center*, New York, 1931–40

The American millionaire John D. Rockefeller was the only man who dared, at the time of the world economic crisis, to commission a gigantic project such as this one: a complex of 15 buildings including a skyscraper (seven more buildings had been added by 1973). This city within a city built primarily as a business center offers a wide range of arts events and services for the general public. Faced throughout in limestone, the complex bears witness to Rayond Hood's concept of building a coherent group of tall buildings which would stand out as a self-sufficient entity against the rest of the city, both reducing the chaos of the New York traffic and improving the quality of life.

Modernism under Siege

Architecture and Power

1930–1945

The Europe of the dictators

The establishment of dictatorial regimes in numerous countries between the two world wars is one of the distinctive phenomena of the 20th century. In their contempt for human beings, and their ultimate willingness to destroy great numbers of them, these regimes differed from each other only in one aspect, whether they were situated on the left or right of the political spectrum.

Why this political polarization was able to take hold in so few years in so many countries has many reasons. While it is true that the responsibility cannot be laid uniquely at the door of the tense economic situation present in the inter-war years and the post-1929 economic crisis and the concomitant housing shortage and high unemployment, nonetheless they were the ground in which extremism could flourish. The roots were already there, in the nationalism of the 19th century. In most countries that had been monarchies before the First World War, there was now an absence of democratic tradition which favored the establishment of dictatorial systems. In a world which had been shaken to its moral foundations, many individual citizens found political freedom too much of a burden. Because of their frequently unthinking faith in authority, the tide of radicalization to left and right was not stemmed either vigorously, or early enough. The ominous progression towards dictatorship began.

The high-flying dreams of a new mankind that had accompanied the October Revolution of 1917 in Russia evaporated. In their place came a communist reign of terror under Josef Stalin, which systematically eliminated all opponents and persisted until he died in 1953. As early as 1922 the first fascist regime in Europe came to power in Italy under Mussolini. In Spain, after an extremely bloody civil war, the fascist General Franco finally wrested power from the Republicans. He was supported in the war by the German Condor Legion, which was responsible for the destruction of Guernica. It was in response to the sufferings of the civil population of that shattered village that Pablo Picasso painted his famous picture *Guernica* in 1937.

In Germany a National Socialist dictatorship was established in 1933 under Adolf Hitler. The persecution of Jewish citizens, political dissidents and intellectuals, and other minorities began immediately. Many of the leading architects of the Weimar era went into exile. The 1930s in Germany were one long trail of tyranny and the denial of human rights, beginning with the Nazi seizure of power, and proceeding through the burning of books, the night when Jews were beaten and their shop-windows broken, and the outbreak of the Second World War, to the decision at the so-called "Wannsee-Konferenz" of 1942 to

1930: National Socialists and Communists gain seats in the German parliamentary elections. The Frankfurt School, headed by Max Horkheimer and Theodor W. Adorno formulate the "critical theory of society." *The Blue Angel,* starring Marlene Dietrich, comes to the cinema. Death of Sir Arthur Conan Doyle, author of the Sherlock Holmes detective novels.

1931: Electoral victory of the coalition of left-wing parties in Spain. King Alfonso XIII abdicates. Spain becomes a republic. Clark Gable begins his film career in Hollywood.

1932: Height of the world economic crisis. Around 30 million unemployed worldwide. Thomas Beecham founds the London Philharmonic Orchestra. A star at four, Shirley Temple is the world's youngest film actress. Exhibition of international architecture at the Museum of Modern Art in New York.

German sportswoman, **portrait photo of a javelin thrower, 1934**

1933: The National Socialists seize power in Germany. Adolf Hitler appointed chancellor. Franklin D. Roosevelt becomes President of the United States. Beginning of the New Deal program of state economic planning. Federico García Lorca's play *Blood Wedding* performed in Spain.

1934: Death of the English composer Edward Elgar. The Polish-born French chemist and physicist Marie Curie dies. She had been awarded the Nobel Prize for physics in 1903 and chemistry in 1911.

1935: The Nobel Peace Prize goes to Carl von Ossietzky. Elias Canetti's novel *Auto da Fè* published. First performance of George Gershwin's opera *Porgy and Bess*.

1936: Beginning of the Spanish Civil War (ends 1939 with the victory of General Franco). Margaret Mitchell's novel *Gone with the Wind* published.

1937: Picasso completes *Guernica.* In Germany, Nazi exhibition of so-called "Degenerate Art" vilifies modern art.

1938: "Swing" reaches its peak under jazz musician Benny Goodman. The 40-hour week introduced in the USA.

1939: German troops attack Poland on 1 September. Start of the Second World War.

1940: Massive German air attack on the English city of Coventry. Leon Trotsky murdered in Mexico. Chaplin's film *The Dictator* comes out.

1941: Japan enters the war by attacking the US Pacific naval base at Pearl Harbor. Konrad Zuse builds the first program-driven electromechanical digital computer.

1942: In Berlin the Wannsee Conference is held to make technical and administrative plans to exterminate the Jews in Europe. Astrid Lindgren's *Pippi Longstocking* published.

1945: Capitulation of Germany. The United States drops atomic bombs on Hiroshima and Nagasaki.

murder European Jews. At the end of this long decade (1945) millions were dead and a wave of destruction had passed over central and eastern Europe.

Memorial architecture

The 1920s and 1930s were not only the time of a new departure in search of a modern society, they also constituted an epoch whose population were still suffering from the shock of the First World War.

All the people from both sides who had lost relations or friends in the conflict had to work through their grief. In national terms, all the ex-belligerents felt the need to remember and commemorate.

Once again there emerged an era of heroic memorials, those national shrines that had already figured so importantly in the architecture of the 19th century. It was a bizarre combination: remembrance of the casualties of the first "modern" war, expressed by means of a 19th-century building concept in the architectural forms of the present.

As a result, innumerable war memorials sprang up in almost every village in western Europe after 1918. Particular importance was accorded to monuments to the fallen erected on battlefields. Within a few years these had become the starting point for a regular tourist industry based around the battlefields.

One of the largest and most impressive of such commemorative monuments is that erected by Edwin Lutyens at Thiepval near Amiens in France, which is dedicated to the

nearly 74,000 British soldiers who went missing at the battle of the Somme and whose bodies were never identified. Lutyens's monument consists of a triumphal arch which goes up in steps like a pyramid, dominated by the color-contrast between the light areas in *freestone* and the red areas in *brick.* Through linking a motif of architecturally historic significance – the *triumphal arch* (victory) – with the motif of the *pyramid* (death), Lutyens created a synthesis that is both full of interesting tension and universally comprehensible. The over-emphatically formal style of the monument leaves no doubt as to its meaning: victory legitimated the deaths.

Lutyens's monumental formal language provides an interesting comparison with the charnel house erected between 1923 and 1932 at Douaumont near Verdun, one of the most fought-over sites of the war, by the architects Léon Azéma, Max Edrei and F. Hardy. The monument holds the bones of 10,000 French soldiers killed at Verdun. The building is long, with rounded corners, but in the center it has a structure similar to a church tower which, like a lighthouse, lights up the battlefield at night.

In Germany it was not on the Western Front (where most of the German losses actually occurred) but on the Eastern Front – where the war against Russia was won – that a nationalistic war memorial was built. The Tannenberg national monument, designed by Walter and Johannes Krüger, was dedicated in 1927. The octagonal, fortress-like building was dominated by eight unfriendly-looking

towers in bluish-red brick, enclosed linked by a pleasant and quite modern looking glassed-in walkway. Tannenberg was a site which could serve a variety of purposes, but the omnipresent cult of the dead was at its center. Under a tall and monumental cross of bronze was the grave of 20 unknown soldiers killed in the battle at Tannenberg in August 1914.

However different these three memorials to the war dead were from each other in formal terms, they were closely related in purpose. They were all places of national significance, dedicated to the memory of the war and its dead, but above all to the glorification of death in battle and so to the formation of myths of the nation-state.

Forward to tradition

At the beginning of the 1930s modern architecture was radically split. While the towns had seen the introduction of many exemplary projects – public housing schemes, private houses, schools, town halls, and factories – covering the whole spectrum of *Neues Bauen* from Expressionism to New Objectivity, there had always been a group of clients and architects who – as with the war memorials – clung determinedly to traditional forms.

Whereas in the United States at the start of the 1930s Modernism was gradually beginning to influence the building of skyscrapers, in Europe it was under increasing political attack. In the Soviet Union under Stalin the Constructivists lost their influence. In Germany, where at the end of the 1920s, projects such as the Stuttgarter Weissenhof estate had set out to make a splash and did, more critical voices were now interrupting the chorus of acclaim. *Neues Bauen* was castigated as "Bolshevik architecture imported from the USSR," without any consideration of the fact that only a very few of the Modernist architects did indeed support the communist ideology. Along with such political polemics which belonged to the social polarization of the times, there were also professional criticisms. The flat roofs of the *Neues Bauen* were unfavorably compared – on the grounds that they fell in easily and were not waterproof – with the traditional hip or saddle roofs; the whitewash favored by modern architects peeled off and their steel window frames rusted, whereas the original wooden ones did not. There were indeed some technical faults in Modernist architecture, but what actually brought it down was the world economic crisis. Another phenomenon was also taking shape: influenced both by political events and wide-ranging economic constraints, a number of architects in Germany and elsewhere turned, in around 1930, to a harder, more monumental language of forms, with a different arrangement of rooms and new dimensions. Instead of friendly white stuccoed exteriors or uncovered cement, suddenly façades started being clothed in *freestone*, usually granite or limestone. There might well be a building with a modern structure and shape underneath, but the stone façade linked the building to traditional values, and thus to security and stability.

The start of Gigantism

One of the projects that stands very clearly on the cusp between the first period of Modernism and the swing back to conservative ambitions in Germany, was the competition for an extension to the Reichsbank in Berlin in 1932, which was announced on the eve of the Nazi seizure of power. It was not only traditional architects who took part; there were also important representatives of Modernism such as Ludwig Mies van der Rohe, Heinrich Tessenow and Hans Poelzig. But even in their submissions one can trace an inclination to monumentalism. The building that was finally erected, designed at Hitler's wish by the house architect for the bank Heinrich Wolff, can be seen as the first official Nazi building. It is in fact an only moderately monumental office building, characterized inside and out by boldness in conception and functional quality. The decor was comparatively sparing, so that there was no excessive "ornamentation" with Nazi emblems.

Very different to this was the case of the new Reichskanzlei (Chancellery). The prestigious new building faced on to the Wilhelmstrasse in the middle of the old Berlin governmental quarter. A grandiose hall over 160 feet (50 meters) long led to the main entrance, which was adorned by a *portico* with four gigantic Tuscan *pillars*.

But not only were the sheer size of the building and the scale of its pillars impressive, the visitor was also intended to be impressed by the two bronze sculptures by Arno Breker flanking the entrance: two naked male figures, one holding a torch and the other a sword, symbolizing "party" and "army." The sculptures,

in conjunction with the architecture of the building, represented the self-image of National Socialism: the Nazi party and its various sub-organizations, and the army were the most important pillars of the Nazi regime in Germany up to and including the moment when Hitler unleashed the Second World War. The inside of the building continued in the plain monumental style preferred by Hitler. Painting and mosaics, valuable fittings in wood and stone, all of an intimidating magnitude – everything combined to present the visitor with an unambiguous picture of the limitless ambition for power of the National Socialists and their leader Adolf Hitler.

But the new Chancellery, the building which was meant above all other to incorporate Hitler's "thousand-year Reich" was not granted a long life: what was left of it after bombing in the Second World War was forcibly removed by the Soviet victors. The costly marble of the Chancellery, where Hitler committed suicide in an underground bunker in 1945, was used by the victors for their memorials.

The monumental buildings of Albert Speer and the reactionary politics of the National Socialists, however, presented only one side

of the picture. On the other side, there were thoroughly modern aspects of the realm of architecture, exemplified, for instance, in the Luftwaffe buildings. These were designed chiefly by Ernst Sagebiel, who had previously been in charge of Erich Mendelsohn's office. Sagebiel's central airport building at Berlin-Tempelhof, which unites modern construction with a feeling of grandeur, remains one of Europe's greatest buildings.

The same principle is to be seen in the 1938 buildings for the German KdF ("Kraft durch Freude" – "strength through joy") car – the Volkswagen. After 1945 the car enjoyed worldwide success as the VW Beetle. The south façade of the factory buildings, which is just less than one mile (1.3 kilometers) long and is reminiscent of a city wall, is given not only a monumental, but an astonishingly modern appearance by the characteristic towers housing the stairwells, which stand out from the building line.

In contrast to this there is the residential architecture of the KdF town, which is today called Wolfsburg. The buildings there, planned by Speer's protégé Peter Koller, were in the *heritage protection style* that had been

Albert Speer, *New Chancellery*, Berlin, seen from the Vossstrasse, 1936–39

With its quarter-mile (422-meter) length, the New Chancellery, inaugurated in January 1939, gave a foretaste of the architectonic *megastructures* which Albert Speer planned for the rebuilding of Berlin under the direction of Hitler. The impression of size created by this *neo-classical* building with its long tracts of offices is mitigated by the way in which the height of the eaves 72 feet (22 meters) is designed to fit in with buildings of the neighborhood, and by the modeling of the façade with its projecting and set-back areas.
It was only on the garden side, not accessible to the public, and above all in the interior that the New Chancellery showed the intimidating face of Nazi official architecture. With their extravagant marble mosaics and tapestries, the giant halls documented Hitler's drive towards ever greater power. In 1949 the Chancellery, which had been war-damaged, was pulled down.

Jacques Carlu, Louis Boileau, and Léon Azéma, *Palais de Chaillot*, exhibition pavilion for the International Exhibition, Paris, 1937

The two 600-foot (195-meter) long, slightly curved wings of the Palais de Chaillot, which now houses several museums, culminate in two symmetrical buildings with towers on top, between and in front of which there is a paved square. Built in 1936 as the foreground to the exhibition, the Palais, in its slightly raised position, forms the visual conclusion to the long reaches of the Champ de Mars. With its monumental linked rows of *pillars* and its lavish decoration with mosaics, the complex is an example of the international *Neoclassicism* of the 1930s, which was influenced by Art Deco.

widespread since the turn of the century, with saddle roof, wooden veranda and sash windows. Wolfsburg is a good illustration of the very varied aims of National Socialist architecture. It also illustrates the unbroken success in West Germany of architects of the National Socialist system after 1945: Peter Koller was once again responsible for town planning after the war.

Cult and seduction

Nowhere are the mechanisms of the regime clearer than in the memorials and places dedicated to the Nazi cult. The effect that an impressive architectural backdrop to a semi-religious cult can have in seducing the masses is particularly evident in these places. Albert Speer's setting for the Nuremberg rally or Paul Ludwig Troost's arrangement of the Königsplatz in Munich were such places, and their main purpose was to provide a suitable site for mass events.

The stone paving, the flanking buildings in granite, the axial direction of the installations towards the Führer: this was the constantly recurring setting of Nazi rituals, which were carried out with military precision. They were accompanied by impressive theatrical effects, such as Speer's "cathedral of light," which caused a "building" created by anti-aircraft searchlights to appear over the assembly.

The culmination of National Socialist architectural ambition would doubtless have been the transformation of Berlin into the new capital "Germania." But the gigantic plans that Hitler and Speer had made, and were now ready to start realizing, were overtaken by the fall of Germany and got no further than the first stage. Speer had planned a monumental, memorial-like north-south axis, along the lines of what he had designed for Nazi rituals, the focal point of which was to be the "great hall."

Its technically innovative cupola, much larger than St Peter's in Rome, was intended to have a classical appearance. The dome was to be 820 feet (250 meters) in diameter, and there would be room for 100,000 people inside the gigantic hall. Beside the "great hall" the old German Reichstag, which had been a ruin since the 1933 fire, would have looked like a tiny relic of a bygone era.

Part of the plan for Germania included confiscating the property of Jewish citizens of Berlin who were deported to concentration and death-camps. But only a small part of the destruction of the historic fabric of the city meticulously planned by Speer and his staff took place at their hands. The rest was taken care of by the war, which destroyed Berlin almost completely.

Between worlds

The Paris international exhibition of 1937 was the last time between the wars that the political systems and their respective architectures met. There were buildings planned for the exhibition that were firmly based in the Modernist tradition of the 1920s, such as the Spanish pavilion by Josep Lluís Sert, with its clear grid construction. However, it was *Classicism* of the simplified international kind characteristic of the 1930s, which had the upper hand.

With their monumental language of forms and colossal pillars, the Palais de Chaillot and the nearby Palais de Tokyo, built in 1937 on the right bank of the Seine, formed a significant backdrop for the exhibition. But it was in the architecture of the German and Soviet pavilions that the claims to universal power of both systems collided. In a skillfully devised *mise-en-scène*, the two buildings were placed opposite each other as the dramatic highlight of the Paris exhibition.

The Soviet pavilion consisted of a stepped building on a podium – almost streamlined in appearance – created by the architect Boris Iofan. But the sculpture by Vera Moukhina that crowned it was its dramatic climax. Storming forward with a challenging stride, two symbolic heroic figures – an industrial worker and a woman from a collective farm, – brandish the insignia of Soviet might: the hammer and sickle.

These figures, poster-like in style, with a generally accessible ideological message, were entirely in line with the pedagogical conceptions of the dominant style in art: *Socialist Realism*. This had completely suppressed the intellectually demanding art of the Russian Constructivists – though the latter, it must be said, had permitted their work to be misused as a means of propaganda directly after the October Revolution.

Standing opposite Iofan's relatively dynamic construction was the undeniably static tower designed by Albert Speer, which the architectural critic Paul Westheim ironically described as "a cardboard box with pillars." As with the Soviet Pavilion, the sculptural embellishment played an important ideological role, in this case the national symbol, the eagle of the Reich, holding a swastika in its claws.

However great the influence of Speer and his buildings was, they should not be regarded as synonymous with National Socialist architecture. The highly official pavilion for the Paris exhibition should not lead one to make generalizations about building under the Third Reich, despite the strict boundaries within which it had to work. There was a hierarchy of building tasks on offer between 1933 and 1945, from the prestige building down to the factory, with a choice of solutions permitting a real, if limited, breadth of stylistic choice.

Classicism in Italy

The situation was rather different in Italy. Avant-garde Modernist architecture had been able to develop early there, in spite of the fascist regime. But even here it was increasingly pushed into the background in the 1930s by the general spread of Classicism.

A good example of such Classicism, based on Roman models, are the buildings for the University of Rome begun in 1932 by Marcello Piacentini, who had been at Mussolini's side as his building adviser since 1922.

His marble-covered rectoral building of 1935 is notable for its monumental *pillared portico,* which extends over the whole height of the building. Taken as a whole, the building displays the features of that type of Classicism reduced to its basic stereometric forms that Heinrich Tessenow had employed at the turn of the century for his Festspielhaus in Hellerau, near Dresden (see page 24), and which was soon to be deployed in France in the Palais de Chaillot.

Piacentini's rectoral building can, however, also be seen as an Italian approach to the architectural vision that was being developed by Mussolini's allies north of the Alps.

Boris Iofan, *Soviet Pavilion* and Vera Moukhina, *Sculptural Group,* International Exhibition, Paris, 1937

Vera Moukhina's two monumental bronze figures (an industrial and a collective-farm worker) seem to be flying almost weightlessly towards a glowing socialist future. Hammer and sickle raised victoriously above them, the powerfully dynamic group was created to serve Stalin's reign of terror.

The future begins

The Globalization of Modern Architecture

1945–1960

VISIONS OF A CIVIC ARCHITECTURE

A shattered world

The devastation of the First World War had led to radical changes in political, economic, and social thinking all over the world, but the situation at the end of the Second World War was even more dramatic. The world of 1945 was very different from that which had existed, still, in 1939.

Hitler's Nazi reign of terror in Germany had led to millions of deaths all over the world, culminating in the horrific crime of the Holocaust. Never before had a war taken so many civilian lives, never before had a war so radically destroyed both cities and country-sides, and thus the foundation of the people's lives. The increasingly technological nature of life in the 20th century brought with it a corresponding advance in the technology of war, which found its melancholy climax in the dropping of the first atom bombs on the Japanese city of Hiroshima by the United States, and a few days later on Nagasaki.

But the end of the war in 1945 did not bring peace to the world. While city and countryside still lay in rubble and ashes, in Europe, Japan, and the USSR in particular, people began to migrate in huge numbers, either because they wished to emigrate or they had been driven out. The map of the world had to be redrawn because of this displacement. France, England, and the United States had fought together with the Soviets against Hitler's Germany, but the alliance shattered soon after the end of the war. The world disintegrated into Eastern and Western power blocs, with the barrier between them running straight through Germany, which was divided into two.

The Western, capitalist-oriented power bloc was formed out of the democratic countries, headed by the United States as the world's most powerful economy. The Eastern power bloc, where communism was the determining ideology, was led by the USSR, where Josef Stalin exercised dictatorial power until his death in 1953. Like the USSR, the other socialist countries were officially "people's democracies," but the people did not have the basic right of every real democracy: to be able to cast their votes secretly in free and equal elections.

Up until the ending of the communist regimes in 1989, East and West stood in irreconcilable opposition to each other: this was the Cold War, which at times, such as the Berlin blockade, or the Cuba crisis, threatened to break out into open conflict. There was fear of a Third World War.

Architectural history was largely shaped according to a Western point of view, as can be seen from the fact that the architecture of the Eastern bloc, in its various phases, has come only gradually, into the public eye, and has begun to be researched only since the opening up at the beginning of the 1990s of the erstwhile Eastern-bloc countries. It transpired that up till the death of Stalin in 1953 the "wedding

1945: Potsdam Conference between Truman, Churchill, and Stalin decides the postwar fate of Europe. Founding of the United Nations (UN). End of the hostilities of the Second World War after the capitulation of Japan.

1946: Posthumous publication of *Le Petit Prince* by Antoine de Saint-Exupéry. The US CARE organization begins sending aid packages into countries suffering from the effects of the war. Death of Damon Runyon, author of *Guys and Dolls*.

1947: Theodor W. Adorno's socially critical philosophy *Dialectics of Enlightenment* published. Maria Callas begins her brilliant career as an opera singer. Thor Heyerdahl sails on a raft from Peru to Polynesia to prove by following migratory routes that prehistoric societies were related. The "New Look" favors calf-length clothes making lavish use of material.

1948: Blockade of Berlin by Soviet Russia (lifted 1949), the Western powers supply the city by airlift. Ben-Gurion proclaims the new state of Israel in the area covered by the British Mandate for Palestine. George Balanchine founds the New York City Ballet. The UN General Assembly promulgates the Declaration of Human Rights. Gandhi assassinated. The Soviet film director Sergei Eisenstein dies aged 50.

1949: East and West Germany constituted as states either side of the boundary between the two blocs. The communist people's army under Mao Zedong conquers the whole of China; the Chinese People's Republic proclaimed. George Orwell publishes *1984*, his novel about a future totalitarian state.

The Berlin blockade: the West supplies the city by air-lift

1950: Armed conflict between communist North Korea and capitalist South Korea. Settled in 1953 by the superpowers.

1952: American fashion for jeans spreads rapidly in Europe.

1953: Workers' revolt in East Germany put down by the mobilization of Soviet tanks. The coronation of Queen Elizabeth II arouses worldwide interest through the use of modern news reporting techniques. Death of Stalin.

1956: Bloody suppression by Soviet troops of anti-Stalinist uprising in Hungary.

1957: The first artificial satellite

(Sputnik) circles the earth.

1958: Hendrik Verwoerd, prime minister of South Africa, makes *apartheid* (separation of the races) state policy.

1959: Victory of the revolution in Cuba under Fidel Castro. Federico Fellini's socially critical film *La Dolce Vita* comes out.

GLOBALIZATION OF MODERN ARCHITECTURE (1945–1960)

cake" style had spread through the whole bloc, and that it was only at the end of the 1950s that attempts could be made to realize a type of architecture appropriate to the ambitious goals which the socialist systems, with their concept of a "new" society, were propagating. Unfortunately, these initiatives, which often produced architecture that was both futurist as well as functional in tone, only lasted a short time. By the 1980s the economic problems of the Eastern bloc had become so great that there were only the resources available to put up what were standardized buildings in mostly prefabricated materials, and in a generally insipid architectural style.

The architecture of East Germany, and its capital East Berlin, had particular significance in the East-West ideological conflict, as East Berlin had to maintain a high profile in the face of West Berlin as the showplace of the Free World, and prestige projects were erected there such as the residential buildings in the Stalin-Allee (today Karl-Marx-Allee) and later the television tower.

The new beginning and continuity

With the Second World War, most of the social visions which had been the mainspring of modern art and architecture in the 1920s had evaporated. In their place new ideals of a peaceful and just community quickly evolved, but these all too often proved to be of limited feasibility when faced with the confrontational reality of the Cold War.

It very quickly became clear after 1945 that, despite the drastic experiences of the Second World War, there was in art, as in politics, no such thing as a "clean slate." One style had certainly lost its credibility with the downfall of the Third Reich: the *Classicism* employed by Albert Speer and Paul Ludwig Troos for their Nazi prestige buildings. On the other hand, the Modernist *International Style* (see pages 30 et seq.), which had no undesirable political connotations, came alive again after 1945, particularly in the United States. German architects such as Walter Gropius and Ludwig Mies van der Rohe who had emigrated there were able to look back to their earlier work, and to take it further after 1945.

In addition, as lecturers in the universities they became role models for a complete generation of young architectural students. Despite the numerous cultural and political rifts caused by the Second World War, the language of forms associated with the International Style in architecture carried with it an important element of continuity from the prewar era.

Shattered countries had to be rebuilt, and *reinforced concrete* and glassy façades became the hallmarks of a new era. From south America to southeast Asia, architecture took on a unified style, which put its stamp to a greater or lesser degree on all cities, sometimes pushing regional architectural forms into the background, or causing them to disappear from the profile of the city altogether.

Walter Gropius, *Graduate Center,* Harvard University, Cambridge, Massachusetts (USA), 1950

In 1935 the architect and ex-director of the Bauhaus in Dessau (see page 33), Walter Gropius emigrated, via England, to the USA, where in 1950 he once again designed a building for educational use, this time for Harvard University, where he himself taught.
Although the arrangement of the volumes and the supports on which they rest have a clear affinity with the Bauhaus building, the spirit of revolt is gone. In the face of the horrors that heroic ideologies had brought upon the world, stylistic muteness seemed the proper response. The daring of Modernism had given way to the bland interchangeability of the *International Style.*

Philip Johnson, *Glass House,* New Canaan, Connecticut (USA), 1949

It is difficult to imagine anything more transparent. Living space and country space intermingle. All the exterior walls are completely glazed. The steel frame which supports the whole could not be more minimal. Only the bathroom unit is in a closed cylinder. But you could only live so openly if, like Philip Johnson in New Canaan, you could protect yourself from prying eyes by turning the surrounding countryside into your own private property. The high point of building in glass was a dead-end for residential building in general.

Charles Eames, *Eames House,* Santa Monica, California (USA), 1949

It looks at first sight like a system-made factory building. In reality it is a house. The villa, which director, furniture, and exhibition designer Charles Eames designed for himself, made no secret of the fact that it was made of industrially prefabricated parts: it became the prototype of industrial building and *high-tech architecture.*

THE BAUHAUS TRADITION IN THE UNITED STATES

Old masters – new buildings

Two of the leaders of the Bauhaus emigrated to America: Walter Gropius in 1935, followed by Ludwig Mies van der Rohe who finally left Germany in 1938. They brought its traditions with them: simplicity of construction and strict rationality, which had been characteristic of Bauhaus building since the 1920s and which struck a chord in postwar American society.

By the end of the 1930s, Walter Gropius had already taken part in several competitions for college buildings in the USA, and also produced a few buildings. When he built the Graduate Center at Harvard, where he also held a lectureship, he was able to refer back to these earlier designs, although he made a point of arranging the buildings to suit the courtyard system prevailing elsewhere in Harvard.

The Graduate Center casts light in many respects on Gropius's views on modern architecture and the way it is produced. He realized the Harvard buildings in cooperation with his studio TAC (The Architects' Collaborative) in which he saw the materialization of his ideas about creative teamwork. The Graduate Center is also a formal and personal link with the Bauhaus tradition in Germany. The elegant pillared buildings with their flat roofs and long strip windows, which he created for Harvard, were entirely in the tradition of the 1920s language of form. And for the artistic decoration of the complex he brought in old comrades in arms from his Bauhaus days such as Herbert Bayer, Josef Albers, and Hans Arp.

Ludwig Mies van der Rohe understood even better than Gropius how to adapt to American needs the basic principles of his classical-modern formal language, which he had employed in the late 1920s in the Villa Tugendhat, or in the famous pavilion for the international exhibition in Barcelona. His legendary maxim "less is more" was taken by a whole generation of architects not just as a brilliant sally, but as an article of faith.

Johnson and Eames – in the footsteps of the master

Steel and glass were Mies van der Rohe's favorite materials and he knew how to use them – in both residential and commercial buildings – like no one else. The steel and glass mania which Mies unleashed in America found many imitators, including Philip Johnson. Johnson, who had worked for a time in Mies's office but later abandoned the plain language of forms cultivated there, went on to become one of the most brilliant figures of the American architectural scene in the 20th century. His publication, with Henry-Russell Hitchcock, of *International Style* at the beginning of the 1930s brought him instant celebrity. His Glass House in New Canaan emulates the strict purism of Mies.

The house was built, according to Mies's concept, on a steel frame which he *filled in* with nothing else but panes of glass. This highly fashionable house, elegant and aesthetic though it is, inescapably begs the question of how practical, how livable such architecture is. How are you supposed to live in a house made totally of glass?

The same, rather polemical question had been posed by many an architectural critic 20 years before in reference to the open ground plan developed by Mies van der Rohe for the Villa Tugendhat in Brünn. Looking at the Glass House, so clearly built to a program, one has the insistent feeling that this is less architecture for living in than a sort of architectonic confession of faith. This feeling is further confirmed by other buildings carried out later by the extremely versatile Johnson, which also seem to have been programmatically conceived. One striking example is the AT&T Building (see page 87) in New York, which counts today as an icon of post-modern architecture.

Charles Eames took a quite different route from Johnson in his steel-frame residential

MIES VAN DER ROHE

One of the most successful architectural trends around 1910 was *Neoclassicism*, the stern monumentality of which worked as an opposing pole to the mobile flowing forms of *Art Nouveau*. Ludwig Mies van der Rohe, born in Aachen in 1886, was employed early on in the studio of Peter Behrens (see page 23), one of the leading Neoclassicists of his day, and so came into direct contact with the style; he was in fact placed in charge of the execution of Behrens's project for the German embassy in St. Petersburg (1911–12). As a result his first personal projects reveal an intense involvement with the classicist architecture of the 19th century. The mainspring of Mies's architectonic inspiration was the work of Karl Friedrich Schinkel. Schinkel had been responsible, among other things, for the celebrated Alte Museum in Berlin, but also for numerous villas for the Prussian royal family in the neighborhood of the Residenz (royal palace). Mies took from them a fine sense of proportion, clear forms, and a close relationship with the surrounding countryside, and then integrated these qualities into his early villas, such as the Urbig house in Potsdam (1914–17). But his ideal projects, which were the Country House in Concrete (1923) as well as the Country House in Brick (1924), reveal not only his interest in

Ludwig Mies van der Rohe with the "Barcelona" chair he designed in 1929

his great forebear Schinkel, but reflect in their ground plans the discussion going on at the time about the abstract art of Theo van Doesburg. Mies van der Rohe's *Classicism* was therefore a translation of classicist trends into contemporary architectural language, which culminated in his renown architectonic credo "less is more."

But it would be to misunderstand Mies to think that this motto would lead to an architectural puritanism. On the contrary, precious materials such as marble and gleaming high-grade steel were frequently his chosen materials, as for instance in the famous German pavilion for the 1929 international exhibition in Barcelona. The open plan of the pavilion, with its unexpected encounters – with, for instance, a sculpture by

Classical elegance in black steel and glass: the Neue Nationalgalerie in the Berlin Kulturforum, constructed between 1965 and 1968

Georg Kolbe – and its carefully studied delineation of interior space, revealed Mies van der Rohe's astonishing sense of the right dimensions and proportions, and give the visitor a unique sense of space.

The discrepancy between Mies's inclination for simple forms and his preference for costly materials – as exemplified in the Barcelona pavilion – caused the architect Hans Poelzig to frame his revealing bon mot: "We build simply, however much it costs."

Controversy also arose in these years over Mies van der Rohe's Villa Tugendhat, which he built in 1930 in Brünn, and which carried over the principle of an open ground plan, as developed in the Barcelona pavilion, to a residential building. This led to the question whether it would actually be possible to live in a house which broke so radically from the typical design for a luxurious private home.

Mies succeeded Walter Gropius and Hannes Meyer as head of the Bauhaus (see page 33) which was then under heavy pressure from the National Socialists. He moved it from Dessau to Berlin and there tried to save it, in vain. Most of the other projects which he attempted to launch after 1933 as an architect under the Third Reich also failed to take root. In 1938 he answered the call of the famous Armour Institute (later IIT) and went to Chicago. Here, in the 1940s, he created the new buildings in simple *rectilinear* forms for the Illinois Institute of Technology (IIT), whose steel frame construction, faced with brick or glass, became a model for other architects. Mies now succumbed to a desire which he had cherished for a long time, which was to construct a tall building. Whereas his sketches for a tall building on the Friedrichsstrasse in Berlin (1921), a glass skyscraper (1922), and a tall office building in reinforced concrete (1923) never left the drawing board, he realized his dream of building a glass skyscraper with the twin towers on Lake Shore Drive in Chicago (1948–51) and the legendary Seagram Building in New York (1954–58), which became the model for a whole succession of skyscrapers of similar design.

A gleaming icon of glazed high-rise architecture: the Seagram Building, realized by Ludwig Mies van der Rohe with Philip Johnson between 1954 and 1958

However, Mies's classically elegant architecture, which was now totally dominated by glass and steel, had a late homecoming to Germany. His Neue Nationalgalerie in the Berlin Kulturforum, which he created in old age, forms a rationalist pole in opposition to the expressive architecture of Hans Scharoun's neighboring Philharmonie building.

The confrontation of the two buildings forms a dramatic finale to the trajectory of a generation of architects – that of the European avant-garde, whose influence stretched from the decline of *historicism* to the end of the 1960s.

The Berlin museum building is composed of two parts: a temple-like steel hall with an entirely glazed façade, and a large lower ground floor, in which the work of the classic modernists is displayed. In his handling of the tasks of building a "temple" and a "museum" Mies shows himself for the last time as the great classicist and follower of Schinkel. It was after all in his Altes Museum (situated not far from the Neue Nationalgalerie) with its front of ionic pillars, that the two tasks were successfully combined for the first time.

Wallace Harrison, Max Abramovitz,
UN Building, New York, 1950

"We are planning a world architecture," said Le Corbusier, who as a member of the architectural commission contributed a large part of the preliminary design for the United Nations Headquarters, "and for this kind of work there is no other name … but discipline." So the most public site in one of the most important and cosmopolitan metropolises in the world was chosen for this most important of world building projects: the East River in New York. Le Corbusier sketched several outlines for the building. The low, level conference center and the upward-striving assembly hall were dominated by the administrative building, a slim, slab-shaped skyscraper. Innumerable critics interpreted this as an unwitting sign that world government had long ago been taken over by bureaucracy.
The building plans, produced by a major American architectural firm, Harrison & Abramovitz, emphasized the oneness of the nations still further. A homogenous gleaming curtain of green glass covers all 39 stories. The same, story-high window module is used 2,730 times. There was another sense, however, in which the UN administrative building represented world architecture: similar *curtain wall*-clad tall boxes are to be found everywhere on the face of the globe.

buildings, such as his Case Study House No. 8, built between 1945 and 1949, which arose out of a competition for the development of prototype houses, or the house which he erected in 1949 for himself and his wife Ray in Pacific Palisades, Santa Monica. Eames, who was also famous as a designer, used the same materials as Johnson – steel and glass – yet their almost contemporaneous buildings were fundamentally different. While Johnson's blazoned his belief in the dominant architectural trend of the time, Eames's fascinated by their reserved, almost fragile elegance. They had a characteristic truth to their materials: standard industrial components which could be ordered by catalog. The construction principles of this technicized house-building can be read from the façade, endowing what were, in the main, very simple materials with an aesthetic all their own.

The steel frames of his houses could be filled in various ways, most often with glass. The rectangular grid composed by the cross-bars of the windows, and the sensitive way in which the houses were made to interact with the natural world around them without dominating it, revealed Eames's experience of traditional Japanese frame-buildings. The result was both filigree and balanced: masterpieces of aesthetic architecture.

The new language of the skyscrapers

The skyscrapers designed by Mies van der Rohe ensured that the prestige office and administration buildings of big firms in these years used glass as their prime material. The

appearance of transparency and practicality conveyed by these buildings, their lightness and elegance, made them stand out dramatically among the *freestone*-clad, *eclectically* styled tall buildings dating from the turn of the century.

The core of all these skyscrapers was a supporting steel skeleton, on which the glassy façade was hung like a curtain. The standardized components of this curtain worked together with the exactly matched grid on which they were hung to create an impression of uninterrupted unity. The concepts of the "curtain wall," and the façade in the form of a grid quickly became synonymous with the architecture of commercial buildings in the 1950s and 1960s.

The glass wall was the solution architects had been seeking for a type of façade that would suit the constructional principle of the supporting skeleton. Instead of eclectic architecture whose pseudo-*Gothic* forms aped the massive appearance of a stone building, the glass wall provided a solution which carried over the lightness and variability of the supporting skeleton onto the façade.

In the last 20 years however, this exemplary honesty with materials has been counteracted by a renewed tendency to envelop skyscrapers in sheets of freestone in the place of the previous glass skin. This stone is intended to convey exactly that massive impression which was expressly avoided in the 1950s.

The glass façades of the 1950s ands 1960s demanded ambitious technical solutions from the architects in the interiors as well. Unlike traditional building in stone, glass gives no protection from heat or cold. The perfecting of air-conditioning, ventilation, and air-extraction techniques, as well as heat retaining double-glazing systems provided the conditions for the success of glass façades in tall buildings.

Even the project for the headquarters of the United Nations on the East River in New York, based on a design by Le Corbusier and carried out by Wallace Harrison and Max Abramovitz between 1947 and 1950 followed the trend. For the main building, which was the Secretariat of the UN, a tall slim glass wedge was the chosen style, with the side walls being without windows. The three buildings of the UN complex are so arranged as to constitute a well-proportioned and internally balanced ensemble of *rectilinear* forms. The differing heights of the three buildings for the Secretariat, the General Assembly, and the press, and the way in which they are graded in terms of space give them almost the quality of a three-dimensional abstract composition.

The theme of the steel or concrete skeleton with a glass curtain wall has remained modern, as is documented by the elegant glass buildings of the 1980s and 1990s by Jean Nouvel (illustrations pages 102–103) and by Norman Foster's skyscrapers (illustration page 80). The glassy cube, in various guises, is a leitmotif that runs through the whole architectural history of the 20th century, from the Bauhaus in Dessau, through Mies van der Rohe's Neue Nationalgalerie in Berlin to Jean Nouvel's Institut du Monde Arabe in Paris.

Once the glass wall had been discovered, it turned out to be a highly versatile way of facing a building, particularly a skyscraper. Architects have reacted to the changing tastes of clients over the last 40 years by exploiting the wide range of possibilities it offers: stressing the articulation of the glass wall in a particular grid, as in the Richard Daley Center in Chicago, built by Skidmore, Owings & Merill as well as C. F. Murphy in 1965, or by varying the ground plan, from the rectangular box through to the polygon, as created by Walter Gropius for the PanAm Building in 1963. All of these types of buildings, right through until the postmodern variants, are finally – leaving aside technical innovations in air-conditioning or ventilation – only variations on a theme which was established at the beginning of the century by the introduction of the new building materials – glass, steel, and concrete.

Horizontal versus vertical

Glassy slabs in the style of Mies van der Rohe did not necessarily have to grow upwards. For the American car company General Motors (GM), Eero Saarinen, who was the son of the architect Eliel Saarinen, built research laboratories in the form of a long horizontal ribbon of glass. The building was part of a much larger installation for GM, including an assembly hall in the shape of an aluminum-covered glittering hemisphere.

Saarinen's formal language and use of materials was too technicist to be truly sober. At a time when the United States was carrying

out experimental explosions with atomic bombs on the Bikini Atoll in Oceania without any particular precautions, and the competition between the United States and the Soviet Union to be the first into space was reaching its climax, architecture itself took on a distinctly futuristic aspect.

The centuries-old interaction between client and architect, which has outlasted every architectural epoch and fashion, came into play once again in the commission to build research laboratories for GM: buildings have both a functional and a prestige role to play, so it almost went without saying that the commission implied developing a design that would express the technical expertise and forward-looking attitude of the clients and their products.

REACTIONS

USA meets Europe

The most perfect variation on the theme of steel and glass must be the town hall created by Arne Jacobsen for Rødovre in Denmark (1954–56). Like Saarinen's GM complex the building did not develop upwards but horizontally. A strict grid articulated the three stories of the building. The separate segments were placed at right angles to each other following the same strict system. The administration block, which was both taller and longer, was linked by a glazed walkway to the lecture area lying behind, which was almost totally composed of large panes of glass. The extremely sober and yet highly elegant formal

Eero Saarinen, *General Motors Technical Center,* Warren, Michigan (USA), 1948–56

The administration building (foreground) of General Motors, with its *curtain wall* façade put together with prefabricated units, is comparable with the contemporary steel and glass buildings of Mies van der Rohe, and develops his style further in the imaginative use of materials (enameled metal plates sealed with neoprene strips). The building exhibits a colorful differentiation of shades in its materials, creating the impression of a layering of strata, given a rhythm by the vertical movement of the slender steel skeleton. Architectonically, both the research laboratories and the domed conference building (background), make a statement about the technical expertise associated with General Motors.

language of the exterior was continued in the
interior, as for example in the self-supporting
stairs, which had gleaming steel rails and
reflecting glass balustrades.

The challenge set by Mies van der Rohe's
buildings to the younger generation of architects, to which Jacobsen was responding, was
met – just as radically but in a formally quite
different way – by Alison and Peter Smithson.

Their design for Hunstanton School in
Norfolk, Great Britain (1949–53), refers back
to Mies's concept of steel-frame buildings. But
in contrast to Jacobsen's strictly axial layout,
their building has an asymmetrical ground
plan. Nor did they use only glass and steel:
their steel frame construction was *faced with
brick.* The decisive innovatory factor in their
much-talked-about school building was that
all conduits for water, electricity, and so on,
and all supply shafts were clearly on view. This
unconditional honesty about materials which
showed everything and hid none of the technology of the building is, however, the point at
which the Smithsons began to take leave of

Mies van der Rohe's carefully balanced and
aesthetic architecture. It announced a new
turn in 20th century architecture which was
to be the mark of the 1960s and 1970s, the
so-called "Brutalism."

ARCHITECTURE AS SCULPTURE

Spirals of art

Frank Lloyd Wright had been setting his mark
on American and European architecture and
exerting his influence over numerous younger
architects for over half a century when he
completed his most notable late work, the
Solomon R. Guggenheim Museum (first sketch
1943), intended to offer public access to its
patron's collection of modern painting.

Since the early 19th century a museum had
become one of the most significant building
commissions. Rulers and the aristocracy had,
from the Middle Ages through to the 18th
century, built up private art collections for
their personal enjoyment and edification;
then, around 1800, the middle classes
discovered an interest in art. The transformation of the Louvre in Paris into a museum, and
the building of Karl Friedrich Schinkel's Alte
Museum in Berlin set a model for modern
museum culture and were soon followed by
many other buildings.

This then was the background to the
instructions that Solomon Guggenheim gave to
the 70-year-old Frank Lloyd Wright when
commissioning him to build his museum in the
up-and-coming art metropolis of New York,
instructions that were as lapidary as they were
difficult to follow: the new museum should be
unlike any other. In fact the solution that Wright
found was extremely unusual and totally unique.

Like an inverted cone with its point buried in the earth, the main body of the building rears up, a sculpture in its own right. To get to the pictures the visitor has to go up in a lift to the top; the route then leads the visitor gently downwards in broad spirals which can be divined from the exterior of the windowless cone. The ramp he follows encloses a bright, atrium-like interior court which runs through the center of the building, crowned with a shallow glass dome.

There has been much argument as to whether Wright's museum, the completion and opening of which he did not live to see, is a sufficiently museum-like setting for the pictures of the Guggenheim collection. But it is absolutely certain that Wright created a unique building which reminds one, with its utopian formal language, of the early architectural visions of the 20th century, and thus thoroughly corresponds with the abstract pictures housed therein.

LE CORBUSIER

The new community – the Unité d'habitation

Although the construction of the UN complex originated with a sketch by Le Corbusier, other architects were then brought in to carry out the detailed design of the building (see page 60). However, Le Corbusier, who was always the great planner and outrider of the avant-garde, also entered the public arena in Europe, with projects which served to confirm his importance as the most important architect of the 20th century.

As early as the 1920s the general shortage of housing caused many architects to concentrate on the problem of building homes and *housing schemes*. In the foreground of their plans was the opening up of apartment design to provide more air and light and to rationalize building methods, but social needs were also met by the provision of communal facilities such as laundries and roof gardens in the housing schemes.

Le Corbusier himself engaged with the questions of collective living in his theories on town planning, presented in his book *La ville radieuse* of 1935.

His Unité d'habitation in Marseille (see illustration page 66), built between 1947 and 1952, was a complex designed to satisfy the most diverse needs of its inhabitants in a single building. The Unité had a unique infra-structure, including a hotel, a roof garden, a children's paddling pool, a nursery school, and a shopping center. It is not by chance that the architecture of the building as well as the structures on its roof are reminiscent of a giant ocean liner, the practical yet aesthetic forms of which had often occupied Le Corbusier in previous works. The Unité resembles a large ship at the edge of the harbor at Marseille, a ship which can supply all of its inhabitants' needs over an extended period with its shops and social arrangements, and in this way serves to exemplify Le Corbusier's ideas of collective living.

Le Corbusier, *Notre-Dame-du-Haut*,
Ronchamp, Vosges (France), 1950–55

Walls several feet thick – in fact they are
double – in roughcast concrete bend to
enclose an inwards-turning meditative
space. The massive hung roof shaped like
mushroom cap, separated from the wall
by narrow glass inserts, is dramatically lit
and seems to hover. The variously shaped
and colored windows inset deeply into
the wall emphasize the successive
climaxes of the liturgy.
The pilgrimage chapel is a highly
expressive sculpture, which seems
at first sight to have nothing in common
with the rational apartment blocks that
Le Corbusier was building at the time.
Yet just as the Unité d'habitation gives
material form to a rational concept of a
place to live, so Ronchamp translates
the functional and emotional demands
of its religious purpose. In both cases
the requirement for the building is
rigorously fulfilled.

The 370 apartments in the Unité, which can
cover from one to several floors, are placed
in relationship to each other through a
complex grid of ground plans, which can be
divined from the articulation of the façades.
Unlike the somewhat monotonous grids of
the American skyscraper fronts, the façade of
the Unité is a work of graphic art. A glazed gap
in the facade indicates the presence of the
shopping street which is located inside the
Unité to serve the needs of the inhabitants.
The expressive roof landscape gives the
building, which stands on concrete supports,
an additional air of technicity.

Sculptures in concrete

The Unité also struck a new note in its use
of materials. Raw concrete – *beton brut* –
without which a Le Corbusier building is
unthinkable, took on a more independent
quality in this one, standing on an equal
footing with other materials in the façade.

In all of Le Corbusier's late work we can
see a breaking free from the language of
Modernism which had become a worldwide
norm: it was still developing, and gave a significant impulse to the development of other
architects. In particular, his use of *beton brut*
was an important stimulus to architects such
as Kenzo Tange (see page 83) and Louis I.
Kahn, and found its embodiment in the
Brutalism (see page 69) of the 1960s.

This development in Le Corbusier's work
continued with the church of Notre-Dame-
du-Haut. This was erected between 1950 and
1955, and became one of the most significant
church buildings of the 20th century. There

was nothing here of the cool, clear materialism
of the glassy rectilinear skyscrapers he was also
building at this time. Instead of a standardized
or typified building, which could be erected
anywhere in the world given the appropriate
technology, Le Corbusier created at Ronchamp
a one-of-a-kind sculpture in concrete, whose
powerful visual effect can scarcely be encom-
passed in words.

The dominant feature of the building from
the outside is its roof, which projects far out
from the walls, and then dips in the middle
like the brim of a hat. The inner space has an
Expressionistic feel, with its irregularly set
windows and the curved forms of wall and
roof. If you permit yourself to respond to the
expressionistic formal language of Ronchamp,
become open to the way the lines and the light
are directed, and take in and understand this
architecture with your own eyes, then even this
gradual apprehension will become meditative
in a unique way which expresses the function
of the building as a sacral space.

THE NEW CITY

Le Corbusier's Chandigarh in India

At the end of his architectural career, Le
Corbusier was given the chance to dare to
realize an idea that had accompanied him all
his life: to turn his ideal of a new city into fact.
From 1951 till his death in 1965 he was occupied with the building of Chandigarh, which
had been founded as the administrative
capital of the new Indian state of Punjab.

India did in fact already have, in the 20th
century, considerable experience of the founding of new cities. The English architect Edwin
Lutyens had created the new capital New
Delhi for India when it was still ruled by Britain
under a viceroy. Le Corbusier understood how
to move from the impressive *Classicism* of
Lutyens buildings to a monumentality that did
not employ the Classicist language of forms.
He allowed himself to be inspired by Indian
architecture as well as the Indian way of
life, then mixed them with the specific formal
vocabulary of Modernism.

Le Corbusier realized the buildings of
Chandigarh with Jane Drew, Maxwell Fry, and
his longstanding collaborator, Pierre Jeanneret.
At the focal point of the of the city stand the
Administration Building, the High Court, and
the State Assembly Building. He again made

an expressive use of concrete, as he had in Ronchamp, and created sculptural roof landscapes in the style of the Unité.

But despite the quality of the individual buildings, it became clear that the project was doomed to failure. Planned as a symbol of the "New India," which gained its independence in 1947, Le Corbusier's work of genius was a work for the future, a vision of a city that was right for cars – in a world where most people went on foot because they could not afford any other means of transport. Even an architect of the caliber of Le Corbusier could not implant his elevated architectural vision in the Indian reality of Chandigarh.

Architecture as the expression of a new world: Brasilia and Niemeyer's plans

When democracy set foot in Brazil in 1945, the breakthrough into a new era was also symbolized in architecture in a most extraordinary way. In the mid-1950s, the architect Oscar Niemeyer, who was a convinced communist, and the town planner Lúcio Costa were commissioned by President Juscelino Kubischek to plan a new capital city in the interior of that Latin American country: this was to be Brasilia.

The city was constructed between 1956 and 1963, for a population of 500,000, in a location chosen as a starting point for the opening up of the interior.

As an expression of progress and modernity it was conceived in the shape of an airplane, divided into three components – cockpit, fuselage, and wings – corresponding with city areas, and each of them with a particular function allotted to it: government, administration, residential.

The architectonic and functional center of the newly created city was the "Square of the Three Powers" (illustration page 66). Niemeyer's Chamber of Deputies was crowned with a saucer-shaped construction, and the Senate had a dome. Between the two there towered a pair of distinctive slab-shaped skyscrapers, which contained the offices of the administration. Both the monumentality and the axial quality of the buildings are characteristic of Niemeyer's architecture.

Highly praised at first, subsequently vilified, the visionary project actually fell victim to the reality of the country. The buildings are indeed strong, expressive visual creations, but the architect had not taken any particular account of the climatic conditions of the Brazilian interior. Much more serious turned out to be the magnetic effect which the airplane-shaped city center exerted on the people in the country that was around it. The city is now surrounded by a ring of more or less official slums, which has swollen the number of inhabitants to two million. This has had obvious fatal consequences for the overburdened civic infrastructure of Brasilia, which had originally been designed for a quarter of that number.

Oscar Niemeyer and Lúcio Costa, *Cathedral,* Brasilia, 1956–63

In 1956, President Juscelino Kubitschek of Brazil commissioned the building of a new capital city in the Amazon forest 600 miles (1,000 kilometers) northeast of Rio de Janeiro. Lúcio Costa designed the general plan of the city and Oscar Niemeyer was responsible for the architecture.
Arranged in a circle, 21 supports curve inwards and widen to meet in a halo at the top, which projects an impressive ball of light downwards into the building, bathing it in gleaming colors.
Oscar Niemeyer's buildings for Brasilia, especially the congress building with its two concrete bowls (illustration page 66), the presidential palace "floating" in water, and the cathedral with its mighty concrete rays all have a fantastic yet grandiose quality which places them among the highest achievements of modern architecture.

TOWN PLANNING IN THE 20TH CENTURY

1930–2000

The 20th century marked the transition from town architecture to town planning. The transition occurred as a result of the industrial revolution which took the traditional city beyond its limits, and gave birth to a new ideal: the modern city. The attempt to realize this ideal came to grief in the 1980s, leading to nostalgia for the traditional city. But at the end of the 20th century, the changing economic context brought the question of the city and the possibility of exerting an influence through planning, onto the agenda once more.

The modernist city

Whereas the designs for garden cities and "Usonia" (see pages 40–41) took root in the country, the French architect and socialist Tony Garnier made detailed plans for a model of a modern industrial city. The project, which he presented in 1904 for a "Cité industrielle," had separate areas demarcated for different functions, such as living, working, relaxation, and transport. The traffic system had separate roads for vehicles and pedestrians, through-roads, and access-roads. Green spaces took up more than half of the city area. Set in the midst of these were loose groupings of simple free-standing apartment blocks, built of reinforced concrete using industrial techniques, and affording plenty of air and light.

Garnier did the conceptual preparatory work for the Modernist town-planners. Both his architectonic details and planning ideas became their basic principles. But it was the ambitious abstract projects of Le Corbusier which first gave these ideas ideological force and promoted their final breakthrough. In 1922 he worked out his plan for the "Ville contemporaine." Whereas Garnier's town was small, with buildings a maximum of three stories high, Le Corbusier wanted to provide homes for up to three million inhabitants massed into residential areas with buildings up to 60 stories high. His "Plan voisin" three years later placed his designs in a real location for the first time. He suggested replacing a part of the historic old city of Paris with 18 skyscrapers 650 feet (200 meters) high. The theoretical foundation of this signed manifesto was worked out by the fourth Congrès Internationaux d'Architecture Moderne (CIAM) and published in 1943 by Le Corbusier and the French CIAM group.

This "Charter of Athens" was the manifesto for the new city. Whereas the traditional city drew a boundary between itself and the country, divided up its activities between public and private zones of influence, differentiated between public streets, squares and parks, and private buildings, and separated town planning from architecture, the modernist city would be a single, open space for living that was organized by a central state planning authority. In place of the mixed-use road system open to all means of transport that was to be found in the traditional city, the modernist city would have a traffic system separated hierarchically according to function. The housing question was inseparable from the crisis in the old cities, and should no longer be left in the hands of private speculators, but instead dealt with by erecting whole areas of mass housing, all built to the same standard, and offering light, air, and sun for all.

The Charter of Athens became the guidebook for all new town planning and building worldwide in the decades that followed. Its emphasis on the new, found particular favor with the states founded after the Second World War. East Berlin's city center was one of many dedicated to the collective idea. Over the ruins on either side of the Frankfurter Allee, Edmund Collein, Werner Dutschke, and Josef Kaiser built the first socialist residential complex between 1959 and 1965. But the West built almost as many mass housing schemes of questionable value: right up until the mid-1970s, estates with tens of thousands of separate living units were put up as the old tenement areas were torn down. Centers that had developed over centuries were programmatically rebuilt in the name of making the cities accessible for cars, and motorways were driven through the heart of the old cities.

The chance to build a completely new city occurred only rarely, however. Between the years of 1951 and 1965 Le Corbusier was commissioned by Pandit Nehru to plan the state capital of Chandigarh, which was intended to be the symbol of modern India. Over a space of

around 250 acres (100 hectares) he laid out a grid of through roads. In between these there were residential areas for 150,000 people, with all the 13 different castes of Indian society living separately from each other. The only area shared by all was the line of commercial establishments along the east-west axis, in the middle of which was the civic center. The state government was separated off in its own area to the north of the city.

Similar concepts inspired Brazil to built a new capital city 600 miles (1,000 kilometers) away from Rio de Janeiro on the high plateau of Planatina. The competition to plan the city was won by Lúcio Costa in 1957. Four years later Oscar Niemeyer had already erected the most important buildings, and Brasilia was inaugurated in 1961. Costa's plan was based on a very simple grid of

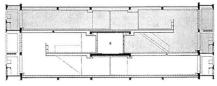

The Unité d'habitation in Marseille by Le Corbusier (1952), and a cross-section through three floors showing two living units (page 64)

four- to ten-lane motorways. The east-west axis is 1.4 miles (2.2 kilometers) long and 1150 feet (350 meters) wide, and along it lie all the buildings housing local government, sports, and the armed forces, and hotels and theaters. It culminates in the "Square of the Three Powers" with the 38-story government building, the bowl of the congress chamber, the dome of the senate, the law courts, the foreign ministry, and the cathedral (illustration page 65). At right-angles to this monumental axis runs the 8.7-mile (14-kilometer) long north-south axis, flanked by residential complexes with green areas around them, in which people live in slab-shaped buildings five or six stories high. The banks and the shopping center are located at the intersection of the two highways.

Brasilia is an exemplary demonstration of the failure of modern town planning. It was successful only insofar as it solved the housing problem. In all

The bowl-shaped congress building, and behind it the skyscraper housing the government offices, on the Square of the three Powers in Brasilia by Oscar Niemeyer

Alvaro Siza Vieira, "Bonjour Tristesse," the "critical reconstruction" of an apartment block in the run-up to the International Building Exhibition (IBA) in Berlin-Kreuzberg, 1982–83

other ways it could not even live up to its own promises. Brasilia's road system does not permit you to cover a distance of a mile simply on foot, you have to go by car, taking a six-mile detour. The international town planning ideas realized here take no consideration of the site or of the traditions of the country. The functionally divided city, intersected by motorways, left nowhere for civic life to grow. It merely represents a collection of buildings, not a city. Despite the enormous open spaces, there is none that can be used by society. Because the plan accounted for every square inch of Brasilia, today three-quarters of the inhabitants live in satellite towns which have grown up without any plan at all. The main lesson that was learnt from Brasilia was that town planning efforts that impose the new instead of giving space to what has developed historically deny themselves from the outset any chance of sustained development.

The renaissance of the city

So, theory looked again at the traditional city. In his book *L'Architettura della Città*, published in 1966, the Italian Aldo Rossi stressed that the form of the city, its ground plan, was valid for every era. Only the use that is made of it must be appropriate to each era. An example he gave was the Placa del Marcato in Lucca, the oval form of which is based on the Roman amphitheatre that stood on that spot. In the 1970s, the Dutchman Rem Koolhaas published several analyses of the metropolis of New York. In his book *Delirious New York* he celebrates the principle of mixed use. The skyscraper which accommodates offices and dwellings, as well as places of entertainment under the same roof, and which, as seen in the Rockefeller Center (illustration page 49) also creates a free space, is Koolhaas's prototype of the city building. Koolhaas's 1972 drawing "The City of the Captive Globe" shows how the most diverse architectonic manifestations can be put together into a unified city by means of a system of blocks. The work stresses the advantages of separating architecture and town planning.

In 1977 the "Charter of Machu Pichu" was drawn up. It was the antithesis of the Charter of Athens, and it demanded, amongst other things, the preservation of historic buildings, the continuity of the city ground plan, the integration of various uses, and the priority of public transport over individual transport.

Thereafter town planning concentrated more and more on the inner city. Between 1984 and 1987, the Internationale Bauaustellung (IBA, the International Building Exhibition), turned West Berlin into a showplace for town planning ideas. Under the slogan "careful city renewal," superannuated buildings were set in order and their ability to last into the future demonstrated in the shadow of the Wall. Under the slogan "critical reconstruction," the ground plan of the city that had been destroyed by the war and by modernist town planning was reconstituted with the most varied examples of contemporary architecture. The IBA was extremely successful in its basic project of regaining the inner city as a place to live. But so long as the project "city" was the preserve of the public authority alone and only council housing was put up, only the form of the city was created; its substance – civic life – was not.

Spain was more successful: in an extraordinary act of concerted effort between 1981 and 1993, innumerable squares were brought to life again in Barcelona, and all over the country schools, tramways, and cultural centers were constructed. At the end of Franco's dictatorship the collectivity, which had been long repressed, reasserted its rights over civic space.

Today's situation

The individualization of society at the end of the 20th century has put a question mark once again over the idea of the city as a community project. The liberalization of the economy is undermining the planning monopoly of the town councils. These had already lost their active role in city development through the crisis in financing brought about by that liberalization, which had enhanced the role of private investors. When there is doubt that the city can be planned at all, aesthetic concepts step into the background.

In the mid-1990s the German Dieter Hoffmann-Axthelm reflected on the question of whether it was still possible to plan under these conditions

and to ensure a continuing development for the city. His *Anleitung für den Stadtumbau* (Guidelines for Rebuilding in the City), takes a position against large town-planning interventions: the basic structure for the city is already there in the historically given layout of the streets. Working upon a structure of small units offers the guarantee that all town-planning goals are achieved and that no part can be developed at another's cost. After the excessive weight of private enterprise in the 19th century and the dominance of the state in the 20th, the "third city" should be based upon cooperation.

His plea for small-scale cooperative development appears completely utopian in the face of larger changes in the cities. All over the world it is not the centers themselves that are developing, but the peripheries.

The regions of southeast Asia are expanding the most explosively. For example, the triangle of Hong Kong, Macao, and Canton is fusing into a mega-agglomeration with unimaginable speed. The number of inhabitants of Canton has doubled in only five years. Hong Kong's satellite city, Shenzen, has a population 115 times greater than 20 years ago. These quantum leaps are occurring within giant building projects . Macao is planning land reclamation which entails filling in an area of water 23 square miles (60 square kilometers) in size. Between Hong Kong and Canton half a dozen overspill cities are planned and whole bays are being filled in to gain valuable building land. Some 300,000 people will live in skyscrapers at least 40 stories high. This growth leads to an unbelievable concentration of population: there are 20 times more people on a single square yard in Hong Kong than in a big city in Europe. The resultant problems, for instance with the traffic, are reminiscent of the crisis in the European cities in the 19th century. History seems to be repeating itself.

Yet in face of the much greater speed and force of the problem it seems questionable to try to deal with it using town-planning methods that were developed over the past 100 years. The cities of southeast Asia have become the experimental terrain for a new model of the metropolis: the chaos city. This "city" is no longer constituted by the collectivity of its inhabitants which expresses itself in a unified type of building, but in the confrontation of conflicting interests, which takes advantage of an open but temporary spectrum of opportunities. In the permanent process of growth and change inherent in such a city, planning has no chance.

Land reclamation projects in Hong Kong, circa 2000. Left in the picture, facing Lantau, the new airport as an island in the sea

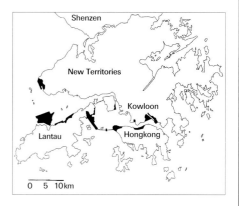

"The Swinging Sixties"

Vision and Reality

1960–1970

SOCIALISM VERSUS CAPITALISM

Let's make a revolution

To a blast of guitar music and bass rhythms from the Rolling Stones and the Beatles, and the sound of Jimi Hendrix's version of the American national anthem at the Woodstock festival, the youth of the world formed into a Protest Generation. Men let their hair grow longer and longer, and the multicolored batik T-shirt replaced the once obligatory, more formal shirt and tie.

University campuses from Berkeley to the Sorbonne developed into the intellectual spearheads of the protest. Their complaints initially were regarding unsatisfactory conditions of study, but their protest became increasingly political, turning against the traditional social values held by the Western world, and denouncing as a falsehood the network of structures – often democratic only in appearance – which made social privilege an everyday fact of life.

It was chiefly the situation in the United States that fueled the protests. The American civil rights leader Martin Luther King, following the example of Mahatma Gandhi, instigated peaceful protests demanding the implementation of equal rights for black Americans, who were still discriminated against, especially in the South. But very soon the tide of protest turned against the role of the United States in Vietnam, where it was waging a barbaric proxy war on behalf of the pro-Western South against the communist-indoctrinated North.

In the Eastern bloc as well, reform movements were widespread. In revolt against daily repression and continually being told what to do and think, the citizens of Czechoslovakia demanded socialism with a human face. Freedom of expression was granted, whereupon the people demanded unrestricted democratization, provoking resistance by the party leaders of the "brother" countries. In August 1968, Warsaw Pact tanks crushed the hopes of the Prague Spring, bringing the world once more during the Cold War to the brink of an open military conflict.

During this time New York finally grew to the stature of the capital city of art, where Andy Warhol made screenprints of a Campbell's Soup tin, turning it into a work of art, and declared to the world that everyone could have their 15 minutes of fame in a world shaped by the presence of the media. Advertising, trademarks, stars, but also anonymous accident victims – Warhol's grids of multiple screenprints struck such a general chord that his series of Marilyn Monroe and Mao Zedong became real icons of the 1960s. The everyday became artistic reality for Andy Warhol, Robert

---

1960: A total of 17 states in Africa become independent: the end of colonial rule. The excess potential for nuclear destruction ("overkill") in the United States and the USSR results in an atomic stalemate. Ten-power disarmament conference begins in Geneva.

1961: On 13 August East Germany puts up the Wall between East and West Berlin. The contraceptive pill is developed and distributed. Death of the American film actor Gary Cooper.

1962: Cuba crisis: Khrushchev agrees to Kennedy's demand that he dismantle Russian rockets. First performance of Benjamin Britten's *War Requiem*. Suicide of Marilyn Monroe.

1963: US President J. F. Kennedy assassinated in Dallas on 22 November.

1964: Arafat takes over the leadership of al-Fatah (the Arab movement to drive the Israelis out of Palestine). International action at the time of the building of the Aswan dam in Egypt rescues the temple of Abu Simbel. In the cinemas is *A Hard Day's Night*, the British film with and about the Beatles.

1965: Nobel Peace Prize awarded to the international children's aid organization UNICEF.

1966: In China, Mao's so-called "Cultural revolution" mobilizes the youth against (among other things) the inflexible Communist Party organization (ended 1969). In the West, beginnings of student unrest against the Vietnam War. Indira Gandhi becomes prime minister of India.

1967: Israel's six-day war against its Arab neighbors. Death of the socialist revolutionary leader Ernesto "Che" Guevara, who becomes an idol to revolutionary youth all over the world. First successful heart transplant in Cape Town. Herbert von Karajan sets up the first Salzburg Festival.

1968: Troops of the USSR, Poland, Bulgaria and East Germany invade Czechoslovakia to halt the path to reform. Assassination of the

A demonstrator holds up a bloodstained Czechoslovakian flag to a Soviet tank as it drives by: Prague 1968

"That's one small step for a man, one giant leap for mankind": Neil Armstrong on the moon

American civil rights leader Martin Luther King and of Senator Robert Kennedy. Starvation in Biafra, the civil-war plagued eastern region of Nigeria. The Club of Rome investigates the "Limits of Growth."

1969: US space mission Apollo 11: Neil Armstrong is the first man to walk on the moon. Pop festival at Woodstock (USA).

Le Corbusier, *Carpenter Center for the Visual Arts,* Harvard University, Cambridge, Massachusetts (USA), 1961

Le Corbusier's last important building and also his last in the United States remains comparatively unspecific. After the failure of his UN project, and the worldwide recognition of the city he designed in India, Chandigarh, Le Corbusier seems poised here between the force fields of Louis I. Kahn and late Gropius. A façade defined by diagonal bulkheads and horizontal platforms, soaring walls and floating ramps, sculptural steps, and free-standing portals, everything that makes the School for the Visual Arts into a school for seeing, is constructed of naked concrete and is entirely without ornament, as befits an architect who had waged an enlightened lifelong campaign against it. The building, which can be seen as the manifesto for Le Corbusier's later architectural ideas, also makes it clear why Brutalism, in its striving for truth to materials, finally confined itself entirely to concrete: no other material was so universally adaptable to any form.

Rauschenberg, Tom Wesselmann, or Roy Lichtenstein, who made pictures like comic strips blown up to a very large format. Art became popular – "Pop Art."

In the 1960s socialist visions began to bloom all over the world, taking issue with the capitalist economy based upon private property and private ownership of the means of production, from a standpoint ranging from criticism to total rejection. Not only the new China of Mao Zedong, the Latin American revolutionaries Che Guevara and Fidel Castro, but also the theoretical acceptance of the social theories of Marx, Lenin or the Frankfurt School spread the idea of a socialist society resting upon equality, solidarity, and justice, which also in turn influenced both architecture and lifestyles.

BRUTALISM

The new openness

As early as the 1920s Rudolph Schindler had built a house for himself in America in which he tried to formulate new ways of collective living in the private sphere, reflected in the layout of the house. At the same time architects such as Gropius, working on housing schemes in Europe, were influenced by socialist views of society.

One of the important ideals which can be traced through the history of modern architecture in the 20th century is the attempt to lay bare the principles on which a building is constructed, and from that the way it works. Load-bearing elements of a construction in *reinforced concrete* were revealed as such by not being covered with glass plates or *freestone*. The different function of the non-load-bearing parts of the façade could be stressed by the use of different material. The contrasts between materials would make the viewer draw conclusions about the role of different parts of the building. Behind that lay the concept of an honest architecture that did not hide its structures behind an interchangeable variety of façades. The American architect Louis I. Kahn (see page 71) formulated this principle very clearly when he postulated that for him, an architectonically designed space was one where you could see exactly how it was made.

Apart from Kahn and, among the younger generation, the Smithsons in England, it was once more Le Corbusier who most espoused this principle in his late work. It was to his use of *beton brut* (French, "brut" meaning "rough," "unfinished"), pure, naked concrete that we owe the idea of Brutalism: an architectonic direction which was founded on the ethical rather than aesthetic concept of a coherent style, and was to remain an important component of architectural forms of expression right through into the mid-1970s.

That Brutalism was an ethical rather than aesthetic concept can be seen from the fact that the idea of honest architecture which it promoted was not bound to the use of partic-

Owen Luder Partnership, *Tricorn Centre,* Portsmouth (UK), 1966

Brutal Brutalism: the Tricorn Centre includes offices, shops, restaurants, even apartments, and swallows up people and cars. Its only contact with the existing city is through the entrances via which visitors disembark into the surrounding streets. Docked in the center of the city of Portsmouth, the Tricorn complex is an autistic phenomenon. The brutal effect of the mega-complex is increased by the fact that the building is entirely made in concrete left rough from its formwork. Buildings such as the Tricorn Centre brought Brutalism and its favorite material into disrepute soon after the center was built. The recognition that the city is less in danger from materials and styles than from particular types of building, has not yet been fully acted upon. Centers such as the Tricorn go on being built.

ular materials. The principles of construction can just as easily be displayed when wood and brick are used as with steel and glass. However, under the influence of Le Corbusier it was the material most relevant for the time, *concrete*, which played the leading role in Brutalist building.

The most important thing was to show the logical principles behind the building. This applied by no means simply to the *façade* but also very much to the ground plan, which – once again in the ideal case – should be developed on the basis of the requirements that the users had for their building. Although the fundamental principles of Brutalism cast a great deal of light on the creation and reception of architecture, they were finally very seldom put into practice. They did after all not only presuppose an unconditional and equal agreement between the architect and his client, but also that one was able to break free of all modish trends – a virtually impossible undertaking, since no one can escape from the straightjacket imposed by the spirit of the time.

The supporters of Brutalism were very seldom able to translate their high theoretical ideals into buildings. What in fact arose were massive concrete forms which seemed to cut

themselves off consciously from the outside world, the antithesis of the glassy elegance of the skyscrapers with *curtain walls* or the expressive strength of an Eero Saarinen.

EXPRESSION IN CONCRETE

Curve instead of corner

Whereas before 1945 airplanes chiefly served military purposes and civil aviation was a much smaller affair, this situation changed dramatically after 1945. The times when pioneers of flight such as Louis Blériot or the Wright brothers just about managed to fly 300 feet (100 meters) were in the distant past, and the first crossing of the Atlantic by Charles Lindbergh was a faraway tale of flying history. In the place of the ocean liners, which had for a long time had the unique privilege of linking the continents, came the planes. The time it took to travel distances which had previously taken several days, now shrank to a few hours.

Civil aviation enjoyed a tremendous boom in the 1950s and 1960s. This boom is still going on today, and the number of flights per year continues to rise. In a world in love with consumption, holidays and business, travel by plane quickly lost the image of an expensive luxury and became an affordable everyday matter for everybody. Gone were the days in which astonished children pointed up in the air, gazing with longing at the planes which circled majestically over their heads.

The increase in air travel was reflected in the building of newer, more modern, and above all bigger airports, which not only had to get passengers comfortably off on their travels, but also had to reflect the spirit of the age.

Whereas Eero Saarinen's research laboratories for General Motors (see page 61), created in the 1950s, had been a model of glass, soberly rectilinear construction, his style underwent a transformation at the end of the decade. In place of restful formal shapes, his work acquired a distinct expressivity. The Expressionism of the first half of the century (see page 24 et seq.) took on new life in his work, albeit in the form of quite different premises. Whereas the Expressionists of the Amsterdam School tended to use brick for their Gothic-influenced architecture, Saarinen's bold constructions would have been unthinkable without the versatility of reinforced concrete.

LOUIS I. KAHN

Louis I. Kahn, born on the Estonian island of Ösel (today's Saarema) in 1901, is recognized as a master with light. His work is characterized by buildings that are basically geometric in form and to which their clarity imparts a majestic severity. His refined skill in directing light gives almost all his buildings an agreeable atmosphere and creates many surprising spatial effects Kahn, who arrived in the United States in 1905, did not step into the international limelight until after the Second World War.

He had studied under Paul Cret at the University of Pennsylvania, where he received an academic education in the Beaux-Arts tradition, graduating in 1924; he did not carry out any projects outside the Pennsylvania area until he built the Yale University Art Gallery between 1951 and 1953. The Yale museum was articulated in two large cubes, which were divided by a cylindrical stairwell and a central service area. This arrangement reflects Kahn's architectonic principle regarding the functional placing of the "service" spaces and the areas which they

Parliament building in Dhaka with presidential garden; rising up in the center of the buildings: the "crown" which lights the assembly chamber

serve, a hierarchy underlining the mental clarity that can always be discerned in the substance of his architecture. Functional ground plans, simple constructions, and the aesthetically sophisticated deployment of both slits and wall-openings to allow light to enter, are the consistent thread that runs throughout all of his creative work. Yet the work as a whole remains extremely heterogeneous.

The Margaret Esherick House in Chestnut Hill, Pennsylvania (1959–61) is still in the tradition of *Neues Bauen*, and pays sensitive homage to the principle of open space with its combination of rough exposed concrete walls and large-paned glass façades. But projects such as the Kimbell Art Museum in Fort Worth, Texas (1966–72), with its round-arched roofs, are dominated by folkloric influences. Yet in both of these it is possible to discern a single, sensitive creative voice. Reacting to the Esherick House, where the transition between inside and outside is defined by the means of ventilation flaps – without negating the edge of the space – Robert Venturi, a pupil of Kahn's, wrote in his post-modern best-seller *Complexity and Contradiction in Architecture*: "It is not a particular style that makes the essence of an interior space, it is

what goes round it and the border between inner and outer." This agreed with Louis I. Kahn's conception according to which a building was primarily a shelter. He started his teaching at Yale in 1947, and never ceased to stress that every room was defined by its natural lighting as well as its construction, a formula with which he was able to unite technological and engineering factors with the sensual effect of a building's inner life.

Kahn's architectonic innovations lie in the use of prefabricated concrete parts, whose dimensions are determined by the radius of action of a builder's crane – "the extension of the human arm." His ideas on the direction of light as part of the structure of a room remain exemplary to this day. Since Louis I. Kahn did not go by hard-and-fast rules and principles, and every design began "from zero," he developed a host of typologies in his 50 years of architectural practice.

In business terms this way of working was constantly getting him into financial difficulties. Kahn lived for his work. In spite of an extremely full order-book, this very busy architect was always surprised when a client offered him a well-paid commission. Kahn would have undertaken for nothing tasks that led him further in his world of ideas. And he is said often to have thrown away all his plans just before the delivery date and start the work anew. When he died unexpectedly in 1974, his company was deeply in debt.

A key time in his life was a year-long stay in the American Academy in Rome, which enabled him to undertake trips to Greece, Egypt, and around Italy itself in the years 1950–51. Although he was already 50 years of age, studying the buildings of antiquity inspired him anew with the awe at their massive materials and heavy parts, which he had acquired from Cret, his Beaux Arts teacher: culture gained solidity by being rooted in the classics.

Using durable materials such as brick, *free-stone*, and bare concrete, Louis I. Kahn created a monumentality situated on the border between architecture and sculpture. His synthesis of the two disciplines is most clearly expressed in the First Unitarian Church and School in Rochester, New York (1959–62), and is also clearly visible in the Salk Institute for Biological Studies in San Diego, California (1959–67). The façade of the church is distinguished by a heavily modulated, almost windowless surface. The building works like a massive *cube*, shaped by horizontal and vertical grooves. The windows disappear into vertical slits which give a visual rhythm to the façade. The brick walls in addition to the terracotta components strengthen the monumentality of the architecture. For his Salk Institute building

Study building with pool: Salk Institute for Biological Studies in San Diego

Louis I. Kahn, about 1962

Kahn once again created windowless cubes – this time in bare concrete – and grouped them round a courtyard. Openings in the walls are placed only where there is an unrestricted view on to the Pacific – so the space outside becomes a determining factor in how the space inside is experienced.

The design concepts of the many-layered wall, and the interplay of closed space and transparency were also operative in Kahn's most important work: the parliament building at Dhaka, Bangladesh (1962–83).

Eight appendages – cubes and "light-cylinders" – are arranged round an inner, cylindrical core. The concrete façade is articulated with grooves filled with white marble and pierced with semicircles, circles and triangles which produce fantastic light effects within. The parliamentary building resembles a citadel, and is crowned with a parabolic umbrella-shaped dome. Undoubtedly Kahn's last project, which was only finished after his death, and for which he was posthumous awarded the Aga Khan prize in 1989, belongs among the jewels of contemporary architecture.

ALVAR AALTO

The Finnish architect Hugo Alvar Henrik Aalto was born in 1898, the son of a land surveyor. At only 23 he achieved an outstanding diploma at Helsinki polytechnic. This was the beginning of a career as the most famous architectural ambassador for his country in the 20th century. After his death in 1976, it was only a few months later that a 50-Finnmark note appeared, bearing his portrait and his most important late work, the Finlandia Hall in Helsinki.

In the midst of a wooded landscape: all the patients' rooms in the TB-Sanatorium Paimio face south

Alvar Aalto during the time of the International Building Exhibition in Berlin, 1957

His plans for both architecture as well as design had long since become major hits on the export market. The use of freely swooping curves, windowless brick walls, and rhythmic glassed façades are among Alvar Aalto's trademarks, placing him among the so-called "other Modernists" who did not confine themselves to white, unadorned *rectilinear forms*. A moderate who was both sensitive and close to nature, he remained all his life at a distance from "radical Modernism" but without his developing any trace of Historicism in his formal vocabulary.

Aalto's architecture, with innate feeling for materials and closeness to landscape, quickly awakened the respect of the European *Neues Bauen* movement. He was inherently a practical man who left only a few lapidary utterances about his understanding of architecture, but his work is considered as the first meaningful Scandinavian contribution to the international debate on architecture. Particularly notable is his synthesis of Finnish tradition (connecting elements in wood) with avant-garde functionalism (the visibility of the inner organizational structures). He created 20 buildings in foreign countries, among them a residential hall for students at the Massachusetts Institute of Technology in Cambridge, USA (1948), and a block of flats for the International Building Exhibition in Berlin in 1957. The Essen opera house was completed only after his death.

Aalto created four buildings that have become icons of modern architecture: the sanatorium in Paimio (1933), the Villa Mairea in Noormarkku (1939), and the community center in Säynätsalo (1952), all in Finland, as well as the 1935 town library in Viipuri (today Wiborg in Russia).

The sanatorium in Paimio in southwest Finland lies within a wooded landscape, and could only be built through joint financing by 50 communes. The guiding principle of the design, which was expressed in Aalto's submission for the competition in 1928, was to put a wide space between the tuberculosis patients and the rooms for the staff. This led to the ambitious scheme of creating a long and narrow building for the patients' rooms, which was a novelty in hospital design. All the rooms face south, to let in as much sunlight as possible. Because of the length of time the patients spent in bed, the ceilings were in dark shades and the lighting was indirect. The building is laid out asymmetrically, with several wings, and seems to draw up the landscape into itself. It is a classic example of modern architecture in which light, air, and sun form the parameters of the design, and served as a model for many other hospitals.

The introduction of light is also a defining element in the town library at Viipuri. The ceiling of the main reading room has circular openings from which light falls onto the interior. Arranged around a large open staircase is a U-shaped reading table, lit from above, from where it is also possible to see the book-issue desk. This library brought the *International Style* to Northern Europe.

The architecture of the Villa Mairea is also an ingenious combination of international Modernism with the vernacular building tradition. The client, who was president of a Finnish wood business, asked his architect to build a house in the middle of a landscape of pine trees, where the rim of the forest formed the edge of a site opening to the southwest. The façade is made of vertical wooden elements, enclosing organically shaped structural parts. The interior, organized on the principle of "flowing space," is especially noteworthy. In his standard work, *Space, Time, and Architecture*, Sigfried Giedion describes the impression it creates thus: "It is architectural chamber music, demanding the closest attention in order to understand how motifs and intentions

International Style and Finnish building tradition: the Villa Mairea in Noormarkku

are carried out, and in particular to recognize fully how the space is handled, and the extraordinary use of materials." The large windows permit the interpenetration of inner and outer space. The forest seems almost to penetrate the house, finding an echo in the slender wooden pillars. In the Villa Mairea, Alvar Aalto created a spatial continuum entirely in the spirit of Modernism, and it is unfortunate that he never put his ideas on paper, since it is almost impossible to deduce his theoretical position about architecture from his buildings alone.

The stepped composition of the community center at Säynätsalo

Although completed only in fragmentary form, his general plan of the center of Säynäsalo, 185 miles (300 kilometers) north of Helsinki, is one of his most important town-planning projects. The only part that was finished is the community center, which is characterized by its stepped construction. Aalto planned for two different levels within the whole and topped the composition with a slanted roof – a striking characteristic in his work – and let grass grow on the steps: a touch intended to link the building with nature.

Alongside his work as a member of CIAM, Aalto also made a name as a designer and a furniture maker. To this day, Artek, of which he was one of the co-founders, produces his strikingly designed chairs in bent plywood. The steel tubing furniture, which he had designed for the sanatorium in Paimio, reflects his connection with Bauhaus design (see page 33) – although he neither learned nor taught there. Alvar Aalto was an architect who preferred building to engaging with the theory of his discipline: "With every building I write ten volumes of philosophy."

Saarinen had experimented several times with flying roofs held up by steel, as can be seen for instance in the ice hockey stadium at Yale University, Connecticut. But his best-known work in this style was to be the terminal for the airline company TWA, which he built on what used to be Idlewild Airport in New York, but today bears the name of the murdered American president John F. Kennedy. Used hundreds of times as a backdrop for feature films, the futuristic building was soon known all over the world.

Like a bird gently gliding through the air on outstretched wings, the arched concrete roof of the terminal shelters the passengers who commence their journey here. The dynamic volumes of the roof flow over the gently curving Y-supports, whose concentrated strength appears to push the roof upwards. Everything flows and glides in and out in the TWA terminal, now convex, now concave, while great glass spaces open up to let the light stream into the interior. With all its modernity and the futuristic ambience that strikes us today as so characteristic of the taste of the early 1960s, the building still radiates a beauty and harmony that very few of the steel and glass cubes of the period are able to convey. Saarinen's TWA terminal is a unique sculptural building, and, in its abstract representation of a bird, an example of *architecture parlante* in the best sense.

At almost the same time (1958–62) Saarinen was confronted with the task of building for an airport yet again, but this time it was not a single departures terminal, but the whole airport: Dulles Airport in Washington DC. Once again he designed a swooping roof for the high main hall, concave this time. However, in contrast to the TWA building, this one has a certain monumental quality arising from the regularly placed supports which are wider at the bottom, a quality that is not dissipated by the wide areas of glass, and which is indeed intended to express the importance of this airport that serves the American capital.

Reinforced concrete appeared to be adaptable and supple in the extreme, and the airy mobile-looking roofs of the 1950s and 1960s would not have been possible without it. However, such structures are only as durable as the materials and construction methods which architects and engineers bring to bear

on them. The potentially limited life of such roofs was made apparent by the frightening and totally unexpected collapse of the Berlin Congress Hall roof in 1980, when one person was actually killed by the falling debris. It had been designed in 1957 by Hugh Stubbins, Werner Düttmann, and Franz Mocken for the International Building Exhibition, and was seen as a sign of German-American unity. It had quickly become a Berlin landmark, referred to by the locals with affectionate irony as "the pregnant oyster" because of its unusual shape. After lengthy discussions, a decision was finally taken to rebuild it with an improved and, it is hoped, safer roof in celebration of the 750th anniversary of Berlin.

A space for music in organic forms

It was back in the 1920s that Hans Scharoun, an architect practicing mainly in Berlin, formulated his principle of not working from a definition of what the façades would be, but by developing a building on the basis of the ground plan. This system, which he evolved chiefly in the course of designing private houses, was intended to create a harmonious intermingling of the various functional areas of a house, from everyday life, through work, to sleep. Unlike Mies van der Rohe, whose Neue Nationalgalerie (New National Gallery) was to appear later within sight of Scharoun's Berliner Philharmonie (Berlin Philharmonics) and which is both elegant and slightly constrained in its rectangularity, Scharoun deployed organically growing forms, whose rounded or sharply pointed shapes stood in striking contrast to many houses produced by the *Neues Bauen*

Eero Saarinen, TWA Terminal,
J. F. Kennedy Airport, New York,
1956–62

The roof spreads over the heads of visitors and passengers like the wings of a bird about to take flight. Underneath everything is open, everything flows. The traveler can see his airplane as he drives up in his taxi to the entrance. Held up by only a few Y-shaped supports, the prestressed concrete construction makes an optimal use of the plastic possibilities of the medium. The way in which Saarinen translates the symbolic meaning required of the building places the TWA terminal among the most impressive examples of expressive-organic building.

Hans Scharoun, *Philharmonie,*
Berlin, 1960–63

Three five-sided volumes turned towards each other under a tent-like concrete bowl determine the shape of the Berlin Philharmonic's concert hall. The geometry is so complex that a new cross-section had to be drawn every 20 inches (50 centimeters) in order to build the hall, which is as complex as the music performed there. Man and music are at the center of this entirely novel construction, with the stage forming the ideal focal point surrounded by banks of seats. All 2,200 members of the audience are in contact with each other through connecting aisles and through the management of space and the acoustics, which are equally good from every seat. All this combines to make the Philharmonie, the design for which goes back to Scharoun's *Expressionist* People's House of 1920, the aesthetic and conceptual summit of organic architecture.

movement at the time. His forms were, however, never an end in themselves, but were designed to give the owners of his houses a living environment that suited their needs as accurately as possible.

The crowning glory of this organic style of building was the Berlin Philharmonics (1960–63), which towers up expressively on the edge of the Tiergarten (the zoo). It was originally planned for another site, where it was to be the hub of a cultural center including a library, museums, and a place for visitors to stay, but so far it has remained the only part to be built. (In the context of the rebuilding of Berlin as a capital city, the debate about rebuilding it at the end of the 1990s has flared up anew and with even more passion than before.) While Scharoun pointedly did not make any grandiose architectural gestures in the entrance and foyer, in the concert hall itself the building opens up in all its beauty. The blocks of seats are juxtaposed to each other like a terraced southern landscape, affording equally good acoustics

and an uninterrupted view from any seat in the pillarless hall. A corresponding democratic element in this layout is that you can get from any seat to another in the auditorium without using the exterior corridors.

Sailing architecture

Seldom in recent decades has any building become such a definitive and universal landmark, even a national symbol, as the Sydney Opera House, designed by the Danish architect Jørn Utzon. In point of fact, Utzon's powerful design, first outlined in 1956, provoked considerable controversy in Australia, which dragged out the building time until 1974. It is hardly surprising that the design, which is so full of movement, found an important supporter in Eero Saarinen when it was submitted for the international competition, and his influence as one of the judges helped Utzon to get the prize. Utzon himself drew his inspiration from many and various architectonic sources. The *classicist* Modernism of someone such as Gunnar Asplund influenced him as much as the organic buildings of Alvar Aalto. There was also the fact that Utzon had gathered experience for a while in the office of Frank Lloyd Wright.

The Sydney Opera House stands on a tongue of land extending far out into the harbor. Its nearness to the water and harbor is reflected in the extraordinary structure of crowding shell shapes that give it its memorable character. The brilliant white shells awaken associations of wind-blown sails and the ebb and flow of sea waves.

Olympic pioneers

The Berlin Philharmonics and the Sydney Opera House are united by more than their exciting architecture, which in itself has become symbolic of their cities. Both of them are assembly buildings that have to receive large crowds of people. Since Max Berg built the Breslau Jahrhunderthalle between 1910 and 1913 (see page 21), halls with self-supporting roofs which could be realized without the need for view-obstructing pillars had become an important theme in architecture.

As we have seen from the work of Saarinen, in around 1960 there was a great deal of experimentation with new multiple tent-shaped constructions, particularly roofs. This produced especially attractive architectonic solutions for the problem of building a hall, which left the purely functional demands of that building project far behind. Numerous roofed arenas for competitive swimming, ice hockey, or basketball were produced, including those for the Olympic Games, where a multitude of spectators was offered not only a dry place to sit, but also an unrestricted view.

Among the pioneers of sports arenas and halls in Europe was the Italian engineer Pier Luigi Nervi, whose elegant reinforced concrete stadium in Florence (1930-35) is one of the icons of modern architecture. It was in the course of building airplane hangars that Nervi evolved a principle for constructing roofs out of intersecting precast concrete beams, making it possible to span enormous spaces. This technical principle had many applications beyond airplane hangars. Between 1956 and 1957 Nervi constructed the Palazetto dello Sport, which was followed by its big brother, the Palazzo dello Sport for the Rome Olympics of 1960. Under the 300-foot (100-meter) wide dome of the Palazzo, 16,000 spectators could be accommodated. The principle of intersecting concrete beams underlying the construction of the dome led additionally to its decoration with an elegant and charming lozenge pattern.

Only four years later Kenzo Tange (see page 83), together with Uichi Inoue and Yoshikatsu Tsuboi, created a possibly even more inspired arena, full of ingenious touches, for the Olympic Games in Tokyo in 1964. The core of Tange's tent-like building was a steel rope that spanned two supports carrying the membrane-like skin of the roof. This roof construction was supported at the edges by a *reinforced concrete* frame. The aim of this so-called "natural structure," with its especially light materials and its woven network of supports, was to be able to span a space offering room for more than 16,000 spectators. The design of the Olympic Arena in Tokyo was a model for the tent-like Olympic buildings in Munich in 1972 (illustration page 81), and Tange was working at this time on similar solutions with Richard Buckminster Fuller and Frei Otto. It was the largest interior space with a roof unsupported by pillars that had been built at that time. But it was more than that; it was also perfectly constructed, a masterwork of *architectural engineering*, offering an aesthetic spectacle of particular charm, a charm arising from the interpenetration of the concave volumes of the roof skin and the wide-branching concrete supports at the side. It is also more than a further variation on the theme of sculptural architecture as already brought to masterly perfection by Saarinen. The powerful architecture of Tange's Olympic Arena develops an almost musical rhythm, which seizes the viewer's attention and directs it along the arched skin of the roof, up to the crown, then leads it gently all over the broad architecture of the hall. If the viewer allows himself to be absorbed by the movement of the architecture and follows its lines with his gaze, he will begin to feel in himself the gentle sway which is the essence of Tange's building.

Jørn Utzon, *Opera House,* Sydney, 1956–74
Looking like wind-filled sails, 12 white cement shells up to nearly 200 feet (60 meters) high stand on a deck of natural stone at the tip of a tongue of land extending into Sydney harbor, irrational and without any direct function but to arouse emotion. Yet they have become the symbol not just for Sidney but for the whole the fifth continent. They stand in two rows on top of the "experience zone": the concert hall, opera theatre, stage theatre, two foyers and main restaurant. The horizontally layered building underneath contains several stories of servicing departments for all the "experiences" presented above. Utzon's 1956 design for the Opera House, which won him the international competition and the contract to build it, places this Danish architect in the organic tradition of Wright, Scharoun, Asplund and Aalto.

Pier Luigi Nervi, *Palazzo del Lavoro*,
Turin, 1961

Pillars and roof are one in the Palazzo del
Lavoro. The radiating beams branch out
into the quadrilateral roof covering. Pier
Luigi Nervi, an engineer, equated good
construction and good design. Whereas
his exemplars Robert Maillart and Eugène
Freyssinet still worked with steel, Nervi
created a daring supporting structure in
reinforced concrete, whose plasticity,
proportion and rhythm endowed it with
aesthetic effect.

Carlo Scarpa, *Rebuilding of the Castel
Vecchio,* Verona, 1956–64

A steel upright supports a *Gothic*
travertine relief: Modernism meets History.
Carl Scarpa's rebuilding of the Castel
Vecchio, which had been rebuilt many
times over the centuries, brought an
exemplary solution to one of architecture's
hardest tasks: how to approach existing
buildings. Everything old that had
survived was restored, everything new
was shaped in appropriate modern
materials and forms. By contrasting and
layering different historical periods,
Scarpa made every epoch visible: history
could be experienced.

APPROACHES TO HISTORY

Tradition and Modernism together: foregrounding an aesthetic

One of the most difficult architectural tasks is dealing with historic buildings. There is often a conflict between the priorities of the owner, who may put function or grandeur first, and those of the conservationists, who will want all the historic remains preserved as completely as possible. With war-damaged buildings a decision is relatively easy to reach: either you make the new building an exact 1:1 copy of the old, as for instance in post-1945 Warsaw – or you look for a different, modern, architectonic solution to replace the building that was destroyed. The result is always a new building: in the first case in a *historicist* garb, in the second case in a contemporary one.

But how do you deal with existing historical buildings that have been changed and rebuilt many times over the centuries, so that every epoch has left behind a different layer? Should one opt for a specific period, such as the Gothic or the Baroque and carry out all necessary rebuilding or restoration in that *style*, as was frequently done in the 19th century? Or should one decide to leave all the historical layers on view, and add contemporary changes in a style appropriate to the times?

This last course was the one adopted by the Venetian architect Carlo Scarpa in what is perhaps his most important work, the restoration between 1956 and 1964 of the Castel Vecchio, which is now used as a museum, in the northern Italian city of Verona. Taking deliberate cognizance of the mixture of styles already present there, Scarpa attempted with

a combination of sensitivity and willingness to experiment, to bring back a considered cultural unity to the building, which would take the demands of modern art into account. The result is a grandiose total artwork, in which the historical strata from individual periods, and indeed the restorations of previous periods, blend with Scarpa's open architecture to form a completely new interpretation of the building. Scarpa made a clear distinction between modern building materials, such as concrete, steel, and glass, and historic materials, so that the various different facing materials are juxtaposed, creating an entirely original charm.

Scarpa, who first became famous for exhibition architecture, used architecture in the Castel Vecchio as a means of putting both the building and its exhibition pieces on display. The result is architecture as *mise-en-scène*, which directs the visitors' gaze as well as the route they follow, and uses surprising and shocking contrasts of materials and colors to put the historic exhibition pieces – sculptures as well as paintings – into a new and totally unexpected light.

THE GLASS OFFICE

Transparency as a sign of corporate identity

It is not only in the area of museum building that new and excellent solutions have been found to answer traditional needs. At the end of the 1960s, some office buildings demonstrated similar outcomes.

A special place must be awarded to the work of Kevin Roche and John Dinkeloo. As early as 1961, they created an open type of architecture, laid out around a garden, in the Oakland Museum in California (completed 1968). During the same period, they repeated in a skyscraper the theme of the garden integrating nature with a building. For the headquarters of the Ford Foundation, instead of monotonous offices all branching off from a central corridor, or great rooms divided off by partitions, Roche and Dinkeloo created a giant winter garden extending over twelve floors, with the glazed fronts of floor after floor of offices opening onto it.

The idea of the glazed greenhouse, which had figured in the earliest stages of architecture in glass, now became linked to the theme of the modern office. In this way, employees were given the feeling of working in a healthy, natural environment, a measure which not only improved the working atmosphere, but also fostered the corporate identity that still figures to this day among the most important motivating and productivity-enhancing factors in business.

For the headquarters of the College Life Insurance Company of America, Roche and Dinkeloo designed (between 1967 and 1971) three identical *pyramid-like* volumes on a quadrilateral ground plan. These futuristic buildings embodied a steel and glass construction on two sides, which was backed by two concrete planes. The staggered siting of the three buildings was intended to allow the accommodation of a potential extension to the complex which was planned for a later date. This could be added on, in the same style, without necessarily creating an over-large and monotonous complex.

The dislike of hierarchy and monumentality, and the demand for democracy that characterized the generation of 1968 also found expression in architecture. The concept of open architecture expressing an open society is the defining feature of the headquarters of the Centraal Beheer insurance company in Apeldoorn, in the Netherlands, built by Herman Hertzberger, Jan Antonin Lucas, and Hendrik Eduard Niemeijer between 1970 and 1972. The building can be extended in all directions, and consists of single interlocking square blocks in which open space and work space intermingle. Like a city within a city, offices and small shops are placed next to each other, and there are views from all the terrace-like projections. Even the offices take up the note of individuality, in that they are very sparsely furnished, giving the users room to complete them in their own style.

Kevin Roche, John Dinkeloo, *Office buildings for the Ford Foundation,* New York, 1963–68

No more cells: in this building all the offices open on to an enormous winter garden accessible to 12 stories. Nature and the city, the individual and the community, appear to have been reconciled. Kevin Roche and John Dinkeloo's building for the Ford Foundation is not just a totally new kind of office block. The construction became the prototype for countless buildings with glazed atria for all possible uses. But unlike the ubiquitous malls, commercial headquarters and hotels built on this model, the Ford Foundation building does not retreat into an inner world. Two façades of the 13-story square building open full on to the city.

The future becomes
the present

High-tech and
Post-Modernism

1970–1980

Victory of Technology

On 21 July 1969, Neil Armstrong became the first man to walk on the moon. "That's one small step for a man, one giant leap for mankind," the American astronaut of the Apollo 11 mission told fascinated viewers, watching live as he leapt from the ladder of the space capsule to the surface of the moon.

The conquest of the moon was the culmination of 10 years of continuous competition between the superpowers (the United States and the USSR) for supremacy in space. For a long time – at least since 12 April 1961, when the Soviet cosmonaut Yuri Gagarin became the first man to go into orbit in space – it looked as though the Soviets would be the first to put a man on the moon. But eventually it was the Americans who won, thanks to immense technical and economic resources, overweening ambition, and a fair portion of luck.

Millions of enthralled television viewers on Earth followed the moon landing for hours, in spite of the uncertain black and white pictures, the crackling and rustling sound, and the almost unrecognizably distorted voices of the astronauts.

The moon landing was a triumph of technology, which planned and realized a high-tech fairytale with military precision. Less than six months later, Apollo 12 took off for the next moonshot. The future had begun. Soon the launching pads at Cape Canaveral in Florida and the Apollo mission control at NASA in Houston, Texas, became familiar sights. Bare scaffolds and ramps, piping and lifts, innumerable video screens, telephones, and headphones gave viewers a direct impression of the equipment necessary to bring to fruition a task of the magnitude of space flight.

Architectural promise – speaking architecture

High-tech constructions, for example the launching pads and the mission control center, became a much more frequent everyday sight. The constructions that architects wrote into their designs became ever bolder. In the wake of *Brutalism* as practiced by the Smithsons in England, exposed pipes, wiring, and ventilation ducts became the trademarks of high-tech aesthetics.

The quintessence of 1970s architecture and its love of technology was the Centre National d'Art et de Culture Georges Pompidou in Paris, called the Centre Pompidou for short, the appearance of which alarmed quite a few of those who first saw it, and indeed continues to do so. It was built between 1971 and 1977 in the Place Beaubourg in the heart of the French capital, and gave the impetus to the "grands projets" with which President Mitterrand also sought to immortalize himself in the cityscape, such as the controversial Bastille opera house built by the Canadian Carlos Ott (opened 1989), or the new building for the Bibliothèque Nationale François Mitterrand (National library) by Dominique Perrault (opened 1996). The Centre Pompidou

1969: Georges Pompidou becomes president of France.

1970: Intensification of the "Troubles" – the conflict between Protestants and Catholics in Northern Ireland. Care for the environment is the issue of the day.

1971: Death of the jazz musician and trumpeter Louis Armstrong.

1972: Murderous attack by Arab terrorists on the Israeli Olympic team in Munich. Signing of the SALT I Agreement for the limitation of strategic weapons between the USA and the Soviet Union. Re-election of President Nixon.

1973: The Watergate affair clouds Nixon's electoral victory. Military coup in Chile brings about the fall of President Salvador Allende and the installing of a military regime under General Augusto Pinochet.

Worldwide petroleum crisis. The Arab states use oil for the first time as a political weapon. The first volume of Aleksandr Solzhenitsyn's description of the Soviet prison camps (*The Gulag Archipelago*) is published, and he is deprived of his Soviet citizenship the following year. Death of the painter Pablo Picasso.

1974: The German Federal Chancellor, Willy Brandt, resigns as a result of the Guillaume Chancellery espionage affair.

1975: End of the war in Vietnam which had begun in 1963. Death of General Franco in Madrid, followed by the building of a parliamentary democracy. Nobel Prize for economics awarded to Milton Friedman. Microsoft Corporation founded by Bill Gates. First showing of the US film *One Flew Over the Cuckoo's Nest*, with Jack Nicholson.

Scene from the film *Star Wars* by George Lucas, with Carrie Fisher as Princess Leia and the robot R2-D2

1976: Death of Mao Zedong. Jimmy Carter becomes president of the United States. A chemical accident in the Italian town of Seveso pollutes the environment with dioxin, causing a severe reaction to chlorine. The 13-year-old violinist Anne-Sophie Mutter begins her career. Disco music from the films of John Travolta becomes popular.

1977: Abduction of the head of the German employers' association H.-M. Schleyer in Cologne by terrorists of the Red Army Faction. First showing of the American science-fiction film *Star Wars* by George Lucas.

1978: Cardinal Karol Wojtyla of Crakow becomes Pope John Paul II.

1979: Nobel Peace Prize awarded to the Catholic nun Mother Teresa. After the flight of the Shah, the Ayatollah Khomeini returns to Iran from 15 years in exile to lead the Islamic revolution.

1980: Iraqi invasion of Iranian territory begins first Gulf War.

is a thoroughly Pop Art object, a museum with universal popular appeal, the sparkling peak of an architectural style wittily exposing to view what would normally be hidden inside.

The architects of the Centre Pompidou, Richard (now Lord) Rogers, who is British, and the Italian Renzo Piano, made little effort to adapt the building to its historic neighborhood. It was a new palace of culture intended for an almost limitless range of uses and included a space for visiting exhibitions and a library, as well as the collection of the Musée de l'Art Moderne. The makers' "carefree" treatment of the historic built environment was much the same as was going on elsewhere in Paris in the 1970s, where only minor importance was accorded to the architectural heritage. Not long before, Les Halles, the old market building near the center of Paris, had been razed to the ground, despite considerable protests, thus eliminating an important element of 19th-century Paris.

Rogers and Piano's building was permeated with the spirit of the time. With its megastructure (550 feet (166 meters) long, 210 feet (66 meters) wide, 140 feet (42 meters) high) it dominated

the originally important smaller-scaled city structure surrounding it with astounding arrogance.

Even today, in its now slightly dated futuristic dress, it conveys the impression of one great building site. It did not have a traditional *façade* but a complex web of interwoven steel tubes exterior to the glazed walls. So that whole of the interior space – some 160 by 480 feet (50 by 150 meters), part of which would have been occupied by escalators – can be released for exhibitions, the escalators are on the outside, carrying visitors in plexiglass-covered tubes up the west façade to the actual exhibition spaces as if through a time-travel apparatus. Brilliantly colored ventilation shafts remind one more of a ship than a museum, though these are yet another quotation from 20th-century architecture, in that they are reminders of the quotations from ship's architecture first introduced by Le Corbusier. Everything is openly on display – supply cables, shafts, and tubes – and metal fire escapes scale the heights of the building: a colorful, cheerful mixture of everything, creating, in a way only possible in Paris, a building whose unique charm lies in being utterly open.

Richard Rogers, Renzo Piano, Centre National d'Art et de Culture Georges Pompidou, Paris, 1971–77

Open and visible ventilation ducts wind through the façade like brilliantly colored entrails. A plexiglas tube pumps visitors through the steel lattice work. The Centre Pompidou is literally a culture machine, as unique as it is un-elitist, drawing people in because it is such a contradiction to its stony environment. The "walls" are so glassy and set so far back that the barriers between city and house, between inner and outer, between art and person, dissolve. The load-bearing elements and means of access are on the outside, so that the whole of each of the six floors, 50 by 150 meters (160 by 480 feet) in area, can be used – as a national museum for modern art, media center, cinema complex, and assembly hall. The Centre Pompidou perfectly expresses the philosophy of high-tech architecture for the first time. A building should function like a catalyst. It is a shell in which technical services are provided and processes are stimulated, but do not become set.

Norman Foster Associates, Ove Arup and Partner, *Hong Kong and Shanghai Bank*, Hong Kong, 1979–86

Normally a tall building should be a powerful symbol externally, but inside have as many useful surfaces as possible; according to this way of thinking, the technology that services the building is of secondary importance, hidden in minimal interior space. The British high-tech architect Norman Foster approached this particular project in a quite different way: the primary elements of his Hong Kong and Shanghai Bank are two groups of four steel frames that project, clearly visible, 600 feet (180 meters) into the air. Each one of them has all its means of access grouped at a single point on its exterior. Between them 47 floors, each 105 feet (33 meters) wide are suspended like bridges. The central space remains open, creating an atrium as high as the towers, which directs light by means of giant electronically steered mirrors into the depths of the building. The technology dominates the building.

The playful brightness of the building is complemented in exemplary manner by the sculptural fountains in the Place Igor Stravinsky, commissioned by the Paris city council and executed between 1982 and 1983 by Jean Tinguely and Niki de Saint Phalle. Inside the giant bowl of the fountain there is a total of 16 individual sculptures – rotating hearts and bright red mouths, water-spurting fantasy figures and musical clefs, as well as turning cogwheels and flywheels. These are intended not only to awaken associations with the work of the great composer Stravinsky, but also to make the square at the side of the Centre Pompidou into a favorite place for people to rest, which, unlike many deserted inner city squares, it has become. The romantic playfulness of Tinguely and Saint Phalle's fountain sculptures as well as the colorful technical language of forms of Rogers and Piano's Centre Pompidou convey a carefree feeling which is very seldom achieved in 20th-century combinations of sculpture and architecture.

Not long after the completion of the Centre Pompidou, Richard Rogers completed the headquarters of Lloyds in London (1979–86) a building that flirted with its own technicism, with curves and gleaming metal parts more reminiscent of a car factory than an insurance company. But in the Lloyds building, the gleaming steel architecture with its giant ventilation tubes descending a distance of 10 stories, strikes a menacing note which is markedly absent from the Centre Pompidou.

Rogers continued putting into practice his ideals of making technology aesthetic right into the 1990s, as for instance in the headquarters of the British commercial television Channel 4 (1995). The architecture of the Channel 4 building looks as technical as the workings of a modern television station has to be. You cross a glass and steel bridge to enter the reception area, whose concave façade is entirely glazed. The canopy over the bridge hangs on a construction of red supports and gleaming steel cables, placed for decorative effect in front of the glass façade. Glazed lifts travel up and down the outside of the building, which also has oversized ventilation shafts – Rogers' trademark.

High-tech forms and a prestigious image go together here in a synthesis which is as impressive as it is of high quality, and prove that the principles of Rogers's truth to construction methods are still capable of producing a pleasing visual effect 20 years later than the Centre Pompidou, and remain as appropriate to their time as ever.

Technical sobriety – Norman Foster

Norman Foster is another leading British representative of the architectural style, who has raised the technology of buildings to a stylistic trademark. The curved building which houses the Willis, Faber & Dumas insurance company in Ipswich (1970–75) clearly displays its structural framework, covered only by a protective sheet of glass. In the Hong Kong and Shanghai Bank also, the load-bearing columns from

which the whole construction of the tall building is suspended are not hidden by the traditional *curtain wall*; rather, Foster has made the monumental suspension system the actual theme of his building.

It was precisely because of his soberly technical architectural language, articulated in a form free of historical connections, that an architect like Norman Foster was destined to be put in charge of the rebuilding of the Berlin Reichstag, the new seat of the German Bundestag (parliament), which he effected between 1995 and 1999. As in earlier buildings, Foster's architecture achieves its form primarily through the materials used and the emphasis on the principles of its construction. Hidden behind its 19th-century façade, the building has a completely new inner life all in glass whose aim is transparency; it is crowned by a *dome*, also glass. It may be that, in terms of preserving a historic monument, violence has been done to the older building and its equally historic transformations in the 1950s, but Foster's high-tech architecture does convey a distinctly progressive view of the world, which is doubtless the one desired by those who commissioned him.

A tent for sport

It is already some years since Kenzo Tange's Olympic arena in Tokyo (illustration page 83) deployed construction and materials to produce a unique high-tech adventure with a breathtaking aesthetic effect. Günter Behnisch and Frei Otto took this idea of an airy tent roof combining weather-protection and maximum transparency and used it for the Munich Olympic stadium in 1972. Its complex roof, constructed of plexiglass plates fitted together, covered large areas of the sports stadium, which held 70,000 people.

Tent constructions of the type developed by Frei Otto had previously been considered suitable only for temporary buildings due to the problem of durability. Otto had made comparable constructions for the National Garden Show in Cologne in 1957, and the German Pavilion at the world exhibition in Montreal in 1967.

A special requirement of the Munich Olympics area was that it should fulfill various functions. It had to be a contemporary sports ground, but it also had to be capable of acting as a park where the people of the Bavarian capital could relax, and it needed to be only a few minutes' tram ride from the city center.

In terms of architecture, a special effort was made to produce a noticeable contrast to the architecture of the stadium that was built in Berlin in the Nazi period for the first Olympic games ever to take place on German soil in 1936. Instead of the *freestone* slabs and *classicist* forms which Werner March was forced to add to his modern concrete construction at the demand of Albert Speer and Hitler, the new Munich Olympic stadium was airy, gently curved, and open. In this way its message to the world community was quite different from its predecessor's; the image of West Germany which it communicated was modern, progressive, dynamic.

SITE, *BEST* **Supermarket,** Towson, Maryland (USA), 1978

The supermarkets produced for the BEST chain by the group of architects calling themselves SITE, Sculpture in the Environment, are entirely original sculptural buildings in places where you would least expect them: suburbs and industrial estates. The element of surprise has become the trademark of the supermarkets and their architects. Unexpected changes – such as a wall set at an angle and sitting diagonally – disturbed and provoked the jaded perceptions of the visitor. But behind this disruption of traditional expectations of how the façades of buildings should look, there was less a criticism of a society that had strayed from the right path, than an attempt, to use architecture to change such a banal and ritualized process as shopping into an all-day happening in an ever more homogenized consumer society.

DE-ARCHITECTURE

Advertising and consumption

Thousands of impressions and images crowd in on everyone daily. The visual signals that thrust themselves upon us from our surroundings every day become ever stronger: from the traffic sign to the billboard, to the television advertising spot. There is no visit to the cinema that is not accompanied by a glimpse of the big wide world preceding the actual film experience. Well-made advertising has even become a form of entertainment itself, in the French film compilation of the best commercials of the year in Cannes. Since Andy Warhol's serial pictures of soup cans brought advertising into art, the aspirations of advertising to become art have heightened.

But all this has only one aim: to attract notice at any price, and to stand out from the competition – starting best of all at the point of sale. This was the line adopted by the American supermarket chain BEST, who had their stores designed by the group of architects going under the name of SITE (Sculpture in the Environment).

In the 1970s, SITE deliberately set out to shock and astonish with their store designs. Monotonous, characterless supermarkets, all built from the same design, had been springing up like mushrooms everywhere. Considering that there were quite enough of such boring stereotypes around, SITE opted for humor, and took the line of making their buildings both surprising and confusing for shoppers. Instead of the usual smooth and flawless façades, customers suddenly found themselves confronted by walls that were apparently crumbling and on the point of collapse, indeed heaps of bricks appeared to have formed beneath them already. In one case there was a wood growing behind the entrance to a supermarket, looking as though it was about to split the architecture apart, and reoccupy its old terrain. Of course all this was an illusion, a trick with the unexpected, intended to make shopping a dramatic experience for the customers. SITE were gambling on the idea that the shock would also force them to recognize that the supposed danger was only a sham, intended to confuse, but finally also to amuse and entertain them.

The SITE architects themselves christened their buildings "De-architecture," thus taking up a critical position against the functionalist boredom of other stores. However dramatic the façade of a BEST building might be – behind it there was just another supermarket.

POST-MODERNISM

The return to style

The critique of functionalism inherent in SITE's sculptural buildings was not the preserve of the SITE architects alone. Elsewhere, clear doubts were being expressed as to whether the architectural concepts of Modernism, which had dominated the history of building for so long and had in the meantime become entirely standard, were the only way to salvation. In particular the premise upon which residential building is based, that it should produce an appropriate social context for the inhabitants, was acknowledged to have been scantily observed in reality. The buildings upon which Modernism was founded had both quality and a spirit of adventure; whereas the apartment blocks now going up were getting ever drearier, without any sense of a standard – slums in a standard box format.

From its inception in the late 19th century, Modernism had striven to banish traditional forms of building and decoration from architecture. *Pillars* and *gables* were replaced with *rectilinear* boxes with flat roofs. Constructed of reinforced concrete and glass, they were entirely without ornament, except for their gleaming white or glazed façades. But under the surface of modern architecture, which covered an astonishingly wide spectrum from Saarinen's richly curved Expressionism to the severe grid-shaped buildings of the old masters of the Bauhaus,

KENZO TANGE

Beside the elevated tracks of the Tokaido Express in Tokyo, there stands on an angularly shaped piece of ground measuring only 225 square yards (189 square meters), a towering cylinder just 26 feet (8 meters) across. This houses lifts and service rooms; the all-glass offices are attached to the sides. From the tower 14 floors jut out, constructed out of *reinforced concrete* prefabricated parts. It is the headquarters of Shizuoka – a press and radio company. At first sight – although only at first sight – it appears to be an extremely effective piece of advertising. In addition to this, it is one of the key buildings of Kenzo Tange.

Tange was born in 1913 in Osaka, and his work combines traditional Japanese thought on building with international Modernism. He is considered to be the leading proponent of Structuralism, on the basis of his theories about building and the city, which he evolved while

Kenzo Tange, circa 1965

mobility." "We propose an axis for the city that will replace the present city center, and will spread step by step over the whole bay of Tokyo. Along this line communication can take place in a minimum of time. There is no simpler or swifter possibility."

Tange proposed to hang the motorways for the new city 130 feet (40 meters) up in the air over the old city and the bay. The ground would be kept completely open, a single "open space." The traffic could not possibly disrupt people's private lives.

Hiroshima (1949–56) and his own home in Tokyo (1951–53). The large room which forms the upper story of his house has no fixed functions. It can be divided into three with sliding doors, according to the needs of the inhabitants.

The house reveals the second great source of the architect's inspiration: traditional modes of construction. At the 1959 CIAM congress in Otterlo, Tange compared the role of tradition with that of a "catalyst, that provokes and promotes a reaction, but is no longer recognizable in the end result." So Tange did not simply adopt the forms of traditional Japanese houses, but also the way they are built: with a wooden skeleton. He constructed the administration building for the district prefecture of Takamatsu (1955–58) in reinforced concrete, a material whose stability is similar to that of wood. It is visually quite similar to a project for an office building in reinforced concrete that Mies van der Rohe produced in 1922. But whereas Mies as a European had to

New town hall, Tokyo

working as professor at the University of Tokyo between 1946 and 1972.

The most radical plan for a city ever devised was the plan for Tokyo presented by Kenzo Tange in 1959, which presupposed a city structure based not on the buildings of the city, but on its infrastructure. Its aim was to point the way for an orderly growth of the city to a metropolis of ten million. "Cities of this size will be needed to fulfill the functions that are essential to the life of a modern society." The most important idea is at the beginning: it is the future function, not the present form, that should be the starting point for town planning. For Tange, the main function of the city was communication. And, at the end of the 1950s, communication meant movement. So the first part of the plan for Tokyo was the plan for transport.

Tange's conviction was that the city as it was, with its buildings, streets, and squares, did not offer sufficient room for the ever-increasing movement occurring within it. Therefore the city must develop "new structures for new

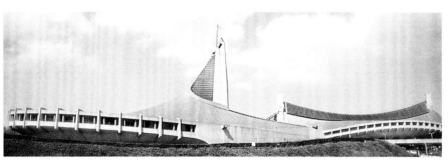

The roof membrane of the Olympic hall hangs on a cable anchored to two concrete masts. This method of support is borrowed from the traditional roofs of Japanese temples.

The starting point of the urban net was to be a row of access towers from 480 to 640 feet (150 to 200 meters) high and 640 feet (200 meters) apart. These would at once be branches of the city traffic system and atria for the buildings, providing vertical access, installations, water pipes, and electrical cables. Platforms where people would live and work would be suspended between the towers. Whereas the framework would be a rigid, unalterable structure, the platforms would be adaptable to all kinds of functions, to suit the changing demands of the users.

Such plans were far from infrequent at the end of the 1950s. But whereas in Brasilia, for instance, somewhat old-fashioned, slab-shaped skyscrapers co-exist with a modern transport system, Tange was able to translate his schema of functions into a coherent city plan, worked out in the smallest architectonic detail. He is an architect who never views town planning and architecture separately from each other.

Tange's ideas have influenced urbanists all over the world, notably Herman Hertzberger and the Structuralists in Holland. In later works, Tange adapts the form of his buildings to the postmodern spirit of the time, yet he remains true to his intentions. His last big project, Tokyo town hall (1986–91) looks at first sight like a skyscraper cathedral. Yet here too the complex is laid out around a citizens' forum, has ramps running through it, and is poised over a motorway that is itself elevated on stilts.

He was building on stilts 40 years previously in his first designs, for the Peace Center in

Shizuoka press and radio company

reinvent visible construction, Tange needed only to follow Japanese tradition.

In the mid-1950s, Tange wrote a book that celebrated the Ise temple as the prototype of Japanese architecture. In 1964 he reinterpreted the soaring shape of the temple's roofs, which had developed originally from tents, for the two Olympic arenas in Tokyo. A cable is stretched in a parabolic curve between two masts, and upon it hangs a steel net which supports the roof skin. The sacral effect of the inner space in the temple is thus transferred to a building which in today's context has an equally religious character.

Gropius and Mies van der Rohe, new currents began moving as early as the beginning of the 1960s – new currents that took a renewed interest in historical forms of building for decoration and *ornamentation*. Some people were no longer willing to follow the rigorous concepts of Bauhaus Functionalism, which they looked down on as boring.

In the vanguard of the movement were the early buildings of the American architect Robert Venturi, whose publications *Complexity and Contradiction in Architecture* (1966) and *Learning from Las Vegas* (1972) created the foundations for post-modern architectural theory. Both publications show the breadth of

Robert Venturi, *Vanna Venturi House,* Chestnut Hill, Philadelphia (USA), 1962–64

The house which Robert Venturi designed for his mother is a new formulation of the Prairie House, with central chimney and harmoniously developed interior spaces, embodying enclosure and transparency at the same time. The façade, according to Venturi, is a "symbolic picture" of a house, looking back to the revolutionary architecture of the 18th century. As one of the first Post-Modern buildings, the house has become a classic.

Venturi's frame of reference that takes in both the tradition and culture of the everyday. On one hand he espouses the internally fractured mannerism of Roman post-Renaissance culture: on the other, he posits architecture as an advertising medium – the principle of the "decorated shed."

Both sides are already on show in the house for Venturi's mother, Vanna. It is an inventory of the petit bourgeois, American suburban house that never really came into contact with the developments of Modernism, if you disallow Frank Lloyd Wright's Prairie Houses (see page 16). The façade expresses meaning without reference to the building as a whole, which is effectively a denial of the principles proposed by Functionalism. And his use of architectonic *noble orders* in the context of a suburban house is a deliberate flouting of these principles.

With its severe, broken pediment, the house follows the principle of "asymmetric symmetry,"

that is recognizable not only in the articulation of the windows, but also in the flat chimney, which turns out to be the back wall of the attic bedroom. The strict cubic quality of the main front, the *flattened arch* over the entrance, the *Diocletian windows* at the back, reveal Venturi as a connoisseur of revolutionary architecture of the type proposed by Ledoux in his houses at the Salines de Chaux (1776). The broken pediment is an element of mannerist architecture, used here as a light shaft for the rooms in the sides of the roof. The "black box" doorway is pure form – a cube – the actual door lies at a right-angle to the front, on the right.

Venturi wanted to show that even in the age of *Brutalism* it was still possible to build poetically. The façade is consciously modeled on the rationalist architecture typical of the 18th century. It is an attempt to win back the "art of building" after the age of Modernism. But the Vanna Venturi house is equally an expression of its own time. It is the first call to post-Modernism, uniting a modernist shaping of space with the idea of the "symbolic image" of a house in the façade. That the "quotation" is broken, is integral to Venturi's approach, which can become directly ironic. Other buildings, apart from villas, have been treated in the same way. In 1960–63 Venturi built the Guild-House, a home for elderly people in Philadelphia, where similar elements were inserted, to give what was a dreary block a new dignity.

Venturi, a pupil of Louis Kahn, whom he admired greatly, thus effected the transition from that which came "after Modernism" to a new variety in architecture, which has today already become classic.

Venturi was even more occupied with architectural theory than with the expression of it in buildings. His purpose was to bring back into the collective memory the architectural canons that had proved valid for many centuries. This canon, with its models such as the principles of using the *orders* of columns, symmetry in building, and so on, had been considered conclusive since Vitruvius and Palladio. Anyone who understood it knew what context of meaning was attached to a particular form, for example the *column* or the broken pediment.

The assumed relationship of prestige and ornamentation had been questioned by the

Modernists in the 1920s, who chose to place the functionality of their buildings in the foreground instead.

From this point of view Venturi's architecture was certainly not modern, but rather on the conservative side. But even when he turns to historical forms, Venturi's buildings are unthinkable without classical Modernism, since they are defined by criticism of it. Venturi's idea was not to refer back to pre-Modernist styles, but to propose an alternative to its dreary and low-quality offshoots. His architecture was therefore a first attempt at going beyond Modernism, the first impetus towards Post-Modernism.

The pleasure in quotation

Venturi was certainly not the only one to show himself open to the *styles* of the past in his buildings. Charles Moore is another of the founding fathers of Post-Modernism, even though at first sight his buildings do not look as though they are peddling the ornaments of bygone eras.

In the case of his own house in Orinda, which is built in wood and appears both restrained and compact, from the exterior the spirit of the building only becomes clear when one observes how it has been conceived. The core of the house consists of two forms resembling baldachins resting on pillars, around which Moore has arranged all the other parts of the building. In this way, the whole forms a rectangle.

Baldachins are canopies resting on pillars, which are erected over holy places. Since the late *Antiquity,* baldachins have been one of the particular *noble orders* of architecture, particularly sacral architecture. It would be inconceivable for any fairly large church of the medieval or baroque period not to have baldachins providing a roof to the altar.

Moore transported an object with a deep sacral meaning in architecture into a place without any sacral meaning – his own home. The ironic break, the intellectual pleasure of playing with a quotation from history, these are the ideas which clarify the use of the baldachin in the interior of the house. If the use of the larger of the two baldachins in the central living area is still at the limits of the acceptable, the use of the second one to provide a roof to the bathtub definitively tips over into the ironic. Moore's passion for playing with historic

architectural forms, putting them in a context where they are out of place, can be found in other areas of the Orinda house. For instance, instead of normal windows and doors, there are sliding doors of a type found in stables.

A house with quotations from vernacular architecture and baldachins which belong in sacral places not only gives free play to many associations, it also says a great deal about the ironic cast of mind of its architect, especially when the house is his own.

Moore's post-modern delight in quotation and in *architecture parlante* is much more clearly visible in what must be his best known project, the Piazza d'Italia in New Orleans, built between 1974 and 1978, commissioned by those of its inhabitants who were of Italian origin. At their wish, the square and its fountain are created on the basis of a stylized outline of Italy, as a boot. The piazza is laid out in concentric circles, at the heart of which lies Sicily, washed by the waters of not the

Charles Moore, *Piazza d'Italia,* New Orleans, Louisiana (USA) 1978

Buildings can and must speak. They require freedom of speech. They can say wise, nice, powerful, and also stupid things. They must make connections with the past and awaken memories. This attitude made Charles Moore the most self-satisfied storyteller of Post-Modernism. For his Piazza d'Italia, Moore transported theater sets depicting Italian geography and architectural history to New Orleans. He copied *friezes* to make sprinklers. He covered *pillars* with steel. Those with architectural training may well be entertained by the irony with which elements from Roman *Antiquity* and the *Renaissance* are mounted. The uninitiated may be more inclined to smile at the expense. The completely circular piazza, carved out of the middle of a shopping center, is far from being the center of social life that its Italian forebears were. But even this polemic against Functionalism is intentional.

Ricardo Bofill, *Apartment Complex Walden Seven,* Barcelona, 1975

The tall apartment block has always been a problematic architectural type. The Spanish architect Ricardo Bofill tried to counter the danger of anonymity by his articulation of the building. It was not a success. The many walkways, bridges, and arcades crossing the five inner courtyards around which the 16-story cluster of buildings in Barcelona are grouped, only serve to make it appear threateningly labyrinthine. The exterior zones are sacrificed to an impractical ground plan. Later housing projects of Bofill's rely upon gigantic, antique-style columns, likewise without success. Behind the *fluted* cylindrical forms lurk exiguous recesses and dark winding staircases. The formalist project becomes too obvious. Post-Modernism brings itself into disrepute.

Mediterranean but the fountain. Behind is a monumental construction of columns, brilliantly colored and full of noble materials, which brings together a unique collection of quotations from the formal language of Antiquity, a confluence of the concentrated architectural power of the Roman Empire and the Italian *Renaissance*.

It seems as though Moore is constantly giving his public a knowing wink, as much as to ask whether they have really got all the abstruse little architectonic references gathered into his Piazza d'Italia. And one does indeed require a certain grounding in architectural history and forms in order to get the joke. Once more Post-Modernism shows itself to be primarily an intellectual movement.

Moore transforms a Doric *frieze* into a sprinkler for his fountain, the *capitals* of the columns are illuminated, and he even gives himself a prominent place in the joke by making in his own likeness two faces spewing out water. The result of this is joyful, humorous architecture, but functional it is not.

The end of Modernism?

In the mid-1970s everything seemed architecturally possible, including things definitely not permissible before: from columns to flat roofs, brightly colored air extraction ducts to expensive marble facing placed next to ventilation shafts. Suddenly everything could be mixed and matched.

The movement which had begun in the early 1960s as more of a quiet protest against the excessively powerful *functionalist* trend in Modernism, had by the 1970s become a raging storm: a dramatic reversion to the *styles* of the past, which polarized not only architects but the whole of society and carried on working right into the 1980s. It was the first architectural Biennale, held in Venice in 1980 at the instigation of Paolo Portoghesi, that brought American and European architecture face to face, and finally established Post-Modernism in Europe.

The most resounding comeback was made by the *column*, an important formal element of Western architecture since the time of the ancient Greeks. The most powerful champion of the column was Ricardo Bofill, but he did not use it at all as the architects of *Antiquity* intended. They thought in terms of the *orders of columns* which prescribed the interrelationship of supporting and supported elements

as firmly as the decoration of columns and frieze. Instead of chiseling the columns out of fine marble as the ancients had done, Bofill and his fellow practitioners at his Taller de Arquitectura office pre-cast them in concrete. He used the gigantic *fluted* columns or monumental *triumphal arches* to articulate the façades of his apartment blocks, as in for example Les Espaces d'Abraxas at Marne-la-Vallée near Paris or at the Temples du Lac at Saint-Quentin-en-Yvelines, in order to invest buildings that had no sacral meaning with a monumental air.

Bofill's buildings are too dramatic. His orders of columns which extend up ten stories do not terminate with any *entablature* as ancient *temples* would have to have done, and memories spring to mind of Albert Speer's gigantomania in Germany or the Stalinist *wedding-cake* style of the 1950s.

Post-Modernism gradually lost the ironic note that had been introduced by Moore and others. In its place came a dogmatic architecture which used the classical quotation in any old way as long as it was expensive. The playful variety of forms which James Stirling and Michael Wilford deployed in the new Stuttgart Staatsgalerie (1977–84, illustrated on page 96) was now the exception, and in Bofill's buildings with their grand gestures, it was altogether absent. Instead, he built apartment ghettos in *classicizing* dress that only offered a very limited alternative to standardized Modernist housing estates.

With classicism so much in favor, it is hardly surprising that at the end of the 1970s Albert Speer, who had been Hitler's architect, enjoyed an unexpected return to favor. His work was republished in folio format and enjoyed a highly uncritical reception.

Architecture was threatening to degenerate into a ragbag of quotations, from which anyone could pick exactly what he liked, package it, and present it in a new context, completely freed of any historical relationship to the current architectural form. A hundred years of modern architectural development seemed in danger of culminating in an infectious *eclecticism*. If Charles Moore could bring Italy to New Orleans for the Piazza d'Italia, why should Arata Isozaki not, quite straightforwardly, quote Michelangelo's Roman Piazza del Campidoglio in the Tsukuba head office in Japan (1980–83)?

The circle closed in the area of skyscraper construction as well; people cold-shouldered the metropolitan elegance of a Mies van der Rohe, suddenly reverting to the cumbrous shapes of *Art Deco* that had first appeared in the 1920s and 1930s in the work of Raymond Hood and William van Alen, but were now tricked out with a *classicist* repertoire that had become nothing more than a fashion.

The versatile Philip Johnson left a lasting mark on Post-Modernism with the American Telephone and Telegraph (AT&T) Building. Clad in pink granite, the building towers up into the skies, emphasizing its vertical lines through the articulation of its windows, for all the world, as if in direct opposition to the horizontal strip windows of Modernism. The monumental broken pediment that crowns the building, trumpets far and wide from whose mind this building sprang. And the entrance in *triumphal arch* mode, which openly and proudly spans several stories, underlines the relationship between the building and its owner. In just the same way as the skyscrapers of the 1920s, the AT&T Building manifests prosperity and growth in architectural form. It is no longer *functionalism* and transparency which are crucial in tall buildings, but prestige.

The play with traditional forms reached its climax with the Humana Building found in Louisville, Kentucky (1982–86), designed by the American architect Michael Graves. A distinguishing feature of the building was its striking pastel coloration, with slabs of pink granite and greenish glass. It was also notable for the fact that Graves tried to break through the traditional *rectilinear* shape of tall buildings and structure its volumes differently. However, viewed in relief, the resultant building is far from satisfactory. Apart from the multiplicity of classical quotations – the loggia, tempietto, and belvedere – there is the overhanging part of the façade, which is partially held up by metal supports and makes the building too much of a hodge-podge to live up to its pretensions to grandeur.

Philip Johnson, *American Telephone and Telegraph (AT&T) Building*, New York, 1982

A *base* shaped like a *triumphal arch*, a shaft of vertical strip windows, the whole crowned by a broken *pediment.* Philip Johnson has dug deep into Post-Modernism's grab-bag of quotations. Dividing the building into the classic three parts, base, middle, and roof, he makes it as plain as possible for a modernist that he interprets a tall building as a tall house. But Johnson does not only use the divisions of Antiquity; Brunelleschi's colonnade in the 15th-century Pazzi chapel in Florence was an important source for the entrance, and the relationship between the pediment and an 18th-century Chippendale bureau was immediately noted. In a time when exciting skyscrapers had been replaced by unexciting tall boxes in steel and glass, the AT&T Building initiated a decisive change of direction for this type of building.

Building in the global village

Crossing boundaries

1980–1990

CULTURES OF EXPERIENCE AND CONSUMPTION

The times before the change: austerity in the East, prosperity in the West

The movement that began in the early 1980s in Poland as a vociferous protest by workers of the Lenin shipyards in Gdansk, organized by the Solidarity trade union under Lech Walesa, climaxed on 9 November 1989 with the fall of the Berlin Wall. Between these two events lay a decade in which the world began to change in a way that was barely perceptible to the individual, but at the end was perceived to have taken a totally new direction.

Under Mikhail Gorbachev, leader of the then all-powerful Communist Party, the Soviet Union began to emerge from a period of stagnation under Brezhnev into the era of glasnost ("openness") and perestroika ("transformation"). After 80 years of dictatorship, the communist system in Russia was economically at rockbottom. Determined reform from within led the way out of stagnation, and the radical reform of society was introduced. Democratization, judicial reform, and de-Stalinization were pillars of the reform movement. After years of oppression and imprisonment, Andrei Sakharov, the physicist, Nobel laureate, and outspoken critic of the Soviet system, became a moral authority. Others, such as the winner of the Nobel Prize for literature, Aleksandr Solzhenitsyn, who had been deprived of his citizenship for his critical attitude, returned to their homeland after many years of involuntary exile. The states that had become part of the Soviet bloc at the end of the Second World War and were members of the Warsaw Pact, were dispersed on the break-up of the USSR. They began the change to more or less democratic countries, a laborious process which has not yet come to an end in the 1990s.

The world order still seemed quite clear and unambiguous at the beginning of the 1980s: over here was West and over there was East – good here, bad there. Then, overnight, that all collapsed. The Cold War that had held the world in its icy grip since 1945 melted away, leaving behind a political and cultural vacuum.

While the Poles in the 1980s lived under the threat of martial law, East Germany struggled to manage scarcity, and the Rumanians starved under their dictator Ceausescu, in Western Europe and North America a euphoric culture of celebration set in.

Wherever there was a historic anniversary, it was celebrated with a bang. In the mid-1980s, the "European City of Culture" system began, with one city each year being selected for the role. The festive luxury of Charles Moore's and Michael Graves' late 1970s architecture found its echo in the deliberately sumptuous tone of the 1980s. Lulled by the sense of security produced by extraordinary prosperity, societies financed almost limitless

1981: Lech Walesa becomes chairman of the Polish trade union Solidarity, which is now officially permitted. Murder of the Egyptian president Anwar el-Sadat, who had initiated the peace process with Israel in 1977. Sensational success of the first performance in London of Andrew Lloyd Webber's musical *Cats*.

1982: Falklands War between Argentina and the UK. Helmut Kohl becomes German Chancellor. Umberto Eco's novel *The Name of the Rose* published.

1983: US President Reagan initiates research into the Strategic Defense Initiative, a defense shield in outer space against enemy rocket attacks ("Star Wars"). Highly criticized, it is halted in 1993. The organism responsible for the viral infection AIDS is discovered.

1984: The Indian prime minister Indira Gandhi is murdered by the Sikhs of her bodyguard. Nobel Peace Prize awarded to Bishop Desmond Tutu in South Africa for his peaceful struggle against apartheid. Milos Forman's film about Mozart, *Amadeus*, receives eight Oscars.

1985: Mikhail Gorbachev becomes general secretary of the Communist Party of the Soviet Union (and head of state in 1990), and introduces

After the opening of the frontiers of East Germany to the West, on the night of 9–10 November, 1989, Berliners from both sides of the city stormed the Wall at the Brandenburg Gate.

perestroika. The American pop singer Madonna also enjoys great success as a film actress.

1986: After a serious fire in a reactor in the nuclear power plant at Chernobyl in the Ukraine, all inhabitants for 18.5 miles (30 km) around are evacuated. Death of the French feminist Simone de Beauvoir, lifelong companion of Jean Paul Sartre.

1987: Signing by Gorbachev and Reagan in Washington of the agreement banning all medium-range nuclear missiles. Beginning of the Palestinian *intifada* (uprising) in the Israeli-occupied territories. The Montreal Protocol is signed by 24 countries which undertake to cut their use of CFCs by half by 1999, to reduce damage to the ozone layer over Antarctica.

1988: Benazir Bhutto becomes the first woman to be elected prime minister of an Islamic country, Pakistan. Worldwide tributes to Nelson Mandela, in prison for 25 years for his opposition to apartheid, and demands for his release. Historic center of Lisbon destroyed by fire.

1989: Bloody suppression of a prodemocracy demonstration in Tiananmen Square, Beijing, followed by a wave of oppression, arrests, and executions. Change in East Germany and fall of Berlin Wall on 9 November leads to democratization and free elections in other Eastern bloc countries. Ayatollah Khomeini imposes a fatwa passing a death sentence on Salman Rushdie, his novel *The Satanic Verses* (1988) is seen as blasphemous. Environmental catastrophe off the coast of Alaska, a damaged tanker spills 40,000 tonnes (190 million liters) of crude oil.

Hans Hollein, *Municipal Museum, Abteiberg,* general view (left), and small exhibition area with group of sculptures by Giulio Paolini (below), Mönchengladbach, 1972–82

The Abteiberg museum marked the beginning of a whole series of museums constructed in the 1980s. The requirement was art as experience. In order to get around the contradictions evoked by accommodating a large event in a small town, the Austrian architect Hans Hollein adopted the new design principle of collage, arranging a collection composed of small sections in a small skyscraper, an underground cube, eleven small halls with sawtooth roofs, as well as various terraces, and formed them out of such diverse materials as copper, steel, brick, and natural stone. In this way the museum fits harmoniously into the small town environment and offers a suitable space for every type of exhibition. Yet: as with all collage architecture, it still smacks slightly of compromise and lack of will.

consumption, with reassuring results in terms of employment figures. In the West, the real social problem seemed to be what to do with ever-increasing leisure.

Post-Modernism soon lost its luster, but the tendency to build palatial banks and tall office buildings at the greatest possible expense stayed on, not only in the expanding economies of southeast Asia from Bangkok to Jakarta, but also in the old world, from Paris to Frankfurt to Chicago.

Although the *columns* and *pediments* of Post-Modernism went out after a few years, new directions in architecture had begun, the hold of classical Modernism had been broken, and the horizon had opened up for different concepts in architecture.

The museum experience: facilities become an event

No category of building is more indicative of the culture of celebration and experience that broke out in the 1980s than the museums, which went up in countries and cities everywhere. The museum had established itself as a middle-class temple of culture in Europe at the beginning of the 19th century, and at the end of the 20th century it was, in terms of architecture, still accorded a central role in not only the transmission of art and culture, but also of the pleasure of enjoying art. While the price of works by painters such as Van Gogh, the Impressionists, or Picasso shot up to astronomical heights, an exhibition culture of a type not known before developed in the new

temples of art. Hundreds of thousands of visitors were attracted to gigantic exhibition events such as "Spirit of the age" or "A new spirit in painting." Art was "in," and afforded museums a lucrative trade in products such as catalogs, posters, and postcards. Architects also now began to realize that they had a chance to make museums something other than the grandiose but ultimately empty shells for works of art that they had previously been. Museum buildings became works of art in themselves, and reflected the artistic ambitions of architects and those responsible for commissioning them.

This had already been the case with Frank Lloyd Wright's ambitious Guggenheim Museum (illustration page 63) in the 1950s, and with Rogers and Piano's Centre Pompidou (illustration page 79) in the 1970s. Despite their differences, the museums have much in common: they have a welcoming atmosphere and create a sense of being the beacon of the age, which continues to attract huge numbers of people to visit them.

Past – present – future

To get an idea of the poles between which museum architecture was fluctuating at the end of the 1970s one needs only to look at two American buildings. On the one hand there is the extension to the National Gallery of Arts in Washington DC, designed by Ieoh Ming Pei and finished in 1978. Its unusual trapezoidal shape, which consists of two triangles pressed together, conditioned by the available terrain, in conjunction with its surface covering of marble, gives it a striking but timelessly classic appearance. The Getty Museum in Malibu, California (1973), on the other hand, is one of the earliest examples of a Post-Modern architectural concept applied to the task of building a museum. In point of fact the building leaves one with highly mixed feelings, as instead of the inspired modern architecture such as that delivered by Wright, Rogers and Piano or Pei, what arose in Malibu was a copy of the no longer extant Villa dei Papyri in Herculaneum, Italy, whose original site was thousands of miles away.

Not only are copies of lost buildings of the past used for museums, but also the structural fabric of real historic buildings. With the discovery of the particular charm that emanates from disused industrial and transport buildings, museum building acquired a whole new arena. The best example of an old railway station being put to a new use is the museum at the Quai d'Orsay in Paris (rebuilt by the architects Gae Aulenti and Italo Rota), which since 1986 has housed the most precious collections of Impressionist art in France.

The 1980s saw the creation of a complete mile of museums in Frankfurt, which stretch along the Main. There is the Museum für Kunsthandwerk (Applied Art), which was built between 1979 and 1985 by one of the most prominent of the 20th-century American museum architects, Richard Meier, with his characteristically purist white façades, as well as the Deutsche Architektur-Museum (German Architecture Museum), created between 1979 and 1984 by Oswald Mathias Ungers, and others, gathering several outstanding examples of modern museum architecture in one small area.

Building artistically for art

It can easily happen that the ambitions of the architect, to create a museum that is also seen as a work of art, clash with the wishes of the artists, who want only a simple shell in which they can display their pictures appropriately. This was certainly the case with the Abteiberg Municipal Museum, which was planned and realized by Hans Hollein between 1972 and 1982 in Mönchengladbach.

Hollein's building was the prelude to a unique wave of enthusiasm for creating museums which was to sweep Germany in the years that followed. From the beginning,

Hollein's building divided critics and visitors to the museum into two camps – ardent supporters and vehement detractors.

Instead of creating one single building, Hollein created a museum landscape in several parts, which fitted together more or less organically. This procedure resulted in a visual plethora of different forms, housing not only the town's own collection but also traveling exhibitions, libraries, and rooms for events and lectures, as well as cafés. This total concept was by no means a new one for a museum. But Hollein found a way of allocating to each function its own area, each one an architectonic unit standing out individually in the terraced museum landscape.

Corresponding to the varied uses of the different museum areas, different materials were employed in a hierarchy of values depending on the part of the building that was involved, from *brick* (a relatively cheap material) for the terraced landscape to *hewn stone slabs* (a grander option) for entrance steps. Metal, glass and plastic were also used. The language of forms in which the parts of the building are expressed is a reminder that Hollein's architecture appeared in the age of Post-Modernism, as for instance the way in which an entirely secular place, the entrance hall, is endowed with the dignity of a temple.

Playing with traditional models

Post-modern! That is the first thought that comes into the head of anyone who is looking at the Neue Württemburgische Staatsgalerie (1977–84, illustration page 96), built by James Stirling and Michael Wilford. Although the central rotunda of the Staatsgalerie reminds one of Karl Friedrich Schinkel's Altes Museum, which was itself borrowed from the Pantheon in Rome, it is in fact much more than a collection of classicist quotations.

Whereas Hollein's museum cannot avoid a certain brittleness despite its ambitious formal choices, Stirling and Wilford have placed the element of playfulness more to the fore. The warm brown tones of the hewn stone slabs, with which the façades are faced, contrast with the brightly painted metal elements in the canopy and the entrance, whose rounded and mobile forms are a deliberate contrast to the rigidity of the stone.

There is a remote reminder in such elements of Stirling's roots in English *Brutalism*.

Playfulness is a strong element elsewhere in the Staatsgalerie: as for instance the Tuscan *columns* half sunk in the floor, or the blocks of *hewn stone* which seem to have fallen out of the façade, and remind one of the romantic ruins of the 18th and early 19th centuries.

But it was not only in Germany that new museums reached new heights of architectonic ambition. One of the most disputed projects of the 1980s was the extensive rebuilding at the Louvre in Paris. A wing of what had once been a French royal palace, once used by the finance ministry, had to be removed prior to a drastic reorganization of the priceless contents of the Louvre, which was to include the provision of underground access to the collections.

On the square in front of the Louvre there is now a glass *pyramid* by the New York architect Leoh Ming Pei, shaped like those of ancient Egypt, which gives an intimation of the massive rebuilding that necessitated these major incursions into the historic substance of so important a complex as the Louvre. The glassy elegance of the construction, often glowingly described as "super-" or "ultra-modern," is in conscious contrast to the *baroque* weightiness of the Louvre.

DECONSTRUCTION

New ways to reality

When standing at various spots in Stirling's Neue Staatsgalerie you suddenly get a flash of that desire to unsettle the viewer, also to be found in the work of the SITE architects, and which consists of making an odd use of structural elements of the building. One example of this is the play with the "romantic ruins" idea, or there is the massive double T-beam, which holds up the canopy and ends in nothing, whereas you would have expected it from a constructional point of view to rest on another beam. Whereas SITE and Stirling use this effect sparingly, the American Frank O. Gehry made it the crux of his style. He began developing it from the end of the 1970s, but it was only in the mid-1980s that he broke through on to the world stage.

As architects often do, he used his own home to demonstrate the powers of innovation that he promised to deploy in all his building. This house, which he built in 1978 in Santa Monica, California, was certainly a very strange piece of architecture, which did not in any way fit the model proposed by the modernists, with their strict, rational, white

Ieoh Ming Pei,*Louvre, Entrance Pyramid,* Paris, 1983–88

Dramatic change was called for, but also continuity. The Louvre was to become a modern museum, the 800-year-old palace of kings was to become a house of the people. And yet the building had to remain what it was: a monument to the glory of France. And so the quiet Chinese-American architect Ieoh Ming Pei accepted the axial *baroque* layout and chose the form of a *pyramid,* which had been the geometrical symbol of grandeur since the time of the ancient Egyptians. But how could he rededicate a monument of kings, designed to keep the people at a distance, to become a symbol of democracy? Pei chose to make the pyramid in glass. The visitor passes through it into ancillary rooms below ground, and from there into one of the most important museums in the world.

Behnisch and Partner, *Hysolar
Research Building*, Stuttgart, 1987

Steel girders shooting out of the building,
distorted stories, a roof that looks as
though the wind was about to lift it off: a
mixture of materials ranging from
corrugated iron through to wood, steel,
glass and concrete, and what is
presumably intended to be the greatest
contradiction of all: this chaotic building
serves for research into solar installations –
an exact science. But the world of natural
sciences is not so securely based at the
end of the 20th century as it once used to
be. Open contradictions come closer to
reality than simple explanations, which is
why Günter Behnisch, the best-known
representative of Deconstructivism in
Germany, chooses to make contradictory
truths perceptible. Deconstructed
constructions exist to make boundaries
tangible, but not to deny the force of
gravity. In point of fact, because this
building does in fact remain standing, it
makes the laws of gravity clearer. The open
clashes of Deconstructivism emphasize
both the individuality of each
phenomenon and its dependence on the
whole. For Behnisch, Deconstructivism is
an image of the individualized society:
democracy in a building.

cubes. However, Gehry's buildings did not fit
the model that was being propagated so
successfully by the post-modernists either,
with their borrowings from both *Antiquity*
and *Renaissance*.

The strange impression created by the
building starts with the steps that lead to the
entrance: these are squares of concrete with
the appearance that they have been pushed
together at an angle, and thus form a kind of
podium supporting the two small wooden
platforms in front of the wooden entrance
door. Over the entrance area towers a strange
cage of wire mesh, while to the side of the
unspectacular entrance door there is a sort of
corrugated construction with a noticeable lack
of right-angles and an expressive corner
window at the end.

Everything that was required for a sensible
construction, with an unambiguous alloca-
tion of supporting and non-supporting parts,
seemed to have been dissolved into what
appeared to be a chaotic mishmash of
cheap building materials that did not appear
to belong together in any way at all. Gehry's
house was a targeted, vehement architectonic provocation, a combination of aesthetic
impossibilities that entirely disrupted habitual
ways of seeing. This vehement early work
was the prototype of Gehry's subsequent
buildings. Its elements do not belong to any

traditional construction, but work together
almost as though they had been taken apart
and shuffled, and then reassembled in a new,
and apparently haphazard, way. The sober
functionality of Construction has turned into
Deconstruction.

Construction – deconstruction

The buildings of the deconstructivists of the
1980s and 1990s are inconceivable without
both the influence of the Modernists of the
1920s, and the art of the Russian Constructivists
(see page 34 et seq.). Their utopian architectural visions, which in fact seldom got off the
drawing board, were taken up by a vanguard of
young architects and turned into buildings.

Also in Gehry's projects, as well as those of
other architects such as Peter Eisenman, there
is a decided "building-site" quality and an
undogmatic use of building materials evincing
an urgent search for a new direction in architecture.

Modernism was recognized to have frozen
into a tradition, but instead of overcoming it by
turning back – as the post-Modernists were
doing so successfully at the time – the deconstructivists engaged with architectural history in
a different way. They tried, by means of unusual
alienation effects, to deprive architecture of its
assumed perfection: "disturbed perfection" was
consequently one of the formal imperatives of

Frank O. Gehry, *California Aerospace Museum,* Los Angeles, 1984

A Lockheed F104 Starfighter hangs over the entrance and every visitor at once understands what this building is about: aerospace. And volumes of air space are what Frank O. Gehry accordingly defined on this small site: wedge shaped, diagonal, circular, stepped to a pyramid, and without any ordered shape. From the outside, they make people notice the small museum; on the inside they afford space for interaction with every one of the large exhibits. What looks from the outside like a crowd of autonomous volumes turns out, inside, to be sections of an interpenetrating air space, through which the visitor is conducted over ramps, viewing galleries, and bridges.
In the Aerospace Museum, the inner necessities of the building project can be logically deduced from its exterior, but this is not always the case with Frank O. Gehry's buildings. For instance an advertising agency building looks from the outside like an up-ended pair of binoculars. His formal games normally only fulfill the function of ensuring that people notice the building.

deconstructivist architecture. At the same time their partially fragmented, partially expressive buildings gave architectonic expression to the lack of direction society had, and to the almost impossible attempt to make holistic sense of the innumerable parts of the reality that make up the Global Village.

The Deconstructivists first received international recognition through the exhibition "Deconstructivist Architecture," which was organized by Philip Johnson and Mark Wigley in 1988 in the Museum of Modern Art. It displayed work by Gehry, and also buildings and projects by Peter Eisenman, COOP Himmelblau, and Bernhard Tschumi. From then on it was only a matter of time before Deconstructivism would rise to become a worldwide stylistic movement, and conquer both the design studios as well as the architectural schools.

The breaking down of functions and forms into their component parts (de-construction), the inclusion of these parts into larger structures – whether of society or the city – and their analysis, found expression not only in the work of architects, but also in the writings of the French philosopher Jacques Derrida – the pioneer of Deconstructivism – who even did concrete work with Bernard Tschumi and Peter Eisenman among others in the Parc la Villette in Paris.

From LA to the world: Frank O. Gehry

With the building of the California Aerospace Museum, which Gehry completed in 1984, Deconstructivism in the United States was ready to make its public debut. Slanting walls, a variety of materials, and interpenetrating volumes made the building into a sculpture. A Lockheed F104 Starfighter, which seems to swoop over the main entrance, gives the building its universally accessible tone as well as announcing very plainly that this is an aerospace museum. But it does more. The fighter gives the façade of the museum a dynamic element, which is echoed in Gehry's unusual diagonal positioning of the volumes of the building. Yet, despite the surprising way in which the parts of the building cut across each other, and the suddenly opening angles of vision and the slanted walls, Gehry's Aerospace Museum has already lost much of the fresh unconcern and the conscious negation of convention inherent in his home in Santa Monica. Compared with his own house, the museum works like a dog on a leash. The surprising use of materials such as corrugated iron and wire mesh, the deliberately project-like and provisional air that had given Gehry's house almost the feeling of a building site, has given way to something more closed, more strictly subordinated to the functional needs of the museum.

Thomas Spiegelhalter, *Ökohaus,*
Breisach, 1989–91

It immediately reminds you of Frank O.
Gehry's house in Santa Monica or Günter
Behnisch's Hysolar research institute in
Stuttgart, but neither playful nor
Deconstructivist goals are involved. The
barrel roof is also a reservoir for rainwater.
The collector for water heating is also a
sunshade, the solar panels, besides
creating electricity, mark the entrance. An
autonomous house, which does not need
to use electricity from the national grid or
any more water than is freely supplied by
nature. The other installations fit
seamlessly into the Deconstructivist
language of forms. It is not clear whether
it really is ecologically sound to use as
many technical resources as are involved
here to make an environmentally friendly
building. What is clear is that
consideration of ecological problems will
be a major demand on architecture in the
21st century.

In the last two decades Gehry has risen
to become one of the most sought-after
architects in the world, and examples of his
buildings can be seen scattered all over the
globe. In Weil am Rhein he created the Vitra
Design Museum, in Prague he produced
a commercial building that looks similar to a
dancing couple (illustration page 101), and in
1997 he completed the Guggenheim Museum
in Bilbao, which has the silhouette of a
stranded whale.

RATIONALIST TRADITION IN ITALY

With cool hearts
In contrast to the occasionally over-emphatic
fireworks of Post-Modernism and the very
serious playfulness of Deconstructivism, there
is the Rationalist tradition. Naturally, it too has
not remained untouched by the revolutionary
whirlwind that swept its way through architecture in the 1970s and 1980s. However, the
rationalists have used that revolution in their
own way, while still retaining a firm hold on
their strict concepts of the building and the
city, which are rooted in both cultural and
regional tradition.

It is not surprising that it is first and foremost
Italian architects who have stayed within
a tradition, such as that founded by Terragni

for instance. It was characteristic of the Italian
rationalists of the 1920s and 1930s, unlike
their German colleagues who had proselytized
for the *Neues Bauen* not least for ideological
reasons, that they saw no contradiction in
the creative interaction and cross-fertilization
of Modernism and tradition. So it was that
rationalism became a traditional strand in
20th-century Italian architecture, which,
despite the partiality the fascists had for
monumental building, has continued unbroken
to this day.

Since the 1960s one of the most prominent
representatives of this architectural direction
has been Aldo Rossi, whose buildings have
been appreciated throughout the world for
many years. His work has both a strict as well
as a monumental quality, with decorative as
well as playful elements. In this way, his finest
buildings almost seem to provide the sensation of being surrounded by the atmosphere
of a southern piazza on a warm and balmy
market day.

In 1969, Rossi began the design of the
Gallaratese apartment building and arcade
in Milan, which was eventually completed in
1973. His radically pared-down façade
consists of seemingly endless rows of monotonous concrete discs with uniform square
openings. In 1971 he and Gianni Braghieri
won the national competition for the cemetery

of San Cataldo in Modena, which they had started building in 1980. The shadows of the empty, glassless windows of the charnel house that are cast by the hard southern light, conjure up the melancholy of the painter de Chirico.

The interpenetration of playful and monumental elements in Rossi's work can be seen clearly when one compares the rebuilding and enlargement of the Hotel Duca in Milan (1988–9) with the apartment buildings which Rossi designed for the IBA, the Internationale Bauausstellung (Building Exhibition) in Berlin in 1987. The clear articulation of the façade in the lower part of the Hotel Duca, using vertical strips faced with ashlar masonry emphasized by intervening areas of glass, is repeated in the upper part of the building. But the façade here is a unified red, pierced with smaller windows instead of hewn stone and glass, which counters the vertical direction of the building. As a consequence, the upper stories appear to rest with noticeable weight on the pilasters, thus giving them the appearance of *columns*.

Rossi used only a few inspired devices to give great formal variety to the façade of the hotel, whereas for the Berlin residential complex he was much more expansive. Here, too, we find a play on different building materials such as glass and *brick*. And we can also observe how Rossi gives a balance to the façade by putting in a horizontal band of differently colored clinker, which contrasts with the vertical emphasis provided by the towers housing the stairwells, which are slightly set back from the building line. These stairwells are also crowned by *pitched roofs*, a type very typical of Berlin, so bringing in a playful element.

Despite the different materials and the emphatic color, the basic forms of Rossi's buildings are strictly *rectilinear*. They also have the additional feature of fitting the historic proportions of the urban space, as well as using indigenous elements such as the *pitched roof*, which not only breaks up the contours of the building, but can be understood as a quotation. This does not, however, have any *historicist* connotations, and is nothing like a copy of the kind that can be found in Moore or Bofill's buildings, but instead entirely maintains the independence of the content.

Aldo Rossi, *Apartment Buildings, Kochstrasse,* International Building Exhibition, Berlin, 1987 (above), *Hotel Duca,* Milan, 1988–91 (left)

Two cities, two building tasks – yet clearly the same forms: the main body of the building faces the street, articulated into base, middle, and roof, a heavy façade, grid windows. The buildings in Berlin and Milan are a translation of the thesis which the Italian architect Aldo Rossi formulated as early as 1966 in his book *L'Architettura della Città.* According to this, the city is composed of a universally valid order of building types, so there is no necessity for each age to invent a new architecture; all that is required is to interpret the traditional canon rationally in the light of current requirements. Eleven years later Rossi made the following analogy between architecture and town planning: "A building is a reproduction of the sites of a city. In these terms each corridor is a street, each inner courtyard a square. In my designs for dwellings I relate to the basic types of living space, which have evolved in the course of a long process of urban architectural development."

Syntheses of past and present

One of the basic tasks of the IBA Berlin, for which Rossi realized his project, was the restoration of the city in the wake of the damage caused by the Second World War (see pages 66–67). This problem was in no way specific to Berlin. In the 1980s there was a generally greater awareness of the problems of dealing with the historic material around the site of a projected building, as well as the ground plan of the city itself – one of the certain benefits of Post-Modernism being that it reawakened interest in historical building styles. But architects such as Rossi also reflected in their theorizing on the historical meaning of cities and the possibility of a further functional development.

SIR JAMES STIRLING

"Master of styles," was the heading that the *Deutsche Bauzeitschrift* gave to its obituary of the British architect James Stirling (1926–92). But he was much more than the creator of the useless *columns* and split *pediments* which tend to be dismissed today as jokes. As the leading protagonist of Post-Modernism, he prepared the ground for the paradigm-change in 20th-century architecture. His buildings are polemics against an ossified Modernism. The theories which he developed with Kevin Lynch and Charles Moore when he was Professor at Yale University led to a reconsideration of values that had been neglected by Modernism: the relationship to history and the

Sir James Stirling, circa 1980

surroundings of a building, as well as the power of architecture to make an emotional statement.

The re-evaluation began with quotations from the icons of architectural history. Between 1959 and 1963, long before the term Post-Modernism was coined, Stirling and James Gowan designed the Institute of Engineering at Leicester University. The overall shape of the tower-like part of the building, with its cantilevered lecture theater, seems a downright copy of the picture, much reproduced at that time, of the Rusakov workers' club designed by the Russian Constructivist Konstantin Melnikov in Moscow in 1928 (illustration page 35). The pillars with a capital in the shape of a truncated cone that turned up for the first time in the Olivetti building in Milton Keynes, England, in 1971, and which became the trademark of the firm which Sir James Stirling and Michael Wilford founded the same year, can be read as a greatly simplified quotation from the mushroom-shaped pillars created by Frank Lloyd Wright in 1939 for the Johnson Wax Company headquarters in Racine, Wisconsin (illustration page 16).

Stirling's Staatsgalerie in Stuttgart (1977–84) is an assemblage of historical quotations. The polychrome masonry echoes the medieval church

buildings of Pisa, and the sequence of rooms corresponds to a *neo-Baroque* suite. Stirling assembles a *Deconstructivist* covered entrance, *Gothic* pointed arches, vaguely antique pillared walks, and Bauhaus details around the ruin-like reference to Schinkel's rotunda in the Altes Museum in Berlin, making a varied and colorful collage. In his plan for the Berlin Wissenschaftszentrum (Scientific Center) Sir James also assembled together a whole repertoire of archetypes from architectural history: a cruciform basilica, a Greek stoa, a medieval campanile, and an antique theater.

Distinct from many of the modish hangers-on of Post-Modernism, Stirling never used other styles for their own sake. The exteriors of the Wissenschaftszentrum, so full of architectural "significance," are completely filled with identical utilitarian offices. The basilica of the Wissenschaftszentrum actually houses nothing but toilets and the caretaker's lodging. The real message of the pale blue and pink striped building is pure polemic against the paradigm of Modernism: the unity of form and function.

In his 1985 extension to the Tate Gallery in London, Stirling criticized another ideal of modernism: the showing of the construction. The façade displays a grid of masonry and plastered surfaces, which has nothing to do with the *reinforced concrete construction* inside. Whereas the galleries inside concentrate on displaying the works of J. M. W. Turner in natural light, the outside tries to fit in with the buildings around, a not unreasonable idea always neglected by self-obsessed Modernists. At the same time, the strong colors and spectacular entrance of the Clore Wing attract an attention from the public which would never have been achieved by the pictures alone. This entertainment value is an ideal which Modernism always rejected.

Stirling was fond of relating a key experience of his, which was that when he was a student he visited Palladio's Villa Rotonda. The plaster was falling off the pillars. Something that was pretending to be marble turned out to be "only" brick. But did that alter the architectonic quality of the building?

This latter was what Stirling always cared about most, as can be seen from his last building, the Braun factory in Melsungen, completed in 1992, for which the Stirling and Wilford partnership also engaged the services of the young Berlin architects Walter Nägeli and Renzo Vallebuona. The mighty building is in fact made up of a large number of highly independent volumes which fit precisely into the winding

valley of the Pfieffewiesen. The complex displays not only the way the plastics manufactured there are made, but also the manner in which the building itself is constructed. For example, the concrete wall of the covered car park which extends along the back of the site, is draped with a mesh of formwork, in such a way that even in its completed state the fluid character of the raw material remains recognizable.

To be sure there are quotations from architectural history in Melsungen, but they are never there for themselves, but to create architectural

As if constructed for the performance of Greek theater: the rotunda in the interior court of the Neue Württembergische Staatsgalerie (New Württenberg National Gallery) in Stuttgart is the summit of Stirling's connotation-rich collage architecture.

qualities. The production shed may be reminiscent of Peter Behrens's epoch-making AEG-Maschinenfabrik in Berlin, but one's impressions are dominated by the wonderful view offered by the curved construction opening on to the landscape. The upturned truncated cones which support the administrative building are certainly a reminder of Le Corbusier, but above all they point to the off-center distribution of forces. You could list innumerable precedents for the colorful slanting window jambs, but their main effect is to give the light which reaches the desks of the office workers an inspirational fluidity. Have more spatial qualities ever been wrested out of a building task normally treated as workaday?

Colorful variety: the Clore Wing of the Tate Gallery in London (left). The curved administration building of the Braun AG works in Melsungen (right) responds to the topography of the surrounding hills.

Carlo Scarpa's museum buildings of the 1960s had pointed the way, impressively, to a means of synthesizing old and new (see illustration page 76). But 20 years had passed since then, and the forms and demands of architecture had indeed changed.in that time. However, despite these changes, the fundamental question had remained the same: should one simply copy the old, or create something new in an environment laden with history?

The city of Venice offers a particular example in this area. The city on the water is a masterpiece of town planning, and its most important monuments are the responsibility of an energetic department dedicated to the conservation of historic monuments. One of the very few new building projects carried out in Venice in the 1980s was a housing development by Vittorio Gregotti, which was undertaken in the Canareggio area. Several factors had to be taken into account in this project, from the position of the site and the existing buildings, which would be a factor in determining both the size and proportions of any new building constructed upon it, to the specific historical development of residential buildings in Venice. For example, there is a typical Venetian tradition of maintaining the separateness of the private and public domains of a building, which makes it imperative that each apartment has an individual entrance, and is not – as is customary elsewhere – served by a communal staircase.

Gregotti's buildings, despite their reserved aspect, not only complied with all of these specifications, but furthermore employed both a rational and modern language of forms that did not insinuate itself into the historic environment, but instead showed much respect for it. Using *pitched roofs*, wooden loggias, and sash windows, Gregotti adopted Venetian architectural elements, but simultaneously lent them a contemporary appearance. He resisted the temptation to endow his apartments with a spurious nobility through the use of incrustations, *Gothic-influenced* arched windows, or other motifs from Venetian grand houses, and also that of utilising *deconstructive,* alienating effects to make the building more noticeable or meaningful in a way in which would run counter to its simple function as a residential building.

THE TESSIN SCHOOL

Architectural landscape with mountains

The rationalist architecture of individuals such as Aldo Rossi or Vittorio Gregotti, and their attempts to bring together traditional and contemporary elements, fell on particularly fruitful soil in the Italian-speaking Swiss canton of Tessin. Since time immemorial the mild climate and beautiful scenery around the Swiss northern shore of Lake Maggiore and around Lake Lugano had made this region a favorite area for the villas of the well-to-do. Since the Second World War in particular, the unique landscape of Tessin was being overpopulated with poor-quality modernist type buildings of an utterly standard kind, which has led since the end of the 1960s to vehement protest by architects. Parallel to the crisis in classical Modernism in the 1960s and 1970s, this area produced its own architectonic direction: the Tessin school, which has been responsible for numerous public and private buildings of recent years. They put architecture that was monumental in place of

Mario Botta, Single-Family House, Vacallo (Switzerland), 1986–89

The side of this three-cornered building that faces the street is closed. The façade facing the valley is open; its two arches interconnect, and there is a semi-circular terrace in front. Like all Botto's buildings, the villa at Vacallo combines almost sacral inner rooms with a confident position in the landscape. Botta, who worked with Le Corbusier and Louis I. Kahn in his youth, obtains this effect with clear, timelessly geometric forms. The result is both dignified and subtle, due to the use of *brick.* While the building seen as a whole is thoroughly monumental, since each individual brick is only the size that the bricklayer can take in his hand, the human dimension is not lost. Because brick also provides visual evidence of the genesis and weathering of a house, and since it has been used from *Antiquity* right up till the time of Rationalism, Botta's buildings also acquire a historical dimension.

vernacular building but also took account of the nature of the landscape and the individual needs of the user.

One of the leading representatives of the Tessin school is Mario Botta, an architect who is himself from southern Switzerland, who early in his career had not only worked in the office of Louis I. Kahn, but also with the most influential European architect of the century, the Swiss-born Le Corbusier. In Botta's early work in particular, such as his buildings resting on pilotis, and in his use of concrete, the influence of both his mentors is clear.

It is possibly in the area of the single-family house that Botta achieves his best work, continuously finding new, surprising, and spectacular solutions, despite the fact that in formal terms he generally confines himself to the use of basic geometric shapes such as the circle, the rectangle, and the square. That this never results in a standard box in the

Arata Isozaki, *Ochanomizu Building,* 1984–87

The gleaming blue *cube* of the new Ochanomizu building by Isozaki rears up in willful contrast to the historic complex of buildings that surround it in central Tokyo. Besides offices, the building contains a large public hall and a room for chamber music. The façade of the tall building, with its severely carved square windows framed in a lighter color, and the monumental *colonnade-like* openings on the top floor, emphasize the independence of the new building and also make a connection to the historical buildings, whose autonomy remains preserved.

classic Modernist style derives from Botta's sensitive combination of these basic geometric forms, as well as upon the deliberate contrast between open and closed wall surfaces. A further characteristic of Botta's buildings is the colorful use of materials in the façades (usually red or yellow *brick*) which, together with variations in the brickwork, produces highly original results.

His round buildings, extremely reminiscent of imagined ideal buildings, are an intense reflection of themes that have occupied traditional architectural theory since *Antiquity*. The concrete results of this intelligent yet sensual process of creation are convincing, for no façade of Botta's is ever boring, and the

element of monumentality is both powerful and yet of a human scale. His formal means are many, and yet he applies them sparingly. Botta avoids all excess, anything overladen in his façades thus concentrates the effect of the means deployed.

One of Botta's most delightful family houses is that in Vacallo (see page 97). The triangular building has a beautifully structured brick façade at the back, which completely shuts it off from its surroundings. On the side facing the valley, however, the building opens out arrestingly with two intersecting arches. In front of the double arch is a gently rounded terrace, which takes up the theme of the arch and extends it into the landscape around.

JAPAN

Architecture as meditation

In their buildings of the 1980s, Botta with his Tessin country houses, and Gregotti with his small residential block in Canareggio in Venice, interwove historical and contemporary aspects in a thoughtful way, and came upon architectural solutions of the highest quality.

The Japanese architect Tadao Ando follows a very similar path in his buildings. He too relates consciously to the principles of a traditional architecture, the Japanese house, which both in size and form had to satisfy completely different requirements from its European or American counterparts.

And yet Ando's buildings do not at first sight work at all like the product of a mind sympathetic to cultural and historical tradition, but on the contrary seem to many viewers to be alarmingly modern. The cause for this lies not least in Ando's favorite building material, *concrete,* which scarcely any other 20th-century architect, even Le Corbusier, knew how to use so perfectly.

With their strict proportions, their studied use of light to enhance the sense of space, and the downright ascetic use of materials, Ando's buildings seem to relate concretely to Mies van der Rohe's dictum "less is more." But by comparison with Ando's buildings, Mies van der Rohe's appear almost luxuriously appointed; their expensive squared stone, their costly polished marble, and fine steel look like deliberate ostentation. Ando uses no such materials, only a combination of concrete and glass bricks, and yet with these he is

Tadao Ando, *Kidosaki House*,
Tokyo, 1982–86

This triple-occupancy house is relatively
large by Japanese standards, and
combines private and communal livings
areas. It is isolated by concrete walls from
the surroundings streets, and access is via
a rounded wall which leads straight to the
heart of the two-story house: a 40-feet
(12-meter) cube. As usual with Ando, the
choice of forms and materials is extremely
restrained, and at first sight the
architecture looks severe. But if you go
along with it, you begin to feel how this
restraint ennobles the form and the
materials. Perception of the particular
attributes of the surfaces is sharpened.
As in an abstract picture, nuances of
color and effects of light unite to offer a
unique experience of space. The large-
paned window areas set up a relationship
with the exterior with its delicate
arrangement of plants, intensifying further
the spatial experience.

able to create spatial effects which – as in
the case of the glass brick Ishihara House
with its shimmering light – have an almost
mystical atmosphere.

The extremely limited range of concrete
finishes deployed by Ando and the rough
surfaces of the walls give a very particular
appearance to his buildings, as for instance
the Koshino House in Ashiya, Hyogo, which
was built in two stages: from 1979 to 1981,
and from 1983 to 1984. Here it becomes
evident that Ando's architecture is not only
rooted in traditional Japanese house building,
but also has been strongly influenced by
Modernist architecture. While the layout of
the site retains the quality of an abstract
composition, the design of the interior has an
almost classical, but clearly monumental tone.
In a world flooded with color and noise,
Ando's buildings have a calming effect. Once
you have become attuned to the language of
his materials, his well-proportioned façades,
and inner spaces, you will be rewarded with a
feeling of meditative repose.

Neither the amusing Deconstructivist
leaning walls of Frank O. Gehry, nor the small-
sectioned town houses of Aldo Rossi can
command such attention as Ando's buildings,
which at first seem so spare and reserved, but
in reality are so expressive.

Tadao Ando, *Glass Brick House
(Ishihara House)*, Tokyo, 1977–78

The building is divided off from the world
around it by thick concrete walls, and so
creates an autonomous realm for its
inhabitants. The glass brick walls create a
luminous spatial effect within, which
reacts to every change in the light.

Tadao Ando, *Koshino House*, Ashiya,
Hyogo, 1979–81 and 1983–84

The parallel rectangular shapes in bare
concrete – embedded in the landscape
of a national park – are a masterly
achievement in the handling of archaic
spatial form. Ando found an aesthetic
means of overcoming the rough materials
through the use of lighting slits and large
openings in the walls. The second
building, also facing away from the road
and erected two years after the first, is
partially below ground, so that the internal
spaces have to be lit from above.
The Koshino house – an exclusive private
home – brings together Modernist formal
language and the beauty of the Japanese
landscape. It stands on a spot that seems
to have been made for it where the
ground falls away to the rear, affording
unexpected views.

Architecture for the millennium

A forward glance

1990–2000

CONTEMPORARY BUT ETERNAL

Change as precondition

With the fall of the Berlin Wall in 1989, the old conflicts between the superpowers of this century seemed finally to have been buried. One almost had the impression that it would now be possible to relax and enjoy the unexpected peace for which we had longed for such a long time.

But if the polarization of the world into East and West is a thing of the past, the apparently boundless optimism and the happy sense of a new start of the early 1990s have died away. They have given way to a new uncertainty, fed by the fact that the old clichés of Good and Evil do not have the familiar meaning in the new world order that once they had.

Signficantly, the cruel civil war in the former Yugoslavia has shown just how fragile the scarcely constituted new world order really is. And in many places in the world, be it in Africa or southeast Asia, it is far from clear how the next few years will turn out. Finally, the number of war zones has not decreased since the end of the East-West conflict; they are simply arising in different places.

So the 1990s have presented a particular challenge, especially in view of the new millennium. Pressing social problems and numerous ethnic conflicts are demanding swift resolution, and the tried and tested economic and social structures of the economically advanced countries have to adapt to rapidly changing global circumstances. With their completely new and, for many people, surprising challenges, the 1990s are not the hoped-for decade of repose but a decade of change and new directions.

Buildings of today for the world of tomorrow

It is as hard for us to see what, in a hundred years, will be feted as the events of the 20th century, as it is for us to know, from our contemporary point of view, which will be the architectural works celebrated as masterpieces in years to come. Such an evaluation requires a critical distance which we perforce cannot have.

Without such a distance there is the danger that what appears to be the most important of today's trends in architecture will turn out to be a false trail, a short-lived fashion born of the spirit of the times, which in 50 years will seem scarcely worth a mention. No one knows which way our path is leading – and the same is true of architecture.

Despite the inevitable obstacles to determine which contemporary masterworks will last, it is possible to point to trends in operation now. Certain tendencies of the 1980s, such as the Deconstructivism of someone like Frank O. Gehry, or the Rationalism of an Aldo Rossi are continuing today, and developing in response to the changing demands of architecture.

1990: On 3 October Germany is reunified after a division lasting 45 years; the first elections since the war to cover the whole country are held.

1991: In the Gulf War, US-led troops secure the withdrawal of Iraqi occupying forces from Kuwait. Signing of the Maastricht Treaty regarding economic and monetary union and the common foreign and defense policy of Europe.

1992: UN Conference on Environment and Development – the Earth summit – held in Rio. UN aid flights and peace-keeping force alleviate conditions in Sarajevo. Number of HIV sufferers worldwide estimated at 10 million.

1993: Power struggle in Moscow; Yeltsin dissolves parliament. Peace accord between Israel and the PLO. Bill Clinton takes office as the 42nd president of the USA. The term "European Union" replaces "European Community" as

Maastricht Treaty takes effect. A human embryo is cloned for the first time; the experiment calls forth worldwide horror.

1994: Nelson Mandela elected the first black president of South Africa; end of the apartheid state. Hollywood takes on the German past in its own way: Stephen Spielberg's *Schindler's List* comes to the cinemas. Opening of the Eurotunnel under the English Channel.

1995: Jacques Chirac succeeds François Mitterrand, president of France for 14 years. Turkey continues to make war on the Kurds, harassing them beyond the borders of the country. "Multimedia" is the word of the year. Christo and Jeanne-Claude wrap the Reichstag building in Berlin.

1996: Refugees suffer terrible hardship in central Africa. After civil war in Rwanda and Burundi, conflict spreads to eastern Zaire. First parliamentary elections in Bosnia

under the strictest security precautions. The "mad cow disease" BSE leads to a ban on the export of beef and cattle from the UK.

1997: The UK returns Hong Kong to China. Civil war in Albania. Bloody end to siege of the Tupac Amaru rebels who had held hostages in the Japanese embassy in Lima, Peru. The New Labour leader Tony Blair becomes prime minister of Great Britain. NATO-Russia summit in Paris: ex-Warsaw Pact countries can now join NATO. The comet Hale-Bopp can be seen from the Earth with the naked eye. The fashion designer Gianni Versace is shot dead. Princess Diana and her companion

Young techno-fans at the "Love Parade" in Berlin in 1995

Dodi al Fayed are killed in a car accident in Paris. Mother Teresa dies at the age of 87. Earthquake damage in Italy, including partial destruction of celebrated frescos by Giotto and Cimabue in Assisi.

1998: President Suharto of Indonesia steps down after 30 years following strong demonstrations against him. "The Voice," Frank Sinatra, dies in Los Angeles. 10th Techno-Festival, "Love Parade" in Berlin.

Frank O. Gehry, *Office Building for the Nationale Nederlanden,* Prague, 1995

The two towers, one glass and one stone, which Gehry designed for a Dutch insurance company press together like a dancing couple. The twin cylinders earned the popular nickname of "Ginger and Fred" after Ginger Rogers and Fred Astaire, stars of the legendary Hollywood musicals – proving that Frank O. Gehry's buildings do awaken associations. This vivid image overpowers the third dimension of architecture: that of volume or space. Behind the façade with its waves of windows leaning in and out, are concealed perfectly normal, regular stories. Like Gehry's buildings in general, it reflects the trend towards virtual reality in the world at large, but does not, unlike Jean Nouvel's work, use its technologies or point out the problems that arise.

If one examines the basic questions relating to the future development of society, one will also find some answers about the future form of architecture. One lesson that has finally been learned from the history of architecture in the 19th and 20th centuries is that society and architecture affect each other. Any architecture that exists only for itself, which just aims to please, without taking on the social and cultural needs of its users, is less likely than ever to be financed, nor will it be able to win a place for itself in the long term.

ARCHITECTURE IN THE VIRTUAL AGE

The power of images

Residential buildings and office blocks, factories and museums: these will continue to be the most important tasks of architecture. But the pressure of rising costs on a world scale will not be without effect on what they will look like, and how they will come into being.

It is almost inevitable that cost-considerations will make rationalization increasingy important in architectural, as well as other, undertakings. Standardization and mass-reproduction – leading themes of 20th century architecture – continue to cover everything from the total plan to the single window. Only a few architects and clients will be able to construct buildings of quality under these restricting conditions. Even under the most

advantageous of circumstances, standardized "average" architecture will continue to leave a large mark on the appearance of our cities. The architectonic highlight, the outstanding design and the end product with quality in every detail, will almost inevitably step more and more into the background.

A decisive role in this rationalization is being played by the invention of the computer, without which our daily lives would be almost as unthinkable as having neither telephone nor car. Although the computer as architect is still science fiction, many areas of the architect's work have for a long time been carried out by computer-supported design programs, and the statics of a building project as well as the logistics of the building site are calculated with the help of the "computer colleague."

In large-scale projects, virtual tours of projected prototype buildings are replacing the tedious job of studying models and scale-drawings. In a matter of moments a computer can take viewers on a tour through courtyards and office buildings, across whole city areas that are still at the planning stage, through any number of interior rooms that have yet to be installed. In the shortest possible time the architecture of tomorrow grows before the eyes of the beholder, and seduces the interested layman by the power of the image.

High-tech architecture, which is the most appropriate translation into concrete reality of such a planning principle, and which has in

The building becomes immaterial.
Everything comprehensible disappears
behind polished high-grade steel and
other ungraspable materials. Four neon
tubes and a mirror dissolve the ceilings
into a "frozen sky." The expansive
construction of diagonal supports is lost
behind the iridescent shell of the double-
layered glass façade. Inside the Galeries
Lafayette, the German branch of the
French department store, a double glass
cone makes gravity seem to disappear, as
holograms and mirrors turn it into a
kaleidoscope. Glass is not used here as it
was in the glass palaces of bygone years,
as a transparent medium through which
to see the truth: it produces multiple
images of visitors to the store; a virtual
public is created.
But here begin the contradictions –
because the business that this building
serves has material interests. People's
perceptions go beyond what they can see.
The optical effects here, however, create a
blind spot for all their other senses.

fact been around since the 1970s in the buildings of Norman Foster or Richard Rogers, will
play a leading role in the next decades on the
global architectural stage. In spite of all the criticism that the worldwide reach of the Internet
has evoked, and all the fears it brings to the
surface, there is a tenacious fascination about
what is now already possible.

Poetry in glass

It was Joseph Paxton's Crystal Palace of 1851
(illustration page 7) which started the extraordinarily successful progress of glass in architectural history. From Bruno Taut's Glass House
(illustration page 19) to Mies van der Rohe's
Neue Berliner Nationalgalerie (illustration page
59), from the villa to the commercial building:
the versatility of the glass façade has covered
so many applications, and the material has yet
to lose its charm.

The French architect, Jean Nouvel, has
added a new, almost poetic facet to the already
rich contemporary repertoire of architecture in
glass. He first received international recognition
with his Institut du Monde Arabe (IMA) in
Paris (1981–87), is on the banks of the Seine,
and which is, according to Nouvel's own
estimation, an "absolutely modern building."

The IMA arose as one of the "grands
projets" initiated by President Mitterrand in
Paris in the 80s. Because of its colonial past,
especially in the 19th and 20th centuries,
France still has close links with Arab culture.

The IMA became a unique showplace for that
culture in Paris, with a museum, rooms for
special exhibitions, a library, documentation
center, lecture hall, and restaurant, adding to
the repertoire of modern museum-building in
the 1980s. The particular merit of Nouvel's
building is the way that it links traditional
Arab elements, as for instance a pillared hall
reminiscent of a mosque, with glassy *high-
tech architecture.*

The balanced stratification of glass elements
gives the building an exciting aesthetic tension
even from the outside. The sightlines that open
up again and again through the glassy transparency of the building are complicated by the
superimposition of intervening constructional
elements. Despite the elegance of its form and
materials, the general effect of the building,
with its interrupted and reflected light, is one
of rich variety.

The design of the southern façade of the
IMA is particularly attractive. Nouvel has taken
various geometric forms in common use in
Arabian architecture, and put them in a
modern sun-shield consisting of 27,000 lenses
that expand or contract according to the light.
This shield is installed in the glass façade and
serves not only as a mundane protection
against the sun, but opens up the possibility
of a fascinating play with light and shade in
the interior. The geometric grid shape of the
sun-shield has a further function, in that its
inflexible language of form bespeaks the

affiliation of the building to two cultures: Arab and European, which are synthesized within it.

Another example of Nouvel's expertise in dealing with the immaterial building material that is glass, is provided by the Galeries Lafayette in Berlin (1993–96), one of the few architecturally ambitious commercial buildings to have been erected in the 1990s on the Friedrichstrasse in the course of the rebuilding of central Berlin after reunification.

The core of the commercial building is the department store that gives it its name, the Berlin branch of the famous Parisian store Galeries Lafayette. It is a fact that in the consumerist culture of the West, the building of a department store is a particular challenge. What kind of attractions can be employed to tempt demanding customers? How can architecture rise to the challenge? One solution was given by SITE in the 1970s (illustration page 82): making buildings that turned a daily shop at the supermarket into a semi-dramatic experience.

Nouvel takes another route. He goes for big-city architecture, characterized by elegance and light, glass and transparency. The heart of the building consists of two glass cones whose bases meet at the ground floor, the one thus tapering upward, the other seeming to bore into the ground.

The impression created by this glass cone is overwhelming, a spectacular aesthetic coup, a new interpretation of the interior courtyard, which is such an important element in the architectural history of the department store. And of course, in a place dominated by glass, there is also the obligatory glass lift.

Even on the outside, Nouvel continues the conceit with the curving glass skin of the façade, which glides round the corner defying the cohorts of granite- and limestone-faced blocks all around it. Nouvel handles the roof zone in a playful manner, in that he deploys neither a pure *flat roof* nor a traditional tiled *pitched roof,* but develops his own particular architectural language by creating a roof whose sloping sides are made of glass.

High-tech expression

Engineers have always been among the innovative and driving forces of architecture. But whereas at the end of the 19th century people, when confronted with the Eiffel Tower and the first skyscrapers in Chicago, were still arguing as to whether the works of the engineers could be considered as belonging to "real" architecture, this argument has long been decided. Without both the functional and aesthetic contribution of the engineer, the history of 20th-century architecture would be inconceivable.

But engineering and modern art can join hands beyond the confines of building as such, as for instance in the constructions and sculptures of Santiago Calatrava, a Spaniard living in Switzerland, whose work is also to be seen in the Museum of Modern Art.

Jean Nouvel with Gilbert Lézenès and Pierre Soria, *Institut du Monde Arabe,* south façade (left) and stairwell (right), Paris, 1981–87

At first sight the south façade looks like an Arabian lattice-work screen, intricately pierced. In fact, it consists of thousands and thousands of motor-driven blinds, large and small. They vary the penetration of light into the building according to the strength of the sunlight, and unfold a play with light and shade with meditative power. The Institut du Monde Arabe becomes a viewing apparatus focused on Arab culture. The spiritual, symbolic world of the Orient is united with the rationally directed world of the West. High-tech elements, which were included in the 1970s for their own sake, are at last used here in the service of overall artistic goals.

Santiago Calatrava, *Pasarela de Uribitarte,* footbridge over the river Nerbio, Bilbao, 1993

Even the approach to Calatrava's footbridge signals an experience to come. The bridge takes off from two elegant, sweeping ramps. But the high point of the sculptural construction is the parabola from which it is suspended. Everything in this building is in tension, seems to be in latent movement – there is nothing stiff even about the bridge itself over the river: it is gently curved. Calatrava's language of forms, reminiscent of organic archetypes, emphasizes this sensual note still more. The architect has understood how to present the apparently everyday act of crossing from one shore to the other as an experience. The bold sickle shape of his bridges is in the tradition of the great Spanish constructors Antoni Gaudí and Eduardo Torroja y Miret, and also the Frenchman Gustave Eiffel (see page 8).

Curving, dynamic forms, whose expressivity is a distant reminder of Eero Saarinen's TWA Terminal in New York (illustration page 73), are a running theme of Calatrava's work. Filigree concrete supports like ribs span his spaces, giving them an extremely lively character that is full of movement, as for instance in his exhibition building on the Spanish island of Tenerife, one of the Canary Islands (1992– 95).

Analogies with living things almost force themselves upon you when you see Calatrava's expressive architecture: the backbone of a fish with the bones all slanting away at an angle from it, or the arched comb on the back of a prehistoric animal. A notable example of this is the Alameda bus station in Valencia that Calatrava built between 1991 and 1995, which is on several levels, dominated by a towering arch held up by filigree supports. The same motif recurs in much of the detailed working-out of his designs for bridges.

An arrow into the future

Dynamism – that is the first impression given by the Vitra fire-station realized at Weil am Rhein in 1993 by the London-based Iraqi architect Zaha Hadid. It was a choice site. Here the grandfather of *Deconstructivism,* Frank O. Gehry had built the Vitra Design Museum, and woven an innovative element into European architecture. And here on the upper Rhine, the British-born Nicolas Grimshaw had also been active, designing the Vitra furniture factory.

Hadid's building plunges like an arrow into the landscape. The jutting concrete canopy of the complex rests on a little forest of astonishingly thin, straight, and sloping pillars, with a dramatic, expressive gesture that lends the building, for all its mundane purpose, the atmosphere of a monument. Slanted walls, walls that cut across each other, and volumes stacked on top of each other give the building expressive strength of an original and restless kind. From a bird's eye view, the building looks like a paper airplane, elegant and aerodynamic

Zaha Hadid, *Vitra Fire Station,* Weil am Rhein, 1993

Leaning blades of bare concrete cut across each other. A gigantic sheet of glass turns the fire-station into a display cabinet. The dramatically pointed slab of concrete which makes up the front canopy seems to float. The leaning steel rods which support it defy the logic of construction.
Now working in England, the Iraqi *deconstructivist* Zaha Hadid has been strongly influenced by Russian *Constructivism.* There could scarcely be a better expression of the essence of the project. Tension is the daily experience of the fire service, and tension is the keynote of this building, housing the fire fighting department of a furniture factory. The eccentricity of this sculptural building has something monumental about it, and its functionality appears incidental. And indeed the fire station has lost its original function; it has become a sculptural museum piece itself in the noted architecture park in Weil am Rhein.

at once, but with its markedly sloping walls it also invokes memories of a ship. Open and closed parts alternate and adjust themselves to a traditional canon of forms. This is architecture driven by an immense outlay of constructive and creative power whose individuality is such that, like the work of Santiago Calatrava, the whole building is consciously raised to the level of a sculpture. The building is as bewildering in its formal structure of interlocking planes, as it is heterogeneous in its deployment of materials, from aluminum and smooth concrete through to the sealed sheet of glass and the strip windows.

The building served as a pillar-less concrete shed for the fire engines of the Vitra furniture factory, but it also housed canteen and sanitary areas and a fitness room. Today it has lost its original function and is an important part of the architecture park at Weil am Rhein, where it serves as an exhibition area for the Vitra collection of chairs, and can also be used for special events.

Hadid's fire station was given much praise, and euphoric comparisons were drawn with the architectural visions of the Russian *Constructivists* of the 1920s, and the spatial effects of Mies van der Rohe's Barcelona pavilion. One should remain level-headed in the face of such excitement. Hadid did produce a strongly expressive fire station, which takes on the avant-garde with its quotations and contemporary forms of expression. Whether her building is in fact more than a milestone of *Deconstructivism*, a modish treasure in an unexpected part of the city, remains to be seen.

THE AESTHETICS OF SIMPLICITY

Reduction instead of expression

The contrast could not be greater between the neo-Expressionist/Deconstructivist buildings and projects of Zaha Hadid or Frank O. Gehry, which for all their artistic intensity are sometimes a little overwrought, and the work of the two Basel architects Jacques Herzog and Pierre de Meuron, who attracted worldwide attention when they were contracted to construct the new Tate Gallery in the old Bankside power station in London. The two architects were once the pupils of the rationalist Aldo Rossi, but their work is also clearly different from his.

Jacques Herzog and Pierre de Meuron, *Stone House,* Tavole, Liguria, 1988

"Less is more" was the opinion of Mies van der Rohe as early as the 1920s. Today, the architects favoring a "new simplicity" have come to see in it the riches of asceticism. Like Mies, the Swiss architects Jacques Herzog and Pierre de Meuron work with clear square shapes and simple spatial geometry. But their materials are more various and used with a greater variety and with greater impact on the senses; they make a point of them. Building materials become raw materials. In the Goetz Collection building (illustrated below) there is a combination of bare concrete, unworked plywood, and frosted glass. In the Tavole house (left) dry stone walls made of local chalk blocks that look like slate are used to fill the load-bearing modern concrete skeleton. The house, which stands alone in a hilly landscape with crumbling stone terraces for olive trees and vines, bespeaks radical abstraction and a new seriousness in architecture.

As early as the Stone House, which they built in Tavole in Liguria between 1982 and 1988, the two had evolved their simple but aesthetic basic concept. The house is a plain *rectilinear* block, with a *pergola*-like structure in front of it, constructed of a clearly visible concrete frame, with an *infill* of dry-stone walls. The constructional simplicity of the building is accompanied by an enormous aesthetic charm, which arises from a synthesis of materials having such different properties. The building is given its liveliness by the contrasting visual effect of the very different surface structures. In addition to this, the two

Jacques Herzog and Pierre de Meuron, *Goetz Collection,* Munich-Oberföhring, 1993

The telescoped and intersecting volumes of Coenen's Architektuurinstitut in Rotterdam, which includes other, smaller architectural institutions, offer an example of contemporary architecture that is full of visual tension and plays consciously with the various stylistic resources of 20th-century Modernism. The main building of the institute rises up in front of a long archive building, which screens off the area in an extended arc. It is oversailed by a monumental *pergola*-like construction, resting on menacingly pointed steel pillars. Within this dynamic construction, which is as functionless as it is impressive, the almost fully glazed rectilinear exhibition area is contained. By evening light in particular, this area appears to turn inside out, reflected in the surrounding water.

types of material stand for different periods of architectural history – concrete is the load-bearing material of Modernism, whereas the unworked stones of the dry-stone walls represent a tradition that extends back hundreds of years.

This seriousness in the use of form and materials, directed towards the specific function of the building in its location, is a leitmotif of the work of Herzog and de Meuron. In a quite different form, but with related aesthetic effect, we find this leitmotif again in the building constructed in 1993 to house the Kunstsammlung Goetz (Goetz Art Collection) in Munich-Oberfohring.

Once again the body of the building is a strict, diagonally placed *rectilinear block.* As in the Stone House in Tavole, the materials surprise: concrete, wood, and frosted glass. The color effect produced is unique, very delicate, and reserved, which gives the building a kind of airiness close to gaiety, despite its introverted appearance.

Above the fully glazed ground floor, which houses both a library and a hall, and is distinguished by the slightly greenish shimmer that it derives from the frosted glass, there are the three exhibition rooms themselves. They consist of a double frame of pinewood that is filled with beechwood panels. Even in the use of these woods you can see the architects' delicate sense of differentiation. The lightness of the color effects produced by the smooth, almost whitish beechwood elements are contrasted with the somewhat darker frames

in pinewood, which gave a more structured and raw effect through the presence of knots. This rectangular wooden construction is sandwiched between two ribbons of frosted glass. They serve to light the exhibition rooms inside, while completing the harmonious symmetry of the building on the outside.

In this Munich Exhibition Building Herzog and de Meuron achieved the task of creating a very reserved style of architecture which seems to subordinate itself to the artworks being exhibited, while remaining an extremely artistic piece of architecture – an effect created with the most economic means, by the surprising and extraordinarily attractive use of materials.

The extension and rebuilding work done on the Swiss Unfallversicherungsanstalt (accident insurance office) in Basel, by Herzog and de Meuron in 1995, is similar in terms of basic structure, and in the diagonal placement of the building. Especially noteworthy in this project is the remarkable way in which they have dealt with the old part of the building; it was simply packed into a glazed façade that was constructed out of variously treated glass panels. In this way the old building continues to be visible from the exterior, and remains largely unaltered.

However, this procedure does additionally have the effect of establishing a deliberately disturbing new layer over the building by the use of the various types of glass, which are of varying degrees of transparency, and have only a vague relationship to the articulation of the

Alvaro Siza, *Portuguese Pavilion for Expo '98*, Lisbon, 1994–98

Built on the quay of the former harbor basin at the mouth of the Tagus, this exhibition building embodies the new self-confidence of modern Portugal. It is composed of two parts: the exhibition building itself, which opens on to the water with a two-storied arcade, and the "Praça Ceremonial," a broad square shaded by a light concrete canopy, where guests of state can be welcomed. The abutments of this canopy, faced in limestone outside and tiled with red and green "azulejos" inside, have a Roman massiveness in stark contrast to the elegance of the free hanging canopy. On the eastern side of the pavilion is a garden with old olive trees and whitewashed walls, reflecting the beauty of the landscape of southern Portugal. It was intended that after Expo '98, the building would be extended to become the seat of the council of ministers.

old façade lying behind them. Reflections and insights, distortions in the structured panes, and the shadows cast by the sun-blinds and by the supporting framework result in a very pleasing intellectual game between the historic and contemporary elements of the building, molding them into a new whole.

Similarly, the typical seriousness of Herzog and de Meuron is also to be found in the rebuilding and extension that they carried out for the Swiss accident insurance institution. Notably, it stands out in a sharp contrast to the playfully ironic expressivity of many of their contemporaries.

Practical but without severity

The formal agitation of many a Deconstructivist architectural fantasy is as far from the work of the Portuguese architect Alvaro Siza as it is from that of Herzog and de Meuron. That does not mean that he, or they, cannot produce exciting buildings! The best example of Siza's ability to produce modern architecture that is both thought-provoking and exciting is the row of white *rectilinear* structures, which he erected on a sloping location in the west of his hometown of Porto, and which together constitute the faculty of architecture. Built between 1986 and 1995, the buildings stand in a park surrounded by greenery, in relative isolation and repose.

The four rectilinear volumes, which are clearly indebted to the classic Modernist tradition, look very much alike at first sight, but turn out on closer inspection, as with the service area lying behind them, to be very different from each other.

In spite of the use of standard building parts, the variety of form is astonishing. Tall rectangular windows and horizontal window strips give the façades "faces," which are additionally accented by inset and projecting areas, half-roofs set back into the building to provide sun protection, and roofs which project out over terraces. Galleries and large glazed zones in the campus-like area between the buildings give the faculty – which contrasts strongly with its rather closed exterior aspect – an open and airy character.

The students of the architecture faculty in Porto are thus given a rich supply of possible forms for architecture just by looking at the buildings of their university. There is a danger with such a variety of architectural languages that a lack of coherence will ensue, but a master such as Alvaro Siza knows how to avoid this. The individual parts of his scheme fit together harmoniously, and form a loose, but organically coherent whole, which is beautiful, but still offers space for all the necessary institutions, from the workshops to the lecture hall, the exhibition room, the offices, and the obligatory cafeteria.

The functionalism of Siza's architecture does not result in monotony. In fact, its apparent severity turns out, on close consideration, to be a clarity of form and content, which has given Siza his deserved position as one of the most important architects of contemporary times.

Dani Karavan, *Memorial to Walter Benjamin,* Port-Bou (Spain), 1994

On 26 September 1940, the philosopher and writer Walter Benjamin put an end to his flight from the Nazi regime, and to his life, at Port-Bou. In memory of this event, the Israeli artist Dani Karavan designed a monument drawing on some of the conventions used in land art.
In accordance with the course of Benjamin's life and the title of one of his main works (*Passagen*), the work is composed of three paths, each signifying a different point. The third and last of the paths consists of a sloping tunnel blasted out of the rock, whose walls are clad in rusting steel. It is ended abruptly by a sheet of glass, beyond which roars the sea. The only way out is the hopeless abyss.
Rich in connotations, extremely economic in its means, the monument at Port-Bou could be a pointer to the development of architecture in the next millennium.

SCULPTURE AND ARCHITECTURE

The new aesthetic of history

One of the most controversial artists of the late 1980s and 1990s is Daniel Libeskind (Berlin, Los Angeles). It is surprising that his work excites so much passionate argument, since he can look back only on a small corpus of finished work.

His radical language of form and the great intellectual intensity of his engagement with the historical and political context of his buildings attract many people, but it is possible that they also frighten off many others, including potential clients.

One of the few buildings so far realized by Libeskind, who has been the winner of several architectural competitions, chiefly in Germany, is the Jewish Museum – or rather the Jewish department of the Berlin Museum – which was opened in January 1999. Its only relationship to the well-known museum buildings of the 1980s and 1990s is that it is indeed a museum. It does not wallow joyfully in quotations as does the *post-modern* Staatsgalerie in Stuttgart by James Stirling and Michael Wilford (illustration page 96), nor has it the noble elegance of Jean Nouvel's Institut du Monde Arabe in Paris (illustration page 103).

Libeskind's museum is intended to present the history of Jewish life in Berlin. Libeskind has himself characterized the building as a metaphorical symbol, as a museum built around a void, a void which signifies the loss of Jewish lives in the Holocaust.

Like Zaha Hadid's Vitra fire station in Weil am Rhein, the Jewish Museum, which is linked underground to the old *baroque* museum building, reminds one of an arrow or a zigzagging streak of lightening. This has a deeper meaning with Libeskind, in that you can see it as a deconstructed Star of David, relating to the places that were once the centers of Jewish life in Berlin.

The goal which Daniel Libeskind is trying to reach is high, as is the intellectual construct from which he is working. His theme is a difficult and unwieldy one, and his architecture is accordingly gauche, going forward and back, with empty corners and high concrete walls, which deliberately exclude visitors and people who come to look, and takes on the character of a complicated architectonic sculpture.

In spite of, or rather because of, this complexity, it may be supposed that Daniel Libeskind's Jewish Museum – radical, uniquely and intensively involved with its historic location – will in future count as one of the most important museum buildings, not only of the 1990s, but of the century.

Reactions – physically enshrined memory

If the 1980s, with their great museum complexes, look in retrospect like an uproarious decade of celebration culture, the 1990s can be most properly described as a decade of more reflective memorial culture.

This involvement with history and the memory of both people and events has become one of the central themes of the decade, with monuments, exhibitions, and memorials. The reasons for this are – as always – multifarious. Without doubt, the approaching end of three time-spans – the decade, the century, and the millennium – is playing an important role in the process of reflection – on what has been as well as on what is yet to come. But also the shadows of significant anniversaries, such as the fiftieth anniversary of the end of the Second World War, have left their mark.

It is certainly not by chance that much recent architecture can also be interpreted as monumental sculpture. This is especially true of the work of Daniel Libeskind, whose complex language of forms links his works to the history of the location for which they were planned, in a deeply thought-out way. But in the same way as architecture has entered into a dialogue with sculpture, numerous contemporary sculptures reveal clear links with architecture. In many cases it seems as though the barrier between architecture and sculpture is on the point of breaking down.

One of the most impressive and perhaps thought-provoking memorials to express its message by architectonic means is the "Commemorative Passages" for Walter Benjamin, created by the Israeli artist Dani Karavan in 1994 on the border between France and Spain at the little Spanish coastal town of Port-Bou.

The Jewish philosopher and writer Walter Benjamin, who was a native of Berlin, came here in 1940 while fleeing from the Nazi reign of terror, and in deepest despair took his own life. Dani Karavan has depicted this with great sensitivity and visual skill in the architecture of his memorial. Between two rusty red, steel walls each 77 feet (2.35 meters) high, a very narrow stairway consisting of 87 steps, also made of steel, leads down a slope from the burial ground of the sleepy little frontier port. The top steps are roofed over, those below are open to the sky. The stairs lead nowhere. At the bottom there is nothing but the pounding sea, an abyss of hopelessness that Benjamin himself may have felt when he realized his flight was leading nowhere.

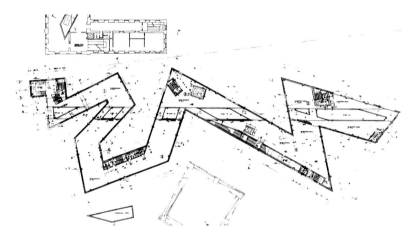

The engagement with history, especially the Nazi regime that had in effect flouted all moral law between 1933 and 1945, is also one of the main preoccupations of a German artist living in Paris, Jochen Gerz. In his works, which demand the participation of the viewer even more than Karavan's memorial, he also continually draws upon traditional architectonic means.

One of his most important projects is the 1993 memorial on the Schlossplatz in Saarbrücken, where the names of all the Jewish cemeteries existing in Germany before the Second World War are engraved on the underside of 2,146 paving stones. Another monument, called *Die Bremer Befragung* (the Bremen questionnaire), inaugurated in 1995, sticks out like a viewing platform from a bridge over the river Weser. An engraved plaque challenges the passers-by to imagine what their own memorial and its theme would be. His involvement with architectonic

Daniel Libeskind, *Jewish Museum,* Berlin, 1989–98

The Jewish Museum is the first design that Libeskind, the most intellectual of the *Deconstructivists* has been able to build. Its outline represents a part of the Star of David. Through this lifeline, rich in detours, runs a straight band of emptiness, signifying the loss of Jewish culture through the Holocaust. Every one of the windows, cut with the precision of a paper pattern into the zinc façade, makes a mental connection to the real places where this life was once lived.
Here although Daniel Libeskind's designs consist only of lines, they produce impressive architecture. And even though the complex academic references will be impenetrable to the uninitiated visitor, the forceful impact of the architecture on the senses delivers the message of the building.

ARCHITECTURE IN THE 21ST CENTURY

Handling resources responsibly

Architecture, if it aims to be good architecture, has been experimental since Antiquity. Each experiment breaks new ground, and seeks an answer to problems relevant to its day. Paxton's Crystal Palace made of glass, Eiffel's tower constructed out of iron, and François Hennebique's early reinforced concrete constructions: all were architectural experiments whose consequences reverberated into the 20th century.

One of the most important problems facing humanity at the end of the 20th century is the fact that the ecological dimensions of our world have shifted dramatically. Architecture must discover viable solutions for the new demands that this poses. For the way in which we handle natural resources will dictate our future. And this does not only mean taking a responsible attitude to non-renewable fuels, the use of which is causing ever greater pollution and environmental destruction. It is becoming ever more clear that things we take for granted such as drinking water, which we in the northern countries think we have more than enough of, have to be handled sparingly and responsibly, and be treated as what they are: a precious necessity for life.

The answers that architecture has brought to the numerous ecological demands and challenges are many and various. They begin with down to earth measures such as putting in insulation walls which – unlike ordinary wood and stone walls – retain large amounts of energy for use in the house which would otherwise get lost in the air outside. Thus the expenditure of heat is lessened, which, apart from protecting natural resources, also brings a financial saving to the owner or the tenant, who needs to spend less on oil or other fuel.

Arranging the ground plan of the house to suit the natural disposition of light and sun is another measure that can significantly reduce the consumption of energy. Solar radiation in particular can be utilized: solar panels collect the radiation which is used for heating the house and the water. Sunlight can also be used to generate electricity via photovoltaic cells, and thus will take over a considerable part of the provision of light in a house.

Nicolas Grimshaw, *Editorial offices and printing works of the Western Morning News*, Plymouth, 1993

High-tech designs, which at first were chiefly a way of displaying innovative construction details, today fulfill all the demands of architecture – a development to which Nicolas Grimshaw has been a major contributor. In his building for the *Western Morning News*, the editorial offices and the printing works are accommodated under the same roof, providing optimal working conditions. The building has the internal and external transparency to be expected from a media enterprise. Located on a hill in Plymouth, the building is a landmark with its distinctive shape like the prow of a ship, and its tusk-like steel supports holding up the all-glass façade. It creates a connection with the history of this maritime city while also symbolizing its economic rebirth as a center of service industries.

form is at its most concrete in the monument against fascism that he realized with his wife, Esther Shalev-Gerz, in Hamburg (1986–93). This consists of a 40-feet (12-meter) high square post that is covered in lead, which was gradually sunk into the ground. The people who passed by it over the years were invited to scratch their opinion of fascism onto the soft surface of the lead before the pillar was entirely sunk into the ground, and their inscriptions preserved there.

Just as Libeskind evokes an engagement with history in his architecture through its appeal to the senses, Karavan and Gerz challenge spectators of their architectonic sculptures to engage with their theme. Only by being drawn into the work can spectators be able to achieve an understanding of it. Contemporary artists and sculptors have taken up a position of intense involvement with historical events and people, which points the way to a future direction for both of these art forms.

Alessandro Mendini, *Museum*, Groningen (Netherlands), 1995

Situated on a canal basin, and accessible only via a footbridge, the *Deconstructivist* museum island of Groningen bristles with shrill, bright buildings leaning this way and that in a hubbub of different materials and forms. Looking at first sight more like an overgrown piece of furniture than a building, the museum houses art of all periods collected in Groningen. The list of artists who worked on this ambitious project reads like a "Who's Who" of Deconstructivism, including Mendini from Italy, Philippe Starck from France, and the Austrian COOP Himmelblau architectural practice. So it is not surprising that in among all the diagonals and curves in steel, artificial stone, wood, and concrete, right-angles are in short supply. The Gröningen Museum's most significant counterpart is the Guggenheim-Museum in Bilbao (opened 1998) by Frank O. Gehry.

Numerous experimental buildings have sprung up of late, trumpeting their purpose with names such as eco-house, or low-energy or energy-saving house, which have a tendency to confuse rather than enlighten the majority of visitors. But all the ecological requirements that such a house has to fulfill – often at enormous expense for those who commission it – need not be detrimental to its architectural impact. This is perfectly demonstrated by the house in Breisach (illustration page 94) created by Thomas Spiegelhalter of Freiburg, who specializes in sculptural architecture. His *Deconstructivist* and technical language of forms is coupled in an exemplary manner with ecological functions.

The porch is made up of solar panels that provide the hot-water supply, and an L-shaped wind and sun shield gives the building formal dynamism while also housing the photo-voltaic module of the house. The barrels on the roof, which emphasize the pronounced technicity of the building's appearance, serve as rainwater collectors.

The building embodies a unique synthesis of up-to-the-minute patterns of use, and an absolutely contemporary language of form that points the way into the new millennium. The architect's responsibility for the future of the environment cannot be overestimated. But this responsibility is also a challenge which will lead to new, exciting architectonic answers in the 21st century.

Richard Meier, *John Paul Getty Center*, Los Angeles, 1992–97

A "new acropolis" was what the John Paul Getty Foundation asked the New York architect Richard Meier to build, in order to display its famous collections of Greek and Roman antiquities, European painting, drawing, and sculpture from the Renaissance, baroque, and classical periods, as well as applied art and photography. The Getty Center consists of six main buildings clearly separate from each other. Nonetheless they can be appreciated as a cohesive complex. Because of the restrained nature of the architecture there is no conflict between the works of art being exhibited and the building. Meier, who was making a name for himself throughout the world for his typical white-tiled façades turned for this, his biggest project to date, to Italian travertine, which glows pinkish in the California sun. In order to achieve a unified color for the façades, all the stone had to be cut from the same quarry.

Architecture in the 21st century

The first decade

A NEW MILLENNIUM

For a lot of people, the beginning of the new millennium was an incisive event, a moment that raised expectations and hopes. But this special date was also marked by fears and anxieties: What would the new age bring?

Accompanied by a worldwide countdown, the third millennium after the birth of Christ began. Notwithstanding the millennium-hype, the development of the world seemed predetermined, thanks to the modern communication technology – above all, the Internet – that increasingly diminishes the contrast between the cultures. The Canadian media scientist Marshall McLuhan had said way back in the 1960s that the world would become a "global village". The sceptics pointed to the drawbacks of these developments. After all, the bloody war in former Yugoslavia in the 1990s showed what dramatic consequences these unsolved ethnic and religious conflicts could have.

Then came 11 September 2001. In an attack on the Twin Towers of the World Trade Center (WTC), constructed in 1973 by Minuro Yamasaki, terrorists killed over 2,000 people. Millions of spectators all over the world watched the attack on one of the symbols of the Western world on their TV screens. Even today, the shock sits deep because the attack exposed the vulnerability of the free world drastically. The terrorists did not hit just any building; they hit both the 1361-feet (415-meters) high towers of WTC, the monument which defined the skyline of New York. Besides its actual function as an office building, WTC was an icon that had a second existence as a two-dimensional symbol of architecture known worldwide. It adorned countless postcards and posters, and also formed the background for many movies from the Hollywood "dream factory".

CONSTRUCTED ICONS

The term icon comes from the Greek word for picture. According to the tradition of the eastern church, it still signifies precious cult pictures, on which the figures of the Holy are represented against a gold-plated background. In architecture, the constructed icons are not the invention of modernity; with the Tower of Babel, whose story is narrated in the Old Testament, they have existed since the beginning of all constructions. The number of these architecture icons has increased since the end of the 1990s. An inspiration for this was the Guggenheim Museum, which was constructed by Frank O. Gehry in 1997 in the North Spanish city of Bilbao. Its silver shimmering components, which seem to have been inspired by Cubism, give the house its distinctive appearance. Since the sensational success of the museum, the "Bilbao effect" is observed worldwide. Whether glassy cool or concrete gray,

Herzog & de Meuron, *National Stadium,* Peking, 2003–2007

The stadium for the Olympic Games 2008, designed by Basel star architects Herzog & de Meuron, appears like a gigantic bird nest. For the expressive interwoven construction of the stadium façade, Herzog & de Meuron used approximately 40,000 tons of heavy prefabricated steel elements. The powerful steel beams overlap in all directions. The inside of the 230-feet (70-meters) high sports complex in turn consists of a sophisticated concrete construction that has a seating capacity of up to 91,000 spectators. After the Alliance Arena in Munich with its colorfully illuminated plastic cover, Herzog & de Meuron have come up with their third sports stadium, a building with an expressive picture effect. This has helped them to reinforce their position as one of the most innovative architecture offices worldwide.

organically swung or acute-angled, thanks
to Gehry's Museum, the "icon-type" is
advancing fast in architecture. With its
media- and market-focused approach and
his modeled plastic methods of building, the
American star architect gave an impulse that
continues like a domino effect. It proved that
symbolically significant architecture can be
used successfully as a marketing instrument

for business and cities. And in addition to
large metropolises, the "Bilbao effect" also
finds its way to smaller provincial cities. For
example, the city of Cottbus in Brandenburg
has a spectacular new library built by Swiss
architects Jacques Herzog und Pierre de
Meuron. The star architects are now working
on the new Olympic stadium in the
explosively growing Chinese capital Beijing.
The underlying aim is to give globally
competitive cities special attractiveness by
means of spectacular architecture – thus
securing for them an advantage in
comparison to other places in the cut-throat
competition for money from investors and
tourists. Enormous sums of money and an
improved image are usually at stake. The
more the constructed icons emerge
worldwide, the greater is the danger of
confusion. Is this house located in Liverpool,
Vienna, Tokyo or Dubai? Is this the art gallery
in Graz, Manchester or Seoul? Is the
architect Norman Foster, Frank O. Gehry or
Rem Koolhaas?

Constructed variety

The first decade of the new millennium is
marked by a large variety of architectural styles.
The computer-assisted designs make possible
the implementation of bold constructions of a
Zaha Hadid or a Frank O. Gehry, which a few
years ago existed only in the imagination of
the architects – or at best on paper. Besides
their sculptural individuality, architects search
for an individual, specific style that can be
expressed through new materials or a
remarkable layout or basic solution. This
applies especially to publicly accessible
buildings like museums or churches. At the

David Chipperfield Architects, *Ernsting Service Center,* Headquarters, Coesfeld-Lette, 1998–2001

The Service Center, that was constructed by the British architect David Chipperfield for the firm Ernstings Family, surprisingly connects monumentality and effortlessness. The informally organized construction is located at the edge of the land belonging to the cathedral of Coesfeld and is subdivided into three larger sections that are set around a row of open courtyards. With the harmonization of this green garden courtyard with Chipperfield's double-story cube of concrete components, a dramatic ensemble grows, which supplements the presentation of a business zone on a new, high-quality facet. This is proven by the high open-plan offices with its wide glass fronts that create a comfortable work atmosphere.

John Pawson, *Our Monastery Lady,* Novy Dvur, Czech Republic, 1999–2004

With his reduced constructions, John Pawson worked hard to be called the master of minimalism. A coronation of his previous work may be the Cistercian convent in the bohemian Novy Dvur with which he supplemented the baroque construction for the monks. Without superfluous details, he enchanted church and cloister by his light effect. Thus Pawson's architecture with his quiet areas and selected building materials proves to be a modern translation of the principles of simplicity, utility and frugality formulated by Bernhard of Clairvaux in the 12th century for the construction of Cistercian convents.

same time, the solutions can be different for the same construction job. The Italian master Renzo Piano created an architectural wave for the Paul-Klee-center, opened in 2005 in Bern, that is included in the landscape. On the other hand, Meinrad Morger and Heinrich Degelo constructed an equally fine and austere impressive building in the black cube of the art museum in Vaduz, Liechtenstein. In Munich, the Maxvorstadt is being connected with the round-designed old town by means of the modern Pinakothek, a building in which Stephan Braunfels concentrated entirely on geometric basic forms. On the other hand, in sacred architecture, the American architect Richard Meier welcomed the new millennium

with his Chiesa del Giubileo in Rome, whose white withes are layered next to each other in such a manner that the spectator gets the impression that the church is a white flower, whose petals are about to open.

CONCENTRATION

Contrary to such constructive and formal splendor, several architects in Europe and Japan feel obligated to an austere, pure architecture. They deliberately concentrate on the basic principles of the building, on the clearly perceived distribution of supports and loads. The frequent result is an unagitated architecture that remains obligated to the tradition of Rationalism of the 20th century. These buildings are so unspectacular at first sight that it is possible to bring order into the constructed environment. With their quiet arrangement, they create an antithesis to the variety of optical and acoustic impressions that thrill us daily in the cities – the harsh advertising messages that crave our attention. With the best of these constructed buildings emerges an architectural minimalism that gets by with few well-balanced means. Yet the concentration on high-value materials and the limitation to clear stereometric forms do not necessarily lead to "poor" or boring architecture. The designs by the British architects, David Chipperfield or John Pawson, thus prove that the formal concentration can go along with an aesthetic opulence which communicates calmness and sublimity. It manages to create functional buildings in which the perception of the spectator is sharpened on architectural details and the significance of spaces. Thus their buildings achieve an astonishingly sensuous effect, behind which exists a mindset that leads back to the roots of the modern architecture of the 20th century. At that time, many architects turned away deliberately from the architectural styles that were identified by the typically exuberant decoration variety of the late 19th century. Till today, this mindset of architectural concentration and silence has not lost its glory.

POWER OF THE REGIONS

Whether in Dubai, New York or Berlin, the range of goods in the big shopping malls is similar everywhere in the world. Whether polo shirts or cars, computers or jewelry, everyone can buy the products of the same company globally. Meanwhile, Russia, China, India and parts of Southeast Asia are flourishing regions that seek to balance the distance to the large industrial nations with their rapid economic growth.

Yet globalization has left its mark not only on the metropolitan centers and megacities. The money from hedge funds and international groups is spreading in a world that knows no capital boundaries. Thus in many places, the change is not only in the economic structures but also within the culture and environment. This development reaches even the remotest mountain villages. To be sure, architects such as Rem Koolhaas construct attractive "flagship stores" for the manufacturers of luxury articles. Though globalization contributes to an attractive product range, it also means the unification and interchangeability of cities and regions. The distinctiveness of a place and its culture is threatened and, along with it, its traditions and architectural structures that have evolved over centuries.

In some regions, architects thus react to the uniformity of the globalized world. They intensively deal with the local and regional

traditions, using traditional designs and domestic materials which are incorporated in their new buildings. The result is an independent architecture with regional roots that refrains imitating older buildings and styles. While in the 1980s, the Swiss Ticino was the center of this development, the focal point shifted in the last decade of the 20th century. Architecture offices such as that of Dietmar Eberle and Carlo Baumschlager or of Helmut Dietrich and Much Untertrifaller are, in the meantime, in search for a regional architecture – Vorarlberg in Austria is one of the important forerunners. Thus Baumschlager & Eberle frequently use renewable raw material wood that not only facilitates a comfortable atmosphere but also has belonged to the preferred building materials in the Alps since time immemorial. It is used both for panel wall constructions and traditional parlors of old houses. In the form of wood products, Baumschlager & Eberle have also used this material in the façades of their constructions and rediscovered it for a modern quality and regionally rooted architecture. At the same time, a demanding wood architecture also means an increase in craftsmanship, where the local craft businesses can maintain the old traditions and thus have larger economic success. A comparable development, as in

Wiel Arets Architect & Associates,
University Library, Utrecht, 1998–2004

In spite of the advance of the electronic media, it is libraries that belong to the exceptional building projects since the beginning of the 21st century. With the university library in Utrecht, Wiel Arets formulated a minimalist modern approach for this traditional construction job with a very powerful effect. The glass façade cover was imprinted with reed, a basic idea that is repeated on the concrete surfaces in the interior of the eight-story building. Otherwise, the library with its smooth red bars fits into the occasionally abrasive architectural language, which has a thoroughly sensuous note and convinces through its tension-laden space concept.

Markus Scherer and Walter Angonese with Klaus Hellweger, *Castle Tyrol,* Meran, 2000–2003

In the case of Castel Tyrol, the challenge for the architects lay in the building substance of a stone castle complex, which had evolved over a period of more than 1,000 years. Thus the base of the reconstruction work was a detailed exploration of the ground. Notwithstanding the restraint in the form of historic building substance from different epochs and their expressive designs of wood, steel and concrete, Markus Scherer and Walter Angonese succeeded with Klaus Hellweger in creating a dramatic dialogue between the old house and its utilization as a modern state museum. Thus Castle Tyrol can be preserved as an exceptional record of the region for future generations.

Francisco and Manuel Aires Mateus, *House in Alentejo,* Alentejo, Portugal, 2000

For Francisco and Manuel Aires Mateus, focusing on a place forms a decisive point of origin in the development of their constructions. This also applies to the house in the region of Alentejo in the south of Portugal. The Aires Mateus brothers have materialized a simple, dazzling white cube, embedded in a soft, swaying landscape with pine and oil trees. The exterior of the house hardly prepares you for the complex space arrangement in the interior. The view of the landscape facilitates an intensive correlation between architecture and environment..

Vorarlberg, is to be observed in the last few years in the North Italian region of South Tyrol, in the Swiss canton Grisons, also in southern Germany where the buildings by Peter and Christoph Brückner are concerned with the regional structures and translate into a consistently modern and, at the same time, regionally anchored architecture. Their interaction with the place, with its qualities and its possibilities, exceeds pure architecture. As the architects are concerned with the people located there, their habits and requirements, they make an important contribution to strengthening the respective region in the global competition which, in addition, contributes to preserving their independence and distinctiveness. This also implies that the architects have to deal with the constructed heritage, and understand and maintain the architectural monuments of a region as important building blocks of its culture and identity. At the same time, the goal is "[to] construct on the constructed" –

the title of a book about the architecture in South Tyrol. It describes the projects for preserving the culturally significant buildings, which are no longer required because of the changed economic situation; examples are not only castles and fortresses but also farmer houses or sheds. By carefully rebuilding and supplementing them, they have become important milestones of the region now and for coming generations. So the architects in South Tyrol, Vorarlberg or Graubünden, are not against globalization, but manage to give it many different facets to strengthen the distinctive quality of the respective regions in the globalized competition.

SUSTAINABILITY

An important aspect of the regional architecture can build upon a longer tradition: using building materials available on the site of construction instead of transporting them with much outlay of energy and financial expense from other parts of the world. Brückner & Brückner, for example, thus use granite for the foundation of a house, which is broken or crushed only a few kilometers from the construction site. Thus regional architecture also follows the principles of sustained architecture. Misused as a vogue word, sustainability has almost come into disrepute, even if it is an important leitmotif for responsible building. Architecture produces not only the houses for tomorrow, but also the building junk and hazardous waste of the day after tomorrow.

The concept of sustainability has its origin in the forestry. During the Baroque period, the aim was to cut only as many trees as necessary for the firewood which could be

Rick Joy Architects, *Desert Nomad House,* Arizona, 2005

With his distinctive dwellings, Rick Joy, a confident architect, delivers something which is rooted within its location. This working with the local circumstances means that Joy must respond to the partially extreme weather conditions that prevail in Arizona – with burning heat in the daytime and cold at night. With his projects, he prefers to work with the traditional building material clay that creates a comfortable and healthy room climate for the inhabitants. An additional guiding theme of his architecture is the targeted alignment of the building body toward the sun. The result is ecologically high-standard architecture which is creatively original and possesses a nearly poetic quality, while respecting the character of the landscape.

grown in the same zone each year. Sustainability thus means observing the world of today with the eyes of tomorrow. This connection played a decisive role in the year 1987 in a report for the United Nations by the former Norwegian Prime Minister Gro Harlem Brundtland. The report showed the long-term perspective for the development policies that should be environment-friendly at the same time: "to make the development sustainable means that the present generation satisfies its needs, without endangering the future generation, to satisfy its own needs."

Thus it becomes clear that it is not sufficient to use the renewable local building materials. A sustained or "green" architecture must moreover observe different aspects: the respective requirements of the people just like the energy-saving provision of water, heat and light. The minimization of heating costs is not only a question of money, but also a question of CO_2-balance of a house in the age of the climate change. It is therefore important for the energy balance of the building to consume as little energy as possible in its construction and use as well as in the production of building materials. At the same time, it is necessary to ensure that a house can be optimally disposed of at the end of its useful existence and, in the optimum case, is completely recyclable. This poses complex challenges to architects with regard to planning, material selection and the technical equipment of the houses. As a matter of fact, today architecture is no longer feasible without close cooperation between the architect and the consultants on statistics

and the energy supply system. More than ever, it proves to be a collaboration of specialists. A building is considered to be energy efficient if the heat and electricity requirement of its inhabitants is limited, energy losses are reduced and energy production is optimal. The ideal case is a so-called "zero-energy house" that does not require any precious, finite fossil or ecologically harmful fuels such as petroleum,

Werner Sobek, *House R 128,* Stuttgart, 2000

The glass experimental house is an ecological, high-tech everyday building, within whose construction insights of year-long research are incorporated. Erected on a hill, it is constructed approximately on a square ground plan. This four-story steel skeleton construction with triple glazing is an emission free, zero-energy-house, thanks to its solar system.

Carlo Baumschlager and Dietmar Eberle, *Munich Re,* Munich, 1999–2002

Today, no one would guess that behind the shimmering blue glass façade of the Munich Re was the plain concrete structure from the 1970s that was found by them. The costly rehabilitation works of Vorarlberger architects shows the possibilities offered by the construction – about the use of energy-saving innovations for the heat recovery and floor cooling. The result is a modern architecture of the highest artistic level.

gas or coal for heating. Instead, it uses, for example, the sun energy stored in solar cells, which functions in the northern regions only if the building bodies are very compactly constructed and excellently insulated.

Besides technology and energy optimization in the planning of new buildings, the conversion and upgrading of already available building substance is an important contribution to sustainability. The life of a house is thus extended and its energy balance is enhanced. While monuments should be maintained in their original structural substance, this is not mandatory in other old buildings; they can be adapted by means of thermal insulation and improved heating systems to the current requirements. But even in monuments, the energy consumption can be reduced, for example by a second pane of window glass or by insulating the roof. Thus such a building makes a double contribution

to sustainability: on the one hand, in terms of its historic meaning, on the other, by improving the energy balance.

SOCIAL ARCHITECTURE

Architecture is more than mere art. And it is more than a building. Architecture is a building block of the landscape and the city. It can make the challenges of everyday life endurable and can provide for a smooth coexistence of people. It has a big responsibility toward people and environment – these should be the focus of sustained and responsible architecture. Therefore it is not surprising that since the beginning of the modern period, architects have not seen their main goal as building magnificent architectural edifices as in the earlier epochs toward the end of the 19th century. Instead, their focal point lay in building for the majority of the less affluent population. Workers and employees should be helped by the industrialization and optimization of the building process for good yet economical dwellings. Finally, light and air should replace the unhealthy damp dwellings. That applied to the residential area of the modern period in Berlin or Frankfurt in the 1920s, as well as to the housing units of the post-war period of Le Corbusier. Certainly there were also setbacks that became the object of criticism. Yet the project of the Modern period, whose representatives critically viewed their own actions and constructions, belongs to the big success stories of the 20th century. And also

Shigeru Ban, *Paper Tube Houses,* Kobe, 1995

Most of the houses seem to be constructed for eternity and they often last years till they are finally completed. In contrast to it, the Japanese architect Shigeru Ban likes to experiment with ephemeral building materials such as paper. With paper, he expands the point of view of architecture and creates new possible uses of these everyday materials. For example, in case of emergencies – maybe after some natural disaster – new lodgings must be erected very quickly. And to make it possible, Ban showed how to make it possible with his paper houses. They consist of materials that are available anywhere in the world. Here beverage boxes serve as a foundation on which the carton tubes stand. These constructions proved their worth as economical emergency lodging for the people who lost their home in the devastating 1995 earthquake in Kobe, Japan.

the idea of a social architecture – architecture of responsibility for people and environment – is in no way finished.

The constructed world has long become just as versatile as the social structures, as shown by the riots in the Paris suburbs, only a few Metro stations away from the center of the city. They are worlds apart – worlds with little mutual contact but with much interdependence. The social differences between the inhabitants of the quarters are very clear and so are the differences in the architecture that they inhabit.

Architectural variety also appears on the Arabian Peninsula and in the sprawling Asian megacities. There are enormous building projects and entire cities are mushrooming. More and more "gated communities" emerge, not only in the Western world but also in the self-contained and guarded urban quarters of high-income earners and the rich. The centers in London and Berlin and other cities adorn themselves with the splendor of a new historicism that, following post modernism, reverts to the architectural symbols of the past times in addition to post-modernism.

It is housing where the gap between the rich and poor is big, representing an additional challenge for the residential construction for the majority of population. In the emerging nations, the situation is just as in the Third World, to improve the living conditions through optimized circumstances. In the Western world, where most of the inhabitants have long reached a comparatively high prosperity level, the social architecture no longer means the satisfaction of basic necessities. Nevertheless, there are, time and again, ambitious programs for the social residential construction, such as in the Spanish capital Madrid. Besides, high-quality individual projects appear, such as the new experimental housing estate in the French Mulhouse, where the first large worker "gated community" of France emerged 150 years ago. To mark the anniversary, Jean Nouvel and other architects were commissioned with the construction of the new settlement, among them the Japanese architect Shigeru Ban, and Anne Lacaton and Jean Philippe Vassal, both French. Lacaton and Vassal, who speak provocatively about their construction, also speak of their "non-architecture" experiment in Mulhouse with the greenhouse motif. They

deliberately use industrial materials such as concrete components, large glass sections and translucent polycarbonate plates, while the interior is marked by spacious rooms.

In addition to the implementation of more concrete housing projects, social architecture must help to preserve the city structures grown over a long period of time and also the social structure of the neighborhoods. All over the world, architects since the beginning of the 21st century face this exciting challenge by making their major contribution to the sustainability of our world. With their buildings, they want to irritate, arouse and create something not known before. Moreover, their architecture must be economical and ecological, and must unite social as well as cultural aspects. Only then will their contribution ensure that the globalized world does not fragment because of personal interests.

Biq., *Starterswoningen,* Hoofddorp, Holland, 2004–2006

The houses of this settlement recall the simplicity of drawings by children. With its gabled roof and partly yellow, partly red brick façades, they offer constructed row- and duplex-houses in the residential construction of economical living space, one's own first apartement for example. The 16-feet (5-meter) wide houses are large enough with their partitionable living space of 295 square feet (90 square meters) to offer sufficient space for a young family with two children.

Anna Heringer and Eike Roswag, *Meti School,* Rudrapur, Bangladesh, 2005

The indescribable wisdom of Ludwig Mies van der Rohe finds an astonishing new confirmation in the school in Rudrapur. The prize-winning clay-bamboo building that was made with materials available on the spot proves to be a fascinating example for the aesthetic wealth that can be developed by a regionally rooted and socially responsible architecture project.

GLOSSARY OF TERMS

The words in *italics* in the main text are explained in this glossary. Those italicized here are further elucidated elsewhere in the glossary or in the names index.

abstraction Tendency in modern art starting about 1850 to simplify forms when representing a naturalistic model in a work of art, especially in painting. The culmination of this tendency is in painting without a subject – abstract painting – as for example in the period around 1910 with the works of *Piet Mondrian* or *Kasimir Malevich*.

academic The nature of the education, conforming to traditional values, formerly offered by art schools. Is generally used pejoratively to refer to conservative art in contrast to innovative movements such as *Impressionism, Expressionism* and the *Secession*.

Amsterdam School Influential Dutch *Expressionist* architectural movement, whose chief representatives, *Johann Melchior van der Mey, Michel de Klerk*, and *Pieter Kramer*, constructed strongly expressive buildings in brick.

antiquity Generic term describing the two high periods of early European culture: Greek antiquity (at its apogee in the 5th and 4th centuries BC) and Roman antiquity (1st and 2nd centuries AD).

arcade A range of *arches* carried on piers or *columns*, either free-standing or attached to a wall.

arch Any upwardly curved element which forms a link between two vertical elements. Extremely varied types of arches have existed since the time of Ancient Rome. The use of different types of arch characterizes specific epochs of architectural history (semicircular arch: *Romanesque, Renaissance*; pointed arch: *Gothic*). Flattened arches are also frequently to be found; these consist of a segment of a semicircular arch. The functional purpose of an arch is to distribute a down force (e.g., the weight of a vaulted roof) into several supports.

architectural engineering Building of a kind which since the days of *Antiquity* could only be carried out with special technical knowledge. In the 19th century this was represented mainly by stations, bridges, and also buildings entirely of *iron*, such as the Eiffel Tower. The 20th century has seen architectural engineering carried to new heights, especially in sports stadia. (See *Pier Luigi Nervi* and *Frei Otto*).

architecture parlante French term meaning "speaking architecture," describing buildings where the form gives an indication as to their use, as for instance in the case of *Fritz Höger's* Chile House, which was built for a shipping company.

Art Déco A style in art in the 20s and 30s, whose name derives from the "Exposition internationale des arts décoratifs et industriels modernes" (Paris, 1925). One of its distinguishing marks is rounded corners.

Art Nouveau Generic term for a movement which had many variants: "Art Nouveau" in France, "Modern Style" in England, "Jugendstil" in Germany, "Stile liberty" in Italy, "Modernismo" in Spain. With its flat-looking *ornamentation* displaying a wealth of vegetal curves, it was the complete opposite to *academic* art.

Arts and Crafts Movement Influential movement in the area of applied art, originating in England in the middle of the 19th century under the leadership of *William Morris, Philip Webb* and *John Ruskin*. They were in favor of a return to the craft tradition of the Middle Ages and were against industrial mass production.

attic (specialist sense) An erection above the cornice, hiding the beginning of the roof. Often used to give emphasis to a centrally projecting volume.

axis (line of sight) A straight line from the eye to the object of sight. Buildings and gardens are generally laid out *symmetrically* on either side of a line of sight, which enhances their effect. Window axes are imaginary lines running from back to front or from side to side of a building.

baroque (Portuguese "barocco" – small stone, unevenly shaped pearl) This idea, derived from the art of the jeweler, was used in a derogatory sense (meaning bizarre or bulbous) by the classicists about the previous era. The terms cover art and culture of the 17th and 18th centuries in Europe. It was very different in the various countries. Generally starting from the formal canon of *antiquity*, the baroque developed colorful and opulent decorations, sometimes made of *stucco*, which created a particularly magnificent impression. It was disliked by the classicists of the 18th and early 19th centuries on the grounds that it was overladen. It was brought to life again from about 1860 in the neo-Baroque.

base Bottom section of a building or sculpture (see *pedestal*).

belvedere (Italian: beautiful view) Originally the description of, among other things, a pavilion (usually in a garden), which can be used to admire a view.

border *Ornamental* decorative panel at the edge of a fabric. Also used in connection with walls.

brick See also *clinker*. Block made of clay in various colors (usually red or yellow) baked till it is hard. Bricks that have been submitted to a great heat are called clinker, and were much used in expressionist architecture.

Brücke, Die A group of artists from Dresden, founded in 1905 and including among others Karl Schmidt Rottluff, Erich Heckel, Otto Müller, Max Pechstein and Ludwig Kirchner. Their strongly expressive and highly colorful works, influenced by *Gothic* models and primitive art, founded the German *Expressionist* movement in painting.

Brutalism Idea introduced by *Le Corbusier* originally relating to the use of unfinished, bare concrete, and taken up by the *Smithsons* and others in Great Britain. Brutalism stands for architecture that is truthful about its materials, and where nothing is covered up, so that functional relationships are directly visible.

capital The top of a column, a form deriving from the architecture of Antiquity. It differs in shape according to which *order* it belongs to (Doric, Ionic, Corinthian or Composite).

cast iron art An art form found in the decorative arts and architecture, especially in 19th century Prussia (*Schinkel*, Memorial on the Kreuzberg, Berlin 1818–21) which was attributed a high degree of national importance.

cement Waterproof building material made of a mixture of burnt lime and clay. An important ingredient of *concrete*.

ceramic tiles Tiles made of fired clay, for the most part glazed and colored (see *faience*).

Charter of Athens see *CIAM*

School of Chicago A group of American architects such as *William Le Baron Jenney* and *Louis Sullivan*, who took part in the rebuilding of Chicago in the late 19th century and built skyscrapers that became signposts for the new.

CIAM (Congrès Internationaux d'Architecture Moderne). International forum of the avant-garde for modernist architects founded in 1927 under the leadership of *Le Corbusier* and Siegfried Gidion. The congresses, which were highly ideological and formalistic, took a different theme each time. So, the outcome of CIAM II, in 1929, led by Ernst May, was a report titled "The minimal-living unit." In 1930 in Brussels there followed "Rational building methods," when Gropius was one of the speakers. CIAM IV (1933) was devoted to the functional city. From this emerged the "Charter of Athens," which bore the stamp of Le Corbusier's concepts. The Charter of Athens presupposes the division of the modern city into zones corresponding to their main functions: living, work, leisure and transport. Against a background of increasing criticism of the International Style and the advent of *Brutalism*, the 10th and last CIAM took place in Otterlo in 1959.

classicism Return of the classical formal repertoire of the architecture of *Antiquity* in Europe and North America in the late 18th and early 19th centuries (see *Schinkel*).

climatization A technical system for optimizing the balance of incoming and outgoing air in buildings. Especially important in museums, whose treasures require a constant climate, as well as buildings holding a lot of people, as for instance public halls and skyscrapers.

clinker *Brick* that has been baked at a very high temperature, so that the pores sinter, that is to say acquire a glassy waterproof surface.

concrete A resistant, relatively light and cheap substance, made of sand, gravel, and *cement*, which sets hard as stone, and can be cast in a desired shape using *formwork*. It was brought to perfection in France in 1879 by Hennebique in the form of reinforced concrete. This system enhances the load-bearing properties of concrete by the addition of an iron or steel skeleton, so that enormous roof areas can be spanned. The adaptability of concrete to a variety of usages has made it one of the most important building materials of the 20th century (see *Perret, Le Corbusier*).

colonnade Hall or walk with pillars. A roofed area with rows of pillars and *entablature*.

column Cylindrical support characterized by its swelling form (entasis). A column has a base, clearly differentiated from the structure underneath, and a *capital* which tops the column, and connects it to the *entablature*.

conservation Efforts, beginning in the 19th century, to preserve works of art from previous epochs (preservation), or to repair them (restoration).

Constructivism A theory of art held by *Tatlin* and *El Lissitsky* in the early days of the Soviet Union, according to which architecture must be reduced to its necessary functional (see *function*) elements, so that it is dominated by pure construction.

cornice A horizontal molded projection which crowns a building.

Cubism (Latin: "cubus" – cube) A style adopted by Picasso, Braque and Delaunay from 1907 onwards, whereby natural forms are reduced to their geometric basic construction. The corresponding movement in architecture was that of the Prague Cubists.

curtain wall A non load-bearing *façade* or wall of glass, granite or plastic hung in front of a load-bearing construction.

Deconstructivism This movement became known through the exhibition "Deconstructivist Architecture" organized by Philip Johnson and Mark Wigley in 1988 at the Museum of Modern Art. Deconstructivist buildings differ from Modernist or Post-Modern buildings through their intersecting, splintered, and sharply inclined forms. They express a general sense of destabilization which has been widespread in the West (and not just in the West) in the 1980s and 90s. The viewer's first sensation on seeing many of these buildings is astonishment, aroused by their apparent technical impossibility, their astonishing use of materials and their unusual formal language. The chief representatives of Deconstructivism, which has now become an international movement are *Gehry, Libeskind, Hadid*, the COOP Himmelblau, Peter Eisenman, and Bernard Tschumi.

De Stijl A group of artists formed in Holland in 1917 under the influence of *Piet Mondrian*, and which included, among others, *Theo van Doesburg, Gerrit Thomas Rietveld*, and *Jacobus Johannes Pieter Oud*. Their aim was to produce applied arts and architecture in an *abstract* language of forms freed from the decoration of traditional architecture.

Deutscher Werkbund An association, founded in 1907, of craftsmen, industrialists, and architects to promote the production of art on a national scale, and extend its economic relevance and industrialization.

Diocletian window Also known as Thermal window. A semi-circular window, subdivided by two vertical supports. First appears in Ancient Rome.

dome A type of roof having the shape of part of a sphere, which has been in use since Ancient Rome. Has frequently appeared in the West since the *Renaissance* in palaces and sacral buildings, but it is also found in quite ordinary buildings in Islamic architecture.

Doric One of the three most important *orders of columns* of Ancient Greece, which has a squat shaft with no base and broad *flutes*, and is crowned by a spreading *capital* and a frieze with triglyphs (surface in the *entablature* decorated with grooves).

dry stone walls Traditional walls where the stones are piled on top of each other and not bound together with any agent such as mortar.

eclecticism A mixture of several historical *styles* in a building. It predominates in *Historicism* but is also to be found in *Post-Modernism*.

entablature That part of an order which is above the column, including the architrave, the *frieze,* and the *cornice*.

epoch Historical period in which a particular *style* and its characteristic *ornamentation* develop.

Expressionism Art movement in the early 20th century, chiefly in western and eastern Europe, covering painting (*Die Brücke*, the *Fauves*) and architecture (the *Amsterdam School*). The distinguishing features of Expressionism in architecture are forms with a lot of movement and color and frequently with detailed ornamentation. *Brick* and *clinker* are the building materials most frequently used.

façade (Latin: "facies" – the external form) The "face" of a house, usually the front wall or the side that is most intended to be seen. The appearance and articulation of a façade often reveal the characteristics of an *epoch* or of a particular *style*.

Fauves (French: the wild men) A group of artists headed by Henri Matisse, roughly contemporaneous with the Dresden *Brücke* Artists, who created an art characterized by vivid movement and studies from nature.

faience Brightly colored pottery deriving its name from the Italian city of Faenza, which was the center of its production in the *Renaissance*.

flat roof See *roof*.

flattened arch See *arch*.

fluting Vertical grooves on the shaft of a *column*.

formwork Temporary, generally prefabricated hollow structure into which liquid *concrete* is poured. After the concrete has hardened, the formwork is then removed. Bare concrete often shows the traces of the formwork, sometimes this includes the marks of the grain when it was made of wooden planks.

frieze An area, normally just under the roof or ceiling which has been used since *Antiquity* for decoration, either in an *abstract* or figurative way.

function, functionalism Basic to the design of ground plans and façades in modern architecture from *Sullivan* ("form follows function") right up till *Post-Modernism*. This concept, which implies that the function of a building should dominate its design, making it as economic as possible, was chiefly to be found in industrial building, but also occurred in residential building, where it implied doing away with elements considered to be superfluous, such as decoration, and with rooms that were mainly for show. It was chiefly through the Bauhaus that functionalism became the dominant principle in the organization of architecture in the 20th century. More recent movements such as *Post-Modernism* and *Deconstructivism* are characterized by their critical attitude to a one-sided emphasis on the functional in architecture.

Futurism Modern art movement in pre-First World War Italy, inspired by enthusiasm for the future. (In architecture see, for example, the designs of *Sant'Elias*).

gable A triangular surface in the *roof* between two sloping elements. In major building works such as castles, there are often remarkable sculptures in the gables. Split gables (or pediments) are to be found especially in *Renaissance*, *baroque* and *Post-Modern* buildings. These do not join at the top but have an interrupted form, giving a dramatic note to the culmination of the building.

glass architecture Glass has entered architecture more and more since *John Paxton*'s Crystal Palace. *Bruno Taut*'s glass pavilion at the *Werkbund* exhibition in Cologne united glass architecture with *Expressionism*. Glass, often with temperature and sun protection, is also an important material for the construction of *curtain walls* in the work of *Ludwig Mies van der Rohe*, but also in the works of 90s architects such as *Jean Nouvel*.

Gothic A style that includes all branches of medieval art, first identified around 1140, and originating in the Île de France region around Paris. The main identifying features of the Gothic are the soaring grouped pillars and the pointed arch. The Gothic took many forms in the different European countries. Whereas in Italy the Renaissance began in around 1400–1420, a late Gothic tradition continued in Germany well into the 16th century. As early as the 18th century the first *neo-Gothic* buildings began to appear in England, Germany and elsewhere.

grid Even rectangular network according to which towns may be laid out. Also used in relation to the pattern of fenestration, usually of skyscrapers.

Heimatschutzarchitektur (heritage protection architecture) German movement, starting from English models, which took root around 1900. Its aim was to promote architecture adapted to regional traditions and landscape. It was discredited by the Nazis' use of the idea for political ends.

hewn stone Worked form of *natural stone*. See also **stone**.

high-tech architecture Generic term in use since the 80s to describe emphatically technical-looking buildings. Main representatives are *Norman Foster* and *Richard Rogers*, who together with *Renzo Piano* designed the best-known high-tech building, the Centre Pompidou in Paris.

historicism Generic term for types of architecture that relate back to earlier styles (*classicism, the neo-Renaissance, neo-baroque, neo-Romanesque, neoclassicism*). Especially predominant between 1860 and 1910.

housing schemes Systematic large-scale building of new homes, which began at the end of the 19th century, in reaction

against the tenements of the outgoing era. The Netherlands were first, then Germany. The aim was to relieve the housing shortage and to improve the living conditions of those sections of the population with a low income (see *Kramer, Klerk, Taut, Wagner*).

ideal city This idea has kept coming to life again since *Antiquity*. It implies constructing a city along ideal social, economic, and political lines.

Impressionism Movement in painting emanating from France in the second half of the 19th century, which, in rebellion against *academic* art, starts out from pure color, showing scenes that are close to nature and flooded with light.

incrustation Already present in *Antiquity*, this form of covering for *façades* consist of variously colored bits of stone.

infill The material (e.g., brick or glass) used to fill the part of the wall between a system of supports in wood, iron or concrete.

International Style Description coined by Henry-Russell Hitchcock and *Philip Johnson* following the creation of the Weissenhofsiedlung in Stuttgart in 1927, for the modern architecture being celebrated at an exhibition in the Museum of Modern Art in New York in 1932.

iron architecture Since the 19th century iron and steel have been widely used for the load-bearing elements of a building. This structure could then either be filled or serve as the framework for a *curtain wall*. Paxton's Crystal Palace is an example of iron architecture, as are other buildings by engineers, the most famous of which is the Eiffel Tower in Paris, built by *Gustave Eiffel*.

Jugendstil See *Art Nouveau*.

lintel The horizontal upper part of a doorway.

loggia Open portico or hall with pillars.

megastructure (from the Greek for "large") Massive enlargement and extension in the technical age of the previously small-scale historically developed structures of cities. Describes many of the utopian town-planning ideals formulated since the 60s, which

have found expression in *high-tech* skyscrapers.

Moorish architecture Architecture of the Islamic countries.

mosaic *Abstract* or figurative images built into floors or walls, made out of flat glazed chips (tesserae) which fascinate with the luminous quality of their color. Mosaics of various kinds have been created from *Antiquity* up till the present, very often in sacral buildings.

natural stone "Real" *stone* as opposed to man-made substances such as *brick* or *concrete*. Can also be used to define stone that is not worked, as opposed to *hewn stone*.

neo-baroque *Historicist* style whose forms are derived from the *baroque*, first used by *Charles Garnier* in his rebuilding of the Paris Opera (1861-75).

neo-Gothic *Historicist* style, whose formal repertoire is borrowed from the *Gothic*. In Germany around 1820 it came to be considered the national style, since it was believed for a long time that it did not originate in France, but in Germany.

neo-classicism Reappearance of *classicism* in Europe around 1900, e.g., in the work of Peter Behrens.

neo-Plasticism Style originating in *Piet Mondrian*'s painting in which the *Cubist* experience of space is translated into a flat picture. Carried over into architecture by the *De Stijl* group in Holland.

neo-Renaissance *Historicist* reappearance of the forms of the Italian *Renaissance* in the work of *Gottfried Semper* but also in *Schinkel* and Klenze.

neo-Romanesque Reappearance of the Romanesque style with its massive volumes and round arches, in *historicist* architecture, e.g., that of Henry Hobson Richardson or Bruno Schmitz.

Neues Bauen ("new building") Description of facets of modern architecture in Germany after the First World War, especially at the Bauhaus, which was part of the developing *International Style*.

noble orders Buildings or parts of buildings that were originally reserved for rulers and significant personages, such as *triumphal*

arches, pyramids, domes. Other forms, as for instance *orders of columns*, constitute in themselves a noble order.

orders of columns An architectural system developed in Antiquity including various types of column having different regional and historical origins. The chief orders are the *Doric*, Ionic, Corinthian and Composite, which can be distinguished by the different handling of the shaft, the *capital* and the *entablature*.

organic building One aspect of the *Neues Bauen* movement, which put the needs of the inhabitants first in planning a building, often in conjunction with flowing forms. Attempts to build organically are already to be found in the early work of *Frank Lloyd Wright, Eero Saarinen* (TWA Terminal), and *H. Scharoun*.

ornament (Latin: "ornare" – to decorate) Special architectural forms, the purpose of which is to decorate a building or parts thereof. Different epochs developed their own specific forms of ornament, which became characteristic of their style (see *epoch*).

Palladian Architectural style developed by the late Renaissance architect *Andrea Palladio*, derived from the *classical* forms of *Antiquity*. Widespread in the 18th century, first of all in England, then later also in America and Germany, in the context of the *classicist* movement.

pedestal Base for, among other things, sculptures and *columns*.

pergola A covered walk in a garden, usually formed by a double row of posts or pillars with joists above and covered with climbing plants.

pilaster Representation in relief of a *column*, against the surface of a wall, which may be the visible part of an internal pier, and serves as vertical articulation of the wall.

pillar Vertical supporting element in architecture; several pillars can be combined to form a *colonnade*. A pillar embedded in a wall is called a *pilaster*.

pilotis French term for a series of pillars or stilts that carry a building. Buildings on pilotis were favored by *Le Corbusier* (Villa Savoye; Unité d'Habitation). Pilotis make it possible to leave the ground floor open. There can also be structural reasons for them, as, for instance, to protect against earthquake damage (see *Schindler* and his Lovell Beach House).

pointed arch See *arch*.

polygon A many-sided shape which occasionally forms the ground plan of a building, sometimes also in the layout of *ideal cities*.

Pop Art Derived from "popular art," the term describes a movement in the 60s which declared objects in daily use such as soup cans or the VW Beetle to be subjects for art, and thereby exalted them in a surprising way and made them seem strange. Among the leading figures of Pop Art were Andy Warhol, Robert Rauschenberg and Roy Lichtenstein.

portico Entrance where the roof is held up by pillars, looking like temple architecture from *Antiquity*.

Post-Modernism Movement that began in the late 60s with the work of *Robert Venturi* and *Charles Moore* in opposition to classical Modernism, its strict *functionalism* and its ban on the *orders of columns* and on traditional forms of ornamentation. It brought these banned forms to playful new life, especially in America (but also in Italy, for instance in the work of *A. Rossi*).

Pre-Raphaelites A group of English artists of the mid-19th century, linked to *William Morris* and *John Ruskin*. They rejected the *academic* painting of their time, and took as their model the painting of the Italian Renaissance before Raphael (1483–1520).

proportions The relationships of scale prevailing among the individual parts of a building of a particular volume.

pyramid Geometrical form with a square base which then narrows to a point at the top , whose four sides are inclined triangles. The pyramids of early history were the tombs of Egyptian kings; the glass entrance pyramid for the Louvre by *Ieoh Ming Pei* has become a late 20th-century icon.

rationalism (Latin: "ratio" – reason) In general, the trend in 20th century architecture and town-planning to go for rational solutions. Closely related to *functionalism* and the goals of *Neues Bauen*. In modern Italian architecture "Razionalismo" is also used to describe a style (see *Terragni*).

rafters Load-bearing elements (usually of wood) in a roof.

reinforced concrete See *concrete*.

Renaissance (Italian: "rinascimento" – rebirth) Reappearance of the treasury of forms deriving from the art of *Antiquity* in Italian art in the 15th and 16th century, which reached its architectural zenith in the buildings of *Andrea Palladio*.

projection Used in the sense of a volume projecting from the topmost part of a façade, the term derives from the construction of French chateaux in the 16th and 17th centuries. Middle and side projections are also possible.

Romanesque Period in the European art of the Middle Ages, beginning around 1000, which in many areas flows on into the Gothic. The massive forms of the Romanesque, with its round arches and square *capitals* relate it to the architecture of Ancient Rome.

roof Can take many forms. A pitched or saddle roof consists of two roof surfaces leaning against each other, forming a triangular gable surface at the narrow ends. In a hip roof, all the sides of the roof lean towards each other and end in a narrow arris. In contrast to the steep forms of roof the *Neues Bauen* promoted the propagation of flat roofs, confining buildings to a purely rectilinear form.

round arch *See* arch.

rustication (from "rustic", derived from Latin "rus" – countryside) Masonry cut in massive blocks and separated from each other by deep joints, or an imitation of it in roughcast plaster, to give rich texture to an exterior wall and usually reserved for the lower part of it.

saddle roof see *roof*.

Secession (from the Latin for "parting") Name given to groups

of artists who left the *academic* art scene around 1900. The most important was the Vienna Secession, a group of *Jugendstil* artists (see *Olbrich* and *Hoffmann*).

skeleton The load-bearing elements of a building, often in the form of a regular grid and made of steel, reinforced *concrete* or wood.

skyscraper The manifestation of a trend which started in America around 1880 to make the most economic use possible of a piece of land in a big city (*Chicago School*), which was largely independent of the development of a modern architectural language. In the 20s and again in the 90s there was lively competition to construct the world's tallest building.

Socialist Realism Type of art established under Stalin in the Soviet Union which rejected the utopian visions of abstract Constructivism in favor of a figurative rendition of the party line.

span The spread or extent between supports. Wide roof spans, achieved by architectural engineering, are especially necessary in the building of sports arenas (see *Nervi, Tange, Otto*). Construction materials such as *iron* and *concrete* have made possible wider spans than could be effected using traditional building materials such as wood or stone.

set-back volumes Volumes that are stepped to produce a livelier looking façade. Set-backs were essential early on in the history of the *skyscraper* in the USA, in order to let enough light and air into the street.

steel skeleton construction See *skeleton*.

standardization One of the chief aims of modern architecture is to achieve conformity among building elements and materials, so that they will be compatible with each other and be utilizable in the greatest number of contexts at the least expense.

stone Traditional building material. Natural stone or finished, hewn stone may be used.

stereometry A method of measuring geometric solids.

style Characteristic repertoire of forms of a particular *epoch*, which differentiate it in form and content from other epochs (for instance Antiquity, Romanesque, Renaissance, classicism, historicism, Expressionism, Modernism, International Style (or Neues Bauen), Post-Modernism, Deconstructivism).

stucco Any kind of plaster or cement used to make architectural moldings or coat exterior walls. It has been in existence since antiquity and various architecturalstyles have utilized it. *Historicist ornamentation* using stucco was rejected by modernist architects (see *Adolf Loos*).

suprematism (Latin: supremus – "the highest"). The description chosen by *Malevich* for his art, because of its pure, extreme *abstraction*.

symmetry Construction of a building or a garden so that one half is the mirror-image of the other. Especially prevalent in the *Renaissance, baroque* and *classicist* periods.

tectonic The fitting together of independent parts to make a complete building.

tempietto From the Italian: "little temple."

temple Non-Christian religious building. The temples of *antiquity* and their surrounding halls of *columns* have served as models for later architecture.

triumphal arch An architectural form that has existed since *antiquity*, consisting of one or more large arches which often have a great deal of figurative decoration. Originally erected in honor of Roman rulers, they are also found in the *Renaissance, baroque* and *classicist* periods.

vegetal Plant-like. Used in particular to refer to the decorative forms of *Art Nouveau*.

wedding-cake style A general description of the heavily ornamented architecture of Stalinism.

wooden buildings Traditional since *antiquity*, wooden buildings have seen a renaissance in the 1990s on ecological and economic grounds.

INDEX OF NAMES

Page numbers in bold indicate illustrations

Hoff, Robert van't (1887–1979) Dutch architect, who was strongly influenced by the work of Frank Lloyd Wright when studying in the USA. Back in Europe he joined the De Stijl movement, and between 1918 and 1919 evolved a scheme for housing developments. *26*

Hoffmann, Josef (1870–1956) Austrian Jugendstil architect and designer, whose Cubist language of forms (Purkersdorf Sanatorium, 1904) had a great influence on the following generation of architects in the Neues Bauen movement. *11, 14, 15, 17*

Hollein, Hans (1934–) Austrian architect and designer, remarkable for his imaginative Post-Modern creations. Chief work: municipal museum, Abteiberg, Mönchengladbach (1972–82). *89*

Hood, Raymond (1881–1934) Most important American designer of tall buildings in the 20s, who carried over the forms of European Modernism to skyscrapers, thereby overcoming the Neo-Gothic repertoire of forms then prevailing. Chief works: (with John Mead Howells) Chicago Tribune Building, Chicago (1925), McGraw Hill Building, New York (1929), Rockefeller Center, New York (from 1931). *44, 48, 49, 87*

Horta, Victor (1861–1947) Belgian architect, leading member of the Art Nouveau movement. Chief works: Hôtel Tassel, Brussels (1893), Maison du Peuple, Brussels (1896–99). *10, 11*

Hübsch, Heinrich (1795–1863) German architect, whose book *In welchem Style sollen wir bauen* (In what style should we build?) was a decisive contribution to discussion on moving on from classicism. *8*

Isozaki, Arata (1931–) One of the leading Japanese architects. Chief works: Fujimi Country Club House, Oita City (1974), Headquarters of Tsukuba, Japan (1980–83), Debis-Center, Berlin (1996–97). *86, 98*

Jacobsen, Arne (1902–1971) Danish architect, who developed his own individual variant of the International Style, to be seen in the town hall at Rødovre, near Copenhagen (1954–56). *62*

Jahn, Helmut (1940–) Born in Germany, Jahn has become one of the most high-flying builders of skyscrapers of the present day. His designs are based upon the use of glass. Chief buildings: Messeturm, Frankfurt am Main

(1984–88), Sony Center, Berlin (1996–2000).

Jenney, William Le Baron (1832–1907) American architect, member of the Chicago School, pioneer in the architecture of tall buildings. Chief works: Home Insurance Building, Chicago (1883–85), second Leiter Building, Chicago (1889–91). *42*

Johnson, Philip Cortelyou (1906–2005) American architect, who, as director of the architecture department of the Museum of Modern Art in New York, supported the International Style in the United States. He later took a Post-Modernist direction. Chief buildings: Glass House, New Canaan (1949), AT&T Building, New York (1978–82). *58, 60, 87*

Kahn, Albert (1869–1942) American architect, whose generally sober and functional concrete industrial buildings for Ford gave an impetus to the European development of Modernism. *19, 20, 23*

Kahn, Louis Isidore (1901–1974) American architect, chief representative of Brutalism. His designs show a sophisticated study of geometric ground plans and the introduction of light. *64, 69, 71, 98*

Karavan, Dani (1930–) Israeli artist, whose sculptures generally consist of architectonically created spaces with a reference to history. An example of this is the memorial for Walter Benjamin at Port-Bou (1994). *108–110*

Klerk, Michel de (1884–1923) Dutch architect, member of the Expressionist Amsterdam School. With other members he created the Schiffahrtshaus in Amsterdam (1912–16). Chief works: residential buildings at Spaardammerplantson, Amsterdam (1913–20), De Dageraad housing development, Amsterdam, with Pieter Kramer (from 1918). *25*

Kramer, Pieter Lodewijk (1881–1961) Dutch architect, member of the Amsterdam School, worked (from 1918) with other members on the cooperative housing project De Dageraad, Amsterdam. *24, 25*

Krüger, Johannes (1890–1975) and **Walter** (1888–1971) German architects. Chief works: Tannenberg Nationaldenkmal (1927, modified 1935), Johannes Kruger: Landeszentralbank, Berlin (1953–55). *51*

Le Corbusier (real name: Charles-Édouard Jeanneret-Gris,

1887–1965) Swiss-born French architect, who became one of the most influential town planners and architects of the 20th century. He was innovative both in terms of his use of materials (concrete) and in his favored style of construction using pilotis. Among his most important works are: Villa Savoye, Poissy, near Paris (1929–31), Unité d'Habitation, Marseille (1947–52), Notre-Dame-du-Haut, Ronchamp (1950–55). *16, 21, 23, 36–39, 44, 60, 63, 64, 65, 66, 69, 70, 79, 96–98*

Libeskind, Daniel (1946–) Created the Deconstructivist Jewish Museum in Berlin (1991-99): a unique type of memorial architecture embedded in a complex web of topographical and historical connotations. *108, 109, 110*

Lissitzky, El (1890–1941) Russian Constructivist artist and architect, whose work exerted a great influence on De Stijl and the Bauhaus. *34–35*

Loos, Adolf (1870–1933) Austrian architect, whose determination to build in an ornament-free rectilinear style paved the way for the renewal of architecture. *15–17, 43*

Lutyens, Sir Edwin (1869–1944) The most important English architect of the first half of the 20th century, his roots lay in the Arts and Crafts movement. Chief works: Viceroy's House in New Delhi, India (completed 1930), monument to the war dead at Thiepval, France (1927–32). *22, 51, 65*

Mackintosh, Charles Rennie (1868–1928) Scottish architect and craftsman. His most important work, the Glasgow School of Art (1896–1909) is remarkable for its angular, geometric language of forms, and shows the influences both of the Arts and Crafts movement and Art Nouveau. *11, 13, 14*

Malevich, Kasimir (1878–1935) Russian painter, inventor of Suprematism, the logical outcome of which was "pure" abstraction, as in *White Square on a White Ground* (1918). *34*

Meier, Richard (1934–) One of the most successful contemporary American architects, and a member of the New York Five, whose buildings at the beginning of the 70s relate to the tradition of the 20s "White Modernism." Main work: City House, The Hague (1986–95). *90, 111*

Melnikow, Konstantin (1890–

1974) Russian Constructivist architect, who developed from classicist beginnings to become the foremost representative of modern Soviet architecture. *35, 36, 96*

Mendelsohn, Erich (1887–1953) German Expressionist architect, who had to emigrate in 1933. The leading representative of Neues Bauen in the area of commercial buildings, famous for, among others, the Schocken department store. Chief works: Einsteinturm, Potsdam (1920–24), Columbus-Haus, Berlin (1929–30), house for Chaim Weitzmann, Tel Aviv (1948–52). *20, 26, 27, 53*

Mendini, Alessandro (1931–) Italian designer and theorist of design, who developed products for, among others, Alessi, Philips, and Swatch, and since 1989 has been working with his brother as an architect. *111*

Meuron, Pierre de see Jacques Herzog

Meyer, Adolf (1881–1929) German architect, who worked first with Peter Behrens, later in partnership with W. Gropius, with whom he built the Fagus works in Alfeld. Chief works: Planetarium, Jena (1925), and the Palace of the League of Nations, Geneva (1929). *19, 20, 43*

Mies van der Rohe, Ludwig (1886–1969) German architect and designer, outstanding in the creation of modern architecture based on pared-down geometric forms in glass and steel. Chief works: Barcelona Pavilion (1929), Tugendhat House, Brünn (1930), apartment buildings on Lake Shore Drive, Chicago (1950–52), Neue Nationalgalerie, Berlin (1962–68). *14, 16, 17, 22–24, 33, 37–39, 44, 52, 57–59, 60–62, 73, 83, 84, 87, 98, 102, 105*

Mondrian, Piet (1872–1944) Dutch painter, whose pictures, in which everything is reduced to primary colors and basic geometric forms, influenced the style of the De Stijl group of artists. *26, 31, 32*

Moore, Charles (1925–1993) American architect, one of the founding fathers of Post-Modernism. Chief works: his own home at Orinda (1962), Piazza d'Italia, New Orleans (1974–78). *85, 86, 88, 95, 96*

Morris, William (1834–1896) English craftsman and artist, theorist and reformer, founder of the Arts and Crafts movement. Decisive influence on Art Nouveau and the Deutscher Werkbund. *10, 18*

Muthesius, Hermann (1861–1927) German architect, who chiefly built country houses based on English models. Influenced by the Arts and Crafts movement, whose aims he attempted to establish in Germany through the Werkbund. Chief work: Mittelhof, Berlin (1914–15). *19*

Nervi, Pier Luigi (1891–1979) Italian architect and engineer, whose exceptionally large roof spans are aesthetically outstanding. Chief works: airplane hangar at Orbetello (1939–41), UNESCO building, Paris (1953–57), *Palazzetto dello Sport, Rome* (1956–57), *Palazzo dello Sport, Rome* (1960). *75,* **76**

Neutra, Richard (1892–1970) Austrian-born American architect, whose residential buildings (e.g., Lovell Beach House, California, 1925–26) established the avant-garde European language of forms in USA as early as the 20s. *44,* **45**

Niemeyer, Oscar (1907–2012) Brazilian architect, practitioner in the International Style, who became famous as chief architect for Brasilia (from 1956). *65,* **66**

Nouvel, Jean (1945–) French architect, one of the most significant on the contemporary scene, whose buildings contain elements of high-tech and more traditional architectural styles in steel and glass. From this combination he has developed his own new, imaginatively poetic language of forms. Chief works: Institut du Monde Arabe (IMA), Paris (1981–87), Galeries Lafayette, Berlin (1991–96). *61, 101,* **102, 103,** *108*

Olbrich, Joseph Maria (1867–1908) Austrian Jugendstil architect, whose chief works include the building for the Vienna Secession (1897–98) and the buildings on the Mathildenhöhe (Hochzeitsturm, 1907). *12,* **13,** *15*

Otto, Frei (1925–) German architect and engineer, whose suspended roofs for exhibition and sports buildings combine esthetic effect with revolutionary technology (Munich Olympic Stadium, 1972, with Günter Behnisch). *75,* **81**

Oud, Jacobus Johannes Pieter (1890–1963) Dutch architect and theorist, founding member of De Stijl. As the city architect of Rotterdam he carried out building projects of a high quality with limited financial means. *32, 38, 39*

Palladio, Andrea (1508–1580) Most influential architect and theorist of the High Renaissance, whose buildings, based on antique forms, have been taken as models up till the present day (see *Post-Modernism*). *84, 96*

Paxton, Sir Joseph (1801–1865) In his work as a gardener, he designed greenhouses which served as the pattern for his revolutionary exhibition buildings in steel and glass (Crystal Palace, London, 1851). *7, 9, 102, 110*

Pei, I(eoh) M(eng) (1917–) Chinese-born American architect. Pei's architectural practice is one of the most successful in the US. Chief works: Louvre pyramid, Paris (1983–88), Annexe to the Deutsches Historisches Museum, Berlin (1998–2000). *89–*91

Perret, Auguste (1874–1954) French building contractor and architect, whose buildings, such as the house at 25 rue Franklin, Paris (1902–03), had a decisive role in the swift and widespread adoption of what was to become the building material of the future: concrete. *9, 21,* **22**

Piacentini, Marcello (1881–1960) Italian neoclassical architect who rose to become the chief state architect under Mussolini. Chief work: Rectory, Rome University (begun 1932). *36, 37, 55*

Piano, Renzo (1937–) Italian architect, who together with Richard Rogers realized the futuristic Centre Pompidou in Paris (1971–77). His more recent works are characterized by the recognizably individual interpretation he gives to the forms of classical Modernism, as in the Fondation Beyerle at Riehen near Basel (1997), and his delicate use of materials (terracotta-covered façade for the Debis skyscraper in Berlin (1995–97). *79, 89, 90*

Poelzig, Hans (1869–1936) A leading exponent of Expressionism in Germany (Grosses Schauspielhaus, Berlin (1919), design for the Schaupielhaus, Salzburg (1920–22)). His later work has functional, monumental traits (Offices for IG-Farben, Frankfurt am Main, 1928–31). *20, 27, 39, 52, 59*

Riemerschmid, Richard (1868–1957) German architect and craftsman influenced by the Arts and Crafts movement, who was one of the leaders of the Jugendstil in Germany. *11*

Rietveld, Gerrit Thomas (1888–1964) Dutch architect and designer and accomplished maker of furniture in wood. His red and blue chair (1917) and his Schröder house (Utrecht, 1924) translate the concepts of the De Stijl movement in an exemplary manner. *26,* **32-34,** *44*

Roche, Kevin (1922–) Irish American architect who worked with Eero Saarinen, and together with John Dinkeloo realized the Ford Foundation in New York (1963–68). *77*

Rogers, Richard (1933–) English architect, who is one of today's most important architects. With Renzo Piano he created one of the key works of high-tech architecture, the Centre Pompidou in Paris (1971–77), and the headquarters of Lloyd's in London, in a similar style (1979–86). For the Potsdamer Platz in Berlin he designed several commercial buildings in a style dominated by glass with façades of non-linear design (1996–99). **79,** *80, 89, 102*

Rossi, Aldo (1931–1997) Leading Italian architect, whose concepts of architecture, grounded in Neo-Rationalism, had a formative influence on the renaissance of European city building in the 80s and 90s (publication: *L'Architettura della Città* (1966)). Chief works: Gallaratese residential area, Milan (1969–73), Cemetery at Modena (1971–84), Teatro Carlo Felice, Genoa (1982–90), Quartier Schützenstrasse, Berlin (1994–97). *67, 94,* **95,** *97, 99, 100, 105*

Ruskin, John (1819–1900) Influential English writer on the theory of art and historicism. In his publications he promoted the idea of Neo-Gothic architecture based on early English and Italian models. His idealization of the Middle Ages also influenced William Morris's campaign for artistic renewal (Arts and Crafts movement). *10*

Saarinen, Eero (1910–1961) Finnish-born American architect, whose work includes prestige buildings in the International Style such as the General Motors technical center in Warren, Michigan (1948–56), and expressive organic buildings such as the TWA terminal at John F. Kennedy Airport, New York (1956–62). *61, 70,* **73***–75, 82*

Saarinen, Eliel (1873–1950) Finnish-born American architect, who created the main station in Helsinki (1910–14) in Art Nouveau style. In 1922 he took part in the competition for the Chicago Tribune skyscraper. *43,* **44,** *61*

Sagebiel, Ernst (1892–1970)

German architect, who constructed monumental administration and service buildings for the Nazis, such as the Reichsluftfahrministerium (air ministry) and the Tempelhof airport (1935–39), both in Berlin. *53*

Sant'Elia, Antonio (1888–1916) Italian futurist architect, whose visionary designs for city and industrial buildings exerted a great influence on the next generation of Italian architects. **29**

Scharoun, Hans (1893–1972) German architect, whose housing developments (Siemensstadt, Berlin, 1930) and apartment buildings (Charlottenburg, Berlin, 1930) ensured him a place as one of the leaders of Neues Bauen. His highly original ground plans show his adherence to the principle of organic building. Chief works: Ledigenwohnheim (home for single people) exhibited at the Werkbundausstellung, Breslau (1929), Schminke House, Löbau (1930–32), Philharmonic, Berlin (1960–63). *20,* **37***–39, 59, 73,* **74**

Schinkel, Karl Friedrich (1781–1841) German architect, the most important exponent of Prussian classicism (Neue Wache, Berlin, 1818–1821, Altes Museum, Berlin, 1822–1828), but who also chose a Neo-Gothic style for some of his buildings (Friedrichswerdersche Kirche, Berlin 1821–1830). Influenced by English industrialization, he was ready to use modern techniques, such as ornamental cast iron (Kreuzberg monument, Berlin, 1818–1821) and worked to rationalize and simplify the shapes of his buildings (Bauakademie, Berlin, 1836). *24, 59, 63, 90*

Schütte-Lihotzky, Margarete (1897–2000) German architect, who in 1926 began working with Ernst May in the Frankfurt city architect's office. While designing public housing, she developed the Frankfurt kitchen, predecessor of today's fitted kitchens. Chief work: Briansk School, Ukraine (1933–35). *38*

Semper, Gottfried (1803–1879) German architect and art theorist, who built in a sober style akin to that of the Italian Renaissance, with clear and practical forms and spare articulation which reference to various historical styles. Chief works: Hoftheater (opera house) in Dresden, (1838–41 – rebuilt after a fire, 1871–78), Polytechnikum, Zürich (1855–57), Burgtheater, Vienna (1875–83). *8*

Sert, Josep Lluís (1902–1983) Spanish architect working in the International Style, whose Spanish Pavilion at the Paris World Exhibition of 1937 was the antithesis of the classicist monumentalism of the German and Soviet pavilions. *54*

SITE (Sculpture in the Environment) Multidisciplinary group of American architects, founded 1970, who aroused interest with their dramatically staged supermarkets for the BEST chain. *82, 91, 103*

Siza Vieira, Alvaro (1933–) Portuguese architect, influenced by classical Modernism, who has developed his own contemporary language of forms, which is remarkable for its aesthetic effect, and its artistic organization of space. Chief works: faculty of architecture at Porto (1986–95), rebuilding of the Chiado, Lisbon (from 1988), Centro Galego de Arte Contemporánea, Santiago de Compostela (1988–94). *67, 107*

Skidmore, Owings & Merill (SOM) American architectural partnership composed of Louis Skidmore (1897–1962), Nathaniel Owings (1903–1984) and John O. Merill (1896–1975), who enjoyed worldwide success with their tall offices buildings. Chief work: Lever House, New York (1952). *61*

Smithson, Alison (1923–1993) and **Smithson, Peter** (1928–2003) British architects, influenced by Mies van der Rohe, leading exponents of Brutalism. Chief works: Hunstanton School, Norfolk (1954), *Economist* Building, London (1963–67). *62, 69, 78*

Speer, Albert (1905–1981) German architect, who rose to the position of chief architect of National Socialism under Hitler, through his construction of neo-historicist monumental buildings of exaggerated size. As General Inspector of Buildings, he planned the transformation of Berlin on a gigantic scale into the capital Germania, an ambition thwarted by the course of the Second World War. Chief works: Neue Reichskanzlei (Chancellery), Berlin (1938–39), arena for the Nazi rally in Nuremberg (1934–37). *52, 53, 54, 55, 57, 86*

Stirling, James Frazer (1926–1992) British architect, who first adopted Brutalism (Institute of Engineering, University of Leicester, 1959–63), then became the leading representative of a playful kind of Post-Modernism, as for instance in the Neue Württembergische

Staatsgalerie, Stuttgart (with Michael Wilford, 1977–84), and the Clore Wing of the Tate Gallery, London (1980–85). *86, 90, 91, 96, 108*

Sullivan, Louis Henry (1856–1924) American architect, leading representative of the School of Chicago. The façades of his buildings were articulated in a strict grid, as for example the Guaranty Building, Buffalo (1894), and the Carson, Pirie & Scott Store, Chicago (1897–1904), They were also specifically designed to serve functional needs. This enabled him to overcome historicism, and he was the precursor of the function-orientated architecture of the 20th century. *15, 16, 42, 44*

Tange, Kenzo (1913–2005) Japanese architect, whose use of bare concrete leads to outstandingly aesthetic results (Olympic Arena, Tokyo, 1964). Most of his constructions also exhibit a strongly plastic articulation (Yamanashi Radio Center, Kofu, 1961–67). *64, 75, 81, 83*

Tatlin, Vladimir (1885–1953) Russian painter and architect, leading representative of Constructivism. His main work is the design for the Monument to the Third International (1919–20), which was never built. *34, 35*

Taut, Bruno (1880–1938) German architect who, after an early Expressionist phase (Glaspavillon, Werkbundausstellung, Cologne, 1914), devoted himself to the construction of large housing schemes (Hufeisensiedlung, Berlin-Britz, 1925–30). His criticisms introduced a revision of Modernism as early as 1929. Chief works: Carl Legien Siedlung (housing scheme) Berlin (1930–32), School at Senftenberg (1930–32), Faculty of Literature for the University of Ankara (1937–40). *19, 26, 37, 39, 43, 102*

Terragni, Giuseppe (1904–1941) Leading Italian rationalist, whose buildings, constructed strictly in the International Style, show the close relationship of Italian architecture of that period with the fascist regime. Examples are the Novocomum apartment block (1927–28) and the Casa del Fascio (1932–36), both in Como. *36, 37, 94*

Tessenow, Heinrich (1876–1950) German architect, who was one of the most influential teachers at the Hochschule in Berlin. The calm neoclassicism of

his Festspielhaus (festival hall) in Dresden Hellerau (1910) became a model for many architects. An example of his sensitive aesthetic sense is the transformation of Schinkel's Neue Wache into a war memorial (Berlin, 1930–31). *22, 24, 52, 55*

Utzon, Jørn (1918–2008) Danish architect, whose best known building is the Sydney Opera House (1956–74), with its exciting sail-like roof, which has become emblematic of the city. *74, 75*

Van der Mey, Johann Melchior (1878-1949) Dutch architect, a member of the Expressionist Amsterdam School, leading architect of the Schiffahrtshaus, Amsterdam (1912–16). *24, 25*

Velde, Henry van de (1863–1957) Belgian architect, artist-craftsman, and reformer, whose work shaped the German Jugendstil. His most important architectonic works include the interior decor for the Folkwang Museum, Hagen (1901–02), and the Kunstgewerbeschule (school of decorative arts) in Weimar (1906). Within the Deutscher Werkbund he favored the production of handcrafted objects (1914), but was overruled by Hermann Muthesius, who supported industrialized means of production. *12, 13, 19, 33*

Venturi, Robert (1925–) American architect, town-planner and theorist, whose writings place him among the founding fathers of Post-Modern architecture. They include *Complexity and Contradiction in Architecture* (1966) and *Learning from Las Vegas* (1972). His Chestnut Hill House, Pennsylvania (1962), is an early example of his many-sided and playful use of traditional architectural forms which had been rejected by the International Style. *71, 84*

Vitruvius (1st century BC) Roman architect and engineer, whose ten books *De Architectura* (about 31 BC) are the basis for the interaction with Roman Antiquity of contemporary architecture, from the time of the Renaissance to the present day. *37, 84*

Wagner, Martin (1885–1957) German architect and town-planner, who, as city architect for Berlin between 1926 and 1933, was responsible for the realization of large housing projects by Bruno Taut, Hans Scharoun, and Walter Gropius. Chief work: Strandbad (lakeside

bathing area), Wannsee (1928–30), with Richard Ermisch. *37*

Wagner, Otto (1841–1918) Austrian architect, who prepared the way for Modernism with his writings *Moderne Architektur* (1896) and *Grossstadtarchitektur* (1911). Some of his buildings can be regarded as manifestos: the Postsparkassenamt (Post Office Savings Bank), Vienna (1904–06), the church at Steinhof (1903–06) and the second Villa Wagner (1910–12). Widely influential through the publications of the "Wagner Schule" (1897–1916). *14, 27, 44*

Webb, Philip (1831–1915) English architect, who translated the ideals of William Morris's Arts and Crafts movement into buildings, e.g., the Red House, Bexley Heath, Kent (1859–1860). *10*

Wilford, Michael (1938–) Partner and coworker in the architectural practice of James Stirling, q.v. *86, 90, 108*

Wright, Frank Lloyd (1867–1959) The most important American architect of the 20th century, whose early "Prairie Houses" (e.g., the Robie House, Chicago, 1908) exerted a great influence on European architects. His buildings integrated organically with nature, as for instance Falling Water, which is constructed over a waterfall in Bear Run, Pennsylvania (1936), and are characterized by spectacularly cantilevered terraces and cornices which emphasize the horizontal. In the context of town planning he developed the "Usonia" garden city project (1935–38). He also realized dynamic office buildings (e.g., Johnson Wax Company, Racine, Wisconsin, 1936–39). The final achievement of his long and productive career was the Guggenheim Museum, New York (1956–57). *16 17, 26, 31, 41, 44, 45, 62, 63, 74, 89, 90, 96*

ILLUSTRATIONS

The publishers thank the institutions, archives and photographers for granting them the right to reproduce works belonging to them, and for their friendly support in the production of this book. In spite of intensive research it has proved impossible to find the copyright owners of certain pictures. Photographers with justified claims in this respect are requested to contact the publishers.

Alvar Aalton Museo, Jyväskylä: 72 bottom right (Maija Holma), 72 top left and top right

(M. Kapanen)

Sammlung Consuelo Accetti, Milan: 29

Akademie der Künste, Berlin, Stiftung Archiv, Sammlung Baukunst: 37 (Arthur Köster)

Albertina, Vienna: 15 top and bottom

© Tadao Ando: 99 middle,

99 bottom

Arcaid, Kingston upon Thames: 8 (© Richard Bryant), 64 (© Stephane Couturier), 83 middle left (© William Tingey), 84 (© Richard Bryant), 93 (© Natalie Tepper), 96 bottom left, 99 top (© Richard Bryant), 110 (© John Edward Linden)

Architectural Association Photo Library, London: 9 (Morrison), 22 (© Erno Goldfinger), 45 top (© Hazel Cook), 45 bottom (© J. Stirling), 57 (© Cecil Handisyde), 58 bottom (© Dennis Wheatley), 62 top (©John T. Hansell), 70

(© Gardner/Halls), 76 top

(© Dennis Crompton), 82

(© SITE), 86 (© Alan Chandler)

Archive of the author: 51 top

Archiv für Kunst und Geschichte, Berlin: 6 (AKG), 7 (AKG), 11 (Erich Lessing), 12 (Lothar Peter), 15 middle (AKG), 16 top (Tony Vaccaro), 17 bottom (Markus Hilbich), 18 (AKG), 23 top (Dieter E. Hoppe), 23 bottom (AKG), 26 bottom (Markus Hilbich), 27 (Markus Hilbich), 33 bottom (Erik Bohr), 39 top (Markus Hilbich), 47 (Keith Collie), 56 (AKG), 59 middle (AKG), 68 bottom left (AP), 68 bottom right (AKG), 72 middle left (Gert Schütz), 75 (Henning Bock), 78 (AKG), 81 (Markus Hilbich), 87 (Keith Collie), 88 (AKG), 89 bottom (Markus Hilbich), 91 (Hervé Champollion), 100 (Irmgard Wagner), 104 bottom (Markus Hilbich), 113 bottom (Schütze/Rodemann)

© Ch. Bastin & J. Evrard: 10, 14 bottom, 106

Bauhaus-Archiv, Museum für Gestaltung, Berlin: 33 top and middle (Fred Kraus)

Bildarchiv Preussischer Kulturbesitz: 50

Jan Bitter: 115

Mario Botta, Lugano: 97

British Architectural Library Photographs Collection: 16 middle, 28 bottom, 55, 62 bottom, 69, 71 top, 77, 83 top, 96 top left, 101

© Friedrich Busam: 102

Keith Collie: 28 top, 35, 79, 95 bottom, 103 right

Commonwealth War Grave Commission: 51 bottom

Central State Machruschin Museum for Theatre History, Moscow: 34 top

Deutsches Technikmuseum, Berlin; 23 left

© Esto Photographics Inc., Ezra Stoller: 16 middle, 59 bottom, 61

© Klaus Frahm/ARTUR:

25, 36, 76 bottom, 92, 96 bottom right

Christian Gänshirt, Berlin: 107

Klemens-Peter Gast, Berlin: 71 middle and bottom

Getty Images: 48, 59 bottom

Fernando Guerra & Sérgio Guerra (Many thanks to Francisco and Manuel Aires Mateus for the permit): 116 bottom

Roland Halbe/ARTUR (many thanks to Werner Sobek for the permit): 117 bottom

Jochen Helle/ARTUR: 104 top

Herzog & de Meuron (Architectural Design: Herzog & de Meuron, Basel, Switzerland; Engineering and Sports Architecture: China Architectural Design & Research Group, Beijing, China; Ove Arup & Partners Hong

Kong Ltd., Kowloon, Hong Kong; Arup Sports, London United kingdom; Artistic Advisor: Ai Weiwei, Beijing, China) (Many thanks to Herzog & de Meuron for the permit): 112

© Karin Hessmann/ARTUR: 94

© Markus Hilbich: 20 both, 21 top, 74 both, 89 top, 95 top, 96 top right

Hiroyuki Hirai: 118 bottom

Kurt Hörbst _ www.hoerbst.com: 119 bottom

Eduard Hueber: 118 top

Japan Photo Archiv, Gerhard Wolfram: 83 middle right and bottom, 98

© Bruno Klomfar: 116 top

Ian Lambot/Foster and Partners: 80

Landesbildstelle, Berlin: 53, 59 top

Daniel Libeskind, Berlin: 109 bottom

Bildarchiv Foto Marburg: 19 top, 21 bottom, 38

Philipp Meuser: 63 bottom

Stefan Müller, Berlin (Many thanks to Hans van der Heijden for approval): 119 top

Museum of the City of New York: 43 (John H. Heffren), 44 bottom (The Wurts Collection), 49 (The Byron Collection)

© Norman McGrath: 58 top, 85

Netherlands Architecture Institute, Collection Van Eesteren, Fluck en Van Lohuizen Foundation, The Hague; Inventory number III.ISI/ Panel 54: 31

Anna Neumann, Berlin: 111 bottom

Frank den Oudsten, Amsterdam: 17 top, 26 top, 32

Klemens Ortmeyer: 113 top

Karl Ernst Osthaus Museum, Hagen, Foto Achim Kukulies, Düsseldorf: 13 bottom

Wolfgang Pehnt, Cologne:

14 top

Picture Alliance/dpa: 109 top

Uwe Rau, Berlin: 67 top

© Ralph Richter/Architektur-photo: 13 top, 111 top

Christian Richters/David Chipperfield Architects Ltd. (Many thanks to David Chipperfield for the permit): 114 top

Bernhard Schurian, Berlin;

108 both

Mark Skalny (many thanks to Rick Joy for the permit): 117 top

Spacelab Cook-Fournier/Kunsthaus Graz/Photo: Nicolas Lackner: 113 middle

© Margherita Spiluttin: 105 both

Staatlich Museen zu Berlin - Preussischer Kulturbesitz, Kunstbibliothek: 26 middle (Petersen)

Staatliche Museen zu Berlin - Preussischer Kulturbesitz, Nationalgalerie: 30 (Jörg

P. Anders)

Bildarchiv Steffens, Mainz: 54, (SLIDE/Pontanier), 65 both

(© Rudolf Bauer), 66 bottom (Bildagentur Buenos Dias,

Peter Koller)

Wolfgang Steinborn, Darmstadt: 63 top, 73

Stiftung Deutsches Technikmuseum, Berlin, Historisches Archiv: 23 left and middle right

Ezra Stoller © Esto: 16 middle, 61

© Hisao Suzuki: 114 bottom

Transglobe Agency, Hamburg: 60, 103 left

Tretyakov Gallery, Moscow:

34 bottom

Horta, Victor © VG Bild-Kunst, Bonn 2013
Van de Velde, Henry © VG Bild-Kunst, Bonn 2013
Wright, Frank Lloyd © VG Bild-Kunst, Bonn 2013
Gropius, Walter © VG Bild-Kunst, Bonn 2013
Grosz, George © VG Bild-Kunst, Bonn 2013
Brandt, Marianne © VG Bild-Kunst, Bonn 2013
Le Corbusier © FLC / VG Bild-Kunst, Bonn 2013
Scharoun, Hans © VG Bild-Kunst, Bonn 2013
Nouvel, Jean © VG Bild-Kunst, Bonn 2013
Köster, Arthur © VG Bild-Kunst, Bonn 2013
Feininger, Lyonel © VG Bild-Kunst, Bonn 2013
Mies van der Rohe, Ludwig © VG Bild-Kunst, Bonn 2013
Minne, Georges © VG Bild-Kunst, Bonn 2013

Front endpaper: There were giants on the earth in those days . . . and here are two of them – Vincenzo Lancia driving the 130 hp GP Fiat of 1907

Rear endpaper: No man, sir, said Dr Johnson, *was ever great by imitation.* No car was more influential than the shatteringly original Mini of Issigonis

THE LIBRARY OF MOTORING
General Editor: Raymond Baxter

The Designers

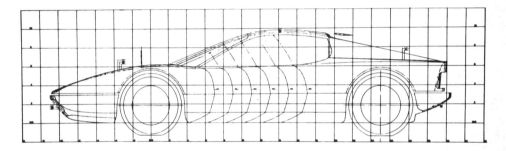

L.J.K.Setright

WEIDENFELD AND NICOLSON LONDON

© L. J. K. Setright 1976

Designed by Behram Kapadia

ISBN 0 297 77050 0

Filmset by Keyspools Limited, Golborne, Lancashire
Printed by Morrison & Gibb Limited,
Edinburgh and London

Contents

Photographic acknowledgments

Front endpaper: 1907 Fiat 130hp GP (Fiat Centro Storico); *13* Bugatti 57 SC Atlantic (Eric Butcher); *14* 1913 Bugatti Type 13 (National Motor Museum, Beaulieu); *16* 1923 Bugatti 2-litre GP (National Motor Museum); *17* Bugatti Type 57 SC (Klemantaski); *18* 1939 Bugatti chair (Klemantaski); *19* Type 35B or C engine (National Motor Museum); *20–1* 1932 Bugatti Type 51 GP (National Motor Museum); *23* Dowson-Issigonis Lightweight Special (Klemantaski); *28–9* Alec Issigonis and Forrest Lycett (Klemantaski); *30–1* Early Morris Minor (British Leyland Motor Corporation); *34–5* 1966 Fiat 124 (Fiat Centro Storico); *37a* Vincenzo Lancia (Charles Pocklington); *37b* Lancia Lambda (National Motor Museum); *39* Lancia Aprilia (Charles Pocklington); *42–3* Mercedes-Benz S (Klemantaski); *44a* Auto-Union V16 GP chassis (National Motor Museum); *44b* Auto-Union V16 GP engine (National Motor Museum); *45* Auto-Union GP (Klemantaski); *46* Ferdinand Porsche (National Motor Museum); *49a* 1932 Voisin (National Motor Museum); *49b* 1929 Voisin (National Motor Museum); *56–7* 1921 Vauxhall E Type (National Motor Museum); *59* Tatra Type 87 (National Motor Museum); *61* 1939 Fiat 1100 508C/MM (Klemantaski); *62–3* Lotus Climax and Lister-Jaguar (Klemantaski); *65* Bristol 401 (Bristol Owners' Club); *67a* Bristol 404 (Bristol Owners' Club); *67b* Bristol 405 (Bristol Owners' Club); *68* 1954 Bristol 450 (Bristol Owners' Club); *73* 1937–8 Rolls-Royce 40/50 PIII (National Motor Museum); *75a* Lago Talbot (Klemantaski); *75b* 1968, Lamborghini Espada (Charles Pocklington); *76–7* Fiat Dino Coupé and Spyder 2400 (Fiat Centro Storico); *78* Sommer Biondetti 8C2900B Alfa Romeo (Klemantaski); *80–1* 1946/7 Studebaker (Classic Car); *82–3* 1949 Jaguar XK120 (Klemantaski); *84* Lyons and Heynes (Klemantaski); *86* Zagato Bristol 406 four-seater (Bristol Owners' Club); *87* Zagato/Bristol 406 two-seater (Bristol Owners' Club); *90–1* Mercedes-Benz 540 (Mercedes-Benz); *95* 1928/9 Tatra (National Motor Museum); *100–1* BMW 326 saloon (National Motor Museum); *101* Jack Channer (Bristol Owners' Club); *105* Lotus 6 (Klemantaski); *108* Lotus 18 (Klemantaski); *109* Lotus Elan and +2s (National Motor Museum); *110–11* Lotus Elan 1500 chassis (National Motor Museum); *113* Bugatti Type 59 (National Motor Museum); *114* Fiat 508C (Fiat Centro Storico); *115* Maybach's Mercedes (Mercedes-Benz); *116* Ferrari 4-cylinder engine (Geoffrey Goddard); Miller (London Art Tech.); *117* Cadillac model A (National Motor Museum); *118–19* 1938 Auto-Union (Klemantaski); *120* Bristol 401 (L. J. K. Setright); *125* Hispano-Suiza Alfonso (National Motor Museum); *126–7* 1928 Hispano-Suiza de ville (National Motor Museum); *129* 1933 Hispano-Suiza V12 (Eric Butcher); *130–1* 1914 Mercedes GP engine (Mercedes-Benz); *132* Bentley with Bentley (National Motor Museum); *133* 1922 Bentley 3-litre engine (National Motor Museum); *134* Le Mans 1928 (National Motor Museum); *135* Bentley Six 6½-litre (Klemantaski); *136* Lagonda V12 (Klemantaski); *138* Ferrari 1½-litre (Klemantaski); *139* Ferrari V12 with Barchetta body (Klemantaski); *140* Bugatti Type 251 and Gordini (Klemantaski); *141* Delage 2-litre V12 GP (National Motor Museum); *142* Delage 1½-litre engine (National Motor Museum); *143* Delage 1½-litre engine (Klemantaski); *145* 1933 Delage D8SS (Eric Butcher); *146a* 1929 Salmson 1100cc engine (National Motor Museum); *146b* 1963 Facel-Vega Facellia (National Motor Museum); *151* Rolls-Royce Silver Ghost (National Motor Museum); *152* Rolls-Royce 20 (National Motor Museum); *154* Henry Ford I and II (Ford Motor Co. Ltd); *155* Early Ford production line (Ford Motor Co Ltd); *157a* Monoposto Alfa Romeo (Klemantaski); *157b* Wilhelm Maybach (Mercedes-Benz); *161* Wilfredo Ricart (Klemantaski); *163a* Karl Benz (National Motor Museum); *163b* Hans Niebel (Mercedes-Benz); *164* Rudolf Uhlenhaut (Mercedes-Benz); *165* 1934 Mercedes-Benz engine (Mercedes-Benz); *166* 1954/5 Mercedes-Benz GP engine (Mercedes-Benz); *168* Dr Fred Lanchester (National Motor Museum); *169* 1902 Lanchester chassis (National Motor Museum); *171a* c. 1913 Lanchester 38hp (National Motor Museum); *171b* 1910 Prince Henry Vauxhall (Vauxhall Motors Ltd); *175* Opel Commodore GS/E coupé (General Motors Ltd); *177a* 328 BM 1939 (Klemantaski); *177b* Bristol 405 and 406 (Bristol Owners' Club); *180* Aristide Faccioli (Fiat Centro Storico); *181a* Guido Fornaca (Fiat Centro Storico); *181b* Carlo Cavalli (Fiat Centro Storico); *182a* 1923 Fiat GP (Fiat Centro Storico); *182b* 1912/15 Fiat Zero (Fiat Centro Storico); *187a* 1932 Itala (National Motor Museum); *187b* 1932 Alfa Romeo (National Motor Museum); *188* 1950s Lancia V6 (Charles Pocklington); *189* Lancia D50 GP (Klemantaski); *190* 1927 Fiat 806 GP (Fiat Centro Storico); *192* Tranquillo Zerbi (Fiat Centro Storico); *193a* Hotchkiss 3½-litre (Eric Butcher); *193b* 1938 Talbot-Darracq (Klemantaski); *Back endpaper:* Formula 70 Mini Minor (British Leyland Motor Corporation).

Picture research by Judy Aspinall.

Foreword

The mobility of the individual – at least in the western world – is what has made the past 50 years different from any previous half-century of human experience. The internal combustion engine – and specifically the private car – have provided the key. Within living memory the world has become smaller for all whose fundamental freedom of movement has not been restricted by political considerations. Even in those countries where the state chooses to intervene in what the rest of us may consider our personal liberties, there is evidence that car ownership is becoming recognized as a worthwhile reward for the industrious worker.

It is paradoxical that at such a time western voices question whether the undeniable convenience and erstwhile pleasures enjoyed by the owner–driver outweigh the cost to society. Environmental considerations and energy-expenditure have assumed new dimensions, and certainly answers to those questions must be found before the passing of the century.

Meantime we have come to take for granted that which our great-grandfathers would have found almost incomprehensible. We think nothing of propelling ourselves in close company with our neighbours at speeds well in excess of one mile per minute! Sometimes we kill ourselves or others in the process. But viewed coldly, the chances of doing so are statistically minute. Evidently they are acceptable to most people, for the causes of recession in the world motor industry appear so far to have been essentially economic. And when accidents do occur, the overwhelming majority are caused by human error rather than mechanical failure.

This represents a technological achievement of staggering proportions, were we to stop and think about it–which of course we don't. The modern motor-car, with all its faults, is a remarkably successful machine. Even when grossly abused it will continue to function – some more efficiently than others. It has a control system capable of operation by the least mechanically-minded maiden aunt. It has a versatility of performance from walking pace to better than twice the speed of the fastest animal. It can be made comfortable regardless of climate, and can gobble terrain and distance far beyond the range of human capability. True, no-one has yet built a car to climb Everest, but it may come, just as scientists routinely motor to work at the South Pole, and the astronauts drove themselves across the lunar landscape in their moon-buggy.

All this has not been the result of accident, but of evolution. It is the product of designers – men who have worked individually and in teams to overcome problems as they have arisen, and to break new ground in concept and function.

This book is about them. Its author is well qualified for the subject as a creative individual himself, both by nature and training.

Leonard Setright read law in London and practised for some years before becoming a professional writer. He is a regular contributor to technical and other magazines in several countries. This is his fourteenth book; his previous subjects have included Grand Prix racing cars and a notable history of the aircraft engine.

His dress, manner and conversation have a certain studied elegance not common amongst technical writers since the passing of such as Laurence Pomeroy, and, in their own ways, Tommy Wisdom and John Eason Gibson. Setright is as much interested by the men who designed them as by their machines – by the machines as artistic creations more than as technical achievements.

He is a romantic, though he may strike me for saying so. And surely in this book his is a romantic tale to tell.

Raymond Baxter
May 1975

Introduction

LET US NOW PRAISE FAMOUS MEN

Men renowned for their power,
Giving counsel by their understanding,
And declaring prophecies. . . .

There be of them, that have left a name behind them,
That their praises might be reported.
And some there be, which have no memorial;
Who are perished, as though they had never been. . . .

Long ago Ecclesiasticus set us an example that has been too little emulated by motoring historians. Famous cars and infamous ones have enjoyed extravagant attention, but few of the men who created them have had their stories told or even been given credit for their work.

If Lanchester was cleverer than Uhlenhaut, was he therefore greater? Did Porsche swear more freely or offensively even than Royce? Had Birkigt and Leland not first worked on guns, would their cars therefore have been inferior to those of Bentley who first worked on locomotives? To know something about the man is to know something more about the cars he designed.

To know something about the cars is also to know something about the man. 'Every man's work,' [as Samuel Butler the younger observed] 'whether it be literature or music or pictures or architecture or anything else, is always a portrait of himself.'

Both these approaches, from the artist to the artefact and *vice versa*, have been used in this book, which seeks simply to attain a better understanding of one in the light of the other. To do this, I have rashly categorized my men, though the system teetered precariously over the need to fit Porsche into one or other of my arbitrary classes. It would have capsized, for sure, had I tried to include Ledwinka; but alas! I could not include everybody. I would have liked to ramble on in discussion of Bizzarini, Dallara, Duckworth, Kuzmicki, Mackerle, Ricardo, Roesch and umpteen more; but the laws of digestion, if not the law of diminishing returns, persuaded me not to attempt it. I have dwelt summarily or at length on threescore and ten; and thereabouts seems a well-ordained place to stop.

LJKS

1
Artists

'*B*ugatti was pure artist; his only scientific knowledge resulted from experience which increased with the years and a natural mechanical ability aided by a gift of observation. He did not believe in calculations, formulae or principles. He joked about pages of mathematical figures and about integration signs which he called violin holes. He had happily the wisdom to surround himself with talented engineers whom he paid generously, but demanded from them total anonymity.'

These words, culled from the writings of Jean Grégoire, himself something of an artist in car design, reveal all that is essential of the approach, the abilities and the acumen of the man who must stand for all time as the epitome of the artist designer, a type whose work owes more to inspiration than to perspiration. To design a car, it is desirable to be a master of metallurgy, electricity, production engineering, mathematics, polymer technology, aerodynamics, marketing and men. Yet, however desirable all these abilities may be, none of them is essential. Nor is an academic training, nor a practical apprenticeship, nor even a proficiency in draughtsmanship of any sort, be it conventional two-dimensional engineering drawing or conceptual three-dimensional freehand perspective. A man can manage quite well without some of these facilities, tolerably well without several of them; but if he lacks all, or nearly all of them, he can only succeed if he be a genius.

A genius of this sort is obviously rare and, with the mounting pressures of modern technology and market-enforced conformity, it is more difficult than ever before for any genius, however brilliant, to make his mark without a fair grounding in the disciplines already listed. The difficulty must only be relative, however, and should not be confused with an absolute impossibility. Forty years ago, it must have seemed equally hopeless for any but the best theoreticians to succeed as car designers, yet we have seen since then the success of some who were theoretically quite unqualified for the task.

The simple truth is that designers are of two kinds, the creative and the reproductive. The latter, to be successful, need not a single original idea; all they need is to be primed with theoretical knowledge, guided in draughtsmanship, furnished with examples and goaded to the task of doing what somebody else has done before, but doing it more efficiently so that it is faster, more roadworthy, prettier or (as is most often the object of the exercise) cheaper. The reproductive designer is not to be dismissed as of no value or importance; he has an important part in the overall scheme of things, refining what has previously been crude, adapting what has previously been inappropriate and making generally available that which has hitherto been hard to obtain. Such men abound in the later chapters of this book. The creative designer, however, is an entirely different being. Trained or not, he will not rest until what is in him has been brought out of him. He may be devotee or dilettante, master or servant, professional or amateur – but what matters is his own inborn appreciation of what is right or wrong.

It is very difficult to make sense of this proposition, for there can

Ettore Bugatti with his son Jean

be nothing innate in engineering knowledge – it must surely all be acquired. Yet there are more ways than one of making the acquisition; where some need painstaking tuition, others need only to look. There is a very good analogy in music: every human has the physical necessities of a musician, the ability to sing, to blow or bow, and to exercise the fingers to a dexterity that is no more remarkable than any other kind of athletic or domestic prowess, be it sprinting or knitting – but only those with an inborn feeling for pitch and rhythm and the harmonic series can ever be musically proficient. There is no need to labour this point, especially since Shakespeare dealt with it so succinctly when he made Hamlet harry the courtiers with his flute: we have already hit on the essential gift, which is an appreciation of what is harmonious. A car is not a thing, it is an aggregation of things, a compound complex of numerous, mutually-supporting components that are infuriating because they are also mutually interfering. The man who can see how to eliminate these incompatibilities, how to make each component in such a way that it does its various tasks as well as can be while detracting from the performance of all the other components as little as can be, can see how to design a car; and if he has not that sight, no amount of formal tuition will ever illuminate his vision.

The best of Bugatti's work was not only utterly persuasive but also unlike anything from elsewhere. Of his road cars this Type 57SC Atlantic coupé was the most extraordinary on both counts

It cannot be argued from this that the designer who produces something truly creative is thereby qualified to take his place among

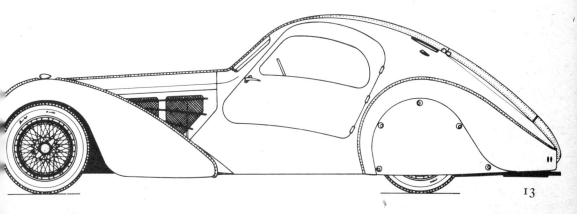

that distinguished class we describe as artists. The clever governor system devised by Henry Royce for the Silver Ghost, the reflex camber principle applied by Frank Costin to all his bodies, the linking of an airfoil directly to the wheels in Jim Hall's Chaparral, are all examples of genuine originality in car design; but it would be fair to say of these three men, as of most of the others whose work we shall review, that each of them produced only one truly epoch-making design, everything thereafter being evolved or adapted to the needs of the time. It has been said that every car designer has just one design in him and that all consequent designs have been produced by a sort of Darwinian process: but the designers whom we can call artists are distinguished by being exceptions to this rule.

This is true even of Bugatti. Practically every one of the many cars he designed between the Kaiser war and the Hitler one belongs recognizably to a continuous line that declares its parentage in every characteristic, a true demonstration of the *pur sang* that was the make's pride. However, Bugatti did not only interest himself in cars; he was interested in a host of things, and his designs were just as eloquent, as idiosyncratic and as extraordinary – while yet contriving usually to be surprisingly convincing – when they were of boats, aeroplanes, steam-engines, bicycles or his own personalized shoes with separate stitched compartments for every toe.

Not all Bugatti's work was beautiful. In his early years his ideas were apparent but his style had not matured, as the clumsy (by his later standards) engineering of this 1914 Type 13 shows

Ettore Bugatti has been variously represented as intuitive engineering genius, temperamental artist, free-thinker and patron of the arts of good living and furious driving. It is doubtful if any of these reputations is not exaggerated, but it would be more unjust to suggest that Bugatti be dismissed as the first quantity producer of over-the-counter racing cars or that he was a brilliant public-relations man, fronting a gifted but firmly-repressed staff of properly-qualified design engineers. He was a man with an eye for proportions and a feeling for materials, as demonstrated by the occasion when, after a careful look at a rival car in a race at Monza, he informed its driver that one of the engine bearers would fracture before the race was done. The driver was Segrave, who was simply annoyed by what he thought to be an impertinent piece of psychological warfare, but Bugatti's own team drivers were respectfully intrigued when their master warned them not to follow Segrave's car too closely. Events proved Bugatti correct: an engine bearer did break during the race, which was something that Bugatti's own components very seldom did. He did not design them with the aid of a slide rule and tables of tensile strengths and elastic moduli; he simply knew how steel and aluminium behaved and therefore freehanded shapes that would ensure the proper distribution through the mass of metal of the forces to which it would be subjected.

We have already mentioned that he was the first quantity producer of production racing cars. The Type 35 Bugatti was not the best of his cars, but it was his masterpiece – literally the work by which he established his mastery for all the world to see and marvel at. Unlike most racing cars, the Type 35 was strongly influenced in its design by marketing considerations; and, admittedly, most of the large number of racing successes attributed to the machine were gained in minor events by amateurs whose custom had been attracted by Bugatti's elegant artifices. The fact remains that the Type 35 was primarily a beautiful artefact, unsurpassed as a vehicle for sensual gratification, whether visual, tactile or aural. For those unfortunate enough to be unable to see it as something outstandingly beautiful, there remains the fact that it was distinctly uncommon. It set no engineering fashions, inspired no copyists (though Alfa Romeo were later to adopt its unusual rear suspension, which Bugatti pioneered much earlier in the Bébé that he designed for Peugeot) and established no norms or standards; yet it remained in contention for a very long time, and neither Grand Prix racing in particular, nor the history of the motor-car in general, would have been the same without it.

Bugatti's aim in producing the Type 35 was one that none of his rivals would then have contemplated in 1924– to produce a racing car which had a reasonable chance of being competitive, but which was so constructed that he could sell it in reasonably large numbers and at a reasonable price (which must nevertheless earn him a profit) to amateur drivers. This was not the only reason why so many detail features of the car were models of efficient simplicity, nor why so many others were crude pieces of gross effrontery. The considera-

tions that influenced his pencil were not only aesthetic, but also severely practical: he had available only the simpler and more basic types of machine tools in a factory employing workmen of outstanding virtuosity and, accordingly, he designed machines that could only be made satisfactorily by highly-skilled artisans, whose need for mechanical aids would be modest. It was thus almost as a matter of course that his engines had clean, sharp, rectilinear lines, that every control had that superbly precise and backlash-free feel that suggested assembly by a jeweller, and that the components of the engine's built-up crankshaft were held together by outsize bicycle-type cotter pins.

What matters now is the most enduring and important achievement of the Type 35. It elevated the racing car to a level of aesthetic sublimity which has seldom been equalled and perhaps never surpassed. Not only was every part of the car beautifully made, all these parts were also combined into a whole in which they were all concordant and contributory to an overall, cultivated beauty. It is

By 1923 Bugatti was learning to be more than a mere iconoclast: his lines were beginning to have a recognizable character. The tiny GP car of that year heralded many things to come . . .

admittedly hard to contradict those detractors who suggest that, if Bugatti's engine had been designed with less concern for eye-appeal and more for the laws of thermodynamics, the car might not have been somewhat lacking in power; but it must be equally difficult for them to deny the proposition that, if the Type 35 were never as powerful as the rivals it encountered in major events, it must have been endowed with superior qualities of reliability and roadworthiness to be as competitive as it nearly always was.

An examination of the engine, essentially similar to those of his earlier cars and clearly related also to the aero-engine upon which he worked during the 1914–18 war, reveals what truth there was in the first half of this proposition. It was a beautiful straight-eight engine whose cylinders gave it a lower ratio of stroke to bore than that of any other competitor. This suggested that Bugatti was espousing the twin causes of ample piston area and high crankshaft revolutions; but he squandered the piston area by employing an arrangement for his valves which, while it may have served satisfactorily in earlier touring models, was hardly adequate for racing purposes. There were three valves set vertically in the cylinder head and operated by a single overhead camshaft: of these three, two were excessively tiny, regulating the inlet ports, and the third was large, to control the exhaust. Bugatti was convinced of the importance of clear and unobstructive exits for the waste products of combustion, and there are those today who are beginning to adopt the same principles; but in fact he did everything wrongly in the upper stratum of his engine. The valves were long, and their guides short, their seats far distant from the cooling water. Condemned to an even hotter existence were the two sparking plugs to each cylinder, which were even less adequately cooled, and which were cantankerously located on the cool side of the combustion chamber, when other designers were already well aware that it was safer to fire the charge from its hotter side.

... of which one of the last was the clearly related 'tank' streamliner on the Type 57SC that won at Le Mans in 1939

It was to be years before Bugatti corrected some of these solecisms, by adopting conventions that he learned from the American Harry Miller, who inspired him to make a far better 2-valve twin-cam head for the Type 50 and subsequent models, though already he had adopted some conventions such as the rockers interposed between cams and valve stems to replace the peculiar and worrying curved tappets of his earliest engines.

His way round other conventions was more stimulating, and verification of the second part of our proposition (that, if the car were down on power, it must have been well up in roadworthiness) can be enjoyably sought in an examination of the chassis, which remained a convincing and surprisingly little-emulated example of how a chassis, confined broadly within the conventions that obtained before the coming of fully independent suspension, might best be built. Everything about it – the cast aluminium-alloy wheels with integral brake drums and detachable rims that allowed a car to continue running on a deflated tyre, the longitudinal frame members so deep at mid-length and so slender at their extremities, the manner in which these were united by the engine as well as by a number of tubular cross-members, the elegant proportions of the steering linkage, the care with which the axles were located and the pains taken to ensure a geometrically and kinetically precise operation of

Not all Bugatti's good work was on cars. He designed this chair, photographed at Molsheim but now in the Bethnal Green Museum, London

Although the hubs and separate brake drums (for wire wheels) betray Type 35A origins, this Bugatti chassis has one of the supercharged 35B or C engines. Here is the classical architecture of his masterpiece: note especially the springs passing through the tubular front axle, in emulation of the 1922 GP Fiat

the brakes – revealed Bugatti's awareness of the importance of structural stiffness (in torsion no less than in beam) rather than mere mechanical strength, his intuitive understanding of stress distribution and his deep-rooted concern over the consequences of laxity in the designer, his workmen, the machinery itself or the men who had to maintain it.

Nor can we forget the unfailing beauty of Bugatti's bodies. That of the Type 35 was influenced by the importance of attracting paying customers for replicas of the car that made its début at Lyon in 1924 for the French Grand Prix. For the same race a year earlier, Bugatti had fielded a team of cars that were nicknamed 'tanks' but which were, in truth, tiny all-enclosed streamliners of rectangular cross-section and lenticular (plano-convex), longitudinal section, a kind of airfoil that evidently reduced the car's drag considerably but impaired its directional stability even more. Once the body of the Type 35 had set a fashion, however, Bugatti racing cars emulated it with lasting success right up to the last and most beautiful of them all,

Clothed and beautiful, the Grand Prix Bugatti looked incomparably right in its proper road-racing environment. Maybe some of the engine details were bad, but the customers for this production racer loved what they saw

the soul-stirring Type 59. At the same time, he produced touring-car bodies with all the practicality, elegance, chic or majesty appropriate to the various chassis for which they were intended, ranging from the modest family tourer that was the little Type 40 to the uncompromisingly megalomaniac Royale, a 12·7-litre straight-eight luxury car that was the Type 41 – not forgetting the dashing Type 55 Super Sport, or the refined and accomplished variations on the theme of the grand touring Type 57. A customer for any of these might never concern himself with the location of a valve or the fabrication of a crankshaft: but everything that he could see and everything that he could feel was done as beautifully and bewitchingly as possible.

Of course Bugatti was an artist: everybody knows that he came from a family of distinguished artists, that he took to the motor industry because his mind and spirit were more adventurous and his hands a little less magical than those of his sculptor brother Rembrandt, that his clothes were peculiar, his horses impeccable, his factory and estate immaculate and his personality as extrovert and imperial as any in the history of the motor industry. Of course he had his helpers – there is not a man in this book who had not. Of course he had his detractors, for the man who buys a Bugatti in any state other than that in which it was despatched from the factory is buying trouble. Of course there were sage and qualified men prepared to swear that his square-section gearbox shaft, or the firing order for the eight cylinders which put such a heavy load on the centre main bearing, were heinous offences against the laws of physics. Of course Bugatti made many mistakes, but he also made cars of unrivalled beauty to the onlooker and inimitable appeal to the driver: he had the eye and hand of an artist, and art knows no laws but harmony.

It has been mentioned that Bugatti was prepared to learn from Miller. This was a reciprocal arrangement, for Miller was ready to learn from anybody. As a designer, Harry Armenius Miller must stand out as unique. Others might be described as artists, craftsmen, scientists, or even as simply inspired, but Miller alone admitted to an inexplicable occult inspiration as the source of his ideas, which seemed to come to him without any real working out. It also seems certain that he possessed some kind of clairvoyant facility, notably in his ability to forecast the precise time when people would die; but, as far as his role in the evolution of the car is concerned, and especially of the racing car, which was his prime concern during his heyday, it is apparent that he was not a practical engineer, nor in any way a theoretical one. He was a fund of inspired ideas, often years or decades ahead of their time, and he was fortunate enough to have working with him men of consummate ability in transmuting those ideas into substance.

Because of the important part these men played in establishing the Miller legend, it is not always clear just how much was originated by Miller himself, but it seems likely that his was the inspiration for the design of a front-wheel-drive layout for a racing car with a conventionally-oriented engine, and for the related adoption of the De

The Dowson-Issigonis Lightweight Special, built with hand tools on a shoestring, has some claim to be considered the most advanced racing car of the 1930s. It is one of the most passionate designs of all time

Dion suspension that had been generally forgotten since the 1890s and which, after extensive use on American race tracks and in some Cord touring cars, was finally taken up to very good purpose by Mercedes-Benz in 1937, since when it has always been in use somewhere. In one other thing, Miller was an undoubted first, although it had nothing to do with engineering ability and probably nothing to do with clairvoyance either; he was the first man in the world to make a thoroughly successful business out of merchandising racing cars.

Miller's father, a cultivated German who had trained for the priesthood before coming to the USA where he worked as a school-teacher in Wisconsin, spelt his name Mueller. His mother was Canadian and Harry, one of five children in Menomonie, not only spelt his surname the English way, but also rejected the education planned for him, so as to take a job in a machine shop at the age of 13. To Harry's credit, he worked hard, so that before long he had his own business, and was increasing his knowledge and experience in various branches of the automotive industry, notably in the design of carburettors, but also in the manufacture of pistons. When America entered World War One, he had already established his own piston factory, probably the first in the USA to make pistons of aluminium and, by this time, was well known as a specialist in carburettors, the first commodity with which he was to make really substantial money. It was in about 1909 that he built the first carburettor of his own invention, calling it the Master.

In those days, when the average carburettor was hopelessly incapable of providing proper mixtures of fuel and air in correct proportions over a wide range of operating speeds and flow rates, the Master Automatic was a good deal better than average; but for engines that had to do a lot of full-throttle work and do it particularly well, it was eminently satisfactory, being taken up with enthusiasm for racing cars, police cars, fire-engines and even aircraft. In particular, the racing-car applications brought Miller into contact with the lively American racing fraternity, much of it gathered along the West Coast where Miller had his factory in Los Angeles. His purpose-built racing carburettor kept them happy until well into the 1920s, when a superior carburettor produced by Ed Winfield (a former employee of Miller) supplanted it. Years later, Winfield paid his compliment to Miller with an evaluation of the man's place in the scheme of things: 'He was the originator in the automotive field of doing an artistic job on his machinery. He was more of an artist than an engineer. The one thing he insisted on – and that was pure Miller influence – was having everything well proportioned and well finished, regardless of structural quality. Others around him could worry about that.'

Miller had built cars and engines before then. In fact, he had built his first car, a ramshackle device with a dog clutch and no gearbox, for his own use as early as 1905. It was late in 1914, though, that the first real task based on racing-car manufacture (as opposed to the repair work that had kept the shop busy for some time) tickled his fancy. This was to recreate the Grand Prix Peugeot that had been blown up early in the season by the racing driver Bob Burman. Miller undertook to do the work in four months and, with the aid of Offenhauser, another designer, took the opportunity to improve upon the Peugeot design in many details. It was natural that he should employ his own light-alloy, single-ring pistons, reasonable that he should replace the feeble Peugeot connecting rods by his own tubular forged pattern which was to remain a characteristic of the Miller engine for many years, and hardly surprising that valve and port sizes should be amplified. More interesting was his substitution of a single overhead camshaft, after the style of the 1914 Grand Prix Mercedes, for the twin shafts standard in the Peugeot that Ernest Henry had designed.

Fortunately for Miller, the Burman car as reconstituted proved fast and competitive during 1915, although a tyre failure was to cause it to crash and kill its owner early in the following year. By that time, Miller was busy building an aero-engine for the barn-storming pilot Lincoln Beachey – a 6-cylinder unit generically similar in section to the Grand Prix Mercedes. It ran very well but, eventually, Beachey killed himself in a test flight to prove some new controls, and the whole project foundered. Nevertheless, it brought Miller's name to the attention of the aviation business and, in 1916, came a commission for a lightweight, high-performance aero-engine, which Miller neatly tied in with another for a complete racing car. He was thus able to build half a dozen engines, two for flight and four (with much longer stroke) for the cars. He settled on a barrel-type crankcase with integral block and detachable head, in which the combustion chamber and valve layout were much as in Henry's engines, except for the single overhead camshaft.

When racing driver Barney Oldfield saw it, he decided he wanted something similar but even better, and, after conferring with Miller, had a new engine devised in which the head became integral with a separate block and with desmodromic valve operation from two camshafts. This engine was designed to run up to 4000 rpm, a very high figure for the times, but it attracted less attention than the car in which it was mounted. This, which was christened the Golden Submarine, was (with the exception of its naked wheels, axles and dumb irons), a completely and quite beautifully streamlined affair, and it scored some notable racing successes. The fame it brought Miller was to stand him in good stead after the war, during which he was heavily engaged in the development of the King and Duesenberg versions of the Bugatti aero-engine, and also created a very large V12 aero-engine for yet another glamour man of American aviation, 'Dutch' Thompson.

At the end of the war, the Miller factory returned to normal work on carburettors and the like, only to be disturbed by a commission from a brewer to produce a radical racing car that might evolve into a volume-production sports car. The project eventually fell through, but it was work on this that gave Miller's design engineer Leo Goossen the chance to prove his abilities to Miller; when the racing

25

driver Tommy Milton ordered a new car, they were ready for him. In fact, Miller must have seen him coming, for this important customer was fobbed-off with an engine like Oldfield's; irate, Milton came back and insisted on something better, the specification of which he worked out with Goossen. The car was a 3-litre twin-cam straight-eight that in most respects was a copy of the successful Henry-designed Ballot, but its exceptional performance was due to a clever new cam contour that Milton admitted pirating from another designer, Hall-Scott. Any part of the engine that was not otherwise inspired by the Ballot was derived from the straight-eight Duesenberg that Milton brought to the Miller factory to be copied or improved. Half a dozen complete racing cars similarly powered were then ordered by the racing driver Cliff Durant, and they were successful enough in the remainder of the season for Durant to order a team of new designs for the new 2-litre formula that took effect in 1923.

For Miller, this was like a dream come true. Instead of scratching from one project to the next, he could now go into business making racing cars on a regular production basis. Anybody else would have taken the chance to rationalize his production and make economies, but the last thing Miller ever could be was a businessman; and he reacted by devoting the new source of funds to making his cars more perfect in appearance and finish, more jewel-like in detail, more delicate in their fine balance of lightness and durability, than ever before. Fine materials were bought from the small specialist firms that made high-grade alloys of steel and aluminium, brilliant artificers were set to machining engine and transmission components to the barest possible tolerances; even the side rails of the chassis were hand-beaten in the shop from mild-sheet steel over cast-iron formers, with such artistry that there was no trace of a tool mark on them when they were finished.

Everything in the new 2-litre cars was beautiful – and most beautiful of all was the engine that Goossen drew up to the broad dictates of Harry Miller. It was a twin-cam, dry-sump, barrel-crankcased straight-eight, ostensibly similar to the earlier 3-litre engine; but Miller had accepted the recommendation of Colonel Hall (of Hall-Scott) that the 4-valve pentroof cylinder head should make way for two valves in a hemispherical combustion chamber, after the style pioneered by Fiat in 1921 and convincingly demonstrated by the Italian firm in the Grands Prix of 1922.

Miller had his own contribution to make, however, and he did this in the light of his experience as a carburation expert: the straight-eight had a separate inlet tract for each cylinder, passing through one of the paired barrels of four Miller updraught carburettors. He went further in pioneering the use of ram pipes to achieve resonant tuning of the inlet tract, an artifice that he developed – in the absence of a dynamometer – by running trials at a convenient oval track with a selection of ram pipes of various lengths and a stopwatch. It was to be a decade before this feature was emulated by F. W. Dixon on his Rileys and, in view of the tremendous success of Miller's cars in 1923 and 1924, it was surprising that this particular feature was not more widely adopted, the reason probably being that the entire racing world on both sides of the Atlantic was captivated by supercharging, introduced to sports cars by Mercedes, to Grand Prix racers by Fiat, and then to the American oval tracks by Duesenberg.

For 1925, the last year of the 2-litre formula, everybody had superchargers, Miller included. Thanks to the gifted Goossen, Miller's centrifugal supercharging was effective and reliable, but Miller had something else that no other competitor had, something that was not Goossen's idea, nor Miller's, but which came from that inventive practical engineer Riley Brett, who worked for Jimmy Murphy – front-wheel drive. Murphy had been so taken with the idea that he set Miller to find a way of incorporating it in a racing car, only to be killed before Miller could deliver it.

There had, of course, been front-drive racing cars before in America, Barney Oldfield having been very successful with a v4 Christy in the first decade of the century; and Miller's first thought was to emulate the Christy layout, which featured transverse installation of the engine. With an in-line 8-cylinder machine, this was hardly feasible, and an alternative arrangement was eventually devised in which the engine was located more or less conventionally, that is to say longitudinally, in the chassis, behind the front axle line, but set back-to-front to drive a combined gearbox and right-angle transmission flanked by brake drums, from which jointed half-shafts led to the wheels, mounted at the extremities of a dead-beam axle. It was in effect a steerable De Dion layout, and its impact on the driver's technique was quite revolutionary. By keeping the throttles open, drivers found that they could take the corners at Indianapolis much faster than ever before, although, if they lifted off, the cars became very difficult to control. The feature was judged valuable enough to have a substantial premium put on it, and Miller in his typically unbusinesslike way chose arbitrary round figures for his wares: 5000 dollars for a supercharged engine, 10000 dollars for a rear-drive car and 15000 dollars for a front-drive car. He did not go short of customers.

In 1925, he went a bit short of competition victories, however, for in that year it was the odd Duesenberg that played the hero while the Millers acted the crowd parts. It was the year in which Goossen set himself to design the engine that would take over in 1926 and remain in contention until the end of 1929, these being the years of the new $1\frac{1}{2}$-litre, or 91-in formula. Superficially, he produced a short-stroke version of the existing engine, but it was refined in every minute detail. In fact, the front-drive '91-in' Miller, which campaigned under a multitude of titles including Duray-Miller, Packard Cable Special and others, was the high point of Miller's achievement. It won everything in sight. It set a world's closed-course record of 148·17 mph that stood for 24 years. It took the International class flying mile record at 164 mph, driven by young Frank Lockhart, for whom the Miller was a basis for further development – a measure of which was the extra 98 bhp that Lockhart found beyond the 154 (at

7000 rpm) of the standard Miller engine, partly by adding an intercooler between the supercharger and the engine. Miller, however, would not allow the 'rookie' Lockhart to alter his engine; Lockhart responded by buying one outright and becoming a freelance driver. He had tremendous ability, and might have succeeded in his aim to capture the world land-speed record in his so-called Stutz Black Hawk. This was a finely-streamlined little single-seater powered by two modified Miller 91 eights paired in parallel, ice-cooled, intercooled, highly supercharged and superbly prepared. A tyre burst during a warming-up run, and Lockhart (having already survived one such misadventure) was killed.

In 1930, a new stock-block or 'junk' formula replaced the old order and, although Miller 91 cars continued to do well, Miller gave up the motor racing business in disgust. Joining financier Schofield, he set out to carve a new career in aviation, but the slump hit the firm hard and, by 1932, it was bankrupt. Miller, whose name had been part of the deal, reversed his name and initials to found the Rellimah Corporation, in which he was joined by Goossen and Offenhauser.

They tried a variety of things, as Miller was to continue to do until he died in 1943. Perhaps Miller, whose decline would make less inspiring reading than his rise, could see what was coming and knew himself to be a has-been. His name at least will never be forgotten, and his engineering style has lasted longer than anyone else's. With this much to its credit, his memory can afford due deference to Leo Goossen, the real designer who created his memorial in metal.

While men like Bugatti and Miller had a gift for appreciating the distribution of stresses in a solid metal component, Issigonis applied a similar talent to box-like fabrications of metal sheet. He, too, is a freehand artist, whose ideas find expression as rapidly as they flow from his brain in perfunctory, pencilled perspectives that may be large-scale guides to his artificer assistants or thumbnail doodles on the back of an envelope; and during the last part of his career, when he was the chief car designer for the British Motor Corporation, his drawings often went no further than that. His small team of assistants – he hated the idea of working with a large drawing-office complement, insisting that communication then became impossible – could quickly fabricate by hand the structure that he sketched and described and, from that point, he would work as a sculptor works, moving masses into different juxtapositions until his trained eye and conditioned instinct told him that they were right. The story of his final proportioning of the Morris Minor is famous, but will bear retelling as an example: the car had been completed as a mock-up, but Issigonis thought that it looked wrong, feeling that it needed to be wider. He had his men cut it straight down the middle and move the two halves apart until the proportions of height to width looked right, whereupon the addition of a 10-in gusset was the final step in clearing the mock-up design to go on to the detailers in preparation for production.

How right Issigonis's eye and instinct were was rapidly confirmed

Issigonis, later Sir Alec, the champion of the small car, with bespectacled Forrest Lycett who made the utmost of an 8-litre Bentley

when the Morris Minor came on the market, for it was an immediate success and remained a success for so long that the British Leyland Motor Corporation became quite embarrassed by it. Time and again, they sought to drop it from their production to make way for new models, but an enraptured public would not allow it – the little car was literally the embodiment of nicety, everything being judged so beautifully that its balance, its handling and its roadholding soon became legendary.

The early postwar Morris Minor which made Issigonis justly famous

Part of the secret lay in the suspension of the car, this being something in which Issigonis had long taken a particular interest. He was by no means one of those designers who could only work in the off-hand manner just described, as though conducting an orchestra of metal shapers: his earlier years in the industry had required him to earn his keep and his employer's respect as a design draughtsman. He never went to the other extreme of being a designer obsessed with academic theory, the extent of his formal education being limited to a diploma course in mechanical engineering. Like Bugatti and many another great man who knows what is right and is quite content to let some menial calculator confirm it afterwards, he loathed mathematics. 'All creative people hate mathematics,' he said. 'It's the most uncreative subject you can study, unless you become an Einstein and study it in the abstract philosophical sense.'

Of his intelligence and intellect, there can be no doubt whatever. Issigonis is an extremely cultivated man, wide-ranging in his conversation, perceptive in his judgements, gently mocking in his wit, devoted and sincere in personal relationships. One sometimes wonders what a gentle man like this is doing in the motor industry, but, with a marine engineer for a father and all hope of a broader education being dispelled by the family's enforced flight as refugees from Smyrna (now Izmir) in 1922, it seemed that training in mechanical engineering would give the then 17-year-old Alexander Arnold Constantine Issigonis a start on a career in which he would at least be familiar with the basics. After passing his examinations, his first job was in a London design office, where he worked on a semi-automatic transmission for cars; this was doomed to failure because General Motors brought out synchromesh at just about that time, so Issigonis accepted an invitation to work for Humber in Coventry. There, he came under William Heynes (later to be the chief designer at Jaguar) and specialized in suspension design. He made a lot of progress, developing or helping with new forms of independent suspension for the Humber and Hillman models of 1936; then he moved again, this time to the Morris factory near Oxford. Once more he specialized in suspension problems, studying and learning to admire the work of Maurice Olley, that expatriate Englishman who had gone from Rolls-Royce to General Motors and there revolutionized chassis and suspension design with the first theoretical examination of the science of steering, roadholding and handling.

The interest was of more than professional concern for young Issigonis, for by that time he was engaged with his friend George Dowson in the construction of a tiny racing car intended primarily for fun in the hillclimbs that were such a feature of motor sport in Britain before the war. This was the Lightweight Special, one of the most extraordinarily advanced competition machines in relation to its time ever built and, without doubt, the most brilliant amateur construction of all the specials that proliferated in that decade or perhaps any other. It really was a lightweight, totalling only 587 lb, of which the highly-tuned Austin Seven engine accounted for no less than 38%. The rest of it was a monocoque construction conceived by eye, pencil and scrap paper in what was to become the best Issigonis tradition. The basis of the hull was two beams of plywood faced with aluminium sheet, given tremendous torsional stiffness by everything that could possibly be integrated with them, starting from the front suspension bearers (themselves stressed sheet structures) and continuing with the engine, a large tubular cross-member, a stressed scuttle, the seat pan and the final drive gearbox about which two swinging half-axles pivoted, their arcs being determined and their loads distributed by radius arms to give a semi-trailing, wishbone type of geometry. At the front, the suspension was by tiny paired wishbones, the springing media at both ends of the car being rubber. Removing some of the rubber bands from the rear to lower the car introduced Issigonis to the secrets of negative camber that eluded other swing-axle practitioners for decades to come.

The whole was made by Issigonis and Dowson, most of it by hand. Yet it was not the work of mechanics – it was a work of art and a means of acquiring science. There was scarcely an ounce wasted in it anywhere, nor any significant space – and when, 20 years afterwards, Issigonis was creating the legendary Mini, all his experience with suspension, his knowledge of structures, his concern with minutiae and his originality of ideas served as a valuable support to that art he had developed with the Minor, the art of putting things in the right place. That really was the secret of the Mini. There had been other cars with front-wheel drive, some of them even with transverse engines. There had been others with rubber suspension, with the outstanding stability born of having a wheel at each corner, and with bodies that had been aggressively boxy in shape so as to secure the maximum habitable space within limiting dimensions. Goodness knows, there had also been many other cars employing the BMC A-type engine that Issigonis was condemned to employ, when the firm's chairman (Sir Leonard Lord) set him to produce a technically-advanced bestseller. What Issigonis did was to arrange the necessary components in a way that had not been done before, subjugating the machinery that traditionally occupied the lion's share of the motor-car to the requirements of the people who would buy and occupy it. It was, as almost every one of Issigonis's cars has been, an essentially humanistic concept: he was not designing cars for engineers, nor for motoring enthusiasts, but for people.

There had been an occasion when he allowed himself some laxity in this, when for a brief postwar period he went to work for Alvis, there to propose an extremely advanced car with a $3\frac{1}{2}$-litre V8 engine. a monocoque hull and an ingenious transmission system involving two 2-speed gearboxes in series, the latter being an electrically-controlled overdrive device. Another feature of the Alvis was a coupled suspension system devised by his friend Alex Moulton, who later attended to the suspensory requirements of the Mini and its numerous derivatives. This Alvis never went into production, the company being dubious about the risks of tooling up for something so unorthodox and preferring the security of their military contracts. After his experience with them, Issigonis learned how to inspire his masters when he returned to the Austin enclaves of BMC, and the decisions they took jointly on his recommendation were undoubtedly brave – for instance, the insistence that Dunlop develop tyres suitable for the 10-in diameter wheels that Issigonis demanded for the Mini. The success of the car, success that was popular rather than profitable – though through no fault of its designer – confirmed the authority of this unorthodox man, and confirmed above all perhaps his philanthropic logic: it was a car for the people, a car in which no less than 80% was theirs to occupy as they liked. He joked about the voluminous door pockets in the Mini, saying that they were calculated to contain just the right materials for a correctly-proportioned dry Martini cocktail – 27 bottles of gin and one of vermouth. Issigonis is a man of great sensitivity and the awareness associated with an artist, but with this kind of boyish exuberance he does his best to conceal the fact.

That same sensitivity and awareness, the same essentially human concern that pervades his engineering logic, is displayed by Dante Giacosa, perhaps the most important of the many superbly able designers who have taken charge of Fiat car production in all the long history of that great company. The essential difference between the two men is that Issigonis got where he did in spite of his character and temperament, Giacosa perhaps because of his. Fiat was already that kind of company, thanks to the inspiration and guidance of the man who, in successively senior appointments from 1928 to 1966, guided and developed the company until it became the industry's most astonishing entity, and until founder Agnelli's grandson was ready to take his place as the chairman. This man was Professor Vittorio Valletta, not an engineer but a graduate and subsequently a lecturer in business administration and related studies. It was he who masterminded the development of a firm that could survive the incalculable moral and material damage of the Second World War, and who supervised its rebirth by concentrating on maintaining its workers' welfare and its customers' interests. In a sense, he was continuing the policies of the firm's founders, who might best be described as wealthy intellectual socialists; and so, after the long and often painfully-interrupted formative years, it became Fiat's policy not to confront the people with the future but to lead them gently into it.

The beginnings of a new generation of cars conceived more perfectly in this spirit than ever before became apparent in the mid 1930s. Prior to that, in 1932, had appeared one of the most popular Fiats ever, the Type 508, known as the Balilla. This was, if ever there were, a car for the people: it was compact and light, economical and lively, adaptable to a variety of body styles and to a steady improvement of individual components. Intended to be as cheap as a mass-produced car in those difficult days should, its utilitarian aspect was offset by as much refinement as the fortunes of the people would allow: its hydraulic brakes, 12V electrics and hydraulic dampers would have been considered luxuries in more expensive cars elsewhere. Its unfashionably short piston stroke heralded the new era of tireless high-cruising speeds for the new *autostrade*. Better still, it had in it the makings of something even more convincing: this became evident in 1937, when a new 508C was introduced with independent front suspension and an enlarged cylinder bore which gave a displacement of 1089 cc and attracted the name Millecento – a name which became official in 1940 and stayed in the Fiat catalogues for no less than 30 years. By the standards of its time, the 1100 (as it was styled in the English-speaking markets) was a prodigy in handling, ride, comfort and performance: it was then the only people's car that was also a driver's car.

Yet it was not alone. As its pillarless body suggested – for it looked like a cross between the 1935 1500 and the 1936 500 – it was one of a new generation. This was a true impression: those three cars between them marked the emergence of Dante Giacosa as one of the greatest benefactors of the motoring world, and the establishment of Fiat as a firm of more national and more social significance than was normally attributed to mere motor manufacturers. What distinguished Giacosa's 1500 (a more luxurious machine than the others, though still essentially modest) was that it was the first of the three to display the new approach, and that its drag coefficient was the best achieved up to then by a touring car, without sacrificing in any way the comfort of the passengers or the aesthetic sensibilities of the times. What distinguished his 500 was simply its size; with a 13 bhp 569 cc engine in a proportionately tiny body (the wheelbase was two good paces) the Topolino, as it was called, was the first really small car to be properly refined, and the first to be free from savage compromises of habitability and roadworthiness.

When Valletta was rebuilding the sadly-damaged company after the Hitler war, the first priority was to produce cars to existing designs, just as in other parts of war-torn Europe. Soon, however, Giacosa introduced replacements. In 1955, the Topolino gave way to the rear-engined 600, a 4-seater economy and utility car that exemplified a new order of very compact and responsive machines that enjoyed immediate and immense popularity, the 850 and, perhaps above all, the new 500 relaying the same message in other price categories. The 500, with its air-cooled, 2-cylinder engine owing nothing to motor-cycle practice (as was often alleged) but a lot to Fiat's aero-engine experience, was to run for more than three million examples before it made way for the Type 126 derivative of 1972.

Long before then, however, Giacosa had recognized that the rear-engined formula could not dominate popular motoring, much as certain French and German rivals hoped it would. The Fiat 124, which was born in 1966, was ostensibly a plain and ordinary front-engined rear-drive family saloon. The fact that it set new standards in performance and in stability and structural safety, in detailed refinement such as 4-wheeled disc braking and elimination of most maintenance needs, and in sheer suitability to the needs of the

The Fiat 124 was the work of Dante Giacosa and Oscar Montabone, but was also a monument to the reign – or rather the regency – of Dr Valletta, who guided the company through its most critical years

motoring population at large – not only in Italy but also in the USSR and virtually anywhere in the world – was what marked it out as a high point in Fiat's history and, above all, as a cogent expression of the philosophy of Professor Valletta and the rare sensitivity of Giacosa.

There is no doubt that Giacosa was an artist, because, above all, he was an humanitarian designer, but there is also material evidence to support his categorization in this chapter – the exterior envelope of the 124 might have been a potentially dowdy box, albeit for the best of reasons, but virtually every individual mechanical component within it was a thing of beauty, as had been the case with the majority of Fiats in earlier times. By the time the 124 emerged, Giacosa was nearing retirement and, under his supervision, much of the work on the car was done by his successor Oscar Montabone, a man of enormous proficiency, schooled in similar principles; but even when the Fiat 128, primogenitor of a whole new generation of front-wheel-drive family cars and still, in 1975, the equal of any of them, came on the scene two or three years later, Giacosa's influence was still visibly strong in its design. Only then, when critics accused him of aping Issigonis, did Fiat reveal that Giacosa had designed transverse-engined, front-wheel-drive cars of essentially similar layout in the late 1930s. He could be as original and as imaginative as any – and his solution to the problems of compacting a front-wheel-drive transmission with a transverse engine is theoretically, functionally and visually better than any other yet seen.

Of course Giacosa, like any chief designer of a large firm, was not a factotum, but was the inspirer and overseer of a large and professionally competent team. Indeed it is in these circumstances that the designer of artistic temperament fares best, when he functions not as a manipulator of the end-product, but as the conductor of an orchestra of men whose individual contributions must be integrated, blended and built up into a cogent and satisfying whole. Vincenzo Lancia was one such, his greatest achievements (the Lambda of 1923 and the Aprilia of 1937) being attributable almost wholly to his inspiration and government of a small team of clever and competent design draughtsmen. For example, the famous Lancia sliding-pillar independent front-suspension, introduced on the Lambda and featured in every subsequent model until the Aurelia broke the pattern in 1950, was designed, not by Lancia himself, but by his technical assistant Falchetto. It was Lancia himself who decided that his new car should have independent suspension: while driving his mother in one of his earlier cars (a Kappa), a front spring had broken and the resulting upset had caused him to think furiously. He told Falchetto to devise a suitable kind of suspension, and Falchetto settled down to a night's concentrated thinking. The next morning he presented Lancia with a sheet of paper on which a large number of different systems had been sketched, including practically every type that has been used by any manufacturer since, and one or two that have yet to be adopted. Falchetto created the choice, Lancia made the choice – and, as a result, his cars became bywords for outstanding road-

Snapped up by an eager Fiat when a youngster, Vincenzo Lancia had already started his own firm when he was pictured here as a works driver in the 1907 Fiat racing team

Lancia's first and most personal masterpiece was the beautifully structured and impressively roadworthy Lambda

holding and steering that was light and precise at all times.

Modern analysts criticize the Lancia IFS because of the variations of toe-in that occur when the car is tilted in roll, its one-piece track rod being unable to accommodate the ensuing variation in effective track; but in those days, when all steering was laid out according to the geometric principles expounded by Lankensperger and propounded by Ackermann, and when the subtleties of tyre slip angles were not understood, Lancia's system gave an anti-Ackermann effect when it was wanted. It was not insight on his part, though it may have been intuition: apart from the solecisms in the cylinder heads of his long line of narrow-angle v engines, Lancia never made a serious technical error. He had after all started off his independent career by designing and making cars himself, and as early as 1906, when the Lancia firm was incorporated, he established the philosophy that shaped all his later designs. He was an artist among craftsmen from the very first, even from the days when he was a lad supposedly studying book-keeping, but spending a lot of time admiring the premises and processes of the Ceirano workshop.

As a boy, Lancia was an adventurer and a dreamer; as a man, he was impulsive, industrious and generous, a great patron of the opera, a passionate enthusiast for the music of Wagner and one of the fastest and most furious drivers of his time. He was still driving in the Fiat factory team, even after setting up his own company, and, by then, had already decided that his own cars should be unconventional – although it is arguable whether, at that time, cars could be thought of as being conventional anyway.

Perhaps a better description of the Lancia ethos is technical nonconformity, with no concessions being made to cheapness or simplicity in manufacture if they involved any displacement of engineering ideals. By the time he came to ponder the design of his Lambda, which first saw the light of day at the London and Paris Shows of 1922, he had been debating the problems of ship construction and was tempted to embody the same principles of stress distribution by building a car in which the body and chassis were integrated for more efficient resolution of the forces to which it was subjected. Likewise, after considering the fashionable and mistaken aesthetic notions which prompted many engine designers to create slender spacewasters of architectural formality and dubious rigidity, he determined to build engines that were short and stiff in all directions. Lancia did not invent any of these features, but he was the first designer to combine all in one car, to put it into full production and to persist with this combination throughout his life.

His addiction to narrow v engines was understandable, for not only were they short and stiff in all planes of the single main cylinder block, they could also be crowned by a monobloc casting embodying all the cylinder heads; and, with evenly-spaced bores and a separate crank throw for each connecting rod, they could run smoothly without suffering agonies of bending or torsional flutter. Beyond these basic attributes, however, they had very little in common with one another: over the years, Lancia employed 14 different angles,

from the 24° of the Di Lambda to the 10° 14′ of the Appia, and, in fact, there were three different angles for the three different sizes of Lambda engine. These engines were not without their short-comings, most notably in the porting arrangements of those complex cylinder heads in which the inlet and exhaust passages burrowed their ways in a convincing imitation of a rabbit warren, without much regard evidently being paid to charge heating, gas dynamics or excessive shedding of heat to the coolant.

By the time Lancia came to produce his second masterpiece, the Aprilia, he had two engineers (Sola and Verga) to concentrate on the engine, and a technical chief (Baggi) to oversee the whole operation. Lancia himself was preoccupied with a new 5-cylinder lorry engine that was giving him a lot of distraction at the time, but he gave the car continuous scrutiny between the laying down of the project in 1934 and the final approval of the production prototype in 1936. The terms of reference he gave his team were to create something bold, unconventional, streamlined, spacious, lively, stable, small, modestly-engined and competitively-priced. This was equivalent to commissioning a string quartet for three players, but Lancia con-ducted everything with a sure hand. In particular, he insisted on cropping the tail and flattening the roof of the teardrop-shaped stressed-skin hull that Falchetto had produced with the aid of the aerodynamicists and wind tunnel of the Turin Polytechnic; and, in retrospect, as the argument of the next chapter will suggest, he was right. In practice he was right beyond doubt, for the brilliant little

Aprilia was a tremendous success, returning to production after the Hitler war and remaining on the market with its enlarged ($1\frac{1}{2}$-litre) engine until 1950. Alas, before the car went into production in 1937, Vincenzo Lancia died when not yet 56 years old. Was he an artist? Without a doubt – apart from his temperament, the only other necessary evidence is the shape of his original Lambda prototype.

If we consider the artist as a man with a baton rather than a man with a pencil, we are irresistibly drawn to the case of Ferdinand Porsche. It is a difficult decision that places him in this chapter: he was emphatically not a chassis man, nor much of a body shaper, but an important figure in the story of the motor engine and a man well enough qualified – albeit on a *post hoc propter hoc* basis – to be treated as a theoretician. His detractors used to maintain that the man could scarcely draw a line; and yet, as the governor of a busy, independent design office, he could so guide his draughtsmen's interpretations of his directions that what was eventually created was bursting with artistic conviction. When at his busiest, his principal tools were a formidable brain and some fearsome invective; and, despite the length of his career, his tremendous output testifies to the frequency of those occasions when he was very busy indeed. There is a great deal of continuity in his work: look at his dedication to swing-axle rear suspension, to the teardrop body, to relatively large and slow-running, lightly-stressed and deliberately reliable engine design, and it is easy to see him as the artist obsessed with the *idée fixe*. The Auto-Union Grand Prix car, the prototype people's cars of Zündapp and NSU, the Volkswagen and, possibly, the postwar Porsche 356, are all fundamentally similar.

There have, of course, been other designers obsessed with a single principal notion that they have carried through to a realization expressed artistically rather than mechanically: Jean Grégoire, with his front-wheel-drive car based on an aluminium-alloy chassis frame and bulkhead structure, is an example cast in the same mould, if not of the same stuff, as Lancia. Porsche, however, was in fact one of those creatively fecund individuals whose vision penetrated the obscurantist orthodoxies of more than mere cars. After all, he started off with an obsession for electricity, pursued despite the furious opposition of his father, until it carried him to the creation of an all-electric transmission system, relying on electric motors set in the hubs of each wheel. Initially, this was propounded for cars made by Lohner; but once Porsche had taken the step of introducing a petrol engine to generate the electricity for the motors, rather than relying upon hopelessly inadequate accumulators, he was soon applying the mixed transmission system to much more extraordinary machines.

In the Kaiser war, he built fantastic military trains of linked, self-steering, electrically-propelled carriages, all deriving their motive flux from the dynamo car that led them uphill, down dale, around corners, over Alps, or even car by car across bridges too flimsy to bear the weight of the whole train. A magnified version gave self-propelled mobility to the biggest artillery piece ever to travel by road, an enormous Skoda mortar, which fired 1-ton shells from its 26-ton barrel. In the Hitler war, the same mixed drive distinguished that most famous of *Panzerwagen*, the Tiger tank. Between the wars, he dabbled in many other things, including helicopters and an inverted V12 engine that became the Daimler-Benz 600 series, acknowledged by at least one rival manufacturer as the best-designed aero-engine to see service in the 1939–45 conflict. There were agricultural tractors too, and all their hydraulic and mechanical ancillaries. From the point of view of royalty income (and even more from the standpoint of its popularity with other designers once the patents ran out in 1950), there was his use of torsion bars as springing media in place of the leaf and coil springs that had formerly been the rule.

Does all this make Porsche an artist? The quantity does not, nor does the variety. It was not an artistic spirit that made him the begetter of torsion-bar suspension and the creator of the first front-wheel-drive car – the original Lohner electric chaise of 1900. There is, however, something more that argues his inclusion in this distinguished company – the quality of his line. Whether he drew it or merely demanded it of the minions over whose shoulders he glared and swore during each working day, the line of a Porsche design is almost always too consistent in character and persuasive in its beauty to be the product of a mere technological equilibrium. The engine of the Prince Henry Austro-Daimler, the engine of the s, ss, and ssk Mercedes-Benz, the engine of the big Grand Prix Auto-Unions and the engine of the Volkswagen, all have in common the same kind of curvature, the same appearance of thin, fragile, ultra-lightweight shells, enclosing large and super-efficient voids. It was quite uncanny how Porsche could make something big, substantial and utterly opaque look light and cavernous, as though it were a papier-mâché *Doppelgänger* for the genuine heavy metal. Was it simply because so many of Porsche's designs were unorthodox, and that we were therefore not led to think automatically of their contents as we do when seeing a piece of traditional enclosed structure? Even if the explanation is simply that curves of this sort were currently fashionable in Germany, to be observed in everything from a domestic radio cabinet to the superstructure of the ss *Bremen*, might not this indicate Porsche's sensitivity to line and proportion and physical beauty?

All the evidence tends to suggest that he was no great shakes as a theoretician; very often the difficult bits (the original detail specification for the Auto-Union P-Wagen, for example) were done by his brilliant assistant Karl Rabe, a man scarcely known for his own ideas, but whose eventual claim to fame was that he made so many of Porsche's ideas work. If it were not Rabe, then it might have been his aerodynamicist Mickl who wielded the slide rule: when Porsche wielded it publicly, it seems to have been mainly for effect. Porsche's own pet independent front suspension, with his transverse torsion bars acting on the trailing links of a 4-bar parallelogram system, caused the front wheels to roll through the same angle as the car,

Overleaf: Bemused by the modern rear-engined projectiles bearing his name, we tend to forget that Porsche began as the first protagonist of front-wheel-drive (for Lohner) and went on to propound magnificent orthodoxies such as this exemplar of the Mercedes-Benz s series, based in the late 1920s on the chassis designed by Paul Daimler

Porsche believed in large lightly-stressed engines. *Left:* The modestly-rated v16 Auto-Union GP engine could have proved him right . . .

. . . had it not been betrayed by the geometrical solecisms of Porsche's suspension designs in this otherwise exemplary chassis (*above*). It was an instance of his assistant Karl Rabe, who was responsible for the detailed specification, being unable to overcome the shortcomings of his master's visionary ideas

Opposite: The GP Auto-Union was very fast and very difficult to drive. When Rabe delved and Porsche span, which was then the clever man?

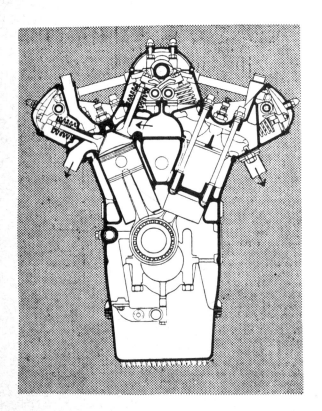

about a ground-level front roll centre. His favourite swinging half-axles, not his idea but no less enthusiastically maintained for all that, produced a roll centre at the rear several inches higher than the hubs, combined with every mentionable horror of camber variation, jacking effect, toe-in and bump steer. Could any serious theoretician really hope to reconcile the two in a car that weighed only three-quarters of a ton and mustered 545 bhp? Even allowing him a brief freedom to try it, is it possible that a serious theoretician would persist with the arrangement for years to come, even in cars that might be lacking in power but whose drivers would often be lacking in skill?

A simpler conclusion would be that Porsche was utterly hopeless on chassis design, a view strengthened by the atrocious behaviour of the blown straight-eight Mercedes he built in the 1920s, following the success of the blown 2-litre four that he inherited when he joined the firm after quitting Austro-Daimler. He is recorded as having given complete approval to the design of a supercharged Grand Prix Cisitalia that was built in prototype form in the early postwar

There is, as shown in Chapter Seven, a kind of apostolic succession among car designers. This laying-on of hands by Dr Ferdinand Porsche in his later years appears in a different light

years, and for which his son was largely responsible: yet the suspension of that car, intended to out-perform such doughty opposition as the Alfetta, and to be so powerful as to justify the provision of selective 4-wheel drive, set at nought the experience garnered in the 1938–9 Grand Prix Auto-Unions in which a De Dion rear axle, in emulation of the very successful Mercedes-Benz, replaced Porsche's pet swinging half-axles to good purpose. The Cisitalia reverted to a form of independent rear suspension that once again imposed camber variations and toe-in aberrations without any means for controlling them.

Even in engine design, he could sometimes show the cloven hoof: after scrapping Paul Daimler's straight-six to substitute a bigger and more powerful engine of his own for the new s series Mercedes-Benz in the late 1920s, he produced what was basically a superb engine, and then spoilt it by making wrong decisions about the cylinder head design and material. Much has been written and said about what happens to one of these cars if driven for long with the supercharger clutch engaged, but it is not generally realized that the supercharger was supposed not to be used at all unless the fuel were benzol rather than the usual petrol. However, occasional errors can be forgiven in anybody: even though man might be a divine creation, his design has shown the need for some development work. We may argue long and inconclusively about how well Porsche was qualified to be cast as a theoretician, great though his practical knowledge and experience were; let us at least give him the credit for having been, in an admittedly special sense, an artist.

A man who was both, whose cars were among the finest of their day, and frequently among the ugliest, was Gabriel Voisin. It must be remembered that he was 40 years old before he embarked on the design of cars and, by then, he had completed a career in aviation that would in itself amply justify his inclusion among the immortals of engineering. Whether he was really the first person to fly a powered and fully-controllable aeroplane is still a matter for argument or, rather, a matter of definitions; but when one remembers that not only had he more than 27000 cars to his credit when he retired, but also more than 10000 aeroplanes, a great variety of engines, inflatable hangar buildings, prefabricated houses (as early as 1919) and even a portable 200-seater theatre building erected by a $\frac{1}{4}$-hp motor and pneumatic pump, it is clear that Voisin illustrates – like Porsche and Bugatti – the truly creative intellect.

Most important is his time devoted to aviation. It is impossible to spend much time in that industry, and emerge from it with a successful reputation, without acquiring on the way not only a mastery of technological processes developed to a much higher standard of perfection than in most other industries, but also an appreciation of the true relationship between beauty and function, between line and load. Voisin also exhibited a trait present in virtually all the designers discussed in this chapter, perhaps to a greater degree of aggressiveness than any of the others, even Bugatti – he was passionately convinced that the way he did things was the right way, and what everybody else did was wrong. To look at the body styles he created for some of his more exceptional chassis, especially in the mid-1930s, would be enough to make one wonder whether it were really a case of everybody being out-of-step except our Gabriel: but his reasoning was rigorous. Weight and weakness were the enemies, whereas his bodies were designed to be constructed of aluminium and wood in such a way as to be very light and strong. So deeply was he committed to these principles that he refused to guarantee any of his chassis if a coachbuilder mounted a body of more than a certain stipulated weight – the limiting figure was usually well below the abilities and tastes of traditional coachbuilders, and made them view Voisin with considerable distaste and occasional open hostility.

Hostility was something that Voisin learned to live with from a quite early stage in his car-designing career: with his aviation background, he knew the importance of low aerodynamic drag, and built his sports cars accordingly, only to have them outlawed by the racing authorities who argued that streamlining gave his cars an unfair advantage. His prompt retort was to enter a stripped version of his ordinary road-going sports car in the French Grand Prix – and, although it mustered far less power than any of its serious competitors, it got along well enough to finish in fifth place at the end of the 1923 event held at Tours. The transmission, the axles, steering, brakes and all the internal components of the engine were absolutely standard, the only modification being the addition of two cylinders to bring the engine's displacement up to the permitted two litres; and with this amplification of what was basically the standard 4-cylinder 8 cv Voisin c4, to give it a power output of not more than 65 bhp, the car maintained an average speed 16% slower than the 102-bhp Sunbeam that won. Later that year, Voisin brought out new sports cars with bodywork designed on similar lines to those of the Tours Grand Prix cars and with either a small 4-cylinder engine or a big 4-litre six basically the same as that of the immensely-respected touring car.

By the beginning of that year, Voisin had already collected 94 first prizes in races and hill-climbs, including a number of records over some of the most important and daunting of the Alpine passes. It was really in its proper element, on the open public roads, that the Voisin demonstrated its abilities best: it was never designed to be capable of development into a specialized track machine, but to be capable in standard form of very high performance in ordinary everyday conditions. It shone, therefore, on such runs as the high-speed dash from Paris to Nice, the second half of it wriggling up and over the Maritime Alps, the whole journey being done with sealed bonnet and subjected to the critical attentions of the Press. Before the Kaiser war, the best time for the journey had been 16 h 15 mins in a 60-hp De Dietrich, and in the early 1920s the run was revived: Delage did it in 14 h in a $4\frac{1}{2}$-litre car of his own, and in 1921 the redoubtable André Dubonnet brought the time down to 12 h 55 mins in the new 45-hp Hispano-Suiza that had been hailed as the finest and fastest road car in the world. Shortly afterwards,

Evidence of Voisin's aviation background is apparent in the shaping of this 1929 12-cylinder record car

The 14CV 6-cylinder Voisin of 1932 was bodied by its creator in a less outlandish style than he was to adopt a few years later

the 18 CV Voisin with its 4-cylinder engine reduced the journey time to 11 h 30 mins, equal to an average speed of 51 mph, and it was another two years before an Hispano reduced this by another six minutes.

It was the 18 CV Voisin that really made the firm's motoring reputation. It was generally known as the Type C1, and much less generally known was the fact that the design originated with Citroën. Voisin had been concerned about the effects of the postwar depression in the aviation industry, and sought a quick means of getting into car manufacture: this particular design was destined never to be put into production by Citroën, and Voisin was able to acquire the rights to it without much trouble. Its engine was a Knight double-sleeve-valve type, such as had become popular with Panhard et Levassor; and, like that company, Voisin became thoroughly addicted to sleeve valves as a result. The C1 was a splendid machine, especially after he developed its engine to give much more power than had originally been predicted for it. The whole thing was

49

extremely strong, beautifully refined and uncommonly quiet. It was also very fast. There has hardly ever been a Voisin that was not. Very few of his products could ever be called sports cars, but even the largest and most luxurious or the smallest and humblest could be described as a high-performance car, frequently being capable of reaching maximum speeds or maintaining averages higher than anything to be expected of rivals in their appropriate classes. The satisfaction derived from virtually every aspect of their behaviour was ample justification for the idiosyncrasy of their design, for the passionately rational and provocatively radical theories that Voisin propounded with all the authority and impatience of an Uccello demonstrating perspective to the fifteenth-century Florentines.

It was not only light weight and sleeve valves that featured in Voisin's diatribes. Reliability and running costs he considered of fundamental importance, too, and so was easy gearchanging. After a brief dalliance with the infinitely variable transmission of De Lavaud in 1929, he adopted with glee the Cotal electrically-controlled epicyclic gearbox which thereafter figured prominently in the specification of nearly every high-class French car until about 1950 and could well be profitably revived today. Not content even with that, Voisin pursued the ideal of engine flexibility to such an extent that he contrived engines with more and more cylinders, with a straight-eight and then a series of v12s echoing an engine of that format with which he had toyed as early as 1919. His engines were technically masterpieces in their aluminium-alloy foundry work, artistically masterpieces by the aesthetic standards of the day: in a general absence of understanding of the importance of inlet and exhaust manifold design (something that seemed to be closed in a book that only Harry Miller might read), it was considered the done thing for a really elegant engine to appear clean and monolithic beneath the bonnet, with everything possible secreted within. Porsche designed auxiliary enclosures to hide the pump, dynamo and magneto of his big 6-cylinder Mercedes-Benz engines, while W.O. Bentley betrayed his locomotive-shed upbringing by a plethora of bolt heads and bits and pieces, even though the manifolding was still poor. Bugatti tried hard enough to satisfy both sets of criteria, but Voisin – thanks in no small measure to the forgiving nature of a sleeve-valve engine's breathing – was quite successful, and little more than a carburettor protruded from the sheer flanks of his engines.

Would that his body designs had appealed similarly to the tastes of the day. The conventional bodies on the c1 allowed it to become extremely fashionable, and many were the great names in French and American society, from Rudolph Valentino and Maurice Chevalier up to François Mitterand, who basked in the reflected glory of this exceptionally fine touring car. The big v12s were another matter altogether for, by the time they were built, Voisin's incorrigible reasoning had led him to the creation of big, light, strong, roomy and heavily-constructed bodies that looked as deplorable as their logic was inescapable. As for the legendary straight-twelve, consisting of two 6-cylinder 3-litre engines in line ahead, producing a top speed of 125 mph, the whole thing was a shortlived flight of fancy – or perhaps a flight into a reality that only Voisin himself could fully comprehend. His objects in creating this car were two: one, to fight back against the depredations of Packard on the luxury market, the other to make a high-speed car that would remain completely controllable and pleasant in its handling, even at the highest speeds of which it was capable. One must not lose sight of the fact that the big Voisins were meant to be driven at 90 mph with as much control and assurance as might seem remarkable in other luxury cars at 60 mph, but the 12-cylinder Voisin was faster still and its creator was not entirely satisfied with its high-speed handling. He reasoned that the big engine placed well forward had an unfortunate effect on the polar moment of inertia of the car, and an in-line twelve would allow much of that weight to be brought nearer the centre of gravity of the whole car, even if it meant that the rearmost portion of the engine intruded into the cabin. It was duly done, on two prototype chassis of different wheelbases, bodied in established Voisin style; and the car received critical acclaim from the Press. Alas, it was too late, for a group of financiers obtained control of the company, and Voisin himself was finished. Cars bearing his name remained in production for another two or three years, but they were cars with which he had had nothing to do, and of which he was thoroughly ashamed, cars based on remaining Voisin chassis but disgraced by the insertion of a Graham-Paige engine bereft of its usual supercharger.

It was the end of Voisin cars, and almost coincided with the end of artistry in car design, though fortunately that revived in the late 1950s. It was not the end of Voisin personally, however. After the war, his next creation was as logical and surprising as all his others: the Biscuter was a tiny, ultra-light, hyper-economical runabout built in some thousands for the Spanish market which was critically short of cars in the early 1950s. It was clever; but it was almost certainly not art.

In the full design sense, it is unlikely that anything ever will be again: cars simply are not manufactured that way nowadays. Art is something that is associated only with body-styling and, although it plays an astonishingly important part in governing the work of engineers, it also reduces them to an individually impotent regiment of faceless, nameless, characterless boffins and bondmen, specialists sitting on a committee. Men who could design a whole car and do it in such a way as to stimulate its comparison with works of art would probably not be allowed to exercise their talents in this day and age, when the designer is subordinated to the dispirited tin gods of government agencies and consumer councillors. Today's legislated motorist is not interested in the surgically-precise steering of a Lancia being hurled through a fast bend, or the fact that its creator loved opera. He is not impressed by the camshaft-driven gearbox serving the cooling fan of a 38/250 Mercedes-Benz, nor by the fact that its designer Porsche loved deflating the ego of Nazi officials, even as high-ranking as Hitler himself. He is supremely indifferent to the niceties of Bugatti's rear suspension and the fact that the man loved horses. He might only be prompted to take notice of the hub-drive hydraulic servos giving anti-lock braking capability to each wheel of a Voisin, if further reminded that Gabriel Voisin loved women. All that today's motorist seems to require is currently fashionable ostentation in styling and the knowledge that his car will survive being driven at 13 mph into a block of concrete. The age of artistry in car design, like the age of chivalry, is gone. As Edmund Burke observed, 'That of sophisters, economists and calculators has succeeded; and the glory of Europe is extinguished for ever.'

2
Body shapers

$\mathscr{S}$hakespeare would have difficulty in understanding modern English. In each generation the vocabulary changes and so, to a lesser extent, does the grammar until, by small degrees, imperceptibly, the usages of the native tongue that he so much embellished have grown quite different. There is a limit to the changes that can be made in a given time without the language becoming incomprehensible – and precisely this same statement applies to the analogous language of car styling. Designers have, at any given time, a certain formal vocabulary that they can use and even extend slightly in the manner of idiom or slang. Thus, high or low waistlines, bulging hips, fastback or notchback roof lines and flowing or cropped tails may constitute items of vocabulary in the language of car styling. The so-called streamlined style which flourished in cars of the 1930s was a kind of slang or idiomatic usage; whereas the fundamental re-statements of how a car ought to be shaped to accord with the requirements of aerodynamic theory, re-statements originating from such designers as Voisin, Burney, Jaray and Rumpler, represented efforts to change the grammar, the conceptual substructure. Too great a change too soon is unintelligible, even though the statement may be important. Conversely, it is possible to retreat a certain distance into the past and make statements that are distant enough to be romantic while not yet being archaic: this is something that Morgan could do as successfully now as HRG and MG did earlier, though this is a question of vocabulary rather than of grammar – the Morgan would not sell as it does if it had a crash gearbox and 19-in wheels.

To many people, the main need to provide some sort of clothing for the mechanical components that go together to make a car, and also some sort of enclosure for its driver and passengers, are the only factors dictating the car's morphology. In fact, of course, there is something more: there is a whole set of conflicting requirements and of influences that at first sight might seem irrelevant. For example, the relative prices of steel and aluminium sheet might govern the choice of one or other material for certain body panels, and the different working characteristics of these metals would, in turn, then influence the sort of contour that must be evolved for the panels if they are to be produced economically. The sheer cost of building a body can have an enormous influence on its design so the area and weight of sheet metal and ancillary materials, including interior trim and (most important because it is both heavy and costly) glass, are body factors as vital as the relative structural strengths and stiffnesses of different shapes.

All these influences can be quantified and are fairly well understood by car designers; but there remains a further set of influences which are less well understood, and these are the effects of various aerodynamic phenomena on the efficiency, safety, comfort and performance of a car. Most modern manufacturers will tell you that their cars are either practical or aerodynamic, and sometimes they claim both, while others will insist that no design that is not aerodynamic can be practical. In general, there is precious little truth in any of these assertions, precious little understanding of what is meant by styling, and even less of what is involved in the science of aerodynamics. Indeed, it has only been from time to time in the history of the motor-car that aerodynamics – the study of the movement of bodies through the atmosphere – has been considered relevant to the design of motor-car bodies.

The trouble with early essays in aerodynamics, most of them devoted to the streamlining of racing cars in one way or another, but seldom in enough ways to be effective, was that, although they were to some extent effective in reducing drag, they also gave rise to side effects that could not be fully understood without thorough scientific investigation. Such investigation was quite beyond the scope of private firms and really needed State involvement, though assistance from the aircraft industry was the next best thing. The same disadvantages applied to streamlined road-going cars that were offered to the public in the early 1920s by Rumpler and by Benz in Germany and by Burney in England. The ideas sounded specious enough, but the cars did not look convincing, and the public was sufficiently ignorant about the whole business to remain unattracted.

Only in Germany in the 1930s did the desirability of reducing drag fire the imagination of public, industry and State alike. This was due to a set of circumstances peculiar to Germany: in the first place, there were some splendid new *Autobahnen* where motorists could go from strength to strength through joy, where traffic was still light and the opportunities for sustained high speed were tempting; and in the second place, petrol was becoming (for reasons that were later obvious) a commodity of immense strategic importance and was not to be wasted, so cars were encouraged to be low-powered in order not to waste the precious stuff. There is only one way to go very fast in a very low-powered car – streamline it – and that is what the Germans did.

Among the most notable designers to show their hands, and one of the first to acquire a reputation as a formalist of academic authority, was Freiherr König von Fachsenfeld, who designed a faintly gormless-looking body on one of the great and traditionally angular SSKL Mercedes-Benz 2-seaters, turning it into a racer of enormous speed, successful at the ultra-fast Avus track for which it had been specifically designed. This was just a foretaste of things to come, and the bodies of the technically revolutionary Mercedes-Benz Grand Prix cars of 1934 to at least 1937 were clearly derived from the postulates of von Fachsenfeld, whose textbook *Aerodynamik des Kraftfahrzeuges* became accepted as a pioneer, but authoritative, treatment of the subject for a long time after its publication in 1936. Other notable scientists in some ways attracted even more attention, notably Professors Kamm and Everling, who were among those who were conducting systematic programmes of research into aerodynamics. As we saw in the last chapter, strenuous efforts to create streamlined bodies had been made a decade earlier by the likes of Voisin and Bugatti, not to mention all

Overleaf: All the artifices of construction, the luxury of finish, the pinched orthodoxies of design and the reactionary disciplines of fashion are evident in this elegant body on a Vauxhall of a certain and unmistakable age

the contenders for the land-speed record, and even such primitives as the Porsche design for the Prince Henry Austro-Daimler, whose so-called 'tulip' body (with concave flanks giving an interesting pre-echo of the body designs by Michelotti in the 1960s) was intended to reconcile adequate space for four occupants with minimal frontal area. Perhaps the greatest and first (not only in rank but also chronologically) of all the wind-cheating body designers was Paul Jaray, who was no less great a theoretician, artist or practical engineer than any of the others, but was far more successful in getting his designs actually built in substantial quantities.

Jaray was born in the 1880s in Vienna, whence he moved to Prague to finish his technical education and start one of the first books about aerodynamics. His ideas were very advanced, as may be judged from the instigation of the cantilever aircraft wing in 1910, a little ahead of Junkers. From then until 1923, he was principally concerned with aircraft, both heavier and lighter than air, and his most notable work was with the latter variety, for he became chief designer at the Zeppelin airship works.

It was the Zeppelin designers who took over from the ballisticians of the nineteenth century as the pacemakers of aerodynamics. They had a particularly good wind tunnel to help them, run by the engineer Klemperer, and, with its aid, they established the ideal streamline shape with its circular section, ogival nose, tapering tail and a critical ratio of length to diameter – 6:1, any deviation from which caused increased drag either through turbulence or skin friction. It was therefore hardly surprising that Jaray should have been competent to publish the first effective patents covering streamlined cars in 1921.

What prompted him to take an interest in cars was the rudimentary 'raindrop' streamliner of Rumpler; but, whereas Rumpler's ideas were merely two-dimensional, Jaray, with Klemperer's help, devised a proper three-dimensional adaptation of the Zeppelin teardrop shape to the motor-car. It was necessarily flattened underneath to match the road, but was well rounded on all other surfaces, the tail tapering to a horizontal edge, while the cabin superstructure (like half a teardrop) was blended in above it. In 1922, Jaray's prototype proved on test to give a drag reduction approaching 25%, compared with standard bodywork on the chassis he bodied. Then he built a single-seater racing car for Ley, increasing the 60-mph maximum speed of the sports version to over 80 mph on a mere 26 hp.

Jaray's work was then interrupted by illness, which prompted him, after his recovery, to leave Zeppelin's and make his home in Switzerland. There, he began a programme of frantic design and development work, concentrating on combining drag reduction with unimpeachable road-going practicality – which included not only things like vision and access, but also the provision of outstandingly good ventilation and the elimination of any spurious aerodynamic effects such as lift and directional instability. All sorts of motor manufacturers were his customers, not only the expected German ones such as Adler, BMW, Maybach and Mercedes, but also

foreigners such as Chrysler, Fiat and Tatra. The 1927 Chrysler
streamliner was based on work by Jaray and, although its looks did
not appeal to everybody, its 30% improvement in fuel economy was
proof that his ideas worked. The Tatra 77, built in Czechoslovakia,
was also based on Jaray's work: for this uncommonly capacious 6-
seater to achieve 93 mph under the impulsion of only 65 hp was an
outstanding achievement at a time when the latest and most
exiguously-bodied Le Mans racers needed 90 hp to reach the same
speed.

As time went by, the lines of Jaray's bodies became more acceptable to the public. It was another case of the language being able to
change only slowly, with no more change at any given time than the
public could accept without shock. He was always constrained by
the chassis of the time, too: they tended to be high and narrow,
according to the current fashions, forcing his bodies to echo these
proportions. As changing tastes brought cars and their occupants
nearer to the ground, Jaray took every opportunity to make his cars
lower and sleeker; and by the end of the 1930s he had perfected his
bodies to the point where their drag coefficients ranged from 0·3 to as
little as 0·19, when the typical touring car of the time had a coefficient higher than 0·5. Among the most notable was one that he
produced for a 55 bhp Adler, which managed to average 100 mph on
a long *Autobahn* run: this Adler used formal ideas for which Pininfarina was to be given the credit 11 years later.

One of the problems of the body designer is that his work is so
easily copied, and so impossible to protect by patents or any other
form of registration. Misunderstanding is another problem: the case

of Kamm is typical, for his efforts were crowned with a success that was largely misunderstood, and he is remembered today mainly because of the tail shape he designed, though there are relatively few people who understand why it works as well as it does. In the 1930s, many engineers had learned to accept the postulate of the ideal streamlined body with its long tapering tail; but such a tail was grossly impractical for a car that was to be used in traffic or in the tight streets of old European towns and villages. The long tapering tail is too long for ordinary road conditions, but any attempt to steepen the taper caused airflow to break away. Kamm's idea was to minimize the separation area, to reduce the amount of turbulence created over the tail area of the body where the air could no longer faithfully follow its contours. The important part of his design (as expressed on the specially-bodied BMW 335, known as the K-Wagen) was that he recognized that the car is not a solid body, and that the air passing through it for engine cooling modifies the airflow as it emerges again. Kamm proved that the strategic siting of air intakes and exits could control the flow around the upper and after-most parts of the body; and having, by these means, postponed the separation of airflow until as late as possible, he then simply cropped the body at the point of separation and gave it a virtually flat posterior – saving space, weight and drag all together.

The body of knowledge amassed by these designers was heeded at the time, but further progress was interrupted by the war, and that knowledge has been largely ignored ever since. Some of the reasons were technical: there was a great deal of confusion over the phenomena of lift that seemed to work at cross-purposes with the designer's ideal of low drag, even though the principles involved had been explained by Jaray so much earlier. However, the principal reasons for abandoning the aerodynamic ideal were mainly psychological and aesthetic.

We shall be looking into these reasons later, but first it is proper to point out that – apart from racing and sports-racing cars which are clearly a special class, free from the pressures and inhibitions that impair the design of road-going cars for the public – there have been dozens of manufacturers paying lip service to streamlining, but only five consistent, sustained efforts to achieve good aerodynamic car form in the years since the Hitler war. These were by Citroën, Porsche, Saab, Bristol and Costin. The early postwar Porsche cars were shaped according to a mixture of ideas derived from the work of Mickl, Glockler and Abarth, and were thereafter the result of teamwork by a number of designers working together, rather than of any particular individual. In the case of Citroën, whose DS of 1955 established a characteristically logical style that has endured ever since, the work must be assumed to be that of a team of designers, if only because the organization of Citroën is such as to prevent any possibility of an individual being given credit for the work.

In complete antithesis is the clearly recognizable work of Frank Costin. Beyond doubt, he is one of the greatest aerodynamicists,

probably the most outstanding of his time; and although his best-
known work among motoring enthusiasts is probably his bodywork
designs for some of the most distinguished and distinctive competition cars of the last twenty years, he also has to his credit a number of
noteworthy production cars, including the Lotus Elite, a Marcos,
and his own Costin Amigo. Although outstanding as an aerodynamicist, he is equally accomplished as a structural engineer, and
remarkable for being an influential innovator in both disciplines. In
this, he bears comparison with but one other, Jim Hall of Chaparral;
but whereas Hall is an acute iconoclast and a fairly ready delegator,
Costin is a shrewd and solitary thinker who does nothing that ought
to be revolutionary, since it is all supported by a classical engineering
science that is available to any of his competitors who have the wit
and experience to understand it.

Born in 1920, Costin began to garner experience when he joined
the old General Aircraft Company after leaving school. During the
war, he worked with other aircraft manufacturers, and after it he
served De Havilland for many years, including an important spell as
aerodynamic flight-test engineer in charge of the experimental

department. It was while he was still with De Havilland that he began to seek recreation in motor sport, and this interest led to an association with Colin Chapman, the proprietor of the then-tiny Lotus firm making some clever little sports cars. The Lotus of the early 1950s, typically the Lotus 6, was a petite piece of mechanical gossamer, but about as aerodynamic as a barn door – and with the body he designed for the next production model in 1954, the Lotus 8, Costin transformed it into an arrow, obtaining for it so much extra speed that Chapman was encouraged to pursue more thoroughly both suspension design and competition honours.

Thus began an involvement with the motor-car that was, within three years, to earn Costin the greatest respect among those *cognoscenti* who could identify his work, though at the time he enjoyed little public credit for it. By 1956, he had evolved the Lotus 11, a creation so refined that Costin's attentions went even as far as the driver's seat height: airflow tests with nylon strands (wool tufts he thought too coarse and crude) established whether the driver's head was low enough for laminar flow to be maintained over the headrest bearing, or high enough to cause turbulent flow. Sometimes it was critical to within half an inch of helmet movement, but Costin is a precise man, and the Lotus 11 was a precision instrument: it did well in major events, notably Le Mans and Sebring, and in time became the Lotus 15. By then, Costin had produced something even more remarkable.

Both these cars, the little Lotus-Climax and the larger Lister-Jaguar, were bodily and to some extent structurally the work of the uncompromising Frank Costin

This was the Vanwall, the crude, Cooper-framed Grand Prix sow's ear that Costin and Chapman were consulted about in the hope that it might be made into the silk purse of metaphor. Its engine was promising, but the rest quite forbidding. Costin assisted Chapman on the chassis (there is nobody quicker to spot a redundant tube in a spaceframe), but, more important, created a superb body. It was like nothing else on four wheels – and that, in view of the state of the art of the time, was almost an assurance that it would be right. As with most of his masterpieces, it was perfectly reasonable according to the knowledge of the time, but extremely advanced according to the practice of the time.

His brief was a difficult one, for the car had considerable frontal area and height, so Costin had to produce a body that would be low enough in drag coefficient to compensate for this handicap. He knew as well as anyone that a square foot of frontal area was worth yards of streamlining, but succeeded in bartering excessive frontal area for low drag: and in 1957–8 the Vanwall was incontrovertibly the fastest racing car of its time, by a margin that was quite out of proportion to the power output of its engine.

Costin then moved on to better things. Lotus were evolving that lovely little heartbreaker, the Type 14 Elite, and it was Costin's task to attend to the aerodynamic aspects of its design, the basic styling of which has been attributed to John Frayling. That he succeeded was amply evinced by the distinguished competition record of the car, and by its low road-going fuel thirst; but how he did it makes an interesting study of applied knowledge. The Elite embodied the principle of reflex camber, one known to the aviation industry for some years (the wing section and even the fuselage of the Lockheed Constellation exemplified it well), but which Costin was the first to apply to a car. The camber line – the mean centre line of the body section when seen in elevation – is shaped like an ogee, drooping towards the front and rising to the rear; and Costin established that it provides aerodynamically-induced stability at high speed, undebased by ground effect and consistent with a body of very low drag. The Elite proved him right, and so has every car that he has shaped since.

Such cars have been surprisingly numerous, for he became a popular and even a fashionable consultant. Bodies for the Lister-Jaguar, the record-breaking Speedwell Austin-Healey Sprite, a special Lotus Elan for Stirling Moss, a nose for the TVR, studies for

Ford, and even a low-drag body for the British 4-man bobsleigh team, were interspersed with hydrodynamic and structural projects for manufacturers of boats, earthmovers and printing machinery. There were also ventures in which he did more than just shape bodies: the original Marcos was typical of the situation in which Costin had too often found himself, when his ability to create futuristic and effective machines by unconventional design proved that his strict but radical logic was misplaced in business, for which he had no commercial flair.

The Marcos was made of wood, and was lighter and stronger than anything that might have reasonably been compared with it. Quite apart from his knowledge of engineering with wood, there was another good reason for the admirable stiffness of the Marcos frame: it was probably the first car to have what laymen call wrongly a monocoque construction in what is really a stressed-skin hull comprising a number of torsion boxes.

His skill with structures brought Costin some other interesting work at about that time: the spaceframe for the 1959 Lister-Jaguar was basically quite elegant, even if it needed a few diaphragms to integrate it. Monocoques, if we must call them that, figured in a chassis for BRM and in the Costin-Nathan sports car, followed by a beautifully-refined spaceframe for a Formula Four racer in which two triangulated bays were joined at their apices and braced by a pair of tubes to unload the joint – perhaps the purest and simplest car spaceframe ever built.

By this time, Costin was itching to produce his own road car. After a streamlined and very fast Formula Two racer, the Protos, was finished in 1966 and proved faster than any other car of similar power, Costin settled down to design his Amigo. It had about it everything that was typical of his work: the structure was a complex of wooden torsion boxes and possessed exemplary stiffness, the envelope shape was a minimal-drag reflex camber affair, every detail being minutely scrutinized. Even the exterior mirror was redesigned and wind-tunnel-tested until its drag was halved. The whole car represented the triumph of engineering over salesmanship: it was implausibly fast (130 mph from an absolutely standard 2-litre Vauxhall Victor engine), ineffably competent in every kind of manoeuvre, mechanically simple and utterly practical – but only a handful of people could appreciate it. The financial backing that Costin secured to cover construction of a pilot batch could not be extended to permit the car to go into production, and the project foundered.

It is scarcely surprising that Costin was a product of the aircraft industry, in which the determination of correct envelope shapes goes to the very root of the product's functional viability, whether commercial or military. So was Jaray: and so, too, was another car-body designer of outstanding ability, albeit of scant reputation, Dudley Hobbs of Bristol. The car division of the Bristol Aeroplane Company did a lot of work in the 1940s and 1950s, developing high-speed low-drag bodies that still had aerodynamic stability; and in many

Confirmed by the MIRA
laboratories as one of the most
superbly streamlined cars of
all time, the Bristol 401 was
the work of engineer Dudley
Hobbs in the late 1940s

ways the most outstanding of these was that of their second production model, the Bristol 401, which came on the market in 1949 while the BMW-inspired 400 was still in production. The new car was essentially a 400, graced by a new streamlined saloon body such as might be expected from an aircraft builder intent on showing his skill. Once again, the inspiration was foreign, coming from Touring and Pininfarina of Milan; but the inspiration was merely stylistic, and Hobbs improved upon it enormously. Above and beyond all the refinement of construction, of detail work and metallurgy, where he really excelled was in achieving great aerodynamic efficiency. Even today, the 401 body ranks aerodynamically as one of the best production cars yet seen: the Motor Industry Research Association measured the drag coefficients of 118 assorted cars (only seven of them prewar) in or about 1969, and the old 401 was bettered by only four others, only two of them being better by a significant margin. By 1975, MIRA had brought the study up-to-date with examples of the latest saloon cars to go into production, and included in their studies measurements of drag coefficient, not only in the zero yaw condition, but also at a 20° yaw angle, which is significant in determining the autostability of the car when travelling at high speed in a cross wind. After all those years and with so much new knowledge supposedly acquired in the interim, the 401 (whose body first appeared, it must be remembered, as long ago as 1948) ranked equal fifth.

It is interesting that all the modern cars that bettered the results of this old one had fairly smooth and extensive undershields, whereas Bristol tried one experimentally and found that it made no difference. However, all that was visible on top was completely smooth. There were no excrescences to spoil the cleanliness of those curves, no protruding door handles, mascots, fuel-filler caps, bumpers or anything like that. The bumpers were deep light-alloy pressings which appeared to be integral with the body, but were, in fact, mounted on energy-absorbing rubbers that allowed a 2-in displacement. The doors were opened by a push-button flush with the surface, while all other hatches and holes were opened from inside the car, incidentally making it quite remarkably burglar-proof. Pursuing smoothness as far as possible, the rear window was bonded in, without any of the conventional framing and beading that so often mar the surfaces of cars whose basic lines may appear satisfactory. Proof of the pudding was the fact that this superb shape improved the top-end performance of the 401 considerably. Since the gearing remained the same as in the 400, as did the engine, the maximum speed was not all that much higher, but acceleration from 70 mph, or thereabouts, was a good deal stronger despite the greater weight of the 401, attributable not merely to its expansive form, but also to the more extravagant luxury of its interior. This was no coarse sports car, remember, but a highly-refined and superbly-finished luxury car for a very small and discriminating class of customers, who would have rejected cheapness and crudity as unhesitatingly as stylistic vulgarity or defective steering and roadholding.

After the 401 was designed, it was subjected to a good deal of investigation, with the aid of wool tufting, smoke tests, and scale-model, wind-tunnel work; but it is important to emphasize that this was done after the body was designed, after it was put into production: the fact that it was found to be so good is eloquent testimony to the ability of its designer.

Dudley Hobbs came, like many of the others in the small design team of the cars division, from the aircraft side of the Bristol company. He had been specializing in wings, structurally and aerodynamically the most critical parts of an aircraft; and he has continued to apply his knowledge and experience to this new subject matter ever since. The fact that the very latest Bristol, the Type 411, is as stable and wind-quiet as the earlier ones and is, despite its relatively conventional appearance, evidently better streamlined than a cursory glance might suggest (for it undoubtedly goes faster than any other full 4-seater of similar power), shows that he has not lost sight of, nor faith in, those principles which guided his early work.

Of the cars that came between, the Bristol 404 and 405 are surely the most notable. From the windscreen forward, they can be considered identical and particularly interesting. Some of the practical details were quite brilliant, such as the finding of a new home for the spare wheel: in one of the most simple and persuasive pieces of logical thinking in the history of car-body design, this was put into the left-front wing, just behind the wheel arch, where it could be removed through a pivoting valance panel. On the other side of the car, a similar compartment housed the battery and most of the electrical gear, including a very impressive terminal block acting as a

The Businessman's Express, the Bristol 404, shared with the 405 the best parts, from the windscreen forward. It was one of Hobbs' most fetching designs

The Bristol 405 of 1954 offered the same wind resistance as the 401, being inferior in the posterior and superior in the anterior. Its four doors were awkward and Bristol never repeated the mistake; other features were brilliant and remained in subsequent models for 20 years

66

Not merely slippery but also without peer in its aerostability, the 1954 version of the racing Bristol 450 applied aviation science to automobile control. The finrails maintained attached flow over the roof and kept the aerodynamic centre of pressure well aft

sort of quick-access brain-centre for the entire electrical system of the car. The virtues of this arrangement were numerous: first and most obviously, the heavy masses were concentrated close to mid-wheelbase, where they would least affect the polar moment of inertia either in pitch or in yaw. Secondly, the spare wheel was accessible without the need to disturb any luggage and (in Britain and other right-hand drive countries), could be reached and removed from the safety of the pavement or verge. Thirdly, the battery was fairly close to the engine compartment, and there was no danger of any significant voltage drop between it and the starter motor, whilst its location in a draught of warm air prevented it from getting too hot (as it might under the bonnet) or too cold, with the result that its performance was unusually consistent, and its need for topping-up remarkably infrequent. Morphologically, the front of the 404 and 405 was fascinating in that the radiator air intake became entirely functional without losing any stylistic appeal: its shape was modelled on that of the leading-edge engine air intakes of the big Bristol Brabazon airliner, and was a shape so efficient that the area of the aperture could be reduced considerably, to the general benefit of penetration and front-end design.

Because of the extensive fenestration along its flanks, imposed by a management decision to produce a four-door car (a mistake they never repeated), the drag coefficient of the 405 was higher than that of the 401, though, interestingly, its frontal area was lower in exactly the same proportion so that its overall wind resistance was the same. The shape of the car was particularly timeless, for it acknowledged no stylistic patterns of the day, and therefore looks just as modern in the 1970s as it did in the 1950s. Perhaps more than any other, the Bristol 405 really looked like something built by an aircraft manufacturer. The 404 might have revealed this even more clearly had its production form followed more closely that of the prototype. That experimental car was known as 'The Bomb', for, in addition to the quite large fins on each rear wing, there was a very large central fin on its tail. The second prototype had a bolt-on fin, but it was decided that customers would not accept anything so *outré*, and the finning was reduced to vestigial relics of the original – little more than a stylistic echo of the functional fins on the racing Bristol 450.

That competition coupé had two large fins starting from its sloping tail: the fins were extended into the actual crown of the roof, so that airflow could be guided from the windscreen over the roof and down the central part of the tail between the fins, the protruding rail effect over the roof helping to maintain attached airflow. These cars, which, unlike the 401, really were designed in a wind tunnel, were respectably successful in long-distance sports-car races, consistently winning class and team awards at Reims and Le Mans. Bristol's assistant chief designer, Denis Sevier, said in a 1954 paper that the fins helped in fast cornering as well as on the straights, while the drivers commented that gusts which could put rival cars all over the road on the very fast Mulsanne straight had very little effect on the Bristols. That was more than 15 years ago, but proper finning never caught the popular imagination. The public did not understand it, thinking it a mere styling gimmick that had been invented in Detroit, so the fins of many production cars withered away until nothing remained of them but a Farinaceous rear wing on certain Peugeots. After all those years and all that effort, manufacturers' interest in aerodynamics seemed to wane. You do not have to look any further than into the street to see that there are not many low-drag cars about nowadays.

In the face of so much evidence to the contrary, the designers of our popular cars generally deny all the advantages of low-drag and aerodynamically-induced stability. They are showing some signs of being influenced by the wedge shape currently fashionable among certain racing cars – although the wedge is, in fact, not an efficient shape for generating downward thrust, nor for minimizing drag. In general, neither the constant increasing of cross-section towards the rear, nor the addition of stabilizing fins, nor even the maintenance of a nearly-constant cross-sectional area over the whole length of the vehicle (a good means of achieving attached flow, directional stability and a low-drag coefficient, and a clue to the surprisingly high performance of single-deck buses) seem to find any adherence among the styling departments of car manufacturers. Despite the convincing demonstration by Mercedes-Benz with their modifications to one of their saloons before the war, when they reduced by 47% the power required to achieve the same maximum speed, a modern Mercedes-Benz looks closer to the original production car than to its more efficient, experimental derivative. It is possible today to build a low-drag, aerodynamically-stable car: why then are we still using precious petrol to move the air and not the car?

The answer lies in styling, that strange institution by which car manufacturers try to sell the public what it wants, or perhaps what it thinks it wants or, most truly of all, what they can make it want. There are, it seems, two diametrically-opposed approaches to the designing of a car body. For the likes of von Fachsenfeld, Burney, Jaray and the others, the shape of the body was the basic design parameter. Bristol demonstrated that it takes logical priority over even the engine, but the traditional approach, which is unfortunately still with us, sees body styling as superficial, added on to the real mechanical car. This is the 'icing on the cake', or 'fashion' theory, grimly associated in the critical mind with aggressive marketing and planned obsolescence. This was at one time quite defensible, having its origin not only in ignorance, but also in the early practice of manufacturers of supplying rolling chassis to specialist coach-builders. The body builder, confronted by the many fixed spot heights defined by this rolling chassis, usually including the radiator and even the front wings, had little scope for originality: and a classical style emerged which laid emphasis on the precision and elegance of statement within a very rigid idiom. When it was felt that something like perfection had been achieved, emphasis shifted to the comfort and amenities provided within the structure.

In an evolutionary process of this sort, it seems to be axiomatic that only one aspect of the body may be changed at a time. Any car which departs from the norm in more than one way will be unacceptable, as Voisin's car was to the French motor-racing authorities, and as Burney's streamline car was to the British public. We are brought back to the language analogy: in Shakespeare's day, a Dadaist writer would have been either burned at the stake or put in an asylum. The forces of conservatism are strong, and only gradual evolution is possible.

Throughout the 1920s and 1930s, this evolution centred on two areas. One was the bonnet, which varied progressively in length and height in relation both to the car's wheelbase and to the height of the windscreen; the other was the wings of the car, or mudguards as they were originally called. It is interesting to see that the stylists, especially in America, often arrived at the same formal solutions as the aerodynamicists of this era, but by a different route. At any given time, people can conceive of a car as being only slightly different and, by 1930, the front wings of cars had developed from a flat plane, or simple curve, to a complex, three-dimensional curve. Custom body builders had done this long before, but mass producers could not afford the expensive labour necessary to create such shapes in volume; and it was a technological revolution in car manufacture, rather than a stylistic one, that made possible the change.

Responsible for it was Edward Gowan Budd. Born in 1870, he was a little too late to be considered one of the founders of the motor industry, but undoubtedly he was one of the pioneers of the car as we know it today. His concept of the body built up from steel pressings was perhaps the most fundamental piece of rethinking to have occurred so far in the history of the car, and had a more profound influence on what came after than the work of any other man.

Budd began to study pressed steel and its uses in 1899, after a brief period at the Franklyn Institute in Philadelphia where he studied mechanical engineering. In particular, he realized that pressed steel, if correctly used, could replace the more traditional wood and iron in industry and create a lighter, cheaper and better substitute in many products. For a while, he worked on railway rolling-stock, at the same time making a study of current and potential welding techniques, upon which the fruition of his ideas would depend. Finally, in 1912, he set up his own company, and embarked on a crusade to popularize the all-steel body. It is not strictly true to say that he (with or without Joseph Ledwinka) sold the first all-steel motor-car bodies, for several American vehicle manufacturers were experimenting with the idea at about that time; but he was the first to supply all-steel bodies in volume production when, after having sold examples to a number of firms including General Motors, Studebaker, Willys and Oakland, he secured a contract from Dodge for 70000 bodies in 1916, to be followed by 99000 the following year. These were all of the open-tourer pattern, composed of about 1200 separate pressings; but the possibilities inherent in the system were so appealing to the rapidly-growing American car industry that, by 1916, Budd was building bodies fitted with a permanent steel hard top and, in the following year, had developed an all-steel, fully-enclosed four-door saloon body. This was put into production in 1919, when Dodge achieved its highest production record, leading them on to sell their millionth car by 1923. In 1924, Budd began to collaborate with André Citroën, who had earlier been fired by the mass-production techniques of Henry Ford and had set up the first similar manufactory in Europe. That collaboration was to lead to great things: Budd showed his forward thinking by producing a prototype car in 1930 featuring an all-steel body and front-wheel drive; and it was this prototype that Citroën developed to become the deservedly famous *Onze Légère* (popularly known as the *Traction-Avant*), destined to become one of the most popular and long-lived cars in Europe until it was superseded after 20 years by the magnificent new DS.

The revolution wrought by Budd brought technological spin-offs in its wake as surely as any other breakthrough in design, from the cannons of Crécy to the sputniks in space. His elimination of wood from the car led to the development of new kinds of vehicle upholstery and the burgeoning of the spring clip industry; the drumming of unsupported metal panels led to acoustic deadening compounds being developed; the failure of contemporary welding techniques to meet Budd's demands encouraged the rapid evolution of arc welding; and the absence of wood (supported by the fact that upholstering could be carried out after the body was built) allowed new high-temperature paint-baking techniques to be introduced, with a resulting increase in the quality of finish achieved and tremendous improvement in its durability.

It is interesting to see how these production techniques influenced the work of one of the most distinguished carriage-trade body designers of the 1920s and '30s, the American Howard Darrin. When he set up with Tom Hibbard as a custom body builder in Paris in 1922, he commented that his familiarity with American constructional techniques gave him an easy entrée to the European trade. 'In Paris at that time there was what might be called a vacuum caused by four years of war, and lack of capital and many other things, and automobile coachbuilding had not recovered. Also, the old ideas still held force. Now understand, the French coachbuilders were terrific. They had terrific sports cars, in fact they had terrific cars of all kinds, but their construction was not up-to-date. And they were difficult to export to different climates because wood, and in some cases cloth, as in the Weymann bodies, was used for panels. This was a great handicap. Tom and I actually stepped into a situation in which we couldn't do anything wrong. Believe me, we weren't geniuses. We actually weren't very experienced, but we had one thing in our favour – our way of thinking. We thought ideas should be young and numerous old customs disregarded. We were riding high. We were consulting engineers for nearly every top motor-car company in the world: General Motors and Stutz in America, Renault and Citroën in France, Minerva in Belgium, Rolls-Royce, Armstrong Siddeley and Barker in England, Daimler-Benz in Germany. For those companies to which we contributed design and styling, we built sample bodies or show cars. Never, never had such an opportunity been given anyone.'

As Darrin said, they were not very experienced. He had built a couple of open-tourer bodies on Delage chassis, after selling out the airline that he had founded in 1920 and which had been America's first scheduled service. Hibbard had been founder of the firm that made Le Baron bodies from 1921, attracting the custom of Minerva, Hispano-Suiza and Isotta-Fraschini. In fact, Darrin's start came when he was an electrical engineer with Westinghouse and was approached by Willys in 1916 to design an electric gearshift. His study of the car, while doing this work, prompted him to feel that cars might offer him a more interesting career than electrical engineering; and his war service in France then made him so fond of that country that he resolved to return to it.

Basically, Darrin was an artist and an entrepreneur, but he was not without engineering background, and had the intelligence to exploit such features of American production cars as might be applicable to the custom trade that he was so successful in obtaining – for instance, panels that were curved, where other designs remained flat – while his shrewd assessment of the handicaps imposed by structural woodwork allowed him to produce cars that could be exported freely. As a result of all these things, not to mention the excellent contacts he made in the industry, he built – first in association with Hibbard, and then, when his partner joined General Motors, with the banker Fernandez of Paris as a wonderfully provident and influential new partner – as many Rolls-Royce bodies

The best of British? Barker coachwork on Rolls-Royce chassis was no worse, no more opulent or irrelevant, than that of the other famous London coachbuilders. It revealed the British as a nation almost as immune as the Swiss to the real joys of motoring

as any other manufacturer outside England. He even designed cars that, for political reasons, had to be built in England – one, for Lord Mountbatten, was constructed by Barker. Likewise, when he built bodies in Paris for Rolls-Royce of America, the bodies were then delivered to Brewster, the R-R subsidiary in New York, the addition of whose nameplate was deemed to make the body acceptable.

Apart from building cars, Darrin's other great enthusiasms were flying and playing polo and, in the course of a trip to America indulging both these fancies, he decided to return there permanently. In 1937, he set himself up with the title Darrin of Paris, observing that this convinced most Americans that he was French and that, in Hollywood, this was perhaps better advertisement than all the work he had ever done. One of the first things he did whilst there was to create one of the most superb bodies ever to grace a Rolls-Royce: it was mounted on a 1930 Phantom II, and was made at the request of Countess Dorothy di Frasso. She specified only that it had to outshine the Rolls of her great social rival Constance Bennett; and, indeed, this extraordinarily glamorous conveyance, one of the most formal town carriages of an age when the elegant and expensive dress car was at its zenith, probably outshone anything else of the kind ever built before or since.

Certainly nothing that Darrin did subsequently was of such quality; the bodies he produced for the few remaining American manufacturers revealed that, whatever his stock of young ideas, his vocabulary had failed to keep up with the change in the language as spoken on the far side of the Atlantic; his work was inconsistent with new idioms. To be fair, it is known that much of his styling was corrupted by production engineers, sometimes in a spirit of deliberate resentment and sometimes through sheer ignorance and insensitivity. It is worth remembering, though, the Super 8 Victoria that he created for Packard shortly before the war. He had made bodies for a number of Packards already when he was invited by the president of the company to discuss a formal collaboration – but this was resisted by the Packard engineers, who complained that custom bodies were a risky business, being mostly made of wood and consequently neither reliable nor durable. Darrin promptly climbed up on the car he had brought with him and began to jump up and down on it, demonstrating convincingly the strength of the cast-aluminium scuttle structure that was one of the features of his construction.

Today, the carriage trade has been virtually extinguished. Darrin recognized the fact in due course: 'It must be realized that the progress to be made in the art of both beautifying the automobile and making it more acceptable to the public, is a combination of engineering, architecture and, naturally, of styling. This combination no longer exists in America for any individual. It is for this reason that Italy, with its many custom builders, has been able to develop stylists who are not only experienced and qualified in the construction of automobile bodies, but are also very familiar with chassis problems, allowing them to approach the automobile as a chassis body entity, and enabling them to follow designs through to actual construction.'

Of these Italians, the outstanding examples must be the houses of Farina and Bertone. The original Bertone body shop was opened as long ago as 1884 by Giovanni Bertone, for the repair of carriages and wagons; his first motor-car was an SPA in 1921. He worked for the company for many years, as he did for Lancia, and in fact it was not until 1934 that, due to a shortage of business from the quantity manufacturers, he began to build one-off bodies to private order. It was then that he was joined by his 20-year-old son Giuseppe, nicknamed Nuccio, the man who is most associated with the name today. However, when (after the interval of the war) the Bertone factory resumed work, it was again for series manufacture on behalf of a major company, in this case Fiat. A few special bodies were built for Lancia, Ferrari and Borgward, and then, with the strength of a contract from S. H. Arnolt of Chicago to support him – Bertone created two special bodies for the MG for Arnolt to sell in the USA – he let himself loose with some far-fetched styling exercises intended to excite the world at large and attract custom.

The most important of these was a series known as the 'Bat', standing for Berlinetta Aerodinamica Tecnica, and they were as intriguing and beautiful as they were outlandish and impractical. He expected these to lead him to some kind of fortune – but what really forced Nuccio Bertone to make the grade was another little

The Parisian *carrossiers* preferred to let craftsmanship wait on artistry. When the owner of this Lago Talbot, bodied by Figoni et Falaschi, complained that it overheated in town, he was blandly assured that *of course* such a car would overheat if condemned to such usage

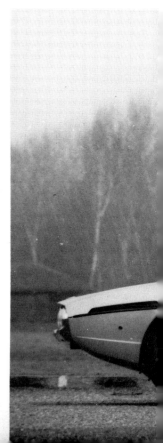

The Alfa Romeo Giulietta Sprint made Bertone rich; a succession of Lamborghinis, starting with the Miura and including this Espada, made him famous

car that he displayed at the 1954 Turin Show. It had been constructed hastily at the urgent request of Alfa Romeo, who were supposed to be introducing a new low-price popular model and who, as a nationalized firm, were in some embarrassment at having taken so long about it. Furnishing him with some chassis, they left it to him to produce a car that might only be produced as a small series, but would at least give the public evidence of their good faith. What Bertone created was the Giulietta Sprint coupé, the first of a long series that, with minor changes, has endured to this day, when it can be seen in the form of the 2-litre Alfa Romeo GTV.

Such was the demand for the Giulietta Sprint that Bertone was forced to open a new factory and settle down to series production in quantities far greater than he had envisaged. As a consequence of this, he and the other important styling houses in Italy all set off on this new course, guided by the knowledge that, with business of that magnitude, it would be commercially feasible to employ the most brilliant artists to create eye-catching fashion exercises, whose sole function would be to advertise the firm's creative ability at the great international motor shows. As with the dream cars beloved of the styling divisions in the large American corporations, these might sometimes lead to new trends in body design.

In a business of this sort, the individual designer is often lost, sometimes deliberately. Between 1965 and 1972, Bertone produced 500 designs, never being particularly anxious to reveal who was responsible for any one of them. Some were of tremendous significance, not least the fabulous Lamborghini Miura, which was reputed to be the work of Giugiaro, but was mostly done by his assistant.

The Sommer/Biondetti 8C2900B Alfa Romeo, which so nearly won at Le Mans in 1938 and is now in the Doune Collection of the Earl of Moray, was bodied by Touring of Milan in a style that constituted a link between the pioneer designs of Jaray and the postwar Cisitalia by Pininfarina that is so often thought to be the archetype of the mid-century *Gran Turismo* fashion

Previous pages: The Bertone coupé on the Fiat Dino 2·4 was a superb car, one of the truly great. Pretty but quite inferior, the Pininfarina spider version revealed a more elementary appraisal of the Fiat's brilliant potential

Much the same story could be told of the house of Pininfarina, another father-and-son business that waxed mighty and kicked against established fashions, creating in the process what became known as the 'Italian line'. Probably the most significant car to emerge from Farina was the early postwar Cisitalia 1100 coupé, a cleaned and lightened simplification of the more elaborate pontoon-style sporting bodies that had been built before the war, on chassis by Alfa Romeo, Delahaye and others. The Cisitalia furnished the inspiration for most of the successful advanced styles of the 1950s, some of which brought Pininfarina sufficient volume of production orders to create a 'custom' bodybuilding factory as large as any in Italy.

The first serious efforts to integrate art and engineering for modern mass production were made in Germany in the early 1920s. This was in the Bauhaus design school, where the impetus came from the architect Walter Gropius; and the influence of this school was so great that by 1928 it was possible for no less than four separate industrial design consultancies to be established in New York. One of these four was that of Raymond Loewy, and he was immediately successful. The time was now right for a fresh approach to the design of industrial products; for a long time the mere facts of the car, the radio, the refrigerator and so on were sufficiently exciting to overwhelm any critical appreciation of the relationship of form to function in each, but large-volume production had made such strides (especially in the USA) that aesthetic appeal was fast becoming a major factor in marketing. Although cheap and humble products were most in need of the professional designer's services, it was the really big corporations who possessed the resources to test the validity of the claims made by Loewy's new profession: therefore, his first important designs were of locomotives for the Pennsylvania Railroad and refrigerators for Sears Roebuck – these latter, sold as the Coldspot series, being so successful as to fix a style that remained universal for 30 years. Very soon it became clear that the criteria of the industrial designer could validly be applied to the motor-car, and by 1939 Raymond Loewy found himself put in charge of styling for the Studebaker Corporation.

His first task was to clean up the existing designs and rid them of their more obvious failings, but during the ensuing war years it was hardly appropriate to risk anything that savoured of iconoclasm. When the air had cleared, however, Loewy took his chance; the new Studebaker displaced all the old clichés of car design so effectively that before long it had become the model upon which the majority of others were fashioned.

When these 1946–7 Studebakers appeared, there were brief jibes from the sceptics who maintained that it was impossible to tell whether the cars were coming or going, but it did not take long for the world to be sure that this utterly novel styling was the coming thing: within a few years, it was commonplace for ordinary saloons to feature a 3-box, turret-top composition in which the rearmost box (the luggage boot) was as substantial as the foremost or engine

compartment, and in which the area of glazing to provide vision to the rear was almost as great as that at the front of the turret within which the passengers were lodged. It was a re-proportioning that struck at the very roots of car styling and engineering, one which was perhaps more fundamental and successful than any since Maybach's 1901 Mercedes and Budd's 1916 Dodge, or before the 1959 Mini of Issigonis. With its unaccustomed symmetry and its wrap-round glass, the Studebaker set fashions that persist today.

Alas, fashion is a commodity that defies accountancy. For a while Studebaker prospered, but it was not for long. It may even be questioned whether that brief prosperity was of Loewy's making, for as Alfred P. Sloan wrote in his outstanding book *My Life with General Motors*: 'With the resumption of production after World War Two it was necessary because of shortages, particularly of steel, for the industry to operate under material controls. These

Maybe it reminded us of Janus, but many later cars should remind us of Raymond Loewy's 1946–7 Studebaker

allocations favoured the smaller manufacturers (Kaiser–Frazer, Nash, Hudson, Studebaker and Packard) whose product presentation at that time was concentrated in the medium-price range, with the result that the proportion of the market accounted for by their cars increased sharply. Competition in this period was largely confined to production – that is, whatever a manufacturer could make, customers were waiting to purchase. In the years after 1948, normal competitive influences began to reassert themselves in some areas of the market, and the sales of the smaller manufacturers in the medium-price group declined.'

Loewy, it seemed, had shot his bolt; and if the entire car business profited from his work, his immediate employers unfortunately did not. The last attempt to save Studebaker involved Loewy in one of his most dramatic designs, the 1962 Avanti. He was justifiably proud of this high-performance machine, with its ergonomically-integrated controls and functionally-coherent shape, for integration and cohesion in these things was the essence of his work – as may be seen by looking at his designs for Aga cookers. The American public was by no means educated or eclectic enough to buy the cars in adequate numbers, however, and the company foundered. A rescue operation mounted by a consortium of businessmen saved the Avanti for a limited production, which endured for another 10 years; but more important was the fact that its lines – subject to the mutations of the jeans era – were echoed in many commercially successful cars, including some current models. Once again, Loewy was proved correct in his assertions.

To be right once in car styling or design is a circumstance within the working life of many men. To be right twice is a privilege for very few; and Loewy, in his subsequent attempts, came nowhere near that mark of genius or conceptual larceny which is to be right three times. None of the other self-styled industrial designers, who now populate the lofting rooms or tramp the streets between them, has fared much better. The old adage about each man having only one design in him seems to apply perhaps more rigorously in body design than in any other branch of car creation. This need not be seen as a criticism of the work of all those men who have each produced one outstanding design: it is more a recognition of the validity of individual style. Nobody exemplifies this better than Sir William Lyons, whose series of bodies for the ss and later Jaguar cars built by his own company is distinguished by the most recognizable and inimitable style of all.

Lyons has been described as one of the most outstanding men in the motor industry, a reputation that is due as much to his tremendous strength in business dealings, and his utterly autocratic management of his firm, as to the artistry of his creation. He started in 1922 building sidecars for motor cycles, in a little partnership called the Swallow Sidecar Company; but his flair as a body stylist soon found expression in the Swallow-bodied Austin 7. Thereafter, he turned out a succession of cars based upon essentially humdrum mechanical components made by Standard, but so well styled and so competitively marketed that SS Cars, as the company became known in 1935, never looked back until 1945, when it tactfully restyled itself as Jaguar Cars Limited. Even then, the policy of appealing to the customer who could see a good deal more clearly than he could think continued in force; the bodies were still eye-catching, the mechanical elements still humdrum. Not until the XK 120 introduced an outstanding new engine in 1949, and the E-Type brought a remarkable new suspension in 1961, was this tendency reversed, so that by the end of his long career (he retired in 1973) Lyons could take pleasure in the thought that, as Lord Stokes put it, '90% of the motoring population would like to have an XJ Jaguar; the other 10% would like the same thing with a Daimler grille and badges'.

It was a pardonable exaggeration, but no more than an exaggeration: the Jaguar, which had begun life a quarter of a century earlier as a car for cads, *boulevardiers* and poodle-fakers, had matured into an extraordinarily impressive car that was capable of giving the most demanding drivers and the most sensitive passengers equal satisfaction. The Jaguar, whatever model you consider, was never by absolute standards a cheap car, and this made the ownership of one in itself something in which to take a certain pride. By comparative standards, the Jaguar was never anything *but* a cheap car, and this was the other element that made it so incredibly popular. The secret lay in selling enough, and it was the lines of the cars, always recognizable as belonging to a distinguished breed, and little if at all affected by stylistic trends apparent elsewhere, that attracted the customers.

Interestingly, Lyons did very little actual drawing in the later stages of his career. He preferred to direct a handful of trustworthy and sympathetic men working full scale in the metal, rather as Issigonis did at BMC. Working like this, it is only possible to make gradual changes, which is why the succession of Jaguars maintained such outstanding continuity of style and were never in any danger of progressing at such a rate as to offend current tenets of acceptability. The only exception was the E-Type, which looked rather different because it was derived, not from its road-going predecessor the XK 150, but from the racing D-Type.

That historic car was most definitely created on the drawing-board – not by Sir William Lyons, but by an aerodynamicist from Bristol, Malcolm Sayer. His work on the D-Type earned the unstinted approval of experts at Farnborough. The shape he created for the car, basically elliptical in longitudinal and transverse sections, was an evolved form of a special body built for record-breaking purposes in 1953 (it reached nearly 180 mph in that year) based on a development of the racing C-Type Jaguar. The refined contouring of the final D shape did more than reduce aerodynamic drag; it also encouraged the adoption of constructional techniques that had hitherto been foreign to the firm. The centre section was an elliptical-section tub of stressed 18-gauge magnesium-alloy sheeting, suitably stiffened by bulkheads at front and rear, and welded to a multi-tubular frontal frame carrying the engine and

The 1949 Jaguar XK 120 prompted a wholesale revision of standards and values. It looked like no previous Jaguar yet was typically Jaguar, even though its shape faithfully echoed that of the 1940 Mille Miglia 328 BMW

front suspension. It was from this structure that the road-going E-Type was developed, to become immediately upon its introduction the most glamorous and eye-catching object one could possess.

The interaction of appearance and construction has always been crucial to the development of the motor-car. We have already discussed the evolutionary changes that took place in the 1920s and early 1930s, but, as tooling skills were raised to steadily higher levels, it became increasingly conceivable that the bulbous shapes being created might accommodate the previously excrescent headlamps and the wings might even merge with the bonnet. Thus, in the USA, Ted Allen's Cord 812 of 1937 and Chrysler's Airflow of 1934, and even the La Salle of General Motors, were idiomatic re-statements of what Wikov had done in 1931, and what so many more were to do before the end of the decade. The commercial failure of the Airflow was probably more the result of clumsy handling of the new form rather than of the essential formal ideas, which were just as much attributable to the engineering artistry of Budd as to the aerodynamic inspirations of Jaray. In Europe, the reaction to these revolutionary developments was either to resist them at any price, or to do the

Bespectacled Sir William Lyons, creator of the most personal and glamorous series of body styles in quantity production throughout the last quarter of a century, spectates at Le Mans with the chief engineer of most of his Jaguars, William Heynes

same sort of thing but to do it properly.

Probably the most significant reaction was that of Fiat, who aligned themselves with the second group and produced in Giacosa's celebrated Fiat 1500 saloon a car whose coefficient of drag was measured in the wind tunnel and demonstrated to be the best achieved up to then by a touring car, without sacrificing in any way the comfort of the passengers or the aesthetic acceptability of the lines. Besides its own contribution to streamlining, the lowering of the bonnet and the new characteristic curvature of the nearly integral front wings and headlamps set the seal on a new fashion which persists in the Volkswagen of the 1970s.

It is interesting to recall the commentary of the *Giornale d'Italia* on the Fiat 1500 when it first appeared: 'It was time to turn bravely towards streamlining, which means more speed and less fuel consumption, that is, progress. Fiat have done well to abandon the old forms, renouncing firmly outworn conservative methods of construction. In the case of the 1500, one must give credit to the designers who knew how to reconcile the needs of streamlining with aesthetic considerations, keeping their distance from certain horrible designs from beyond the Alps' [presumably the now-legendary Citroën which appeared a year earlier] 'and from overseas' [the Chrysler] 'which seem designed for quick obsolescence rather than as a technical stimulus towards new horizons. The bodywork is beautiful and comfortable as well as – at last we can use a word which would seem to be outlawed – rational.'

The contrasting fates of the Chrysler and Fiat streamliners show how factors like the competence with which formal ideas are handled make it difficult to assess public reaction to aerodynamically-efficient shapes. Whatever that efficiency, the myth has arisen that aerodynamic shapes do not sell – and yet people want cars that look fast. The stylists' solution to this problem has been to employ shapes and angles that do not endow the car with extra performance (often the reverse is the case), but which suggest that they do. The means by which such suggestions may be conveyed prove on analysis to be rather surprising.

Because the car is so obviously a product of technology, it has often been assumed that the history of technology can account for its morphology. Yet it has failed to do so in several crucial cases, despite a wealth of cogent demonstrations of how important the connection is – best summed up in the words of Bristol's Denis Sevier: 'It can be shown that maximum speed, acceleration, the power required, therefore engine size and weight, cooling system, optimum rear-axle ratio, and intermediate gear ratios, fuel consumption and tank size, braking, wind noise, ventilation, ride and steering characteristics and, finally, safety, are all determined by a motor-car's proportions and styling.' Why, then, did the industry not progress as a technological approach would lead us to expect? What other factors were involved?

Ernst Dichter has indicated the non-rational motives of consumers. Designers such as Bertone, who referred to the Giulietta

85

Sprint as 'a lively, cheeky car that attracted equally young people, and men of a certain age' acknowledge the importance of compromise between rational and non-rational requirements. So did another distinguished Italian body designer, one of the brothers Zagato, referring to his Super Sport body on the Lancia Flaminia: 'For this car we set out with a functional aerodynamic line, and we have tamed it, taking care of the aesthetic appearance and renouncing, naturally, something of the aerodynamics.' In fact, it has long been a tradition of Zagato's styling that the weight and frontal area should be pruned to the practical minimum, the reduction in frontal area being considered worth the sacrifice in purity of aerodynamic form; and since bonded-in glass has made it possible, it has also been a preferred Zagato method of producing a clean exterior surface to restore some of the aerodynamic purity previously lost. All car stylists acknowledge this compromise between rational and non-rational requirements, but not all are able to identify them, while there can be very few who go on to consider whether they are peculiar to the consumer.

At this point, the study becomes one of psychology, rather than one of art, with people operating somewhere along a continuum between rationality and non-rationality. The philosopher Kant pointed out a long time ago that we do not merely perceive the world about us, we order it. Sense data do not flow through our minds in a random flood; we filter, select and discriminate. This filtering is at

All body designers are forced to compromise; Zagato admit to it. Their insistence on light weight, accompanied by some reconciliation of streamlined form and minimal frontal area, produced this four-seater on the Bristol 406 chassis

More typical of Zagato in its curvatures, this unique two-seater on a short 406 Bristol shows how much difference two seats and a foot of wheelbase can make

times rational and adaptive, but at others it amounts to no more than a penumbra of prejudice and intuition, and it is the less evidently rational of these filtering processes that seem to exert a dominant influence over our behaviour, conditioning the choices we make. Decision-making in the motor industry similarly involves participation by individuals occupying different points along the continuum, from artist to engineer, and from builder to advertiser. Today's motor-car is the result of the tension within the company structure being resolved in a way that has little or nothing to do with the technicalities of motor-car design, but a lot to do with the strengths and weaknesses of individual persons and their non-rational reactions to novel ideas. It is possible to isolate and study this non-rational element and understand it in terms of mythology; it is also possible to see the car as a message, that is as a component in an act of communication, but with the context and therefore the meaning of the message changing as the design moves through the usual sequences, by way of manufacture and market place, into obsolescence.

From the styling point of view, the history of the car can therefore be written as a dialectical progression through a number of stages, in each of which the rational and non-rational modes of thinking are differently reconciled. It began with the functional stage in which form was a symbol of function, and the new enthusiasts recognized a special mechanical ethos. This was followed by a long classic stage when we saw the unification of form in graphic terms, inspired less

87

by technology than by mythology – the tall, long bonnet with a little engine hiding somewhere beneath, the long, flared mudguards suggesting speed higher than the car might achieve, the elegant interior trappings proclaiming to the onlooker the luxury that was at complete odds with the probably diabolical ride quality. The all-steel body brought technological changes that we have discussed, leading in turn to an age of formalism in which rival models were differentiated by quite arbitrary styling changes. Finally, when this formalism had gone too far, we saw in the late 1950s and 1960s a new conflict between formalism and rationalism, when both the reality and the myth were isolated, and both came under attack. By the 1970s, this promised to lead to the apparent end of the car as a convincing social symbol, returning it to a purely functional duty, so that the entire cycle might possibly be repeated all over again.

Or is it simply the sudden scarcity and expense of fuel that has prompted a greater awareness of low drag and all the bodily features that ensure it? On the latest evidence, the attempt to sell truly aerodynamic cars is not doomed to perpetual failure. Indeed, a precedent exists for manufacturers actually to educate the buying public. By 1930, many firms were providing easier gearchanges, in order to encourage drivers to use the engine to best advantage. There seems to have been little demand for this from the public, who tended to judge a car rather on its top gear flexibility, assuming that they *would not* change gear if they could possibly avoid it. Nowadays, without synchromesh, the majority of them *could not* change gear.

One of the exquisite ironies of this study is the realization that, in market situations dependent on consumer research, this could never have happened. For chapter and verse, see Ford development. It is significant that it was Citroën, with their haughty disregard for the customer's appraisal of what should be done and how, who embraced aerodynamics as a fundamental determinant of design and made an aesthetic and commercial success of it. Thus, they gave us the DS – for a long time one of the most outstandingly stable, low-drag body designs on the market – and more recently have followed it with the even more efficient GS, SM and the latest CX, all of them with exceptionally low-drag coefficients.

It must be admitted, too, that the generality of today's cars are aerodynamically more efficient than they were twenty, thirty or forty years ago. Outstanding among them must be listed NSU (whose RO 80 was, they insist, designed by a team of engineers, and not by any stylist), Lotus and Matra. However, the generality of today's cars, and even these exceptions, are not as good as we know they could be and, in trying to account for this, it is too easy to postulate a sort of conspiracy theory according to which the manufacturers and petrol companies combine to deprive the poor motorist of his inheritance. The truth is somewhat more complex, and involves conspiracy rather between the customer and the manufacturer, or his mouthpiece the advertiser.

In this symbiotic relationship, what is bought and sold is the shadow, not the substance, the myth rather than the reality. The modern Icarus still does not want to know the chemical composition of wax, nor the laws of aerodynamics. The conjurer must promise not to show us what is up his sleeve. When Nuccio Bertone insists that his cars are not dream cars, he does not mean that they are undesirable, but that the benefits they offer, based on aerodynamics, are real. His may be a luxury market, for the specialist coachbuilders of Italy have generally too limited a production capacity to make other than relatively expensive cars – accepting that, for example, Bertone's pretty little 850 Sport coupé is expensive in relation to the basic Fiat 850. Of all production cars, there are several that give us encouragement. Even the Kamm tail finds its echo in the Citroën cx, the Bristol finrailed roof in the Renault 16 and the Volkswagen Passat (another design by Giugiaro), the sports racers of the mid-1960s in the Lotus Europa and Fiat x1/9, the singledecker bus in any one of many estate cars. These last, in particular, may be the means whereby dreams and reality can coincide. Already more efficient than many of their fastback or other saloon equivalents, they may – if given the glamour of the Reliant Scimitar GTE or the Lancia Beta estate – yet propel us into the romantic sunset.

In these circumstances, it is impossible to classify those designers who have been significant in shaping car bodies according to their talents or importance. Perhaps the really important men now are not necessarily designers themselves, but heads of styling departments, men of enormous power and hopefully of broad and open mind, who can say to this artist 'Go', whereupon he goes, or to that artist 'Come', and he comes. Undoubtedly, the greatest of these centurions is William Mitchell of General Motors, a man who has inspired all sorts of beneficial trends in the styling of cars all over the world, largely because he is not only a fluent artist, but also a motoring enthusiast, one who drives as wholeheartedly as he designs. There are a few other men who might be similarly described, though they have not attained such heights in their profession; Trevor Fiore comes immediately to mind. As for the others, it is surely not commercial success, but recognizable sustained individuality that distinguishes the really great body shapers, as it does the really great painters or sculptors; and on this basis the men who should be revered as great masters must be Costin, Hobbs, Jaray and Lyons. It may come as a salutary shock to many people to find that three of these four are English, practitioners of an art that is popularly reputed to be an Italian-American speciality. What is perhaps a more entertaining subject for speculation is how the rapidly-developing and extremely idiomatic German school of design of the late 1930s might have continued had its course not been so rudely interrupted. A drophead or cabriolet body by a German coachbuilder looked suspiciously like that by any other German coachbuilder, but altogether different from all non-Germans and immeasurably better. Given another five years, their saloons might have been endowed with similar character and the balance of things might thereafter have turned out very differently – as, indeed, it would have in numerous other respects.

Based on the all-independent 280 chassis, the supercharged Mercedes-Benz 540
was often more rakishly bodied than this; but nothing could be more
unmistakably German than that cabriolet top. Why could – or would – nobody
else do it?

3
Chassis constructors

The chassis is a structure constituting the foundation upon which all the other parts of a car are assembled. A more modern view, reflecting the changes in design philosophy with the passing of time, defines the chassis as that structure which connects the parts in their proper spatial relationships and accepts the loads they create. In either definition, *structure* is the important word. However, the later definition more clearly implies the requirements of that word, which are that the chassis should retain its dimensional integrity despite the stresses imposed on it by the suspension, the drive train, or other loads. It must neither sag (which would indicate a lack of beam stiffness) nor twist (which reveals a want of torsional stiffness), from which it follows that it must be more than merely strong enough for its duties: it must also be stiff enough.

This need for stiffness was generally ignored by car designers during the first 50 years of motoring. In the days when front and rear wheels were mounted on rigid beam axles, it was commonly and erroneously supposed that they would be immune from the effects of chassis distortion; and the simple frames on which most cars were based were designed according to rudimentary mechanical principles that had something in common with bridge-building, but little connection with any disciplines more closely related to automobile engineering. The basis of the conventional frame was two longitudinal girders, made of channel-section steel and set parallel to each other; and these were spaced, rather than braced, by transverse members of similar construction. The whole thing was fastened together by bolts or rivets and was torsionally very weak, while its beam strength was often due to the generosity of material. The only significant contribution to the stiffness of this structure was generally made by the engine, which was commonly mounted rigidly between the main frame longerons; but when, in the 1920s, designers of luxury cars sought to isolate them from engine vibrations by mounting the engine on flexible bearers, the final degradation of the chassis as a structure seemed assured.

The knowledge was, in fact, available at the time to counteract this decay. In the aviation industry, distinguished engineers such as Wagner, Northrop and De Bruyne created between 1925 and 1931 some extremely advanced forms of stressed sheet construction, extending ideas that had been embodied in a monocoque airframe as early as the Deperdussin monoplane of 1913.

However, the majority of car designers were of inferior quality, and those few who recognized these advances were tempted to dismiss them as irrelevant. There were one or two isolated examples of cars exploiting stressed sheet metal to create the beginnings of a kind of primitive unitary structure, such as the Lancia Lambda and the 11·9 hp Lagonda of the 1920s. In general, though, the old girder chassis held literal sway, and only Bugatti provided a frame that did more than offer a convenient datum about which to construct the car. The others sometimes relied upon the superimposed bodywork to contribute to the overall stiffness of the vehicle, and they were rewarded for their indolence with splits, cracks and tears in the

Independent suspension, the backbone frame, and much else, began in the work of the genius Ledwinka during the years he spent with Tatra. This triumph of accessibility was a light touring car that did well in tough competitions such as the Targa Florio: paradoxically, its swing-axle independent rear suspension depended for its success on badly surfaced roads. Porsche's mistake in appropriating the idea was in not appreciating its limitations

bodies. Weymann contrived a body structure which deliberately allowed itself to flex with the chassis and yet be free from creaks and rattles; the rest sought the palliative of flexible body mountings or simply made their chassis of stouter metal.

The definitions so far given for the word 'chassis' allow it less breadth of meaning than it enjoyed in former years, when it was often the practice of a manufacturer to sell a rolling chassis for some coachbuilder to grace with a body, to make a complete and finished car. Then the chassis would not only include the suspension, engine, steering and all mechanical adjuncts, but also even the wings. In casual use, the word 'chassis' may still include by implication many of these elements, particularly the suspension; and in this chapter particularly, the word must be taken to mean the basic structure that has to bear loads fed into it from the engine and drive line, and from the suspension, together with that suspension and its related tyres and running gear. The whole thing is, or should be, an entity in which every component may have a bearing on the performance of every other: if the object be to create the basis of a car that will ride and handle satisfactorily, then everything affecting these phenomena is material, starting from the tyres and working through the suspension and steering linkages to the basic frame or hull of the car. There is no need in this chapter to consider the work of those many designers who have proved themselves quite capable of creating eminently stiff fuselages or elegant spaceframes, stiff backbones or even such ingenious contrivances as the endo-skeletal foundation of the Rover 2000. Such men are, and have long been, numerous, and they are correspondingly unremarkable. The same may be said of those who, from time to time, contrive a suspension system that works passably well. However, when we consider those designers who have proved themselves capable of creating an entire chassis complex, from the tyres up, such that it satisfied all applicable criteria, and indeed made a significant contribution to automobile engineering knowledge, we find such men astonishingly few in number.

This is due simply to the fact that, in the scale of automobile engineering history, the chassis has been a very late developer. Vincenzo Lancia took the subject seriously in the early 1920s when he created the Lambda, as we saw in Chapter One. Maurice Olley took it a lot further with his studies of ride and handling in the 1930s for General Motors. In the late 1930s, the Germans investigated chassis design with great curiosity, and some ingenuity, notably the designers of the Mercedes-Benz and Auto-Union Grand Prix cars of the time, but also such pioneers of the modern sports car as BMW – in which connection it is interesting to note that the chassis of the BMW 326, a design far superior in every way to that of the sporting 328, was designed for them by Budd, whose contribution to the all-steel body and to the evolution of the front-wheel-drive chassis was mentioned in the preceding chapter. It was not until the 1950s, however, that chassis design really came of age, with an intensified study of the peculiarities of the pneumatic tyre accompanying rapid developments in its design and construction.

The peculiarly non-linear characteristics of tyres demand an unusual imaginativeness on the part of the car designer if he is to comprehend the part they will play in the behaviour of the whole car. The interdependence of vehicle and tyres goes far beyond the mere need to specify tyres of certain dimensions to suit a given car. The design of the car itself may have to be modified in order to adapt it to a chosen tyre which may be particularly demanding in vibrational characteristics, sensitivity to camber, steering offset or other suspension characteristics. On the other hand, the tyre may have to be modified to suit a car which presents particular problems, of weight, speed, ride quality or even such apparently unrelated matters as brake cooling. Either way, a great deal can be done to ensure compatibility of these two components in the vehicle-tyre system, though some adjustment may still have to be made to meet the needs of certain driving styles, if the drivers cannot themselves adapt to the characteristics of the vehicle. Other external factors must be taken into account, such as geographical peculiarities of climate or road surface: the bumpy contours and loose surfaces of roads in the mountainous areas of central Europe made independent suspension at all costs, even using swing axles, appear entirely desirable to the 1930s designers of cars intended for use there, but the same suspension proved dangerously unsuitable for cars exploiting the greater speed and grip possible on the roads of western Europe and the USA.

Were it not that he ignored tyre characteristics, the great Dr Frederick Lanchester would undoubtedly rank as the first and still one of the most distinguished designers of all time. Instead, the first to investigate their effect on car behaviour was Maurice Olley, an Englishman who worked for Rolls-Royce, and subsequently became famous in his work for General Motors. His first involvement there was in the development of ride quality, and the related introduction of independent front suspension; and, although he took pains to disclaim any suggestion that it was a one-man show, there is no doubt that his was the brain that resolved all the outstanding problems. As a matter of interest, those whose help he acknowledged included Henry Crane, Ernest Seaholm (chief engineer of Cadillac), the famous Charles Kettering, and (for what he described as 'tolerance and constant support') Lawrence P. Fisher, then general manager of the Cadillac division of General Motors, who had personally engaged Olley and who accused him of being the first man in General Motors to spend a quarter of a million dollars in building two experimental cars!

When Olley came to Cadillac from Rolls-Royce in November 1930, he was surprised to find Rolls-Royce so popular. A Rolls had at that time just completed a phenomenal test at the new GM proving grounds, and had been torn down for inspection; at Rolls-Royce, however, there was an awareness that everything was not as good as it might be. For several years, they had been engaged in a concentrated drive on ride quality, the technicians at Derby being intrigued by the fact that cars which were considered acceptable on British roads were far from acceptable when exported, even to the improved roads of the USA. They were beginning to realize that this was not because American roads were worse, but simply because the waves in them were of a different shape.

A great deal of work had been done at Rolls-Royce along the lines of swinging cars from overhead pivots to measure their moments of inertia, measuring the stiffness of chassis frames and coachwork, and measuring the suspension rates of the springs as installed on the actual car. The British factory had also developed one of the very first practical ride meters, which consisted simply of an open-topped water container: the amount of water lost from it in a measured mile gave an indication of the smoothness of the ride at the

97

chosen speed for each test. Some of this practice was introduced to Cadillac in 1930, and soon Olley had them swinging cars, measuring installed spring rates and all the rest of it. He also had them build a bump rig similar to the Rolls-Royce machine (it was the first in Detroit) and used it to produce a synthetic ride on a stationary car.

In the course of all this investigation, Olley became fascinated by the relationships between spring rates and dampers and, in particular, by what he and others since have always called the K^2/AB ratio, which is the moment of inertia of the car in pitch divided by its wheelbase. Early in 1932, he built the K^2 rig, which consisted of a complete seven-passenger saloon on which it was possible, by moving weights, to produce any desired changes in relative deflections of front and rear springs, and in the moment of inertia of the whole car. No instrumentation was used on this to measure ride: the engineer simply assessed it subjectively. As Olley observed: 'This was the best method, because we did not know then, and do not know today, what a good ride is.' But they could make so many fundamental changes in ride on this rig in a single day's running that their impressions remained fresh, and direct comparisons were possible.

It was at this stage, early in 1932, that Olley began to feel the urge to investigate independent suspension. The K^2 rig was spelling out in unmistakable terms that a flat ride (which was an entirely new experience) was possible if the front springs were made softer than the rear – something that traditional car designers would have considered a dreadful error. All previous attempts to use soft springs with the conventional beam front axle failed because of steering shimmy and a general lack of stability in handling. The next step, therefore, required a couple of experimental Cadillacs to be built with independent suspension. The reason for using two was that GM had taken an interest in the very compact system devised by André Dubonnet, but also wished to study a double wishbone layout. An independent rear suspension was also tried, for Olley had it in mind that as soon as possible GM should also get rid of the conventional rear axle – a step that he insisted, to the end of his career, was long overdue. From these cars, in which many of the GM engineers rode, it was evident that Cadillac had something very special in the way of improved ride and handling. Finally, by March 1933, they were ready for full-dress demonstrations to the top brass, the General Technical Committee, which met to ride in the two experimental Cadillacs and also a Buick on normal suspension but with an infinitely variable transmission.

After the demonstration runs on the three cars, the Committee began by discussing the new automatic transmission, and it was immediately turned down by Vic Grant, who was Vice-President of Sales. It was hardly a surprising reaction: in March 1933, there was not a bank open in the USA, and anyone who owned a farm was thankful that at least he could eat. Grant rejected the automatic transmission and the 100 dollars cost that went with it as something that a Buick buyer could very well do without. 'But,' he continued, 'if I could ride like you've shown us, for a matter of 15 bucks, I'd find the money somehow.' Olley records that the meeting impressed him as a marvellous demonstration of American enterprise in action: in the face of the conditions then existing, the expenditure of millions of dollars to which GM was committing itself indicated courage of a type that was outside his previous experience. Charles Kettering managed to put it in perspective: 'It seems to me we can't afford not to do it.'

With this vindication of his first work for his new employers, Olley was justified in further investigating the peculiarities of ride and handling, and all the interactions of suspension and steering, that now became much more manifest in the independently-sprung cars. It was he who first worked out how to translate the peculiarities of tyre behaviour, things such as the constantly-changing relationships between cornering force, slip angle, self-aligning torque, speed and load, into their effect upon the actual trajectory described by the car, compared with the course directed by the driver through the steering mechanism. It was Olley who created the terms 'understeer' and 'oversteer' and suggested rough working definitions of them that, perhaps unfortunately, have been accepted by later generations of designers as some kind of irrevocable gospel. Not only did he work all this out for himself, he also went to a great deal of trouble to explain it to others, not only to learned institutions but also to the men in the workshops; and his teachings are acknowledged by many of the greatest designers today (including Channer of Bristol and Chrysler-Rootes, Chapman of Lotus, and Issigonis of BLMC), as providing the foundation of the chassis-engineering knowledge that they went on to develop so well.

Jack Channer came to the subject with a completely open mind, having been taken on by the Car Division of the Bristol Aeroplane Company as a stress man after doing similar work on airframes for the parent company. Finding himself with insufficient to occupy his time in the very early days, he set himself to study the dynamic behaviour of the car, and reasoned that this should start from the points where it reacted against the road. Accordingly, he sought detailed information from all the tyre companies and this led to particularly fruitful collaboration with Dunlop and Michelin, in the course of which Channer began to appreciate, as perhaps no designer had before, just how a car reacted to every kind of steering motion, suspension flexure, load distribution change, and so on. Within a couple of years, he made himself the greatest expert in Britain – and probably in the world – on suspension design, a component manufacturer commenting that he was the only man in the industry who could, if asked, quote roll couple distribution figures for his cars, at a time when his opposite numbers either had not the foggiest idea what it meant, or were forced to admit that they had not bothered to find out.

Thanks to his work, the steering, handling and roadholding of the Bristol – already good because of the sound basis afforded by the BMW 326 chassis from which they were developed – were raised to quite extraordinary levels, far superior to those of their contemporaries. It was through Channer that Bristol became pioneers in the use of radial-ply tyres and of the Watt linkage to determine the roll centre and lateral location of the rear axle. For a later prototype that the firm was unfortunately unable to put into production because of the government's reconstruction of the aircraft industry, he devised what must be the most perfect De Dion suspension ever seen. Then, for space reasons, he rejected it in favour of a rubber-sprung semi-trailing arm suspension, so contrived as to give wheel motions likewise superior to those of any kindred arrangement, allowing the prototype (known as the Bristol 220) to reach extremely high cornering rates with virtually zero roll, while exhibiting handling qualities of a similarly high order.

Today, Jack Channer is a senior chassis designer engaged on advanced projects at the British Technical Centre of the Chrysler Group, where he went after spending a little time with ERA. He was deeply involved in the design of the suspension for the Hillman Avenger, which proved to need remarkably little modification before acquiring itself an enviable reputation for cornering and handling in modified saloon car racing.

Another man whose skill in vehicle design begins from a thorough appreciation of tyre characteristics, but whose concern has been entirely with racing machinery, is Jim Hall, who will always be associated with the mighty and often misjudged Chaparral. This car, or rather series of sports racing cars, was built in Texas during the 1960s and early 1970s and, in its early years, attracted great admiration as a brilliantly innovative technical exercise conducted very successfully and more or less privately by the apparently amateur partnership of Jim Hall and Hap Sharp. Both were wealthy men owing their fortunes to the petroleum industry. It therefore seemed feasible that a private venture of this nature might well produce such distinctive machines, if only because of the enthusiasm and original thinking of the proprietors being unfettered by the formal handicaps of a large motor-manufacturing organization, such as those with whom they were competing.

Later, it became clear that the operation was no longer merely one that had earned a patronizing interest on the part of General Motors, but one that had become a clandestine means whereby that organization (or certain sections of it) might reap the benefits of using motor racing as a proving ground for various ideas, without contravening the official General Motors rule on abstention from motor racing.

None of this complexity of organization or design existed when the first Chaparrals were built. They were constructed by the California firm of Troutman & Barnes, to a commission from Hall for a front-engined car with a spaceframe tubular chassis, a fairly conventional design by the standards of its time, with which Hall enjoyed reasonable success. In 1962, he and Sharp had Chaparral Cars incorporated at Midland, Texas, where a small but very competent factory was set up in open country, a few miles out of town. An important feature of the location was that it allowed a private

Jack Channer leaning on the lash-up body of the all-independent rubber-sprung Bristol 220 prototype that was doomed never to go into production. Channer made himself without peer among chassis designers as a specialist in ride and handling

The chassis of the BMW 326 saloon, derived by ex-Horch designer Fiedler from an earlier BMW chassis with frame designed by Budd, formed the basis of the Bristol 400 upon which Channer's development work was first concentrated

test track to be built there, embodying a sinuous 2-mile road circuit and a steering pad. Far from merely providing an opportunity for test drivers to form subjective impressions of prototype and development cars, this track was a model of objectivity: its curves were of carefully-calibrated radii, and a series of photocells was laid to track the cars, whose performance would be subsequently analysed from data provided by the photocells, wired to recording and computing apparatus in the factory. It was thus possible for very advanced tests of roadholding and handling to be carried out in privacy, exploiting the undoubted talent of Hall as a driver.

Hall was also a talented engineer and, after graduating in mechanical engineering at the California Institute of Technology, he built up the experience necessary to become one of the outstanding driver–engineers of motor-racing history, by arranging to participate in the 1963 Grand Prix season, driving a Lotus. At the same time as he was studying the art of motor racing, he was applying his science to the construction of a new second-series Chaparral car.

This made its first appearance in October 1963. With its GM engine and Collotti transmission behind the driver, and most of its running gear obtained from Lotus, it was reasonably conventional for a sports-racing car, being remarkable only for the lightness of its chassis construction. The basic structure, comprising a multiplicity of torsion boxes that constituted a monocoque hull requiring

only a little superstructure to complete the bodywork, was composed almost entirely of glass-reinforced plastics, painstakingly moulded and locally reinforced with metal to comply with Hall's postulates of 150 lb weight and 3000 lb ft per degree of torsional stiffness between axle centres.

The series 2 Chaparral won its first race in April 1964. A month later it won again, but now it had within it yet another example of Hall's radical approach to high-performance motor engineering, in the form of an automatic transmission. Like many other features of this and later Chaparrals, it was shrouded in secrecy; only years later did we discover that it was not strictly automatic at all, consisting merely of an hydrokinetic convertor coupling with a lock-up clutch and a simple 2-speed constant-mesh spur gearbox with dog engagement. Hall's next campaign was to harness aerodynamic effects to improve the stability of the car, and to exploit the cornering power of the latest low-profile racing tyres, then being introduced by Firestone.

Working very closely with the tyre company, Hall knew that the latest tyres generated higher cornering forces if subjected to greater downforce than was applied by the weight of the car. Obviously, to increase the car's weight would be undesirable, since it would increase the mass being accelerated and braked; but an aero-dynamically-induced downforce could be achieved by careful shaping of the body, with scarcely any weight penalty. Logical pursuit of this argument led to the use of an airfoil mounted on struts that were attached directly to the rear-wheel hub carriers. The idea had been tried in the past, notably by Michel May, on an experimental Porsche sports car in 1955 (May later worked for Ferrari) and much earlier by Fritz von Opel on the experimental rocket car that was built for publicity purposes in the late 1920s. The first thorough development, however, was by Hall, who realized that, by applying the aerodynamic downforce direct to the tyres through the hub carriers, the suspension could remain unaffected. A further refinement was a provision for the airfoil to be adjusted by the driver: the two-pedal control made possible by the transmission allowed a third pedal to be linked to the wing: pressure on the pedal feathered the wing to the zero-drag position for maximum speed along the straight, while release of the pedal for any reason caused the wing to revert to its maximum angle of incidence. How advanced Hall's thinking was is well illustrated by the fact that the idea was not effectively copied until two years later in Formula One Grand Prix racing, where it received little further development before being banned by the FIA in 1969.

This car, the Chaparral 2C, was developed in subsequent models for some years, until new rules governing the CanAm series of sports car races banned movable aerodynamic devices, while airfoils were virtually proscribed by European and international rules. Hall responded with the last and most revolutionary Chaparral of them all in 1970. The 2J employed new means to provide the necessary downforce: housed in the tail was a small 2-stroke, 2-cylinder,

45 bhp snowmobile engine, driving a pair of large extractor fans which faced rearwards through the vertical wall of the slab-like tail. These fans sucked air from beneath the car, the area of road it covered being sealed by skirts of Lexan polycarbonate. In this way, the 2J was sucked down onto the road surface, the total downforce generated combining with the vast tyres to permit cornering rates almost certainly higher than any other car in any category of racing could achieve.

Propelled by a 7·6-litre Chevrolet engine, the 2J was consistently the fastest car in the 1970 CanAm series, but its ground effect mechanism was the object of much vilification and jealousy on the part of other competitors, who successfully sought to have it banned. Thereupon, Hall, recognizing that the regulation of motor racing was now governed by alien considerations to impose a mindless egalitarianism upon a sport that had once been a cradle of innovation and a harbour of genius, announced that he would take no further part in it. In the circumstances, he no longer really belonged to it, and no more Chaparrals were made.

Jim Hall is a very rare example of a chassis designer with great breadth of vision allied to innovative genius. He makes an interesting comparison with a more common kind of American chassis engineer, the type who accepts prevailing dogma on major issues, but worries away at minor details to produce a machine of delightful engineering refinement. A good exemplar would be Frank Kurtis, a man who supplied the winning chassis at Indianapolis no less than five times, and whose work was always superbly constructed and finished. He was the first to use torsion-bar suspension on these racers, a medium which became almost universal in American track racing cars, and he played a major part in setting a pattern for Indianapolis machines that lasted virtually unchanged for a decade. The cars all featured tubular-steel chassis frames, arranged as a pair of longitudinal beams, each composed of parallel tubes joined by triangulating members, and they had rigid beam axles at front and rear. When the suspension of such an axle is properly arranged, it can give very good results on a smooth road surface, and Kurtis took immense pains to perfect his suspension. The axles were confined to vertical motion by longitudinal Watt linkages, and laterally by the same, or by a neat little asymmetrical three-bar linkage known as the 'Jacob's Ladder'. Disc brakes were fitted from very early on, and development as the years continued saw the suspension system offset to move the centre of gravity of the car to the left, because all the races were run on anti-clockwise oval circuits, imposing a repeated series of left turns. Carrying the idea further, Kurtis learned to shift oil tanks and other accessories onto the left side of the car, to tilt the engine over on its side, and eventually to evolve a car that was wide, well balanced and very low indeed.

Kurtis was in motor engineering for the greater part of his life. Born in Colorado in 1908, he was soon involved in the booming midget-car racing business, which gave him his start. His finish amounted to a voluntary retirement at the age of 54: until 1962, he had built chassis for Indianapolis (not to mention a series of 2-seater sports cars that were quite successful in domestic events), but then the new rear-engined Lotus Fords began to demonstrate that the era of the old-fashioned, front-engined roadsters was drawing to its end. Some of his contemporaries followed the lead of the English cars, but Kurtis preferred to call it a day.

The man who caused his discomfiture and displacement was Colin Chapman, then making his first forays into the brickyard that, within a couple of years, he was to dominate. The associated names of Colin Chapman and Lotus became famous rapidly in the early 1950s and have remained so for a generation, the merits of Lotus cars arising almost entirely by virtue of their chassis design (Chapman never designed an engine), in turn an expression of all the elements that make up Chapman's remarkable character. He was tremendously industrious, prepared to work all the hours that God sends; he had an exceptionally strong sense of the rightness of design, which he sought with a passionate logic, scorning the shabby compromises of other engineers and designers in the industry; as a shrewd businessman, wholly committed to the deadly serious pursuit of his own goals, he was prepared almost remorselessly to exploit every opportunity available to him, either material or human, driving other people as hard as he drove himself. Chapman is not a genius except in his infinite capacity for taking pains; he is not really an artist, although there is a mathematical beauty in many of his structures; nor is he a tyrant, though he has left a wake of broken and despairing men. History has proved him to be one of the most intelligent, purposeful and creative designers of high-performance cars, one whose work has been emulated more than that of almost any other.

Most of all, he is a worrier, a man whose creative processes – be they the design of a car or of a component, in the winning of a race or the settling of a contract – are marked by an obsessive and almost malignant objectivity. There are two stages evident in it, the first being a logical assessment of the true nature of the problem, so as to arrive at the proper (not merely the best, nor the most convenient) resolution of it. The second stage is not so much applied mathematics as astringent miserliness; every scrap of superfluous weight, every item that is irrelevant or otiose, every poundsworth that can be replaced by a pennyworth, is pruned away as though Chapman's commercial object were to sell air. The package that results may not appeal to those conditioned to judge a car by the shut of the door, the depth of the upholstery, or the weight of the paint; but to the driver whose sensual and cerebral appreciations of motoring offer more relevant criteria, the Lotus is as much a machine for driving as a house by Le Corbusier is a machine for living. It has been typical of every road-going Lotus and of the majority of Lotus racers that the steering and roadholding should establish standards by which those of all other current cars might be judged, while the performance is out of proportion to its meagre material endowments.

No model better illustrates this Vespasian achievement of great

Light weight and structural purity were the cornerstones upon which Colin Chapman built his early cars, of which this Lotus 6 was typical

ends by modest means than the Lotus 3, which first made the name of Colin Chapman known to every motor-sport enthusiast in the land. Built in 1951 for 750 Formula racing, it complied with the regulations for these club events, but it was so scientifically different from the amateurish hacks with which it competed, so tiny and light and fast and stable, that the incredulous amazement greeting its early performance was soon replaced by a resentful and unmerited jealousy. This gave way in due course to a demand for replicas, an opportunity that, like any other presenting itself to Chapman, was not to be missed – he established the Lotus Engineering Company on the first day of 1952.

He was only a spare-time proprietor, working during the day as a structural designer for the British Aluminium Company, where his talents and engineering degree had taken him. In the evening and for half the night, Chapman laboured on the cars; the fort was held during the day by his partner Michael Allen. Before long, they progressed to making the Lotus 6, a sports car based upon a multi-tubular chassis that was a nearly complete spaceframe, most of the missing diagonals being replaced by stressed body panels, riveted to the tubes of the framework. This chassis was sold as a kit to which proprietary engines and running gear might be added, and it was so successful that, by 1955, a hundred examples had been built, giving Lotus in turn an enviable reputation on the racing circuits and hillclimbs of Britain. Long before it went out of production, however, Chapman was irritated by it. He has been like this about practically everything he has made, painfully conscious of its shortcomings, and almost pathetically anxious to do better next time.

Salvation came in the person of Frank Costin, brother of the Mike who had for some time been helping Chapman when not gainfully employed with the De Havilland Aircraft Company. Frank was with De Havilland too, but before long he became fired by the same enthusiasm as had already driven so many other willing slaves in the Lotus galley. With his aid, Chapman produced the Lotus 8, in which structural purity vied for priority with aerodynamic refinement. For development of the prototype, Chapman formed Team Lotus, staffed by unpaid volunteers, while a full-time paid mechanic did the work of the company that still produced the component-form Mark 6 – and Chapman continued to burn the candle at both ends. By the beginning of 1955, he and Mike Costin began full-time work for Lotus, in time to see the Mark 9 make its appearance, cleaner and simpler, shorter and lighter than the Mark 8, and withal a little stronger and somewhat easier to work on. Frank Costin had devised the body shape with all these things in mind, and also with the benefit of knowledge he had acquired during development work on the Mark 8 – work which included being strapped to the bonnet so that he could study the behaviour of airflow under the front wheel arches, at speeds up to 110 mph.

Such was the impetus of the Lotus competition career that Chapman was encouraged to embark on his first pure racing car, a Formula Two single-seater for 1957. This was the Lotus 12, a car that has never really emerged from the obscurity that its mediocre success earned it, but which is of absorbing interest as the first embodiment of a number of design principles that Chapman was later to incorporate in other more successful models. In essentials, the Lotus 12 was designed primarily for light weight and low drag, so as to be able to exploit the power of the Coventry Climax engine to better purpose than it would be when used in rival cars. To this end, it had a spaceframe chassis and a very closely-fitting body, within which the driving position was lowered as much as possible (despite the central transmission line) by the use of a special all-indirect gearbox, built integral with the final drive housing. This gearbox, designed for Lotus by Richard Ansdale and Harry Mundy, was a very clever 5-speeder offering everything that a racing gearbox should have, except reliability. By the time the reason for persistent failures was discovered (under power the gears flung most of the oil away from themselves and thus committed suicide), it was too late. Two other features of the car were, however, successfully proven and were to remain in use for many years. One was the magnesium disc wheel, based on the principle of the convoluted or wobbly web: in this, the architectural notion of a sine-wave wall (which is notably stiff in relation to its mass) is translated into metal, the disc portion of the wheel being effectively a crimped quasi-cylinder so that its undulations are steeper near the hub than they are near the rim. The effect is to dispose a minimal amount of material to give a strength proportional to the loads to which it will be subjected – always the focal object of Chapman's chassis design – while susceptibility to fatigue failure was reduced by the absence of apertures such as exist between the spokes of more conventional light-alloy wheels.

The other enduring feature of the Lotus 12 was its independent rear suspension, the first example of what became known as the 'Chapman strut'. The object here was to contrive a geometry of rear-wheel movements similar to what had already been arranged at the front of previous Lotus models: structurally, the Chapman strut was analagous to the MacPherson strut system of independent front suspension, the distinguishing feature being Chapman's very clever use of the universally-jointed drive shafts as elements of the suspension.

What followed next was, knowing Chapman, inevitable on at least four counts. The wide separation of the load paths from the Chapman strut rear suspension made the system admirably suited to a stressed-skin body, and it was inevitable that he should be tempted to try it. In any case, his obsession with the creation of automobile structures having the greatest possible stiffness, while employing the least possible mass of material, made it inevitable that sooner or later his elegant tubular spaceframes would give way to a more efficient stressed-skin or even monocoque hull. The ambitions of the young company were such that they were sure to be seduced by the idea of a high-quality closed car that would serve admirably on the road, while having all the most desirable characteristics of a racing car, so as to earn the name Lotus that respect among motoring connoisseurs that had already been won among motoring enthusiasts. Finally, and with equal inevitability because it was a young and still inexperienced company, it could never make that car as good as it could have been, simply because unrealistic pricing made its constructors unable to do the job as properly as it should have been done. In the Lotus 14, all these things came to pass: breathtaking in its beauty, heartbreaking in its fallibility, utterly right in conception, and unutterably wrong in its execution, the Lotus Elite was an aesthetic triumph and a commercial disaster.

In retrospect, there was very little wrong with the Elite, and hardly any of that was the fault of the car itself. What really handicapped it were commercial mistakes: it should have been priced higher and commensurate quality control exercised, but instead it was bodged in detail and the company lost money on every one. Perhaps the greatest mistake of all was offering it in kit form: when a manufacturer as young as Lotus then was seeks a reputation for excellence, it is suicide to put that reputation in the hands of an unknown assembler, whatever the attractions of space-saving at the factory and tax avoidance for the customer.

In the Lotus 18 and especially in its suspension, Chapman made advances as important in their context as those in the body of the Elite. The Lotus 18 can best be judged by the contrast it afforded to

the Lotus 16 that raced in the Grands Prix of the previous season. That car, a development of the Lotus 12, had been an abysmal failure, due not only to mechanical unreliability but also to unsatisfactory roadholding. Starting afresh, Chapman sought to espouse a new ideal, to make a car that would employ with the utmost economy the potentiality of every bit of rubber that it could put on the road. All this was achieved in a car that looked superficially crude, but which was in fact a masterpiece of mechanical simplicity and geometrical refinement, inheriting nothing from the front-engined Lotus 16 but the engine itself and the wheels. The result appeared to be a simple slab-sided box of a car, of which no part other than the windscreen stood higher than 28 inches.

By thus reducing frontal area, Chapman regained what ultimate speed might have been lost by want of aerodynamic refinement. He also kept the car light; to the surprise of everyone else, the removal of the engine from the nose of the car to the tail paradoxically resulted in the front wheels of the new car carrying 4% more of its weight than did those of the Lotus 16. Finally, to suit his scheme for a supremely roadworthy and responsive car, Chapman devised a new rear-suspension system to complement the ordinary, unequal-length wishbones so disposed at the front as to place the roll centre fairly close to ground level. At the rear he brought it down to a similar altitude, again using the axially-rigid but universally-jointed half-shafts as suspension links, so that each could be considered to act as a wishbone would. Well below each shaft was a proper wishbone, its apex almost on the centre line of the car beneath the gearbox, its base anchored in the bottom of the cast light-alloy hub carrier; by bringing this casting very near to the ground, the upper and lower links diverged away from the car's centre line, providing the low roll centre and appropriate control of camber that Chapman sought. Weight transfer from inner to outer wheels during cornering was dramatically reduced, and the considerable roll couple that was a corollary was dealt with by the addition of anti-roll torsion bars to the front and rear suspension (the latter being rare in those days), so that rotation of the car about its

Even in the cars that have superseded this Elan and Plus 2s, Chapman (leaning on the latter) is still committed to the economy of efficiency, making cars that are no bigger, no heavier, no more powerful and no less taut than they need to be

roll axis was limited to a mere four degrees. It only remained to supply some form of longitudinal constraint for the rear suspension, and this was easily done by a pair of parallel radius arms extending from the top and bottom of each hub carrier.

In a very short time, the Lotus 18 proved itself the fastest car in the history of Grand Prix racing. In a little longer, it was being avidly copied by all other racing-car constructors. To copy somebody else's motor-car is like preaching Holy Writ: it is not the substance that matters, but the spirit. Where most of Chapman's imitators failed was in lacking his compulsive urge to take every advantage available to him and to give nothing away. Other people in the past had sometimes succeeded in elevating meanness to the status of a fine art, but it was left to Chapman to perfect it as an instrument for winning motor races. Just as his demands for credit were notorious in business, so his insistence on the utmost efficiency of men and machinery became a byword in automobile engineering. Sometimes this niggardliness took curious forms: no visitor to the factory (in the days when it was at Cheshunt in Hertfordshire) ever enjoyed any hospitality, even a cup of coffee, the boss having decreed that anybody found consuming food on the premises was liable to instant dismissal on the grounds that it made the place untidy. He could not offer perfection, but he could demand it.

The delicacy of perfection is a very precarious thing: and the delicacy of the Lotus chassis evolved in the mid-1960s, so that it was undoubtedly the most perfect in racing, made its durability a very precarious thing indeed. There were times when suspension or steering components would come apart or wheels would fall off, times when a driver noted for his courage grew very petulant about the relative chances of breaking records or his neck, and times when it all held together – the faults were usually of quality rather than of design – so that this beautiful fragile creation might demonstrate that ineffable superiority which declared Chapman to be the most shrewd and perceptive designer in Grand Prix racing. The evidence of this might be sought in the Lotus 25, the first Grand Prix car to have a stressed-skin hull. The weight of this eggshell fabrication was but one-sixteenth that of the total machine, but its strength and stiffness were unimpeachable. To give it further superiority, Chapman reduced the frontal area to a mere eight square feet, by making the driver lean back further than ever before, giving him a steering wheel only a foot in diameter, packing him and his controls and every possible ancillary well down inside the car, allowing as little as possible to protrude.

Not all of this was original work. The inboard front suspension units were hailed at the time as an innovation, though Maserati had employed them in 1948; the supine driving position echoed the designs of Gustav Baumm for a record-breaking NSU motor cycle a decade earlier; the revised rear suspension owed something to the example of Eric Broadley and his Lola. Chapman was not concerned to be original, merely to be thorough. His success makes it not at all fanciful to declare that all subsequent Grand Prix cars have been modelled on the Lotus 25. The only significant developments, apart from the brief flutter of wings for a couple of years from the middle of the 1967 season, have been Lotus-inspired. Even the classic status of the Lotus 72, which came on the scene in 1970 and was still competitive in 1974, bears a clear relationship to the 25, just as the later GRP-bodied production cars (the Elan and Plus 2 with cruci-form chassis, the rear-engined Europa with a similar frame, and even perhaps the latest Type 75 which is eponymous with the original Elite) can be seen as modern and practical realizations of the ideals that inspired the original Elite. On the evidence of five cars in his history – the Lotus 3, 14, 18, 25 and 72 – Chapman is entitled to be considered one of history's tiny band of really great and truly creative high-performance car-design engineers, the only one (unless Jim Hall be admitted to their ranks, as I feel he should) to achieve that distinction by leaving engines entirely alone and con-centrating on the chassis. During the past ten years, of course, he has relied heavily on the services of assistants who have often been highly capable men (notably Maurice Phillipe and Leonard Terry) while the expansion of his group of companies has forced him to exercise a more supervisory role; but just as he still takes the credit for everything, he still takes the responsibility. There is not a car for which he has been responsible (and this includes not only every Lotus model, but also the finally successful version of the Grand Prix Vanwall, which owed its chassis to the wisdom of its builder in consulting Chapman on its design), that is not clearly the work of an engineer more imaginative, more creative, and more critical of established practice than any of his contemporaries.

Chapman's purism weakened in his later commercial designs. The bifidate spine frame of the Lotus Elan was torsionally weakened by the spring locations: torsion bars feeding the suspension loads into the centre of the chassis would have been better, but otherwise the chassis deserves only praise

COLOUR ILLUSTRATIONS

OPPOSITE

Car design cannot progress for a decade without *hic jacet* being metaphorically inscribed on a few monumental constructions, and for all its paradoxical delicacy the Bugatti Type 59 was one such. In it, Bugatti said his last word on the subject of the racing car, in what was becoming a dead language. His artistry was more apparent than ever: the architectural beauty of the whole was greater even than the sum of its parts, which included wheels whose torsional stiffness was imparted by peripheral serrations at the rim corresponding with others on the brake drum, allowing slender wire spokes to act purely radially. It was a surpassingly beautiful car, but not an effective one: within ten years of the birth of his epoch-marking Type 35, Bugatti's art was refined until it was teetering on the brink of degeneracy.

PAGE 114

The common man demanded a lot of his car. Ford gave it cheapness through simplistic mass production; Gropius, promoting functional styling, gave respectability to the wind-shaping of Voisin and Jaray; Austin gave it a new and more humble scale; and the Italian tradition gave it roadworthiness and spirit. Giacosa brought all these together in his Fiat 508c and added something extra, *humanity*: here at last was the popular car that gave the ordinary motorist more than enough, yet never too much. Perhaps this, after all, was the real modern car, the first embodiment of principles that have remained valid ever since.

PAGE 115

Never mind who made the first motor-car; it was Maybach who made the first modern motor-car, defining the machine as we know it today. His partner Daimler had died with the nineteenth century, after doing so much conjectural design; born with the twentieth, Maybach's Mercedes was definitive, more completely so than anything in the next fifty years.

PAGE 116

For thirty years the design of the high-performance engine had been influenced by the work of the Fiat technical office of the 1920s. Only when Lampredi altered the proportions while retaining the basic morphology, and brought to the Ferrari four-cylinder engine the unsupercharged volumetric efficiency previously secured by forced induction, was valuable progress made. Lampredi, now with Fiat, is still continuing his career, but history may see him as the man who killed the supercharger.

Man proposes, God disposes, said Thomas à Kempis; but in America it was different. Miller, regarded with awe and reverence in the racing heyday of the 1920s, had ideas; his man Goossen did the engineering. Between them they created the most beautifully made mobile jewels, brilliant, lustrous, kaleidophonic and utterly uncompromising—like this 1925 supercharged model, the '122-inch' or 2-litre rear-drive car, a stepping stone towards their greatest joint achievement, the front-drive '91'.

COLOUR ILLUSTRATIONS

PAGE 117

Or was this the truly modern motor-car, designed for quantity production by machinery so refined as to guarantee complete interchangeability of car parts? The century of the common man expanded the uses of mechanized construction that had formerly served only to manufacture the arms that made him cannon fodder; Leland's Cadillac model A proved that machine tools had the power to give society a practical mobility.

PAGES 118–9

Though a pioneer of front-wheel drive and architect of some notable cars in the classical front-engine rear-drive idiom, Porsche became committed to—even obsessed by—the rear-engined, independently sprung car. All his strong points, and all his blind spots, were evident in his Auto-Union racing cars, of which this example is a rarity: superficially similar to the 1934–7 750 kg cars, it was an interim design prepared for the new 1938 3-litre formula. It was driven in practice here at Brno for the 1938 Czech Grand Prix, but it did not race.

PAGE 120

The debt owed by motoring to aviation is enormous. No better example exists than the shape (and much of the construction) of the Bristol 401 body, aerodynamically one of the best saloons of all time. Its designer Hobbs and his assistants applied to the car the knowledge and experience gained in the Bristol Aeroplane Company; the excellence of the design was confirmed by *ex post facto* wind-tunnel tests.

4
Engine developers

*I*n the early hours of a morning in the middle 1950s, Colin Chapman left his night's work in the little Lotus factory in North London and set off for home, calling on the way at the house of a friend for some advice on a problem that had been taxing his considerable ingenuity. It was one which demanded either a Socrates or a Procrustes. The car he was labouring to produce was the Lotus 14, the first Elite, but there seemed no way of giving it the necessary headroom, without either raising the roofline to the detriment of aerodynamics, or lowering the floor to the impairment of ground clearance. Chapman needed another inch and a half, and his friend Alfred Woolf suggested that least harm would be done to either boundary if the increase were equally divided, raising the roof by three-quarters of an inch and lowering the floor by the same. Chapman's explosive response was typical of a man who had never had to design an engine: 'I'm not doing that – that's a bloody compromise.'

Engine design allows no such idealism. It follows from this that the cars designed by men who are primarily specialists in engines are those most likely to be infected by that spirit of compromise that comes most naturally to such men. Some of the greatest cars in the history of motoring were produced by designers whose principal concern was with engines. The Hispano-Suiza of Marc Birkigt, sundry models created for Maserati, Ferrari, and the posthumous Bugatti factory by Gioacchino Colombo, the first BRM by Peter Berthon, and the cars bearing the respected names of Walter Owen Bentley and Fred and August Duesenberg, have all been the objects of popular and generally uncritical adulation in their time, and in most cases ever since; yet they were all rather ill-balanced in concept, relying on a soul-stirring engine in a chassis that could seldom command much more than apathy. The general readiness to accept this double standard is easily explained by reference to the beginning of Chapter Three: in the history of the motor-car, chassis design was a late developer, because the phenomena governing ride and handling were scarcely understood. For the first three-quarters of the history of the motor-car, popular concern among the public and manufacturers alike was almost entirely with the motor.

Birkigt at least recognized his limitations. 'I am only an engine designer', he said in one of his rare public speeches, given at a banquet in his honour on the introduction of the 32 CV Hispano-Suiza, perhaps his greatest car. Known in Spain as the Type 41, this magnificent machine (with each of its six cylinders displacing a litre) contradicted him in one notable respect: it introduced his one and only important contribution to the chassis, really efficient 4-wheel brakes, power-assisted by a friction servo and driven by a cross-shaft from the gearbox. The system was far better than any other then available, and was adopted after some show of resentment by Rolls-Royce in 1924 and by most of the leading European manufacturers of luxury cars and racing cars for the rest of the decade.

With the introduction of the 32 CV, Hispano-Suiza more or less took over from Rolls-Royce the role of manufacturers of the best car

The Alfonso, the T-headed Hispano-Suiza that earned Marc Birkigt critical acclaim

Overleaf: Jewels for the rich were for a long time the speciality of the poor Spanish automobile industry. Connoisseurs of coachwork will appreciate the *de ville* body on this 6-cylinder Hispano-Suiza; connoisseurs of the cinema will recognize its owner

in the world. Of course, the Rolls-Royce company would not admit it, and continued to display modest whole-page advertisements in the Press, consisting merely of a photograph of one of their cars in elegant surroundings, and bearing no more by way of legend than the manufacturer's name and address and the words 'The best car in the world'. Hispano-Suiza, in their advertisement, merely displayed one of their cars in elegant surroundings and their name and address.

The differences between the makes were, in some ways, the differences between the men principally concerned, Birkigt being a model of courtesy and tact, who was able to move with ease in the highest level of society. If there were nothing special about the design of his chassis, his cars were still perfectly acceptable to customers who were attracted by the superb engines, because the whole car was superbly made. Within his factories, Birkigt was just as much a perfectionist as Royce: cost accountancy and planned obsolescence were abhorrent to him, aspects of a commercial immorality that could do no lasting good. His complete rejection of all that was shoddy was based on very high standards acquired by the best available means: he was sent by his grandmother (at the age of 11, he had been orphaned from his home in Geneva, where he was born in 1878) to the famous School of Mechanical Engineering in Barcelona when he was 21, graduating there with distinction in engineering and physics before undergoing his statutory period of military service – and, while serving with the artillery, he made a study of the materials used by the ordnance factories. At that time the arsenals were the repositories of the most advanced engineering knowledge of the day: their ballisticians were the greatest masters of aerodynamics, their production engineers commanded the most sophisticated and accurate machine tools, their metallurgists had an unrivalled choice of special steels and bronzes, their designers a greater familiarity with the problems of tribology than those in any

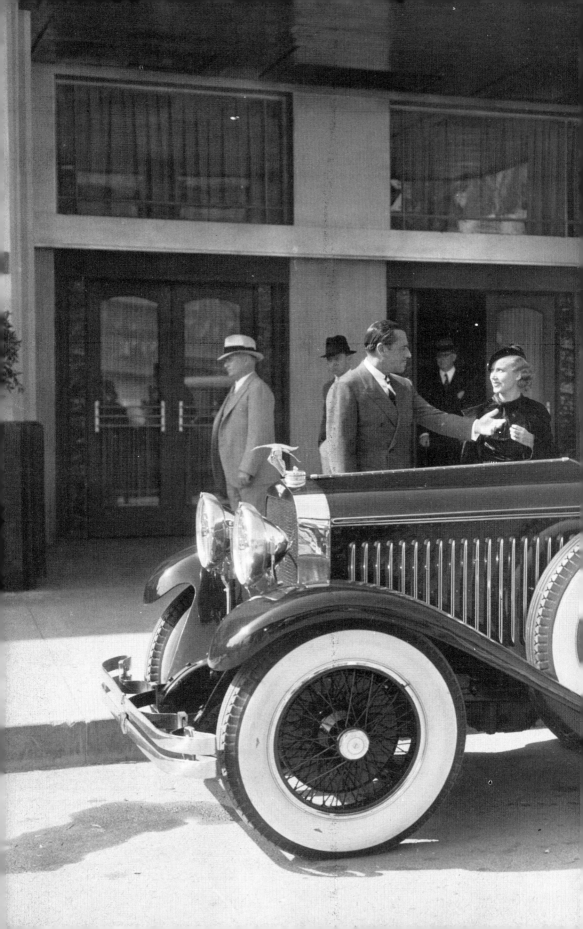

other industry. Birkigt never lost the interest he took in ordnance, for, as well as producing some of the world's greatest cars and most successful and significant aero-engines, he also was responsible for the 20-mm machine cannon that was the most effective air-to-air weapon of the Hitler war.

Because he was engaged as intimately with aero-engines as with cars, it was relatively easy for Birkigt to remain in touch with continuing developments in these technologies, and comparatively simple also for him to apply them to the improvement of his cars. For example, in 1928, he adopted nitralloy liners for the cylinders of his 32 CV car, and its 8-litre offspring the 46 CV, long before most people in the industry had even heard of the material. In fact he pioneered a number of engine features, including dual coil ignition, unit construction of engine and gearbox, and a form of cylinder head design with enclosed overhead-camshaft valve gear that – if it did nothing else – made his copyists famous. Birkigt himself was not so obsessed with his designs as to think them immutable: in 1931, Hispano-Suiza showed his superb new v12 car whose 9·4-litre engine, with its bore and stroke equal at 100 mm, not only discarded the long-stroke conventions that he had formerly accepted, but also contrived to run more quietly with pushrod valve gear than his earlier overhead-camshaft designs. The monumental carriage known as the Type 68 weighed a full two tons, but could exceed 100 mph thanks to the engine's 220 bhp, performing even more vigorously when an optional long-stroke version offered 250 bhp from 11·3 litres in 1934. Not that Birkigt was wholly committed to gigantism: his simple little 4-cylinder Type 48 Hispano-Suiza (a 2½-litre cut-down version of the 1924 Barcelona 6) was standard issue for official use by the Army, Government, and what passed in Spain for a Civil Service; and an even simpler 4-stroke, pushrod, 6-cylinder engine that he designed for Hudson of Detroit remained in production in Spain as the Hispano 60 from 1932 until the company finished in 1943, though the economic situation prevented Hudson themselves from building it.

Of comparable size was the most important car engine Birkigt ever designed. It might not have had the ultra-light construction, the enclosed valve gear or the screwed-in steel cylinder liners of his v8 aero-engine, which was eagerly adopted by the allies in the Kaiser war and manufactured under licence by 21 companies in France, England and America, until eventually nearly 50000 were made, a number equal to the total of all other types produced by the allied countries during the war. What it did, however, was to introduce a twin-overhead-camshaft layout that, once pirated, spread like wildfire and has remained the accepted fashion for high-speed machinery ever since. It was the 2·6-litre 4-cylinder engine of the car that Birkigt's friend and patron King Alfonso XIII of Spain tried as a prototype at the end of 1911, finding it so good that he bade it be named España. He could hardly do better than that, for the car was intended by Birkigt as a successor to the immensely successful T-head 3·6-litre Hispano-Suiza that was named the Alfonso.

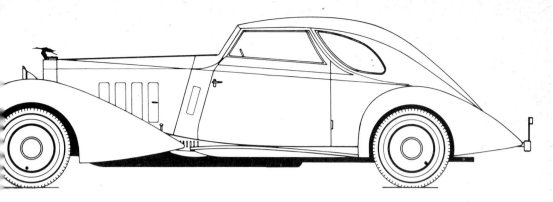

When Birkigt made a pushrod-ohv V12 with equal bore and stroke quieter and even more flexible than his established ohc long-stroke sixes, there seemed nothing more to be said – but somebody should have spoken a word of caution to the coachbuilders, who must have found it difficult to keep a sense of proportion

This new engine had 16 valves, hemispherical combustion chambers, dual ignition and two shaft-driven camshafts: it was the clear precursor of every really respectable engine that has been built since, in everything except its quota of four valves per cylinder, a number which has been in and out of fashion with much the same sort of cyclic frequency as most other features of automobile engineering. Alas, an engineer working for Birkigt, another Swiss named Ernest Henry, whom we have already mentioned, then conspired with their test driver Zucarelli to carry off the designs of the new engine for sale to Peugeot in France, where, within three months, they built a larger copy to propel the car that was destined to win for Peugeot the 1912 French Grand Prix. Up to the level of the cylinder head, this Grand Prix engine looked very much like that of the 7·6-litre *voiturette* that had been originally intended for a race which had been scheduled to accompany the 1911 Grand Prix, though it never in fact took place. Onto this basis, Henry grafted a cylinder head just like that of Birkigt's, embodying his master's ideas so faithfully that there was no doubt of the outcome of the legal proceedings that were soon to be taken against the offenders.

Henry was clearly concerned with the opportunities this design gave to produce an engine capable of very high rotational rates, thanks to the minimized reciprocating weight of the valve gear. In fact, this 7·6-litre engine gave its maximum power at 2200 rpm, admittedly a higher figure than anything in earlier Grand Prix practice (if one excepts the little Bugatti that ran in the 1911 race), but matched by some of the cars which competed in the *Kaiserpreis* and other 8-litre races of 1907. What, then, can Henry's efforts have achieved? At this speed, his engine in developing its 130 hp displaced precisely the same total volume per minute as did the 16·2-litre pushrod Fiat of 1907, when that ran at 1600 rpm to produce the same power. The Peugeot enjoyed a slight superiority in hp per unit of frontal area, but its measured maximum speed, a fraction below 100 mph, was scarcely more than the 98 mph reached by the Fiat five years earlier. The average speed of the Peugeot on the same open road circuit was no higher, perhaps partly due to its intractability which could be attributed to the wider timing of the valves which Henry had adopted, and which would have contributed to the fact that the engine reached new high levels of bmep and mean piston

speed. Thus, in almost every respect, the Peugeot is seen to have had to work much harder in order to do no better than its predecessors. This being so, the enquiry as to what Henry really achieved with his car can only with some temerity be met with the answer – reliability. Not that *his* engines were reliable; it was his weakness that he did not fully appreciate or could not properly cater for the lubrication requirements of his engines, especially in the nether regions, and the oil feeds to his crankshaft journal bearings

The 1914 GP Mercedes engine inspired a lot of other designer Miller borrowed from it, cappi a Peugeot-style (or Henry-styl which is to say Birkigt-derived engine with Mercedes valve-ge Bentley probably saw the one sequestered by the Admiralty i 1914, and did the same

were implausibly primitive. That was why he adopted ball and roller bearings for the crankshafts of his later engines, but still he failed to produce one whose bottom half would allow such rates of crankshaft rotation as its top half encouraged. The point to be made is that the reliability that his engines promised, and indeed the higher specific performances that derived from the same features, were to be enjoyed and cultivated in the many later cars to which the principles that we now know to have been first propounded by Birkigt were more effectively applied than by Henry himself.

No better example of this could be found than in the engines created by W.O.Bentley. This quietly passionate man began his working life as an apprentice in railway locomotive workshops, and seems to have carried over to his cars the notions of scale that he acquired there. So far as his chassis were concerned, the effect was almost always disastrous; everything about them was of heroic dimensions and villainous proportions, the outcome being an aggregation of components (one could not call it a structure) that was grotesquely heavy without being particularly stiff. Indeed, the main chassis rails, though of very thick channel section, were only four inches deep and their inadequate beam stiffness often made it necessary for supplementary trusses to be bolted beneath, an arrangement which improved matters in bending but did nothing to improve the torsional stiffness of the chassis. Bentley's predilections for massive construction served better in his engines, however, which acquired a prodigious reputation for durability. The layout of valves, ports and combustion chamber was essentially that of the engines that he would have taken to have originated from Henry, whose long-stroke Peugeot engines certainly inspired their dimensions. Massive though his engines were, Bentley nevertheless minimized their weight with a good deal more care than he applied to the rest of his cars, making generous use of aluminium and magnesium alloys for the crankcase with its deep sump, and for the camshaft housing which, with only one camshaft communicating with the valves via rockers, acknowledged the influence of the $4\frac{1}{2}$-litre Mercedes that conquered Henry's Peugeot to win the 1914 Grand Prix.

Before embarking on the design of his first 3-litre car engine, shortly after the end of the Kaiser war, Bentley had had plenty of opportunity to acquaint himself with the use of light alloys in engines. Even before that war, he had been active in the development of aluminium pistons, in the DFP car that he raced quite effectively (though he was certainly not the originator of the idea), and for the duration of the war he was involved in the design of aero-engines in which lightness was one of the cardinal virtues. He began by working on the development of existing Clerget rotary engines and went on to design his own which, by the end of the war, had the distinction of being the most powerful rotary engine in service, with an output of 230 bhp.

Thereafter, he appears to have been in a constant quandary about the sort of engines he should produce. On the one hand, he had a

great fondness for distinctly sporting engines in which refinement of running was subordinated to performance: recalling the thrills of riding on a locomotive footplate, he explained his contentment with the vibrations inseparable from an in-line 4-cylinder engine, by evoking the thrill he enjoyed from 'that bloody thump'. On the other hand, he knew perfectly well that the majority of his potential customers were far more interested in silence and the sort of flexibility that made it possible for them to drive everywhere in top gear, as though the Bentley were nothing more than a Rolls-Royce in a track suit. It was for them that he created his 6-cylinder engines of 6½ and 8 litres, and devised an entirely silent drive system for the overhead camshaft in which his original shaft and bevel gears were replaced by a set of connecting rods and eccentrics. In fact, his 8-litre car was as magnificent and as competent as any luxury car of its time; but the time was a bad one and, when his company failed, he found himself working not, as intended, for Napier on the further development of his existing designs, but for Rolls-Royce as part of the office furniture.

For them, he created at their request the 3½-litre Bentley, which was essentially a modification of the existing 20–25-hp Rolls-Royce; and after he quit them and went to Lagonda, he still had to apply himself to the age-old compromises of the engine man, trying to

I have the greatest respect for Mr Bentley, said Ettore Bugatti. *He makes the fastest motor lorries in Europe.* Young w.o. also made a more successful wartime aero-engine than Bugatti did

Bentley's first car had a tall and slender 3-litre 4-cylinder engine, blessed with 'sloper' su carburettors, 16 valves under a single camshaft, and a sporting character. Its chassis was quite unremarkable but it was a very pleasant car to drive

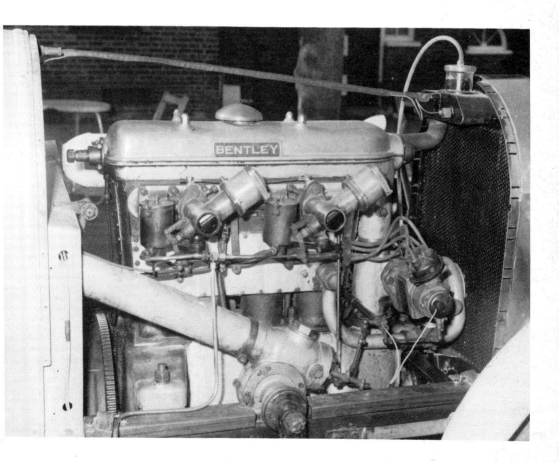

reconcile performance with refinement and flexibility. In 1935, he produced his first version of the existing Meadows-engined Lagonda M45, which became known as the LG 45, the engine being rubber-mounted and given a new exhaust manifold and twin magnetos, while the chassis was graced with softer springs and hydraulic dampers. The following year he redesigned the cylinder head and, with this engine, the Lagonda was faster than it had ever been. His final version of the $4\frac{1}{2}$-litre six – the LG 6 – came in 1937; it had a further-developed engine but was more important for its torsion-bar independent front suspension and hydraulic brakes. This was the chassis that later accepted the splendid $4\frac{1}{2}$-litre V12 Lagonda engine, for which Bentley had also been given the credit; but that credit really belongs to the man who went with him from Rolls-Royce, Steuart Tresilian.

Trissy, as he was often known, was one of the greatest and least-known to the public of all engine designers. He had already had a distinguished career, starting with an honours degree in engineering at Cambridge and followed, shortly afterwards, by his joining the technical staff of Rolls-Royce. There, he was strongly influenced by the man who was perhaps the greatest of them all, A. J. Rowledge, who had come to Rolls-Royce after a spell with Napier, for whom he designed the clever, powerful, long-lived and surprisingly economical broad-arrow Lion aero-engine. Between 1927 and 1936,

By 1928 the $4\frac{1}{2}$-litre Bentley, more powerful if less nicely balanced than the 3-litre, was making the running at Le Mans – not without stern opposition from this Stutz

The 6½-litre Bentley six was conceived as a luxury tourer but was soon pressed into service as a speed model. The late Pierre Maréchal cherished his Speed Six and drove it well, but does it look convincing?

Tresilian worked on car and aircraft engines, including the Schneider Trophy R (for racing) engines that were Rowledge's responsibility, the Merlin, the Bentley 3½-litre, and the Rolls-Royce Phantom III, a V12 that brought back to Rolls-Royce the engine refinement that had been missing since the demise of the original Silver Ghost, along with far more power than ever before. He also worked on a number of other more interesting projects that Rolls-Royce never allowed to happen, until he joined the disenchanted W.O. at Lagonda. Then the war came; Tresilian moved first to Armstrong-Siddeley, and then to an attachment with the US Air Force, before returning to Rolls-Royce just before the war ended. In 1948, he resigned to work as an independent consultant and, in the years that followed, he was involved with Connaught and BRM. An ardent advocate of 4-valve cylinder heads, he met stubborn resistance from Peter Berthon of BRM, whose insistence on retaining two enormous 2-piece poppets for the 4-cylinder 2½-litre engine was probably accountable for the failure of that machine to satisfy its promise.

Tresilian's last years (he died in 1962) were spent with Bristol and, although much of his work was secret and military in nature, he was able to devote some time to the car engine, working with others at the little prototype drawing-office which used to do contract work as well, especially for the Army. One of his jobs there was on a weird monstrosity christened the Flying Pig – a military vehicle that

135

was enabled to jump over obstructions with the help of airfoil blades mounted on the rims of two huge horizontal flywheels, each driven by a $2\frac{1}{2}$-litre BRM Grand Prix engine. As was no doubt expected by everybody except the hare-brained soldier who thought of it, the Flying Pig was a disaster, but everything else Tresilian touched seemed to lead a charmed life thereafter. It was not what he did that was important, but why he did it; on his death, he left a sheaf of notes on engine design, analysing the problems presented at every stage and explaining how they might best be resolved. As a theoretical work it was a model of clarity; as a practical guide it was remarkable for its vision.

When released from Rolls-Royce, Bentley went to Lagonda and rapidly developed their $4\frac{1}{2}$-litre six, making it smoother, faster, and slightly less accelerative. With Tresilian he then made everything better with a splendid $4\frac{1}{2}$-litre V12, but the war checked its promising career

136

Notwithstanding the claims that could be made on behalf of that great and revered pioneer Sir Harry Ricardo (who was truly a scientist rather than a mere engine developer and would accordingly belong to Chapter Six), there is one man in our list of similar abilities and even greater distinction. He is Aurelio Lampredi, nowadays in charge of engines at Fiat. The mere fact of his holding this appointment is sufficient commendation of him, for it is one over which Fiat have never been known to make an error of judgement; but if any further qualification be sought, it must be his work for Ferrari.

The chief designer of the first postwar car to bear Ferrari's name was Colombo, who had worked with Ferrari in the design of the Type 158 Alfa Romeo racing car. Ferrari meant to go racing seriously, and must have known what he would be up against, at least from Alfa Romeo; and so must Colombo, who set himself to design a $1\frac{1}{2}$-litre car which might form the basis not only of a commercially-viable sports car, but also of one that might take part effectively in Grands Prix run under the new $1\frac{1}{2}$-litre supercharged or $4\frac{1}{2}$-litre unsupercharged formula.

There is no doubt but that Colombo was a gifted designer. The ineffable superiority of his Type 158 Alfa Romeo throughout the late 1940s, while Ferrari struggled to become competitive, may be sufficient evidence in itself; but when, disenchanted with the work of this great man, Ferrari sent him packing and transferred the responsibility to Lampredi, Colombo went to Maserati and wrought wonders there. He began with the 2-litre A6G upon which a lot of work had already been done, and finished with the Type 250 F Grand Prix car which appeared in 1954 and grew increasingly competitive in racing throughout the following four years. Then, as if to prove that engineering merit is not alone sufficient, he went to Bugatti and devised the very unconventional Type 251 which ran in the 1956 French Grand Prix. It was dismissed as an abject failure, and was never seen again, despite its embodiment of features that, in retrospect, can be seen to have been far ahead of their time.

In the meantime, Ferrari had the relatively-unproven Lampredi as a source of engineering inspiration. He was not as completely unproven and unqualified as some commentators have suggested, having been responsible for the very sophisticated rear-engined V8 Isotta-Fraschini saloon prototype, whose failure to go into production was no fault of his. What Lampredi had to contend with was not only the opposition, but also the reputation of Colombo. The latter's $1\frac{1}{2}$-litre V12 was initially a sports car, the first real racing car following in 1948. It could be seen following Alfa Romeos or following Maseratis – and, when it was not chasing these, it was chasing its own tail, for it had been given all-independent suspension by the altogether too popular expedient of swinging half-axles. When supercharged, it went faster and fared worse, and even when given 2-stage supercharging and a De Dion rear suspension, it failed to stem the Alfa Romeo tide: in the 1950 Swiss Grand Prix, one of these cars went out with a broken axle, the other

went out with engine trouble. Colombo went out, too. He insisted
that the way to success was in further development of the highly-
supercharged engine, a theory to which the majority of contemporary designers would have subscribed. Assisting Colombo,
however, was Lampredi who maintained with equal vigour the
argument that an unblown engine of $4\frac{1}{2}$-litres capacity, as the
regulations permitted, could give as much power as was necessary
to equal the performance of the smaller supercharged machine,
while using less fuel. Ferrari gave him his opportunity, and he
seized it avidly.

His first trial engine displaced only 3·3 litres, but within months it
was fully developed in full $4\frac{1}{2}$-litre form; and at long last in 1951,
at Silverstone in the British Grand Prix, a Ferrari beat the Alfa
Romeos. Since 1923, when Fiat introduced it, the supercharger had
been the god of Grand Prix motor racing; now, after 28 years, here
was another Italian to preach a new faith. Ferrari was obliged to
Lampredi for moral victory at the end of the 1951 season, when Alfa
Romeo withdrew from racing while their championship record was
still intact. He expressed his thanks by setting Lampredi to provide a
suitable car for the new Formula Two category that would inherit
the Grands Prix for the next two years, and the blue-eyed boy did it
in the traditional Italian way by copying an existing chassis and
putting a beautiful new engine in it.

Lampredi's choice of a simple 4-cylinder engine for this new car
seemed a terrible regression to many people at the time. The
Colombo V12 had dominated Formula Two racing hitherto (and to
be fair, it was later expanded to 3 litres and developed to bring

The most famous V12 Ferrari
engines grew out of
Colombo's first little V12,
designed to serve not only this
tiny and ill-handling GP car
(here driven by the late Peter
Whitehead) but also a sports
car . . .

Ferrari more consistent glory than any other), serving both in road cars and racers. Some of Lampredi's engines were to do similar dual duty, the big v12s driving some very long-legged touring cars in the Superfast and Super America series, the 4- and 6-cylinder machines propelling a series of amazingly rapid sports cars. Before this came about, however, the Lampredi had to make its mark in Grand Prix racing, and that it succeeded shows how shrewdly Lampredi assessed the problems he had to resolve. In view of his success with the big unblown v12 engine, it displayed courage to strike out afresh as he did, producing a 4-cylinder engine of supreme beauty, an engine whose major castings had a fluidity of contour which bore witness to the elegant solution of many problems of stress distribution. As in

139

his big V12, Lampredi used cylinder liners that were screwed into the cylinder head, eliminating the conventional gasket, improving the coolant flow, and allowing close pitching of the cylinder centres which, in turn, allowed the construction of a short engine with a torsionally-stiff crankshaft. For the rest, it was the cylinder head and its associated plumbing that made it so good; its volumetric efficiency was something that promised to be the keynote of all new unsupercharged engines, and was exceptionally high; and with a little development, it reached levels a good deal higher than any unblown engine had done before. It saw Ferrari through two successful years of 2-litre racing and kept him going with occasional successes through the first two years of the 2½-litre Formula, when Mercedes-Benz ruled the roost almost as a matter of course. No entrant with the means of Ferrari could hope to compete with an organization so well endowed as Daimler-Benz, but the proud Ferrari refused to compromise, treating Lampredi as the scapegoat. The gift to Ferrari of the relatively new V8 Lancia and its designer Jano left Lampredi no room for manoeuvre, and he left, finding his way to Fiat a short time later.

Serious efforts to achieve high volumetric efficiency in unsupercharged engines had previously been few and far between. In 1950, there was the Formula Two Connaught, the engine of which was based on a production Lea-Francis 1½-litre engine that had been designed by Hugh Rose, the man who, 38 years earlier, had been responsible for the very successful 3-litre Sunbeam cars that were devised for the race for the *Coupe de l'Auto*. In the 1930s, there had been some similar work done on a morphologically very similar engine, the 4-cylinder Riley, by the celebrated driver and tuner F.W. (Freddy) Dixon. Before that, it is necessary to go back to

Of all Colombo's racing cars, none was less successful or more visionary than this clever Type 251 Bugatti, years ahead of its time and yards ahead of a Gordini at Reims in 1956

Plancton's V12 2-litre Delage, initially an unsupercharged damp squib, became explosively successful in 1925 when given the supercharging that it could exploit better than any other current engine

1920, when Miller was scheming a 3-litre racing engine that could beat the Henry-inspired Duesenberg straight-eight. This Miller engine was the first to enjoy an entirely separate inlet tract for each cylinder, tuned with the aid of ramming air intakes on the carburettors to the critical length for best performance. Doubtless it was because Miller was a carburettor specialist that he had this idea so far ahead of everyone else; and equally doubtless it was the advent of supercharging in 1923 that prevented the technique from being further developed and more widely adopted.

The man who designed Miller's engine in detail, and many others as well in his later years – but who always had to accept basic guidelines on shape, style and dimensions from whoever employed his services – was Leo Goossen, the quiet, gifted and immensely capable design engineer whose contribution to the history of the high-performance engine has been longer and more consistently distinguished than that of any other man in this book. He was, in particular, the originator of the high-performance engine combining four valves in a pentroof combustion chamber with a vertical downdraught inlet port passing between the banks of valves: he first laid out such an engine in 1929, admitting that he had got the idea

for the inlet ports from some unknown make of experimental engine that he had seen in the eastern states. That idea was later to be seized upon by a consultant called Schleicher, who employed it for creating a high-performance version of the existing BMW 315 6-cylinder engine which was reborn for the new 328 sports car of 1937. By 1940, this BMW engine enjoyed further development by Dr Fiedler (who had come from Horch and, after the war, was to be winkled out of political prison by Mr Aldington of Frazer-Nash and taken to England to continue his work with Bristol) to the extent that it, too, might have been a contender in the stakes for high un-blown volumetric efficiency. By that time, however, many of the world's greatest engine designers were busy in the armaments industry, while in neutral America Leo Goossen co-designed the Novi supercharged v8 engine that, for many years to come, was to be by far the most powerful ever to run at Indianapolis. All the draw-ings, calculations and layouts were done by Goossen in his home and on the same drawing-board on which he had schemed the original 3-litre Miller twenty years earlier.

When Goossen came to Miller in 1919 it was from Buick, where illness had forced him to give up his promising work and seek a kinder climate. Like Miller and Offenhauser, the two men with whom he would be associated for so many years, he was a first-generation American born of immigrant parents. His were a Dutch couple who settled in Michigan, where he was born; and because

After making the best of Plancton's v12, Lory created this wondrously intricate and fabulously successful blown straight-eight for Delage to run in the 1½-litre Grands Prix of 1926–7

The internal layout of the 1½-litre Delage owed much to Fiat, but the construction of the engine was quite different and its appearance exquisite. It contained 48 roller or ball bearings and was rather long and heavy, but it gave 170 bhp at 1·53 at boost and in 1927 was eminently reliable

they were unable to keep him at high school beyond the half-way mark in his formal education, he had to find a job in the blueprint room at the Buick factory. While there, he continued to study hard, rapidly acquiring a command of mathematics and engineering theory to match his exquisite and eloquent draughtsmanship. When he left Buick, it was with a strong letter of recommendation from the general manager, who was then no less a man than the great Walter P. Chrysler. When Harry Miller saw that letter, he hired his visitor on the spot; and so Goossen embarked on a new life that was to make him the one and only man who could be considered truly responsible for the design of all effective American racing engines from 1920 until 1965 – or even to the present day, for the 4-camshaft Ford v8 that intruded in 1965 was, in many senses, an extension of his design principles and was not done without his help as a consultant.

Goossen loved his work. He and Miller were perfectly complementary, the most faithful mutual-admiration society in the business. Each knew he could rely on the other. As Goossen explained, 'Miller was a genius, but, being without formal education, he needed someone with my background to put his ideas into manufacturing form and to make them workable. Young as I was, it happened to be me: it seems to have been an act of providence. Miller was most appreciative of my efforts and I remember when six 91 engines were being built and run through the shop at one time and my drawings weren't even looked at. Fortunately, there were no errors and no changes were required, but you can imagine the responsibility and worry that I felt. Miller's confidence in my ability was an inspiration to do my best. That is how we all felt about working for him. That privilege was an indescribable reward.'

When Miller found his new aviation career collapsing about him in the slump, and set up his Rellimah Company, he brought Goossen in again to help him. They tried many things, of which just one was important: Goossen designed a twin-cam, 3-litre, 4-cylinder, 16-valve engine (actually based on a marine engine he created in 1926) that is still racing. When Rellimah broke down, Offenhauser set up his own firm to keep this engine in production. When he went, former associates Louie Meyer and Dale Drake took over, and the famous Offenhauser engine became the Meyer-Drake. When that firm finally ended its days, the Offenhauser name was revived – and still that incredible engine endured. In the un-supercharged days, it grew to $4\frac{1}{2}$ litres and completely dominated American track racing. When the rules allowed it, the displacement was curtailed to 2·8 litres and a supercharger was added. And when finally turbocharging became the fashion, the exhaust-turbocharged 2·8-litre 'Offy' was the most formidable thing ever seen at Indianapolis, capable of rendering over 800 bhp for qualifying runs, or of running 500 miles competitively at a slightly lower rating.

It has always been, and still is, a superb engine, and the name it bears is a credit to that gifted artificer Fred Offenhauser. Yet it is probably not fair to think of it as an Offy, nor (for all its characteristic

features so redolent of Miller practice in the 1920s) as a Miller. If anything, it is a Goossen.

In the 1920s, there were others who were equally keen on what we might call watchmaker's engines, especially in France. For Delage, there was the Frenchman Plancton, whose duty it was in 1923 to make the French company competitive with the 2-litre Fiat that had proved new principles convincingly the year before. Plancton created a surprisingly competitive car in the brief space of four months, and if this time had not permitted any great care to be devoted to the chassis, which was entirely orthodox, incredible care had been lavished upon the engine, which was one of those nicely-detailed and very complicated machines which can work effectively if they are superbly made, as this one was. With all the remorseless logic traditionally attributed to the French, Plancton had recognized that an engine capacity formula put a premium on piston area and high rates of crankshaft revolution, which can be combined by a multiplicity of small-capacity cylinders without the ratio of stroke to bore being different from what is fashionable among other engines of like displacement but fewer cylinders. He accordingly designed an engine whose stroke : bore ratio was virtually the same as that of the 1922 Fiat, while its piston area was 10% greater than even the 1923 Fiat, which came as a rude shock to all those contenders expecting merely a developed version of the 1922 car from Italy. Plancton's engine was certainly capable of running at a crankshaft rate higher than that of any other 2-litre car : it was a 60° V12 on a crankcase that carried its crankshaft in seven roller bearings, while the big-ends and even the camshafts also ran in rollers, and all other rotating members were supported in ball-bearings. Broadly speaking, the principles applied by Plancton could be said to be those of Fiat, but the details were reasonably spontaneous, if not new. The significant thing about the engine was that, although designed for atmospheric induction, it could exploit supercharging more effectively than perhaps any other in racing; and when, in 1925, it acquired supercharging, the Delage reigned supreme. The man who developed it was Lory, who then went on to create an exquisite $1\frac{1}{2}$-litre supercharged straight-eight for the 1926–7 season; this engine was so effective that it could still be made competitive in the hands of a good driver

145

ten years later, even though the lamentably flexible chassis had to undergo considerable revision.

It seemed to be a French speciality in those days to make small and exquisitely-detailed engines for insertion in spindly and care-lessly-designed chassis. They were rather carried away by their filigree traditions, none less than Emil Petit, who did his first twin-cam engine for Salmson in 1921, and made those cars very fast in a very few years. By 1934, when the introduction of the 750 kg formula coincided with the general adoption of independent front suspen-sion and (as a logical and convenient corollary) hydraulic brakes, Petit had the idea of a multiplicity of small brake shoes instead of the conventional pair of large ones, and introduced into the abortive *Sefac* what must stand as the record number of six shoes within each drum. It was entirely characteristic of the unbalanced design of this car that these components should have been cable-operated, as it was that the generally crude chassis should carry a fairly refined 8-cylinder engine consisting of two in-line fours set side by side and geared together, the transmission being aligned with one crankshaft and a large supercharger with the other. It was a classic example of too much motor and not enough car.

As it happened, Petit was later to make the mistake of providing too little motor – not in terms of displacement, but rather of mass. In the late 1950s the proprietor of the French Facel company, Pierre Daninos – a man whose tolerance of foreigners, and particularly his appreciation of foreign component manufacturers, was as diminutive as his stature – engaged Petit to design a 2-litre engine for a small car he was building in the image of the big Chrysler-engined Facel Vega upon which his reputation had previously been based. Petit made the mistake of overlooking the fact that, in the 1960s, requirements for sustained high performance and un-impeachable stamina and durability were much more strict than had been the case in his heyday; and the new car (known as the Facellia, and for which 120 bhp was claimed from its 2-litre, 4-cylinder twin-cam engine) was an unmitigated disaster.

Emil Petit created some simple, internally elegant and potentially lively 2 ohc engines for Salmson in the 1920s. When this 1100 cc 'Grand Prix' engine was supercharged, it drove the San Sebastian model at more than competitive speeds. The carburettor in the picture looks like the rare Griffon type

Salmsons were spidery, but the Facellia was pretty solid, and Petit's engine for it (sometimes alleged to have received the attentions of British consultant Harry Weslake) lacked the necessary stamina

5
Mechanics

*I*n Derby, there stands a statue to the memory of Sir Frederick Henry Royce, and on the base beneath it may be read only the simple inscription – Henry Royce, mechanic. That is exactly what he was, and he knew it; but it is not true, as many of his detractors would have it, that he was a mere improver, incapable of original creative design. One must remember that life as a car designer began for him at 40, prior to which he had established a worldwide reputation as a manufacturer of electrical equipment, especially cranes and particularly-efficient dynamos. One has only to examine his innovations in electrical machinery to see that creativity was not foreign to him: in fact, he was always prepared to work out his own original solution to a given problem, but only after he had satisfied himself that no potential solution might be found in the work of others. He saw no point in deliberately turning a blind eye to the products of other intelligent brains, wasting precious time in arriving independently at what might turn out to be the same end. He was more concerned with quality, his outstanding contribution to automotive engineering being his revaluation of quality as mechanical integrity rather than as the luxurious kind of finish with which it had previously been identified. His great personal quality was a compulsive perception of imperfection, and was one that made his name famous all around the world of motoring and aviation: he could see how much better certain things could be done, and was able to do them accordingly.

It is hard to see where he could have acquired his own standards. His childhood was impoverished, his youth hard, his whole life so consumed with work that he had little time for social intercourse – and, with his generally unkempt appearance and unabashed coarseness of language, he was ill suited to it anyway. Nor was there anything of the intuitive artistry we discussed in Chapter One; he was instead a craftsman with an intuitive appreciation of what was good, backed up by the facility for logical examination of whatever might be dubious. For the rest, his success depended on colleagues who were perfectly complementary in being able to supply his deficiencies – his secretary De Looze, his partner the Hon C.S.Rolls, and the brilliant businessman Claude Johnson who advised him what to make and made sure the world knew he had made it.

Royce's first car was a real mechanic's job, a highly-refined version of the Decauville that he had bought and by which he had been appalled. The curiosity that prompted his examination of the engineering solecisms he detected in contemporary cars set him to a study of motor-car design; and by the time he had progressed to his 4-cylinder, 20 hp model (the one that nearly won the 1905 Tourist Trophy and scored a convincing victory the following year), it was plain to everybody that he had pretty well mastered the subject.

Like all other designers, he had his blind spots. For example, he never really overcame the problems of vibration in a 6-throw crankshaft – but on the other hand, he knew perfectly well how to make a 6-cylinder engine that would give what was required of it at speeds low enough to make torsional flutter a matter of no concern.

Royce could hardly be blamed for this landaulette body, and could only be praised for the 40/50 Ghost chassis that made light of carrying it

This was the short-stroke, side-valved and immensely flexible engine of the 40/50 hp Rolls-Royce that became known as the Silver Ghost and really earned its reputation of being the best car in the world. This is something that no other Rolls-Royce car has ever done; its successors simply inherited the title ready made, and it is unlikely that any of them could really justify their claim to it.

Because Royce was not a deliberately innovative engineer, there was nothing superficially outstanding about the design of the Silver Ghost: but there was in it a wealth of detailed perfection, bearing witness to the fact that he was a gifted mechanic with an uncannily shrewd and perceptive technical (as opposed to scientific) brain. These detailed felicities of design were backed by a quality control more rigorous perhaps than any that has since been known in the motor-car industry, and undoubtedly far more stringent than anything that had been practised before. The whole car, down to its

tiniest component, was made with an expensive disregard for any consideration that might prejudice its quality.

It was not just a matter of employing artisan skills, but rather a matter of design expertise – though the former could be taken for granted, since Royce visited summary dismissal on any man he saw mishandling a tool. For example, forgings were designed so that the grain flow of the finished machine product should be most favourable. In the case of the brake drum, this meant that a forging weighing 106 lb in its raw state ended up as a beautiful drum weighing 32 lb. Even more extreme was the connecting rod, finished at 2 lb from a forging weighing 8 lb, with only the perfect core of the forging remaining and every bit of the rod's surface polished. Indeed, Royce saw to it that every component of the car, if it was not machined, was filed and polished all over to find cracks in the metal, and every highly-stressed piece was examined with a magnifying glass to discover surface cracks. Flaw detection was in its infancy in those days, and even 20 years later Rolls-Royce were somewhat behind the times in their detection methods; but they were ahead of their time in the measures they took to prevent flaws rather than tracing them.

After his experience with the Decauville and study of other cars, Royce was distrustful of other people's methods. Accordingly, his factory made everything possible, even every nut. All rotating parts were balanced, not just the crankshaft, flywheel and road wheels, but also all the gears – even the bevels in the back axle. Copper pipes were always brazed, never soldered; rods and tubes in tension were always straight. Everything ferrous was steel, except the cast-iron cylinders, piston rings and the linings for the handbrake; and the steel parts were always rolled or forged except for four particular pieces which could only be cast. In every little detail, concealed or manifest, perfection was sought. The quality would still be appreciated, as Royce was so fond of remarking, long after the price had been forgotten.

There was another result of Royce's distrust of other people's methods, one that acted to the detriment of his car's reputation. He was always suspicious of new design ideas, of new developments, even if they had been introduced by firms of high repute and had stood the test of years. Four-wheel brakes, and even electric lighting and starting equipment, were deferred for ages, until that conservative old greybeard in the baggy suit had stopped worrying about them, having at last brought them up to the standards that he required.

There was another greybeard perfectionist who brought unexpectedly high standards to the industry on the other side of the Atlantic. Henry Martyn Leland was another who only became involved with motor-cars in late middle age. This American, who had something in common with Royce, also had something in common with that Swiss Calvinist Marc Birkigt: not only a black-and-white moral code, but also an immensely valuable grounding in the skills and sciences of the firearms industry. It was in developing special precision tools for Springfield & Colt that he learned how machine tools could be designed to replace even the most petty manual jobs and do them better, as well as in enormous quantities. He then went to toolmakers Brown & Sharpe, who had already brought out the first universal milling machine and the first practical micrometer, and set about improving and inventing in a milieu where some of the workers accepted tolerances as close as four-millionths of an inch. He fathered the universal grinder and, after another quarter of a century's work on precision machinery, he was ready to instruct the new automobile industry in its uses. He was consulted by Olds, Dodge, Ford and, finally, by Cadillac. Given almost complete control, in this new company (it was established in 1902) Leland introduced the concept of high-quality mechanized production through tolerances so fine that components could freely be interchanged between different cars from the same factory. How well it worked was confirmed by the award to Cadillac of the Dewar Trophy, after examination in 1908 by the Royal Automobile Club of Great Britain – a country that was not merely neutral, but was indeed critical of American methods of manufacture.

With the company thus established and successful, the rest followed naturally, after due allowance for Leland's thoughtful and calculating approach to planning of every sort. Harnessing the brilliant Charles Kettering, an engineering graduate of Ohio University, who was then in charge of inventions at the National Cash Register Company, he made the Cadillac the first car to have modern coil ignition, self-starter and electric lighting – and, as a result, the only one ever to win a second Dewar Trophy. He promoted the design of the v8 Cadillac – it was not the first v8, but it was the first that mattered – employing a brilliant design draughtsman named McCall White who came from Napier in England. Perhaps most important of all, he drove a very hard bargain with William Durant, founder of General Motors, and for a while Cadillac were a sheet anchor when GM looked like running on the rocks. Leland left when war was in the offing, because he felt the need to busy himself with aero-engine production, and Durant would have none of it: Henry and his son Wilfred then founded the Lincoln Motor Company, with the intention of producing the Liberty aero-engine – and thus were laid the foundations of yet another great American manufacturer of luxury cars.

Practically all the other great American motor engineers were mechanics too, but of a cruder kind. Henry Ford was marvellous with his hands – he could manipulate tiny watch screws without using tools – but his mind was a confusion of enthusiasms and prejudices, as witness his reaction to the 6-cylinder engine: 'I've got no use for a motor-car that has more spark plugs than a cow has teats!' Walter P. Chrysler was somewhat better than this, but still an essentially practical man, while others whose names became famous in the high-performance world, such as Fred Offenhauser and the brothers Fred and August Duesenberg, were little more than skilled

Henry Ford, late in life, aboard the first vehicle he built, a quadricycle with a 2-cylinder engine. On the right is his grandson Henry Ford II *Opposite above:* Line production was Ford's most important contribution to the motor industry. The workers are pitched surprisingly close together on this sub-assembly line at the original Detroit factory. *Opposite below:* When the engine of the Model T was lowered into the chassis, the men on the line were given the space they needed

machinists. Their work was good, but it was strictly derivative.

To be fair, we must remember that there has been many a design engineer compelled to emulate others in his work, and to keep to himself the original ideas he can only dream about. William Heynes of Jaguar, for instance, would have loved to try out his plans for a brake system that was quite immune to fade: braking would have been done by closing the vents in air compressors turned by the wheels, the compressed air and all the heat that went into it being discharged to atmosphere. Anti-lock braking would have been virtually as automatic as with the wheel-driven hydraulic system made by Voisin.

Much rarer is the case of the designer whose approach to his work is, because of his lack of technical education, essentially mechanical, but who becomes great and respected because of his intelligent and continued appraisal of past evidence and present trends in his chosen field. It would be wrong to describe such men as non-intellectuals: it is a matter of background rather than of intellect – though Ferdinand Porsche, who could perhaps have been studied in this chapter rather than in the first, was as lowbrow as any famous designer outside America. One of the most distinguished exemplars of this type was Vittorio Jano, whom we shall meet again in Chapter Seven. In the course of his long career with Fiat, Lancia and Ferrari, he produced a series of racing and sporting cars renowned for their performance, their breeding and their beauty. His inspiration seemed to run direct from eyes to hand, without him being troubled overmuch by the toils of intermediary brainwork; and if the result he achieved could bring such credit to his name and his employers', it is not for us to question either his luck or his lapses.

A German of similar gifts and background, but of loftier mind, remains perhaps the most important of all these designers whose understanding of their subject was essentially technical rather than scientific. The name Maybach has a variety of associations, and we will not be considering the work of the younger Maybach, Karl, who was the creator of a 20-year series of cars that were enormous, luxurious, complex, extravagantly good and only remotely relevant; he seems to have been a very well-informed and thoroughly competent megalomaniac. It was his father Wilhelm who was perhaps the most important of all – first as an assistant to Daimler and finally (apart from his work on Zeppelin engines) as the man who realized the architectural form of the modern motor-car. He gave this expression in the 1901 Daimler that was christened Mercedes on the direction of the influential Emil Jellinek.

Just as Royce clung to conventions while putting right everything that he saw to be wrong, so did Maybach accept the postulates of Panhard and Levassor while subjecting them to the pitiless scrutiny of the mechanically-minded man whose vision of what is wanted is not clouded by what is available. Instead of a wooden chassis with flitch plates, the 1901 Mercedes had pressed-steel chassis members; instead of a troublesome and imprecise quadrant gearshift, it had a

It may be more important to have talent than to have academic qualifications. This proposition was never better supported than by the work of Vittorio Jano, whose monoposto Alfa Romeo will be remembered when 'cleverer' men's creations have been forgotten

Many famous designers' praises should be sung to their uncelebrated aides – Porsche's Rabe, for instance, or Royce's Rowledge – but Gottlieb Daimler's assistant became famous in his own right. This is he: Wilhelm Maybach

gate change allowing any ratio to be selected at will, and without too much difficulty. It had a beautiful and very efficient honeycomb radiator in place of the grotesque lengths of finned tube that had been habitual wear before, and its 4-cylinder, 35 hp engine was the first to have mechanically operated inlet valves (instead of the automatic type), with a variable lift device giving the driver an additional means of control over the engine speed. It was a brilliant new car, quieter, more flexible, and altogether better-mannered than anything previously known, and more completely definitive in its design than anything to follow for at least half a century. Considering the preponderance among the world's cars, even today, of designs based on exactly the same basic layout of major components, Maybach must rank as the most accomplished mechanic of them all.

6
Theoreticians

'*C*oming up with ideas doesn't have to be a remarkable process. It's easy to suggest mining metals on the moon; the men who work out the technique for the realization of the raw idea are the achievers.'

It was no jumped-up spanner-wielder with feet unable to leave the ground who said this, nor any calculator come down from Parnassus with his head still in the clouds – from somewhere in between it was Vittorio Jano. A gifted and experienced man he may have been, but he was not a learned man; and it was in these terms that he was dismissed with a faint suspicion of contempt by one of the great engine designers from Chapter Four, with whom I was discussing his peers. It does not do much good to ask a great man about himself, but there is a lot to be learned from asking him about other great men; and, in this case, my engineer revealed a great respect for the Spaniard Wilfredo Ricart, whom he described as a man of profound intellect.

Ricart would probably have accepted this deference seriously. He once told Enzo Ferrari, who had asked him why he wore shoes with extremely thick rubber soles, that a great engineer's brain must be carefully sprung against the inequalities of the ground lest its delicate mechanism be disturbed. Ferrari, unable to detect any evidence of tongue-in-cheek, simply felt more antagonistic than ever to the man who had come to join the Alfa Romeo design staff in 1936, and was to take charge of it in 1940. In fact, Ricart's presence was what drove Ferrari to leave Alfa Romeo and set up his own company, while Ricart settled down to the design of some racing cars that might wrest superiority from the Germans. The first of these, begun in 1939, was the Alfa Romeo Type 162, and it immediately demonstrated that the Spaniard was devoted to mechanisms as complex as his own. The engine, which was claimed to give 490 bhp at the outset from its 3-litres displacement and was expected to give 560 bhp after development, demanded a certain numeracy if it were to be appreciated: it had two carburettors, 3-stage supercharging by five compressors, 16 cylinders, 64 valves, and roller bearings all over the place. The next was the horizontally opposed 12-cylinder engine of the rear-engined Type 512, with centrifugal supercharging and 335 bhp from $1\frac{1}{2}$ litres. Constructed somewhat in the Auto-Union idiom, it likewise handled badly; but by 1940, when it was being tested (one of the two examples built crashed, killing its driver), Ricart was busy on a 4-bank 28-cylinder radial aero-engine of 2000 hp. That, it will be remembered, was the year in which Italy entered the war; but Alfa Romeo continued its work on cars and, in 1941, Ricart occupied himself with a hyper-sports car consisting of the v16 engine in unblown form (with only eight carburettors!) in the rear-engined chassis. Finally, in 1943, he designed a 6-seater saloon that was meant to be Alfa Romeo's first new, postwar car. Apparently it was very nice and not at all extravagant, its unitary-construction body and chassis featuring independent suspension of all four wheels by torsion bars, a twin-cam 2-litre engine in the front, and a gearbox integrated with the final drive in the rear.

A man of profound intellect, Wilfredo Ricart designed Alfas and Pegasos that were excessively logical and compulsively extravagant. The antithesis of Jano, he was perhaps too clever to be good

The sales department even picked a name for it, the Gazzelle, but the factory at Portello was so badly damaged by Allied bombing that the car could not economically be put into production, and older models were revived instead; and, in 1945, Ricart left Alfa Romeo to join ENASA in Barcelona, where the erstwhile Hispano-Suiza factory was now given over to the manufacture of Pegaso trucks and buses.

Ricart's technical apparatus was quite up to this challenge. Before he had gone to Alfa Romeo at the age of 38 he was already a man of varied experience, including the organization of public transport and bus services in Valencia, not to mention the acquisition of a pilot's licence and the design of diesel engines as well as sports and racing cars. For Pegaso, his first job was to be making cars again, though his tenure of office coincided with a notable efflorescence of the specifications of the firm's commercial vehicles. Really, ENASA had no intention of making more than a small quantity of cars on which their apprentices could be employed while learning their trade: these cars were to be jewels for the rich, built in surgically clean workshops with all the painstaking perfection that only apprentices have time to cultivate. Jewels they were: the Z102 Pegaso and its handful of variants was tantamount to a grand touring body on a Grand Prix chassis, with a de-tuned engine that was still more powerful than any comparable production car. The chassis frame was a nest of square-section steel tubing, the suspension was by torsion bars all round with one of the nicest De Dion rear ends ever seen – the dead axle beam passed in front of the final drive, while its locating radius arms converged to a single pivot point in the tail, making the geometry of motion particularly pure, and allowing the designer considerable scope for adjusting the roll axis and introducing or eliminating roll steer. The brakes were enormous 14-in drums, the gearbox a particularly obliging constant-mesh five-speeder and engine a V8 with four overhead camshafts and as many carburettors as the customer wanted – and if he preferred a supercharger he could have that, too! It was a very fast, very roadworthy and very expensive car, that inspired some of the more adventurous European coachbuilders to do some of their best and most imaginative work, particularly Saoutchik of Paris and Touring of Milan, in the years following the car's introduction at the 1951 Paris Salon. Some measure of the scale of the operation, and a clue to the extent to which Ricart's versatility was applied to other ends, comes from the modest total of 125 examples built by the time he retired in 1958, when car production ceased.

That period coincided with a golden age in motor racing in which by far the most convincing display of superiority was given by Mercedes-Benz. First, there was the 300 SL gullwinged coupé, displaying the advantages of direct fuel injection into the cylinders of its engine (adapted from that of the 3-litre Touring saloon) and of a true spaceframe chassis – a spaceframe that was much the more complex and somewhat the more perfect of the two that pioneered the technique in 1952, the other car being Colin Chapman's Lotus 6. Then, in 1964, came the W196 Grand Prix car, which, whether as a dramatic streamliner or a matter-of-fact bare-wheeler, remains the most outstanding racing car yet seen. There can seldom have been a first racing car so full of heterodoxies as this $2\frac{1}{2}$-litre Grand Prix Mercedes-Benz, and never such a car so successful. It bore little superficial relationship to the great racing cars that had preceded it, whether from its parent factory or from others, and its success therefore confirms the value of the original thinking that it represented. The fact that it did not go as fast as might have been expected betrays the lack of really effective competition during much of the

time that it was current, but it is also known that the car had been
originally intended to enjoy a longer competitive life than circumstances eventually permitted it, being designed with a view to
progressive development over a span of four years, at the end of
which it was intended to deploy 400 bhp through all four wheels.
The car pioneered a large number of features that were to pass out of
currency when it was withdrawn, only to be adopted afresh by other
racing-car constructors later; but it was a terrible irony that the
accident that prompted the withdrawal of Daimler-Benz from
racing was one that involved a sports-car version, the W196/110,
with a 3-litre engine and even more brilliant novelties, including the
provision of a large airbrake that was extremely effective (and of
course entirely fade-free) at very high speeds, and could be exploited by an intelligent driver (Moss was the only one to do it, to the
joy of its designer) to modify the car's behaviour in corners.

The designer who was responsible for all these, and who thereafter
devoted the remainder of his most distinguished career to the
development – it would not be unreasonable to call it the perfection –
of the Mercedes-Benz line of passenger cars – was Rudolf Uhlenhaut, conceivably the most complete and the most competent
designer in the history of the motor-car. When he joined Daimler-
Benz he must have seemed little more than a clever and cultivated

lad in his very early 20s, born in Germany, brought up in England and educated in both. Before long, he was singled out to take charge of the new racing service division that had been formed to develop and field the fantastic new cars built for the 750 kg Grand Prix formula of 1934–7. His reaction was typical: confident that he had all the necessary theoretical knowledge, he embarked on a training programme whereby to acquire the necessary practical knowledge of the problems that his drivers would have to face, but might not be able to recount in terms satisfactory to the engineer.

He borrowed a racing car and drove it round and round the Nurburgring, starting at a pace such as he would employ with an ordinary touring car and progressively increasing it until he satisfied himself that he was virtually as fast as the best professional racing drivers. He always insisted that driving a racing car was no different in essentials from driving a touring car, and the results he achieved certainly commanded respect for that view. He, in turn, commanded four engineers of degree status and 50 mechanics in direct charge of 10 complete cars with another 10 spare engines, and could call if necessary on the services of another 220 first-class fitters and mechanics at the factory where the main drawing-office and works was responsible for the design and production of the cars. In those days, Daimler-Benz spent annually a sum equivalent to about £1,500,000 in 1975 values; and during the last three years of prewar racing, seasons in which the team was overwhelmingly successful, it must have been evident to the directors of Daimler-Benz AG that the small portion of this colossal investment that showed the best return was the salary of Uhlenhaut.

When the company was recreated after the havoc created by the war, Uhlenhaut was appointed to take complete charge of car design and development, a position he held until his retirement in the early 1970s. Throughout that period, his work reflected every facet of his incomparably impressive personality: he was charming and courteous, completely approachable and ready to talk with anybody, he was blessed with a formidable intellect that gave him complete command of the science and technologies that were his stock-in-trade, he was punctilious in every detail, the epitome of that thoroughness which we accept is a German tradition; and, finally, he was insistent in applying to his cars the exacting standards of a driver who was capable of lapping the Nurburgring in a W196 at an average speed within 2% of that achieved in the same car by that greatest of drivers, Juan Manuel Fangio. The reputation earned in the last quarter of a century by Mercedes-Benz cars, for quality, performance, roadworthiness and safety – summed up in the word 'integrity' – owes more to this polite colossus than to anyone else. What was particularly nice about him was that he did not allow his proficiency in theory to get in the way; his standard test for thermal insulation of the luggage boot was to put a kilo of butter in it and set off for a hard day's drive into the mountains, at the end of which the butter should not have melted.

Mere theoretical proficiency is not enough, as many men, whose

When Rudolf Uhlenhaut joined Daimler-Benz, Niebel had not long to live. Sound in talent and training, Uhlenhaut rose from racing service manager to the office of chief designer as Niebel's postwar successor

During 1937, Uhlenhaut made the W125 Mercedes-Benz the fastest racing car in the world. This mechanic is working on a somewhat earlier car (identifiable by the inlet manifolding) but the punctilio of D–B engineering is evident enough already

skill on paper and familiarity with slide rule or computer has made them indispensable without ever making them famous, have found. There was Karl Rabe, for instance, the right-hand man to Dr Ferdinand Porsche, who spotted his talent in 1913 when he was only 18, made him departmental chief of the design office six years later, and left him in charge at Austro-Daimler when Porsche left them in 1923. In 1930, when Porsche started his own design office at Stuttgart, it was Rabe whom he sought as chief designer, and who stayed on as chief engineer until his retirement in 1966.

Another clever man was Uhlenhaut's opposite number in the Auto-Union racing team in the 1930s, Eberan von Eberhorst. He was a theoretician of the ivory-tower type, much given to *ex post facto* explanations in strong mathematical terms, but never very creative as a designer. After the war, he was helpful to Aston Martin over their original DB3 sports racer, and to the young and scientifically inclined David Hodkin of ERA, where the chassis of the Jowett Jupiter was designed. Hodkin applied the Jupiter principles also to the design of the G type ERA that was intended for Formula Two racing, and that was later sold to the Bristol Aeroplane Company to form the basis of their Type 450 sports racing car. He earned a good deal of praise for the stiffness of this chassis, and for the ingenuity of its De Dion rear suspension, but in fact his original version of that suspension had to be corrected and revised by Jack Channer of Bristol in the very early stages of the Formula Two car's development; and when eventually it became their own and they could do what they liked with at Bristol, it was modified even further.

The GP Mercedes-Benz of 1954–5 remains after twenty years the most outstanding racing car design in history. Even its engine is in isolation cogent proof of Uhlenhaut's virtuosity

It is, in the nature of things, rare to find a man whose theoretical proficiency extends to all aspects of car design. One of the least-known but most interesting must be Denis Sevier, a tall, quiet and scholarly man who has probably done as much for Bristol as Uhlenhaut did for Mercedes-Benz.

It is impossible to study the little Bristol organization without recalling some of the most sympathetic stanzas of Gray's Elegy, so small is the scale of its operations – though, in strong contrast to the poet's subject matter, this is a matter not of penury but of policy.

At the opposite end of the scale we find the gigantic General Motors Corporation, which furnishes another example of the universal genius in the person of Charles F. Kettering. He was described by GM president Alfred Sloan as 'an engineer and a world-famous inventor, a social philosopher and a super salesman.' In 1912, before he was associated with General Motors, he made history when he brought out the first practical electric self-starter at the behest of Henry Leland, together with a revolutionary new form of contact breaker that became the basis of the ignition distributor as we still know it today. He backed his inventions with companies to manufacture them, and became very successful, and when one of them, Delco, was brought into GM in 1919, his laboratory had already begun its great work on combustion – work that was to rival in its theoretical accomplishment that of the great Englishman Sir Harry Ricardo, and to exceed it in its practical implications. Kettering went on to do much more besides; aircooled engines, diesel engines, gasolines, refrigerants, all came under his scientific scrutiny, and, until he retired in 1947, Kettering was the man who masterminded the whole GM research programme, reporting direct to Sloan – who has recorded that he gave this man considerably more latitude than he allowed anybody else on his staff.

Such men are rare, specialists are common – but it is an occasional delight to encounter a specialist who is decidedly uncommon. One such who has made a notable contribution to car design with his suspension systems is Dr Alec Moulton, son of the Spencer Moulton who became famous in the rubber industry. Alec Moulton lives most graciously and works most seriously in a stately and beautiful home on the edge of Bradford-on-Avon. In the grounds of his home are workshops, laboratories, and monastic cells in which designer–draughtsmen enjoy complete seclusion in which to do their work and prepare reports on it that Moulton insists be of a thesis quality. His interests go far beyond cars and rubber: he is famous as an iconoclast in pedal-bicycle design and deserves to be famous as creator of one of the most beautiful and modern buses ever to go into production, but his principal claim to our attention is as originator of the coupled rubber-based independent-suspension system employed by Issigonis in his prototype Alvis, in the Mini (which was originally sprung simply by rubber), in the Austin 1100 series (in which Moulton added hydraulic interlinking and modulation of the rubber springing, a system that was used by BMC and BLMC in several later models) and, most recently, by the Austin

Allegro and its successors in which the principal springing medium is compressed nitrogen gas (whence the name hydragas, which correctly implies the presence of most of the elements of the earlier hydrolastic system as well). In this progressive refinement of these systems, culminating in the latest form of the hydrogas, Moulton has succeeded where virtually all 'earlier suspension designers despaired or failed, in creating a system in which bounce, roll and pitch can all be separately controlled, making it possible to combine the softest and most comfortable ride with the utmost roadholding, stability and handling ability, whereas in the past ride and handling have always been mutually irreconcilable.

Seventy years ago there was another designer whose understanding of suspension theory was beyond the wit of all others to appreciate until Maurice Olley came on the scene 30 years later. This was Dr Frederick Lanchester, an inventor, a mathematician, a philosopher, a great engineer and a great scientist whose contributions to academic knowledge were as important and brilliant as his car designs were precociously wonderful and pathetically wasted. The car industry and the aircraft industry still live in the shadow of his almighty intellect, which also embraced and enlarged the studies of optics, poetry, sound reproduction, colour photography and a good deal more besides.

Dr Fred – one of the most accomplished gentlemen ever to be wasted on the motor industry

Born in 1868, he began his engineering studies 14 years later; and in 1895, despairing of finding an outlet for his aerodynamic discoveries until aviation should have progressed beyond the glider stage, he channelled his energies into the design and construction of the first wholly-British four-wheel petrol car, which ran early in 1896. Its vibrationless engine formed the basis for the cars which he put into production in 1900. Everything in that first production car contributed to an integrated whole that was designed from first principles without any regard for current practice: it was unlike any other car in practically every detail, and with its exceptionally stiff unitary body and chassis, long cantilever springs, and 4-bar linkages to locate the axles, was enough to show Lanchester as the first, and for many years the only, man to have any real understanding of the requirements of good chassis design. Its 3-speed epicyclic gearbox set him years ahead of his contemporaries as a transmission engineer. Its engine proved by its layout that he understood better than anybody else the essentially mathematical problems of engine design that could only be ignored (as in all other cases they were) if roughness and mediocre performance could be accepted. Finally, in its detailing of such things as fine-pitch threads for small-diameter screws, precision roller bearings and Hindley or 'hour-glass' worm gears for the back axle, it qualified Lanchester as the motor industry's first quality engineer – and although the expression 'quality engineering' (which should be understood as the provision of whatever may be necessary to ensure refinement and longevity) sounds suspiciously like the venal modern 'value engineering', Lanchester allowed the two to be combined, for he envisaged from the beginning a system of large-volume series production that transferred the

168

responsibility for quality from the skilled workman to the advanced machine tool, and embodied all later mass-production ideas short of the conveyor belt.

All these things throw some light on the amplitude and depth of Lanchester's knowledge. His concern to provide a springing periodicity that matched the natural frequency of rise and fall of the human body when walking, which he accomplished by specifying low-rate springs such as no other designer would feel able to use for generations to come, sprang from his ability to analyse ride parameters – just as his anthropometry led him to set the driver's eye level at the same height above the road as if he were standing, the better to judge distances. Having established the need for a soft suspension, his technical knowledge made him aware that it would involve long travel of the suspension; from this, he had the imagination to consider what this amplitude of axle motion would do to the steering – otherwise he would not have taken the trouble to provide the control linkages that he did. He would not have known about tyre slip angles and the like, for in those days not even the tyre manufacturers did; but the evidence in his designs suggests a mind striving for enlightenment here, too, and his car was the first to be designed expressly for pneumatic tyres only.

The same analytical rigour and exploratory fervour (it was this combination that was the essence of Lanchester's engineering) made his engine a thing at which the educated must marvel and that the ignorant could only deride. In those days, it was not necessary to be numerate to be aware of the petrol engine's shortcomings; it was enough to be alive, and to feel in every tooth that the engine was alive too. The special thing about Lanchester was that his brain was not

The 1902 Lanchester displays most of its creator's theories, with its parallel-link axle location, tiller steering, long-travel low-periodicity springing, a driving position that maintained the eye level and perspective appreciation of a man on foot, a stiff chassis, and essentially practical non-derivative bodywork

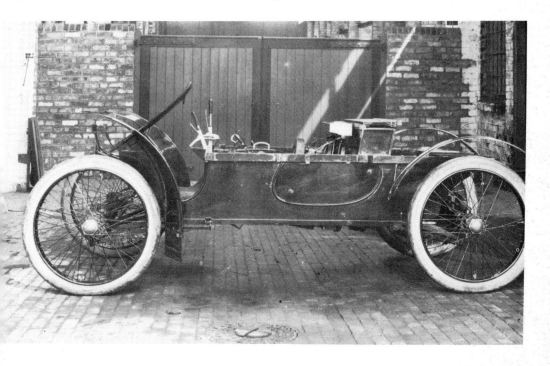

only alive, but kicking: he knew that all this vibration was wrong, and he was clever enough to trace it to its sources and, by drastic redesign, to eliminate them. This, alone, would have set him above his contemporaries, whose concern was never more than to cure the symptoms and leave the disease. In his engine, two parallel contra-rotating crankshafts (each equally *désaxé* from the cylinders, which were horizontally opposed) each carried connecting rods coupled to each piston. The result was a rhomboid motion of these rods which made all the horrid secondary vibrations and other by-products of connecting-rod angularity null by a process of mutual cancellation, while balance weights on the crankshaft webs did the rest.

In the years that have passed since, we have seen precious few attempts to ensure the same smoothness of running: a handful of designers have toyed with the scotch crank (Tresilian was particularly keen on it) and a few more have played with barrel-shaped engines that were usually betrayed by the very cam-plates, swash-plates and wobble-plates that they sought to rely on for harmonic motion of the pistons. Only in the 1970s have we been shown anything better, in the form of the eccentric-crank cruciform radial invented by A.J.S. Baker and embodied in the 1974 Abingdon-Cross engine, than what Lanchester did in 1895. Through all the years between, it was commonly to Lanchester's writings that engineers turned for some guidance through the giddying maze of swings and roundabouts that makes engine-balancing more a job for a senior wrangler than for a junior director.

We shall never know how many of the faults in our cars are due to the junior status that their designers have so often been doomed to accept. *Prima facie*, Lanchester was in a position to command; but in fact he was inevitably subservient to his financial backers, who gave him no peace at all, but badgered him to recant all his high-flown philosophies and get on with the hammer-and-chisel manufacture of cars as depressingly crude as all the others that must have been such an affront to his intellect. Lanchester fought and Fabianized as much as he could; he resisted their pressures to put the car into production before his quantity-production machinery was all prepared; but that was probably a mistake, for it meant that no cars could be ready for sale until 1901, by which time the world was conditioned to accept the very different basic layout compounded by Panhard and Levassor and in that same fateful 1901 to be confirmed in the authoritative Mercedes of Maybach. Likewise, Lanchester resisted for years the demands of partners and customers that he dispense with his own pet control system, which made a fundamental issue of the use of a tiller arm for steering. In this, too, he was probably mistaken, though the prevailing wheel-and-woe arrangement was not without its own faults. Or should that be weal and whoa? If Lanchester was so clever, if he had made such a study of vehicle dynamics, why did he not endow his cars with four-wheel braking?

Never mind: it is too late to ask. Had he not been so beset by belittlers and beraters, had he not had to fight so bitterly to defend what he had already proposed, he might have got around to it – had

Two levers and one pedal had sufficed for the early Lanchesters, but the public insisted on the conventions being observed. The rot set in with the big Edwardian fours and sixes, and by 1912 Dr Frederick's brother George was in charge. Later cars may have been nearly as good, but were not nearly as clever

Famous for his resounding technical arguments with Lanchester, Laurence H. Pomeroy as chief designer of Vauxhall was responsible for the first British sports car, the Prince Henry Vauxhall of 1910. It did not win the Prinz Heinrich trial that year (Porsche's Austro-Daimler did) but it sired the 30/98 Vauxhall, which is praise enough

he not also had a mind of such voracious appetite for variety that it could not keep from pursuing studies as remote from the motor-car as could be imagined. And yet . . . perhaps they were not so remote. Perhaps Lanchester was the finest of all examples of the engineer whose products are bred by cross-fertilization from one branch to another, taking knowledge and experience from here and applying them to make an improvement there. Most of those designers who do not live in ivory towers work in watertight compartments, but to 'Doctor Fred' every field was open. In the end, it does not much matter whether a designer be artistic or mechanistic, filled with humanity or bursting with science: what he most needs, and what Lanchester least lacked, is intelligence.

7
The team

'*C*adillac cars are not the exclusive design of any one person. They represent the composite ideas of a number of inventors, designers and engineers, each skilled by many years in his special branch of work. Every feature of Cadillac cars is thoroughly considered by a special committee of mechanical experts. No feature is adopted until fully proven by long and severe tests.'

Thus, Henry Leland explained in the old days what is modern team practice, in terms that can be little less accurate than when he used them in describing the methods whereby Cadillac – or any other firms in General Motors, not to mention most of those outside – works today. The modern motor-car is a literally sophisticated affair, involving skills and specialities too numerous to mention, too various to combine under one hat – and possibly too incompatible to admit of reconciliation and compromise except when two specialized practitioners fight it out between themselves under the watchful eye of a self-seeking supervisor. 'Divide and rule' is as valid a motto in business as in politics: many are the proprietors who have been browbeaten by their own engineers, but if a large number of engineers is involved they will be so busy fighting among themselves for supremacy that they will be unable to present a united front against a management whose skills are those of accountancy – as are those of far too many managements in the industry.

So, the committee proposes a horse and produces a camel. Management will never be at a loss for a scapegoat when the camel fails to sell, even if it means (though it seldom happens) blaming their advertising men for failing to persuade the public that the camel is a horse after all. Yet a committee can produce good results, and the outstanding success of some present companies in a fiercely competitive market reveals their team tactics as being quite out of the ordinary. One of the best examples is that of Adam Opel AG, another of those unexpectedly autonomous General Motors companies. They are the second largest of all General's divisions, making such enormous strides as the 1960s gave way to the 1970s that, by 1973, they actually outsold Volkswagen on their German home ground. They attained this supremacy with some cars of outstanding beauty and equally notable roadholding, although there was nothing in their make-up that was anything but ordinary.

Whenever a car looks mechanically humdrum and feels delightful – which is a fair description of such Opels as the Manta, the Kadett, the Commodore and the rest of that generation – you may be sure that the explanation is not good design but good development. Whether a car enjoys such development depends on the men in charge: the English specialist motoring press has not forgotten the case of the Morris Marina, the roadholding and handling of which had been passed as amply satisfactory by the senior engineers under Harry Webster, but which the more demanding driving of journalists immediately showed to have failings which called for an urgent redesign of the front suspension.

The Webster team were very sound engineers, of course, but their driving could best be described as artisan. They were not

Handsome, fast and very satisfying to drive, the Opel Commodore GS/E is conceptually simple. It is the work of an enthusiastic team of designers and development engineers working in the modern concerted way, with neither scope nor need for individual assertion

enthusiasts; neither were the customers they thought typical of those in the market for the smaller cars in the Marina range; but the man who bought a 1·8 demanded higher standards, and it was the enthusiasts of the motoring weeklies and monthlies who saw to it that he eventually got what he wanted. At Opel, the team of engineers under Charles 'Chuck' Chapman Jr are as enthusiastic as he is, and it shows in the product. Whether it makes any difference to sales is more difficult to tell: who knows if, for every GS/E that is bought for its cornering prowess, another is rejected for the firm ride that goes with it?

Clever and innovative design, such as the suspension work of Alec Moulton discussed in Chapter Six, could satisfy both kinds of customers; but a really big outfit such as General Motors only takes innovative risks when the moon is blue. Though their research scientists were blessed with universal knowledge and limitless invention, it would make no difference until the moneybags department were confident that the last dollar outside Fort Knox had been safely tucked into the corporate wallet. When no risks are to be taken, design stultifies and development flourishes. For chapter and verse, see Rolls-Royce.

Hence Chuck Chapman's explanation for the effectiveness of Opel's very simple suspension systems: 'Just concentrated design *and development* – we keep working at it until we get it right. Suspension is the major compromise in a car, and we now have better development instruments so that we can isolate separate issues, plus a very good chassis development department. Above all, it depends on the people doing the development – we put a lot of emphasis on the development side. . . . The buck stops here,' (what successful chief would deny responsibility for the work of his subordinates?) 'but generally we get good agreement: we have specialists to evaluate

175

different noises, that sort of thing ... We have an expression: "Let the car tell us what it wants". We design a car as an entity, so we do not lose sight of the whole for the part. We are very much oriented to the road, to the practical rather than theory.'

The system clearly works. There are admittedly strong undertones of the all-pervading Mr Mitchell in the styling, but Opels have a distinct and recognizable elegance that stems from Chuck Jordan who led their stylists in the critical years that produced the Commodore, the Manta and the Ascona. As for the roadholding and handling, look to the earnest chief chassis engineer Karl Brumm, who is not only all that his job demands, but also a very good driver. One might wonder whether there were dangers in having so many ultra-keen drivers on the staff, but Chapman does not. 'Unless you have enthusiasts, how can you function as an automobile company? Yes, we have a lot of enthusiasts in the top management. In fact, I have trouble keeping people away from racing – keeping their minds on other things.'

As the writer Emerson observed, 'Nothing great was ever achieved without enthusiasm.' In the case of car design, that essential enthusiasm may be directed in a choice of ways; and the choice is crucial. If the object of the designer's enthusiasm be motoring, that is, the activity for which the car is no more than a necessary piece of equipment, then it is likely that every possible solution to the basic problems of enjoyable driving will be tried in turn, whether systematically or otherwise; *plus ça change, plus c'est la même chose*. If, on the contrary, the designer's love is the car itself, he will devote himself to perfecting it while everything all around is changing – in which case, since an objective evaluation of a car must relate it to the context of its environment for the time being, it is a matter of *plus c'est la même chose, plus ça change*.

In the early days of motoring, when one man would champion his ideas of what a car should be like and another would urge a contrary argument, while the public wondered whether either knew what he was talking about, the man besotted with his own brainchild was a frequent phenomenon. Old Amédée Bollée, Gottlieb Daimler, Karl Benz, Frederick Lanchester, Henry Royce, Georges Roesch and Gabriel Voisin all suffered at one time or another from not being able to see beyond their own noses. The days of the great individual designer are past, the only exception being explained by the unique and healthy attitude of Colin Chapman, whose perpetual conviction is that all cars are terrible except the latest Lotus and even that is not quite as it should be.

However, if you can gather together a team of designers who all share a common enthusiasm for their joint product, the results are likely to be most gratifying; and it is in the nature of things that such a team will stay together. No better illustration of such cohesion can be found than in the tiny factory and office block on the edge of Filton aerodrome where Bristol cars are designed and built. These are, and always have been throughout their thirty years, cars that are quite exceptionally gratifying – not only to own and to drive, but

The BMWs of the late 1930s were some of the most modern and perhaps the most refined cars in the world. Most famous of them was the sporting 328, the engine of which was combined with the superior chassis of the 326 to form the basis of the postwar Bristol 400

Relying on continuity and conscientious development, the Bristol design team have wrought great changes over the years without ever sacrificing the cars' basic characteristics of quality, elegance, and high performance in all planes and senses. These are the 405 and 406

also surely to make. They are constructed, largely by hand, by men who admit to feeling rewarded in the exercise of the considerable skills demanded of them; and they have all been designed with the same sort of pride *in modo* and pride *in re*, a sort of qualitative loop in which the end is the means.

Indeed, the Bristol team remind one of those bishops whose youthful countenances were explained by Oscar Wilde as due to their still believing at 60 what they were taught at 16. Perhaps they simply know when they are on to a good thing; but it is none the less surprising that a comparison of a modern 6·6-litre Bristol with the first 2-litre should reveal that they have so much in common. The chassis is changed only in detail, the track and general overall dimensions are much the same, the wheelbases are identical. Just as significant is the fact that many of the men who designed and built the one played exactly the same roles in respect of the other.

Most of these long-serving men were recruited from the original divisions of the Bristol Aeroplane Company when the new Car Division was established at the end of the Hitler war. George White, son of one of the company's founders, was keen to undertake the manufacture of high-class cars, and several members of the board saw it as a safeguard against the postwar depression that, from recollections of the company's difficult days after the previous armistice, they properly dreaded. There was no intention of drawing extensively on the skills or labour of the car industry, for it was felt that the abilities of the aircraft industry must be equal to the challenge and more appropriate to the very high class of product proposed.

How well this theory was supported by events, the long line of Bristol cars proves: the men who were most instrumental in creating them from the beginning were all men from the aeroplane company. The chief designer Dudley Hobbs was brought into the Car Division from the airframe works, where his speciality was wing construction: his main concern was with bodywork, styling, ventilation and so forth, and he is still the chief designer today, concentrating on styling and the interior and taking overall responsibility. The assistant chief designer, who had started in the aeroplane company as a student apprentice, joined the Car Division in 1945 and is still custodian of the car's meticulous engineering integrity; it is probably his perfectionist attitude that has been the most important influence in the creation of successively better variations modelled on an inspiring theme.

Their most original thinker was perhaps Jack Channer, who had joined the aeroplane company in 1939 and who began in 1945 a year-long campaign to be transferred to the Car Division, where he made himself the most brilliant suspension and handling specialist in the business. He is not to be found at Filton today, for when the Comet disaster brought the entire British aviation industry into such an orgy of recrimination and research that all Bristol development projects had to be stopped dead in their tracks, he mournfully closed his file on the 50000 miles' development of his very advanced new prototype and went off to seek expression elsewhere – first at ERA and then at Rootes, where he now holds an important design chair in Chrysler's British Technical Centre.

All these men were individually noteworthy enough to find their several niches in the earlier chapters of this book. To combine them in a team inspired by the same ideals, shared by their companions in this Filton subculture, such as Laurie Smith, Jan Lowy, Major Abel and Eric Agar, could not fail to bring egregious results. In the 1950s, Bristol cars were quite idiosyncratic, somehow obviously the products of an aircraft manufacturer, somehow very advanced in their engineering without ever looking unconventional beneath their wind-shaped skins, and somehow far nicer to drive and more competent in every sort of road-going circumstance than their paper specifications might suggest. The same applies today – with restraint in styling taking the place of the 'aircraft look' now that the plane-makers have flown off on a jet-propelled tangent – because the same thinking is applied today. It is that of quiet, economical men whose output of real engineering would stagger an efficiency expert ac-customed to the wasteful protocols of a big corporation – just as government officials were staggered by absence of staff turnover.

An unhappier fate befell what was perhaps the greatest design team of all, the inhabitants of the Fiat Technical Office in the early 1920s who nearly all left to pursue their individual ends in many of the most famous motor manufactories of Europe. To study their joint and several contributions to automobile history, we must return once again to that heady world of motor racing, which from time to time has set the quotidiurnal touring car on new paths. Once again, it is a matter of racing improving the breed only after breeding has improved the race, a matter of tracing the source of some of the most pervasive influences in motor engineering.

In all the years of Grand Prix racing, whose designs have been technically and historically the most important? Chapman, whose Lotus 25 fixed the pattern for the rear-engined monocoque of modern times? The Coopers, *père et fils*, whose cars overthrew the established rule of the front engine? Lampredi, whose $4\frac{1}{2}$-litre V12 Ferrari was the first unblown machine successfully to challenge the classical supercharged cars? We might look rather earlier to the Daimler-Benz team led by Wagner, whose W125 chassis was to inspire designers for the next 20 years; or much earlier to Henry, whose 1912 Grand Prix Peugeot demonstrated the advantages (such as they were) of a relatively small, high-efficiency engine back in the days when, as it says in Genesis, there were giants in the earth. All these were important in their many several ways; but a close look at the history books, and at the cars about which they were written, reminds us of another team of engineers whose work may be un-known to the majority of today's motoring and motor-racing enthusiasts, but whose work was demonstrably the most importantly broadcast of all. These were the engineers of Fiat, and in particular those who were responsible for the racing cars of 1921 and the following two years.

These men followed no examples, but set their own precedents. They did not accept current standards, but established new and higher ones. They stayed on the scene no longer than was necessary to prove their supremacy. Then they were gone, apparently never again to take an interest in Grand Prix racing, while the fickle world they had impressed and entertained quickly forgot that Fiat had been the most consistent – and the most consistently successful – participants in motor racing for a whole generation. They began when motoring itself was in its infancy; when they left, they had created a series of machines whose principles were to be adopted by many other constructors, and to inspire the design of racing cars for generations to come.

Yet it was not just a case of Fiat's ideas being copied, though seldom have ideas proved so widely pervasive. Within a year or so of Fiat quitting the motor-racing scene, their brilliant design team had broken up. Some stayed with the company, but transferred their attentions to the aero-engines that promised to represent their makers and their country more glamorously (in the international seaplane races for the Schneider Trophy) than would the racing cars which were perhaps insufficiently remote from the reality of the company's everyday products. The remainder of this star cast of engineers found their ways into employment with other car manufacturers, often with a motor-racing involvement; and so they carried further afield for another 10, 20, or in some cases even 30 years the ideas that had been prepared and polished in the early 1920s.

These were the men of that exceptional team, men who were successively prophets while they worked together and apostles when, having split up, they moved out into other branches of the European motor industry. In charge of them all was Guido Fornaca, frequently described by various historians as chief engineer but in fact the head of the Fiat Technical Office in that he directed its policies in the commercial rather than the engineering sense. Under him as technical director was Carlo Cavalli, scion of a long line of judges and other lawyers, who was constrained by family pressures to become a lawyer although his inclination was always towards engineering. Eventually he made the break and joined the Fiat staff in 1905 as a designer. There, he played a big part in the design of the heavyweight racers that were so successful during the next few years, especially in 1907. Fornaca soon found that, in Cavalli, he had a very reliable assistant, honest, scrupulous and extremely versatile, for he applied himself not only to the first shaft-drive cars but also to the first aero-engines, to airship engines, marine motors, military vehicles, agricultural tractors and, of course, the brilliant racers. By 1919, at the age of 41, Cavalli had been appointed technical director of the Technical Office, just in time to assist in the birth of a new generation of racing cars.

He had a superb team working under him: Bazzi, Becchia, Bertarione, Cappa, Massimino and Zerbi as design engineers, while in charge of car preparation and team administration was Jano. In a few years all but Cavalli and Zerbi would have deserted Fiat.

Aristide Faccioli was the first and shortest-termed chief designer of Fiat

Opposite above : Guido Fornaca, in charge of the Fiat technical office, in the pits at Monza in 1923 with supporting cast

Opposite below : Here is no jumped-up mechanic off the factory floor but a thoroughly professional gentleman, combining the shrewd and perceptive brain of a lawyer with the talent and enthusiasm of an automotive engineer : Carlo Cavalli of Fiat

In the early years after World War One, the formula governing international Grands Prix admitted engines of 3-litres displacement. It was a time when there seemed no effective alternative to the designs taken from Birkigt and propounded by Henry in the late pre-war years, propositions which led to his elegant straight-eight Ballot which only Duesenberg (heavily influenced by Bugatti) could successfully challenge. Be it French or American, the 8-cylinder racing car was in the ascendant: and by the time of the French Grand Prix of 1921, when the Duesenberg possibly outran and certainly out-braked the Ballot, there was some disappointment that the rumoured new contender from Fiat should not yet be ready. Less than two months later it was fielded for the newly-inaugurated Brescia Grand Prix.

This was the new Fiat 801, a 3-litre straight-eight which finally completed the breakaway from the Henry tradition; and in its necessarily limited career (in the following year the Grand Prix formula was due to admit cars of not more than 2-litres engine displacement) it performed sufficiently well to encourage Fiat to proceed along the avenues that they had explored with this car. Although Henry's fashions were to endure for several years in sports cars, in the highest class of racing it was the turn of Fiat to set the style. This they did with an engine of entirely original conception, with two valves per cylinder instead of four, with 10 roller main bearings and even with roller big-end bearings, with a built-up form of construction similar to that used in the 1914 Mercedes and employed extensively by Fiat in their aero-engines (though originally pioneered by Panhard). This engine had the ability to operate reliably at 4400 rpm, higher even than the 4250 rpm of the Duesenberg, which it also exceeded slightly in piston area and by virtually the same proportion in power. The new Fiat was not entirely successful on its first appearance, however, suffering a number of stops for minor attentions which forced the fastest survivor of the team down to third place behind two Ballots. But it was a Fiat, driven by Bordino, which put up the fastest lap, staying at the head of the field until checked by a puncture on the 12th lap, retiring shortly afterwards upon failure of an oil pump.

If the 3-litre Fiat was not an unqualified success in 1921, it had at least been sufficiently promising to suggest that, under the new 1922 formula, Fiat would need watching. Nevertheless, the rest of the motor-racing world went on its own way, mostly clinging blindly to the tenets of Henry's faith – either indirectly, like Aston Marton who bought Gremillon (one of Henry's disciples in the Peugeot drawing-office) to design them a new cylinder block and head; or directly, like the Sunbeam-Talbot-Darracq combine, whose boss Louis Coatalen bought Henry himself to produce a new Sunbeam. There were some others who went their own bizarre ways, either perishing in the attempt like Rolland-Pilain (whose complex and finely-executed straight-eight could claim neither success nor durability, save in a weakly-contested race at San Sebastian in 1923) or surviving through sheer strength of character like Bugatti.

Technical director Cavalli on the road with Salamano and the 1923 GP Fiat for which he was largely responsible

The 1912 Fiat Zero was meant for quantity production, with some intriguing pressed steel work to prove it. A popular car in large numbers was an advanced idea for those days, but in those days Fiat was full of them, thanks to a brilliant engineering team

183

Henry's Sunbeam was typical of the man. He was very good at twin overhead-camshaft valve gear, not at all bad at cylinder heads, utterly hopeless at crankshafts and bearings, while bemused by the idea of very long piston strokes: so his engines could never run satisfactorily at rates high enough to exploit the power latent in the four-valve heads. The Sunbeam exceeded expectations by developing no less than 83 bhp at 4250 rpm, so that on the basis of piston-loading or bmep it was the best engine he ever did – but if it be measured as the means to those ends he was instructed to achieve, it must be judged one of his worst.

The Fiat that turned up for the great race of 1922 (as ever, the French Grand Prix) gave 92 bhp at 4500 rpm. In other words, the Fiat engineers contrived to combine volumetric and combustive efficiencies comparable with the best that Henry could obtain after his many years of devoted work, together with the high-crank rates that denied him the full realization of his design potential. To the Fiat team under Cavalli, it seemed commonsense that the new 2-litre engine should be created by adapting six of the eight cylinders of the 3-litre car, reducing the stroke to 100 mm and leaving the 65 mm bore unchanged. These dimensions created a piston area rather less than was mustered by the Bugatti; but, because of the excellent breathing through the two large valve ports in the hemispherical cylinder head, because of the exquisite design and consequent high mechanical efficiency of the whole construction, the engine was able to sustain high speeds and loadings with safety and thus to exceed the power of all its rivals. Nazzaro drove the Fiat to win the French Grand Prix in 6 h 17 mins; and officials had to wait nearly an hour for completion of the same distance by the first of the three Bugattis which were the only other cars to finish the race.

All other competitors were so discouraged by the performance that only Bugatti turned up to challenge the Fiats in the other Grand Prix of 1922, which was held on the new Monza circuit. This artificial track promised very high speeds to which the carefully streamlined body of the Fiat was well suited; for its shape initiated yet another fashion that was to endure for a long time, the whole car being painstakingly profiled so as to correspond in plan with accepted notions of the ideal streamlined shape. Fiat were really thorough in this, even shaping the chassis side-members so that they remained flush with the body contours from behind the front springs right through to the extreme rear. Even the outside exhaust pipe was carefully faired-in and maintained at constant height so as to present the least possible frontal area. Nor was low drag cultivated at the expense of weight: this was the lightest Grand Prix winner yet known or to be known for decades to come, weighing 1450 lb.

For the Monza race, Fiat also uprated the new engine. The crankshaft was safe up to 5500 rpm, and now the drivers were cleared to use 5000 and 112 bhp. Nobody else could come anywhere near it, and, if further proof of its superiority were needed, there is the fact that three-quarters of its rivals preferred taunts of cowardice to proof of ineptitude: Ballot, Bianchi, Delage, Rolland-Pilain, Sunbeam and, it is said, Benz and Mercedes, all forfeited their entry fees in the conviction that the Fiats would enjoy a runaway victory. The brothers Maserati were persuaded that valour was more honourable than discretion and raced their Diatto cars until forced to retire at quarter distance, while the Fiats cruised around to win – 6% faster than the only other car (the Bugatti) to finish and with a lap record 6% faster still.

Louis Coatalen knew just what to do. He sacked Henry and lured Bertarione away from Fiat to design a new Sunbeam that would be disparaged by others as 'a Fiat in green paint', its engine virtually identical to that of the 1922 Fiat, its chassis basically that of the 1922 Sunbeam. But Coatalen was not to know that Cavalli was treating the 1922 6-cylinder car as a mere stopgap, while preparing for the following year an entirely new engine of even more advanced design, exploiting revolutionary principles so exotic to Grand Prix racing that the future course of technical development was to be wholly diverted along a new path that would be followed for another 30 years.

In the chassis, body and running gear, it was very like the 1922 car; but the straight-eight engine, with an even lower stroke:bore ratio but with the same kind of detail design, featured a super-charger – the first Grand Prix car ever to do so. It was a vane type of blower of the Wittig pattern, blowing air into the carburettor. This was not efficient, but it was better than no supercharger: the new engine started off in life with 130 bhp at its disposal and, with a record lap in the 1923 French Grand Prix at Tours, demonstrated that it was faster than any of its rivals. Alas, the air intake to the Fiat's blower was unscreened and unguarded, and the grit that flew from tyres on what used to pass in those days for road-racing circuits got into the machinery and wrought havoc. The untoward result was that the red Fiat failed and the 'green Fiat' won, Segrave's Sunbeam completing the distance at 75·3 mph, which may be compared with the 87·75 mph lap record of Bordino's Fiat.

In his Alfa Romeo history, Peter Hull has implied that it was this oversight that caused an argument to flare up in the Fiat Technical Office after the race between Fornaca and Bazzi. At any rate, this row led to Bazzi's departure from Fiat; and since he was a friend of Enzo Ferrari, the Alfa Romeo driver, he obtained a job in the Alfa racing department. Almost as soon as he was there, he advised the Milan firm to lure Jano away from Fiat as well – and this they succeeded in doing. The chief designer, Merosi, was working on the P1 Alfa Romeo racer which was a Chinese copy of the 6-cylinder 1922 Fiat, so when it turned up for the first European Grand Prix at Monza later in the year, it was hardly surprising that it was supercharged. An unfortunate accident in practice, when their driver Sivocci was killed, caused the cars to be withdrawn; and they were never again run in public because Jano became busy on a much better proposition. This was a Chinese copy of the 8-cylinder 1923 Fiat, eventually to emerge as the all-conquering P2 Alfa Romeo in the years after Fiat's withdrawal from racing.

As for Fiat, they did away with the troublesome and inefficient vane-type supercharger and substituted the Roots type, added an intercooler between the blower and the carburettor, fitted a stone-guard, and turned up at Monza with 146 bhp, this being the first time that a Grand Prix engine had sustained more than 4 bhp per square inch of piston area. It won the race at an average speed nearly 7% higher than that of the 6-cylinder car the previous year.

Already the rush to adopt Fiat's new principles of engine design was bearing fruit. The engine of the new 'Teardrop' rear-engined Benz bore a close resemblance to that of the 1922 Fiat, and this style was carried into the Mercedes-Benz amalgamation and pursued in their racing engines for many years to come. Meanwhile, at Delage the designer Plancton built a highly meritorious 2-litre V12, each bank of which was virtually a scaled-down 6-cylinder Fiat with the same sort of combustion chamber, valve-gear reciprocating parts, free use of rolling-element bearings, and even the same stroke:bore ratio. The only important difference was that the cylinder blocks were iron castings, instead of being built up from forgings as Fiat preferred. When eventually it got the supercharge it so needed, this engine was a humdinger; but by that time Fiat had proved their point and withdrawn from racing.

Now the great team of engineers began to break up. Already Becchia had gone to join Bertarione – not at the Wolverhampton works of Sunbeam, but at the Surèsnes factory of the French Talbot concern. There, they added a supercharger to the 6-cylinder Sunbeam, shifting the carburettor from the delivery side to the suction side, thus improving the efficiency of the supercharging considerably, making this car a rival for the P2 Alfa Romeo in speed.

Next to go was the most senior man under Cavalli: Giulio Cesare Cappa, a man who had come to Fiat from Aquila Italiana in 1914 with some good racing-car experience behind him, now left to become an independent consultant, and, after working on a Lorraine aero-engine for the French firm, he took on the job of re-organizing production at the Itala factory. His masterpiece there was the Type 61, a superb 6-cylinder car of refined and elegant engineering. Cappa was very given to complexities, which were fine for prototypes or factory specials, but hardly suited to quantity production, and his cars did not always get the development they deserved. The most notable example of this must be the supremely elegant Type 11 racer, a little 12-cylinder car that survives in the Biscaretti Museum in Turin. But Cappa's work did not finish there: he carried the message on to many other companies, including Ansaldo, OM, Breda, Piaggio and Alfa Romeo. Massimino had gone from Fiat to Alfa Romeo, too, where Jano had taken over as chief designer and where, in due course, a chap called Colombo came to work under him and learn the 'Apostles Creed', as it were. Now the original Fiat team was depleted, but their most brilliant engine man, Tranquillo Zerbi, was still there.

Zerbi was still a young man. Born in 1891, he studied in Mannheim and worked on diesel engines for Sulzer and Tosi before

If Giulio Cesare Cappa had a failing, it was his love of intricate mechanisms – though he would have seen it as a quest for mechanical efficiency. It was something of a hindrance when he left Fiat and worked for Itala. This touring chassis was the most successful of his designs for them

Jano's engine for the Monza Alfa Romeo was compounded of ideas derived from Fiat, where he cut his professional teeth, and from Salmson, whose designer Emil Petit had made a racing 1100 cc *voiturette* of similar disposition in 1927

Jano's D50 GP Lancia was as fast as anything in its time. Given modern tyres it could have proved itself ahead of its time; instead it led him to Ferrari, where he was to produce the V6 Dino as the culmination of 35 years with high-performance cars

Opposite: Alfa Romeo sacked Jano after the failure of his 1937 GP car, saying he was too old. The brilliant work he subsequently did for Lancia proved them wrong, including the D20–25 series of V6 sports-racers that fared so well in 1953–4

Overleaf: The last racing Fiat was this 1927 U12 Type 806, a characteristically brilliant job by Tranquillo Zerbi who had become chief of the technical office. It raced once, went considerably faster than its only possible rival (Lory's Delage), and having won its race it disappeared

joining Fiat in 1919. He was barely 30 when he conceived the epoch-making blown straight-eight, and, when eventually Cavalli had to retire in 1928 through ill-health, it was Zerbi who took his place as technical director. In the interval, he had transferred his attentions to aero-engines, producing the AS2 (which won the Schneider Trophy in 1926) and a long series of other racers and record-breakers culminating in the famous AS6, the double-12 which set the absolute world-speed record in 1933 and 1934. For 1927 he came back to motor racing briefly, though whether as a technical exercise or for reasons of prestige has never been clear. Things had been busy for the two years of the 1½-litre formula: in 1926 Bertarione and Becchia had obtained good results with their straight-eight modelled for Talbot in the Fiat tradition, while at the Delage factory Lory had produced yet another.

Zerbi, however, wanted to do something different. Drawing on his diesel experience, he had experimented with a supercharged, opposed-piston two-stroke; but he abandoned this as impractical and instead designed a 12-cylinder, 1½-litre engine with two valves per cylinder, two crankshafts built up by Hirth serrations (to be adopted in later years by Auto-Union, Porsche and others), eight main bearings of the plain journal type (an important departure from the roller-bearing convention that Fiat themselves had established), one-piece connecting rods, again with plain bearings, and a higher peak-power bmep than ever before. Racing happily at 8000 rpm and 175 bhp, the engine had run up to 8500 rpm and 187 bhp on the dynamometer. The car raced once, in the 1927 Milan Grand Prix. It won – easily – and was never seen again. Fiat had finished with Grand Prix racing. Zerbi was busy with his aero-engines, assisted by Bruno Trevisan, who ten years later went to Alfa Romeo to help them with their big sports cars, and by Ing. Sola, who later went to Lancia and worked on the Aprilia.

By that time the brilliant Spanish designer Wilfredo Ricart (later responsible for the Pegaso) had taken command at Alfa Romeo. Ferrari could not stand him and left to set up his own company,

LA CREAZIONE DEI MOTORI FIAT

Come ho visto uomini e cose

Al terzo piano della « Fiat Lingotto », a destra di chi giunge dalla scalinata, si apre la fuga di un grande luminoso salone, chiuso dalla barriera di due porte vetrate. Quando si parla di barriera non si usa una metafora. Il salone è sbarrato alle persone che non fanno parte del personale; chi vuole conferire con qualche dirigente ed è pregato di attendere in un salotto. Tutto questo con buona grazia piemontese, senza troppi complimenti, ma cortesemente categorica.

Nel salone adunque non si entra, ché questo è il regno dell'ing. Zerbi e dei suoi collaboratori. Ma al tempo in cui io stavo alla « Fiat », in uno dei suoi uffici, ho avuto sovente occasione di salire dall'ingegnere o dai suoi diretti dipendenti, a chiedere dei dati che soltanto essi potevano fornirmi. Acceso, naturalmente, libero il passaggio e, allorquando l'ingegnere era assente od occupato, mi portavo al fondo del salone, dove l'ing. Bona, l'immediato interprete dello Zerbi, ha il suo tavolo di lavoro, ed ottenevo le informazioni desiderate. Informazioni, d'altronde molto parche, rappresentate quasi sempre da qualche notizia assai scheletrica sulla quale la mia fantasia lavorava per dare ai giornali un servizio passabilmente giornalistico; cioè, un servizio che tenesse presente la qualità del pubblico a cui il periodico si rivolgeva e che in genere non era troppo familiare con le descrizioni eccessivamente tecniche.

Voi vorreste ora sapere come sia questo salone dal quale escono graficamente compiuti i meravigliosi motori della « Fiat ». Ed io comprendo il vostro desiderio, perché la immaginazione lavora a figurarsi l'ambiente dove vengono alla luce i prodigi. Il vostro desiderio, vi dirò subito, è stato anche il mio rivissimo quando sono entrato alla « Fiat ».

La « Fiat », come ormai tutti sanno, perché migliaia e migliaia di persone l'hanno visitata, è una fabbrica grandiosa, anzi una successione di fabbriche grandiose, potendo bastare ognuno dei reparti a formare un tutto imponente ed impressionante. C'è, quindi, in essa tanto da eccitare il più acceso desiderio di vederla in azione, attraverso la fuga dei suoi saloni che si perdono a vista d'occhio nella magnificenza della sua grandiosa costruzione a cinque piani. Eppure, il più immediato, il più acuto, il più assillante desiderio non era di visitare la « Fiat », bensì di gettare lo sguardo dentro le pareti che racchiudono il mistero di una continua creazione.

Se ora vi dirò che la mia è stata una delusione, voi non mi crederete. Eppure è così. Ma la causa è mia, come sarebbe vostra, e non delle cose che volete vedere e che potete vedere. La sfilata di sgabelli davanti ai quali, in piedi, i disegnatori tracciano fitte reti come ragnatele mostruose, non vi dice nulla. Vi lascia freddi e indifferenti. Perché? Per la semplice ragione che siete un profano, un incompetente, un ignorante in materia.

Lo studio dell'ing. Zerbi? Cartoni, compassi, linee. Eppoi? La vita della mente che crea i motori della vittoria si materializza attraverso questi cartoni, questi compassi, queste linee. Bisognerebbe saper afferrare la loro voce meravigliosa ed allora sentireste cantare la grande, potente, ineguagliabile musica, dei motori « Fiat » che da anni sfidano tutte le competizioni, tutti gli assalti, tutte le battaglie.

Dobbiamo invece accontentarci di osservare gli uomini, e soprattutto l'uomo che silenziosamente (provarci a tentare un'intervista con l'ing. Zerbi) lavora dalla mattina alla sera allo scopo di portare sempre più oltre la sua volontà di conquista. Non abbiamo tentato neppure noi di avvicinarlo in questi giorni, perché speravamo di andare incontro ad un cortese rifiuto di parlare della sua persona e della sua opera. Le notizie che di lui abbiamo furono già pubblicate una volta ne « L'Informazione ». Ma possono benissimo, in vista di così straordinaria circostanza, tornare a prendere posto anche in questo numero, dedicato alla Crociera.

L'ing. Zerbi è nato a Saronno nel 1891 e si è diplomato in Germania. Nelle officine tedesche e svizzere egli fece i primi anni di tirocinio, a contatto col lavoro manuale, presso le realizzazioni industriali. Ritornato in Italia, dopo un breve passaggio agli stabilimenti Tosi di Legnano, ove si dedicò particolarmente allo studio dei motori « Diesel », fu assunto dalla « Fiat » nel 1919. Sotto la guida di un maestro, l'ing. Fornaca, poté rivelare rapidamente il suo ingegno nel campo delle costruzioni speciali, e cioè: aviazione, macchine da corsa e trazione ferroviaria.

Nel settembre 1927 fu chiamato a capo di tutti gli Uffici tecnici della « Fiat », cosicché sotto la sua direzione passano pure lo studio dei progetti relativi all'automobilismo, il quale costituisce il nerbo della produzione « Fiat ».

L'Ufficio tecnico progettò i motori da aviazione ad altissimi regimi e poscia la serie dei motori A. 20, 22 e 25, nonché i motori speciali A. 8. 2, A. 8. 3 della Coppa Schneider del 1926, del record di velocità del maggiore De Bernardi e della bellissima corsa fatta da Dal Molin sul « Macchi-Fiat » nel canale di Solent, battendo il « Supermarine » di D'Arcy Grieg.

Una magnifica affermazione dei motori di serie è stata la crociera dei 12 apparecchi, muniti tutti di motori Fiat A. 22, che S. E. Balbo condusse da Roma a Londra e da Londra, attraverso la Germania, alla loro base, in perfetta formazione, nonché il I Circuito Europeo, con 8 partiti ed 8 arrivati con motori « Fiat ».

Occorrerà ricordare il record di durata stabilito da Ferrarin e Del Prete nel cielo di Roma? Oppure il volo di Ferrarin e Del Prete Italia-Brasile?

Il motore da corsa da un litro e mezzo, la prima locomotiva « Diesel » elettrica in funzione nelle Ferrovie italiane, gli autoveicoli che entrano in tutti i servizi civili, le automobili che irradiano nel mondo il nome di un'industria italiana che domina una situazione tutt'altro che facile di fronte alla concorrenza americana, questi ed altri sono i terreni della operosità dell'uomo che la fiducia della « Fiat » ha chiamato a coprire un posto di grande responsabilità, coi risultati che ci abbiamo discorso.

Poiché siamo in argomento diciamo che la industria italiana impostasi sul mercato automobilistico del mondo, ha saputo contemporaneamente indirizzare la sua attività verso altre applicazioni senza che nessuna delle singole ne soffrisse, ma tutte traessero vita e vigoria dalla incessante fecondità dei nuclei centrali. Poiché tanto si parla di Ford e compagni, sarà bene ricordare una volta tanto che di fronte alla uniformità di concezione americana la genialità di vedute e la coraggiosa multiformità di azione dell'industria italiana meritano, se non altro, un equo apprezzamento.

E ricordiamo anche che una grande impresa non può essere che il risultato di una maturità industriale raggiunta attraverso lunghi sforzi, accurate selezioni, perfezionamenti instancabili di valori umani e di valori meccanici.

L'ing. Zerbi ha validi collaboratori nell'ing. Zanatelli e nell'ing. Bona, e trova nella Direzione Generale centrale della « Fiat » l'alto organismo che, in armonia d'opere, indirizza e collabora.

La Crociera atlantica solleva oggi il nome dell'ing. Zerbi alla cerchia dei massimi costruttori, ma la sua vita chiusa fra il lavoro e la famiglia non uscirà per questo dalla severità di una disciplina, che a tutti è d'esempio, ammirevolmente.

GIULIO ALBERTI.

L'ing. ZERBI

Il grandioso « Do X » totalmente azionato dai motori « Fiat ».

Un interno « Fiat ».

TELEGRAMMI

L'on. Ferracini al Duce ed al sen. Agnelli

L'on. Ferracini, Presidente della nostra Unione, ha spedito i seguenti telegrammi:

Sua Eccellenza Benito Mussolini
ROMA

La meravigliosa impresa voluta da Vostra Eccellenza, che corona lo sforzo tenace dell'industria torinese, è nuova ragione nostra riconoscenza per Vostra Eccellenza, come italiani e come produttori.

Unione Industriale Fascista
Presidente FERRACINI.

Senatore Agnelli
TORINO

L'Unione Industriale Fascista di Torino, orgogliosa superba riaffermazione valore industria torinese, manda a Lei, creatore e animatore grande organismo che onora la nostra città, vivissime felicitazioni.

Unione Industriale Fascista
Presidente FERRACINI.

Il Podestà al sen. Agnelli

Senatore Agnelli
Presidente « Fiat »
TORINO

Alla « Fiat » ha forgiato i cuori pulsanti della magnifica impresa transatlantica il plaudente grato tributo della Città di Torino.

Podestà Torino
THAON DI REVEL.

Ai cinque caduti nell'ardimento del volo oceanico mandiamo il nostro commosso saluto. Essi sono periti al loro posto di battaglia, con la fronte rivolta verso la mèta. Onoriamoli col patto di essere degni di tanto sacrificio.

Zerbi was preoccupied with aero-engines (including Schneider Trophy racers) in the late 1920s. This page from a Fascist workers' newspaper in 1931 pays tribute to him and, of course, to the others in his team

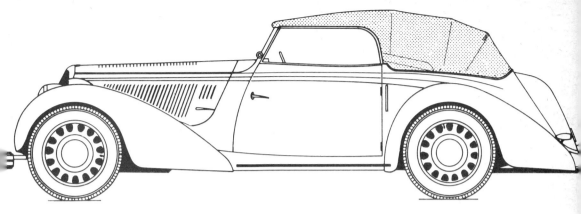

In the 1930s Hotchkiss was run by an Englishman, Harry Ainsworth, but the technical director from 1928 to 1962 was a Fiat man, Bertarione, and the simple but very effective 3½-litre car that did so well in so many Monte Carlo Rallies up to 1950 was yet another tribute to a good school

In 1935 Automobiles Talbot, descendants of Darracq, came under the control of another Englishman, Anthony Lago – and the chief designer was another former Fiat man, Becchia. The very fast 4-litre 23CV Lago Record Talbot was the forerunner of cars that were to win Grands Prix as late as 1951

Auto Avio Costruzione. With him went Massimino and Jano and Bazzi, all ex-Fiat men, together with their protégé Colombo; and when, after the war, Ferrari set up to manufacture cars under his own name, three of these men stayed with him. Jano in the meantime had gone to Lancia, where his last great achievement was the $2\frac{1}{2}$-litre Grand Prix car of 1954. By then, Ferrari had sacked Colombo, giving his job to Lampredi; but when Lancia had to give up racing, and handed their cars and designs over to Ferrari for further development and racing, Jano went with the cars and took over from Lampredi. In the meantime, Colombo had gone to Maserati, where he joined none other than Massimino in working on the A6G and developed it into a highly-competitive Formula Two car, from which evolved the Type 250F which will be remembered as one of the most consistently effective racers under the $2\frac{1}{2}$-litre formula. From Maserati, Colombo went to Bugatti where he designed the ill-fated Type 251, the most forward-looking, unsuccessful and under-developed Grand Prix car of all time. It appeared but once, in the French Grand Prix of 1956 at Reims. At the same circuit five years earlier, the big unblown $4\frac{1}{2}$-litre Lago Record, alias Talbot, was still being raced in Formula One events and was not to be despised in its latest form designed (like the prewar version) by old Becchia just about five years earlier.

If Becchia were still in France, what had become of his erstwhile Fiat colleague Bertarione? He was working in France, too: in 1928 he had taken the job of technical director at the Hotchkiss factory in Paris, a job he held until the year before his death in 1962. He could thus take the credit for some brilliant rallying successes, just as Becchia could for sports and Grand Prix racing victories.

It was, of course, to the big Talbot that everybody looked to challenge Colombo's supercharged $1\frac{1}{2}$-litre Alfa Romeos in the early postwar years, which it sometimes seemed able to do by keeping on going while the thirsty blown cars had to stop for more fuel. In the years before the war, not a single first-class Grand Prix had been won by an unsupercharged car since Zerbi's Fiat won at Monza in 1923 and set the supercharger on its way.

1951 was the year when the supercharger's grip was broken, and it was Lampredi's Ferrari that broke it. Since then the supercharger has never been given a chance; and it may be significant that, of all the designers mentioned, Lampredi is the only one who does not appear to have come under Fiat influence in his formative years. It was a poetic kind of justice that saw him, a little while after his departure from Ferrari, join Fiat where today he is head of the Engines Department. He promises to be a worthy successor to Cappa, Cavalli and Zerbi; but history will have to run for another dozen years or so before we can see whether his influence will be so widespread or his ideas so widely disseminated. It is a situation such as Ecclesiasticus handled well – but which the imitative Kipling handled perhaps better:

Let us now praise famous men,
Men of little showing
For their work continueth,
And their work continueth,
Broad and deep continueth,
Greater than their knowing!

Index

GENERAL